JUST A HOGG'S LIFE
A Royal Navy Saga of the Thirties

THE MIDSHIPMAID

Celia: Jane Baxter   *Commander:* Basil Foster

Celia: "Darling, why didn't you tell me?"
Commander: "I've been trying to explain all afternoon, but one gets so little privacy at rehearsals!"

ANTHONY HOGG

Just a Hogg's Life

A Royal Navy Saga of the Thirties

SOLO MIO BOOKS
CHICHESTER

© Anthony Hogg 1993

First published in 1993 by Solo Mio Books
2 Mount Lane, Chichester, West Sussex PO19 2EX
Telephone: 0243 784014

All rights reserved. No part of this publication may be reproduced or transmitted in any form or by any means, electronic or mechanical, including photocopying, recording or in any information storage or retreival system without the prior written consent of the publishers.

British Library Cataloguing in Publication Data

Hogg, Anthony
Just a Hogg's Life, A Royal Navy Saga of the Thirties
I. Biographies -
I. Title

ISBN 0-9508955-4-7

By the same author

Wine Mine - A Mine of Wine Information (Editor) 1959-1974
Off the Shelf - Gilbey Vintners' Guide to Wines and Spirits 1973-77-80
Guide to Visiting Vineyards. Michael Joseph 1976-81-82
The Wine-Taster's Guide to Europe (USA edition of the above), E.P. Dutton 1979
Cocktails and Mixed Drinks, Hamlyn 1979-80-81-82-87. 108000 copies
Travellers' Portugal, Solo Mio Books 1983-86-87
Everybody's Wine Guide, Quiller Press 1985
The Hulton Diaries 1832-1928 - A Gradely Lancashire Chronicle. 1989

This book was designerd by David Goodman
and produced and typeset by
Woodfield Publishing Services, Fontwell, Sussex UK

Set in 11 point Garamond

Printed and bound in Great Britain

Dedicated to the Greynvile Term
R.N.C. Dartmouth, 1926–29

Only eleven of us now remain from the original forty-nine. Four left the Navy before 1930, nine lost their lives on active service and twenty-five have died since they retired. Sad to report, these now include our top three, who attained flag rank:

Richard Smeeton *Peter Gretton* *Charles Wheen*
Vice-Admiral *Vice-Admiral* *Rear-Admiral*
1912-1992 *1912-1992* *1912-1992*

After keeping the compulsory Midshipman's journal for three years, most of us gladly said, "Good-bye to all that". For some reason, perhaps to deprecate my seniors, I began another in 1934 when Sub-Lieutenant of *Royal Sovereign*'s Gunroom, continuing with page-a-day diaries until wounded in 1940. These are the source of this book.

From Cadet to Lieutenant I served in three capital ships, an aircraft carrier, a cruiser, a new destroyer, a Naval Barracks and two minesweepers. Two of my Captains, A.B. Cunningham and B.A. Fraser, rose to be Admirals of the Fleet; another, B.H. Ramsay to Admiral. Of course I played a great part in their achievements.

Sailing in Cunningham's galley, I advanced from 'that slow and indolent cadet' to 'the galumphing elephant that upsets the trim'. On the Algiers golf course I struck a ball that required him to practise instant avoiding action. On board I introduced an activity exercise called "Chicken Breathing", which had the men too breathless with laughter to breathe. For Ramsay the Midshipmen I trained gave a glorious display of how not to win an obstacle race in a gale. Bruce Fraser needed no help except invitations to parties, which he accepted and enjoyed. I am proud to have proposed and worked for his bust, now by the *Victory* in Portsmouth.

Finally I hope my full description of the Greenwich Night Pageant might encourage a revival one day.

A.H. January 1993

James Hogg, the Ettrick Shepherd, whose statue looks down on the Tibbie Shiels pub.

Acknowledgements

Many people have contributed to this book by answering my questions, mainly about their relations or the fate of mutual friends in the war. I thank them all, naming below those who have been particularly helpful.

Lieutenant-Commander E.F. Baines DSO RN, Mr Kenneth Benton CMG, Captain George Blundell CBE RN, Commander W.S. Bracegirdle DSC RAN, Mr John Charlton of Harvey's, Portsmouth, Captain J.S. Dalgish CVO CBE RN, Commander Robert de Pass RN, Lieutenant Commander R. Ellsworth RN, Mr J.T. Fleming, Lady Diana Fyffe (née Moore-Gwyn), Mr Robert Gieve (Gieves and Hawkes), Vice-Admiral Sir John Gray KBE CB RN, Mrs Marguerite Harwood (née Carver), Sir John Hoskyns, Commander A.C.W. Jones RN, Captain Barrie Kent RN, Mr Rex King, Rugby Librarian, Twickenham, Rear-Admiral D.W. Kirke CB CBE OBE, Rear-Admiral J.R. Llewellyn RN, Captain Sam Lombard-Hobson, Mrs Diana Luck (née David), Commander A.V. Lyle RN, Rear-Admiral Colin Madden CB CBE MVO DSC RN, Captain Roger Morgan RN, Rear-Admiral E.N. Poland CB CBE RN, Dr David Pugh DSC RNVR, Air Commodore G.P Seymour Price RAF, Captain Alan Smalley DSC RN, Captain Sir David Tibbits DSC RN, Lady Walsham, Captain L.E.D. Walthall CBE DSC RN, Mrs G.M. Wheadon, Lieutenant-Commander Richard Wilson RN, Captain John Wells CBE DSC RN.

I also wish to thank Lady Gretton, Lady Smeeton and Mrs Charles Wheen for sending, at very short notice, photographs of their husbands.

Finally my neighbour, Mrs Elizabeth Harmer has word-processed the book in a most agreeable and professional manner while her husband reading its content has been seen to rock with laughter at times.

Anthony Hogg
January 1993

My father, Adam Spencer Hogg.

My parents, Adam Spencer Hogg and Brada Hulton married at Emberton, August 15th, 1901.

Contents

1. BEFORE MY TIME 1
2. RPM'S BROCKHURST 8
3. GIEVES ARRANGES EVERYTHING 24
4. DARTMOUTH AT THE DOUBLE 29
5. MIDSHIPMAN MOD 45
6. AT SEA WITH ABC 60
7. WESTWARD HO! 96
8. HAS ANYBODY HERE SEEN KELLY? 106
9. BOLD GENDARMES IN BARBADOS 119
10. BATTLE WAGON WITH A SQUASH COURT 131
11. THE GREENWICH NIGHT PAGEANT 141
12. SUB-LIEUTENANT THIRD CLASS TO MALTA 155
13. THE TIDDLY QUID 167
14. AN IMPOTENT SCENE SHIFTER 180
15. 1935 – MUSSOLINI'S ABYSSINIA AGGRESSION 203
16. 1936 – HMS GRAFTON – COCK OF THE FLEET
    AND KING'S ESCORT 216
17. 1937 – BRUCE FRASER'S GLORIOUS 246
18. VICTORY AT TWICKERS 272
19. 1939 – NOBBY CLARK'S HARRIER 289
20. FROM A WAR TO A WEDDING 310
    A MUSICAL APPENDIX 321
    INDEX 326

Adam Hogg
1832 - 1887

CHAPTER 1

BEFORE MY TIME

I was born during the middle watch of 6 November 1912. This was a relief; Hogg, which can be a swine, sheep, deer, fish, or louse is not the most attractive of surnames and to be called Guy Fawkes as well as Hogg would have been a calamity. On December 21, the Saint's day of 'Doubting Thomas', I was christened by a Red Dean-to-be in St. Margaret's Church, Altrincham: Anthony Lee Spencer.

Anthony, said to mean 'worthy of praise' was most reassuring; praise rarely came our way in the Royal Navy. Lee being my father's eldest brother, the compliment brought me a legacy of £1000 when this bachelor uncle died in 1925. Spencer was my father's second Christian name by which he was known in preference to Adam.

All Hoggs hail from Hawick or thereabouts. We descend from James Hogg (1770-1835), the Ettrick Shepherd, so Lord Hailsham (Quintin Hogg) once told me and as a Lord Chancellor he should know. James has his place, after Robert Burns, as Scotland's second poet. He came from a family of shepherds living in Ettrick and Yarrow country, two small Tweed tributaries merging in Selkirkshire. Walter Scott (1771-1832) a life long friend persuaded Constable to publish his first book of poems.

Both authors were keen anglers fishing the three and a half miles of St. Mary's loch and doubtless drowning their disappointments by the dram in *Tibbie Shiels* – still the same old 'local' at the southern end where they were often found by a third friend, Thomas Todd Stoddart, author of the first book on angling in Scotland, published in 1835.

In 1806 Isobel, known as Tibbie Shiels, 1782-1878 married Robert Richardson, a stately home mole-catcher, who died in 1824 leaving her destitute with six children. A strong personality she became an inn-keeper, who made her place a *rendez-vous* for artistic anglers that included Robert Louis Stevenson (1850-1894) and Thomas Carlyle (1785-1881). Ninety six when she died, a booklet *Tibbie Shiels* by Michael Robson was published in 1986. With her spinning wheel and Sir Walter Scott's armchair, her hotel by the loch is now a place of pilgrimage, where there is still good fishing, though Stoddart and Hogg's record catch when sharing a boat, of seventy nine trout weighing 36 pounds on 4 May 1833 has yet to be broken.

JUST A HOGG'S LIFE

Born at Ramsaycleuch in the Ettrick forest, James received little education, but was lucky in 1817 to be given a small farm at Altrive by the Duke of Buccleuch. In 1820 he married Margaret Phillips and there were five children. His statue, holding a shepherd's crook and watching for the trout to rise, is close to the westward of *Tibbie Shiels*.

His most important works are: *Scottish Pastorals* 1801, *The Mountain Bard* 1807, *The Queen's Wake* 1813, *Evening Tales* 1820, *The Shepherds' Calendar* 1829, and *Lay Sermons* 1834. Better known than these should be:

> God Save the King!
> Make him victorious,
> Happy and glorious,
> Long to reign over us!
> God save the King

The verses of our National Anthem are shared by James Hogg with Henry Carey (c. 1693-1743) explains *The Oxford Dictionary of Quotations*.

My grandfather Adam Hogg (1832-1897) had founded McIntyre Hogg Marsh and Co., making *Radiac* shirts and pyjamas, with its northern office at 27 Portland Street, Manchester and a factory out at Ardwick. His brother, David, began as his partner but moved to a competitor, Hogg and Mitchell in Londonderry. Their father Robert farmed at Glendearg near Melrose. Preferring politics to tunics David, in 1913 became M.P for Londonderry and, being 6'6" was the tallest member in the House of Commons.

Adam was married to Eliza Gilfillan, daughter of a Royal Navy surgeon, whose family had moved to Ulster from Scotland. Between 1866 and 1878 they had five sons and two daughters, losing Florence the youngest child from a fever when she was only seventeen. The family's Victorian mansion called Silverlands was in Bowdon, the well-to-do residential part of Altrincham nine miles South of Manchester on the Chester Road.

Uppingham was the family's public school, the two eldest sons going straight from there into the family firm, Lee to manage the Londonderry factory, Sandy the business in Manchester. The third son, Spencer managed to persuade his father to let him read Law at Trinity College, Oxford. Photographs show him in the Uppingham Cricket XI in 1888, the Trinity XV 1890-1-2 and the Trinity VIII in 1890-91. Qualifying as a barrister on the Northern circuit, he practised from chambers in Manchester.

The other three children were Eliza Gilfillan, 'Betty' 1872-1954, William Gilfillan, 'Willie' 1874-1949, and Percy 1876-1906, who died of enteric fever when a Captain in the Royal Scots Greys. He was only thirty.

The 1890s were a sad decade; their mother died in 1895, their father Adam in 1897. The brothers, by all accounts, were a rough lot reported to have installed a beer engine in the drawing room. Shy and reserved Betty, the one woman left, found house-keeping for them a thankless task.

In 1897 Queen Victoria's Diamond Jubilee was celebrated with great illuminations in London, a naval review and many balls. At one of these my father Spencer danced with a Miss Brada Hulton, whose father Jessop was a Bolton solicitor and Registrar of the County Court. Quite a beauty aged twenty, Spencer confided to a friend that he had met the girl he intended to marry.

On February 14, 1901 St. Valentine's Day my mother's diary is brief and precise, "Mr. Hogg came to dinner and the night. Proposed." The result in the words of an Alice Delysia song was: "She didn't say yes and she didn't say no". But on March 17 St. Patrick's Day, Mr. Hogg proposed again. This time he was accepted and became 'Spencer' at last. He was just thirty, Brada twenty three.

They were married on August 15 1901 at Emberton, a Buckinghamshire village near the Ouse, where the Hultons held the living for many years; the wedding breakfast was for a hundred and six people. The hymns they chose were *Fight the good fight* and *O Perfect Love*, an inconsistency that never occurred to them until years later when their children roared with laughter. The young people went on the river. The Rector, walking and reading simultaneously along the bank fell in, much to the general delight. My father rowed his bride from Oxford to Windsor, probably explaining the facts of life on the way by day in order to demonstrate them by night, an aim which took several days to achieve successfully. One would have thought that Blanche, her step-mother, in a house that kept two Dachshunds, male and female would have managed to explain them before, but Victorians were immensely prudish.

How pleasant and peaceful the Thames must have been then! Bathing, punting up the backwaters and lying under the trees, with neither the sound nor the smell of an internal combustion engine. And, obligingly, the Great Western railway would deliver the heavy luggage from one overnight stop to the next during each day's row.

Beginning their married life in Eccles near Manchester, my sister – also christened Brada – was born there in 1902 and my brother Martin in 1903. In 1905 the family moved to an attractive, recently built house in an acre of garden called Orchard House, a mile west of Altrincham Station at a point now marked on the Manchester Ordnance Survey as Oldfield Brow. About half a mile towards a village called Dunham Town, my father's elder brother Alex G Hogg, known as 'Sandy', had built himself a large mansion called Tirbracken on park land belonging to Lord Stamford of Dunham Hall now a National Trust property. CH. for Club house on the Ordnance Survey now marks the spot because my brother, who inherited it and lived there with his family after World War II, was obliged to sell the place to a Jewish syndicate, who replaced it in the 1960s by building a club house for their new golf course Dunham Forest.

Regarded as the rich member of the family, my Uncle Sandy, unmarried and managing the northern half of McIntyre Hogg Marsh, making Radiac shirts and pyjamas, went daily to the warehouse, at 27 Portland Street, Manchester. A scratch golfer he competed in the Amateur Championships around 1904 but was knocked out in the first or second rounds. A member of Formby, his great feat was beating Harold Hilton in a tournament which that great champion habitually won.

Sandy Hogg was an early motorist with two cars by 1906 supplied by the Jackson Bros. of Timperley, who came to the rescue when the cars broke down, usually when away at Windermere for example. The house he had built for himself would have done nicely as a Dr. Barnado's home but it was destined never to hear the pitter-patter of little feet because a certain Miss Craven to whom he proposed let the side down.

This was a godsend for my parents who struggled to make ends meet during the first ten years of their marriage. My father's income as a barrister in 1906 was £350, swallowed up by rented chambers, the Clerk's salary, light, heat, telephone. Sandy stood them trips to the Lakes and Llandudno and made interest free loans to my father. Not until 1911 when he was made Stipendiary Magistrate at Salford, followed by promotion to County Court Judge, South Lancashire in 1913, did his finances improve.

Orchard House was a sunny, half timbered edifice only six years old standing in an acre of garden. Its smoke room and drawing room faced south with my parents' bedroom and a day nursery on the first floor immediately above.

My night nursery on the north side, shared with my brother, looked over open fields across the Bridgewater Canal, with Rivington Pike and the hills beyond Bolton visible on a clear day. Having the kitchen range below warmed our bedroom considerably. My father's dressing room and a double spare room looked westwards across another field. One bathroom, a hot cupboard, two WCs and two attic bedrooms for the servants comprised the usual offices, while below there were cellars, largely empty except for bicycles, Threlfall's draught bitter and tubs for bathing terriers.

The Author's birthplace, Orchard House, Altrincham.

My mother as a V.A.D. (Voluntary Aid Detachment) 1914–18.

My earliest recollections are of my mother in a V.A.D. uniform, and on December 9 1917 the bells of St. Margaret's Church being rung because General Allenby had entered Jerusalem expelling the Turks. With no motor car, my vehicle for joy riding was the milkman's open one horse dray. Mr. Steel had an Arnold Bennett moustache and only part of a larynx. Standing up like Ben Hur he would hold the reins with one hand while preparing to fill his pints and gills from a large churn with the other. The milk was from local farms, the customers decanting into their own jugs kept in the larder.

One day with everybody out, my father answered the door. He had no idea where to put the milk and on their return the servants did not like to ask. They found it eventually in the Georgian silver teapot in the pantry. He was not a very practical man - a misfortune I inherited - and would even mount his bicycle from the back, using a step on the hub of the back wheel instead of a pedal.

Among my parents' closest friends were Hewlett Johnson, the Vicar of St. Margaret's and his wife Mary. Every summer they ran camps to some beauty spot in North Wales, first 400 boys then the girls too, giving these town and city dwellers a taste of the country. In 1911, Mary and my mother also started a Mothers (with babies) annual sea side holiday which continued into the Twenties.

My father, who had stood as a Liberal for Exeter in the 1893 election and seen plenty of poverty as a barrister, became the Vicar's church warden finding Hewlett's Socialism a new and fascinating topic.

During the war Sir John Leigh, a cotton mill owner and self-made man, set up Haig's Lawn, a large Bowdon house, as a hospital for wounded officers where Mary Johnson became the Commandant and my mother a V.A.D. Hewlett and Mary were my godparents. On Armistice Day 1918 unable to find bell ringers when the Mayor telephoned the news, he ran into a small party of children walking near the church with their teacher, Miss Church. Away we all went up to the belfry and, acting under his instructions, made a little bit of history by ringing an attenuated peal. Norah Church had first appeared in 1914 as a Governess to teach my sister Brada and her friend Gytha Burgess, who later married Sir Keith Nutthall, killed on active service in 1941. She ran many classes for Bowdon families, including the Holdens, Prestwiches, Burgesses and Heywoods, in one house or another, becoming a friend to them all.

Once a week in winter there was a dancing class at the Bowdon pavilion, still there by the Parish church. Presided over by Miss Ratcliffe of Fallowfield this old dragon in shining black satin stood in the middle of the floor beating time with a leg that looked as if it might fall off her torso any moment as she sang to the polka tune, "And a one, two, three hop, one two three!" Needing a little private tuition I was greatly humiliated by a young lady assistant taking me to the *Ladies* cloakroom. Sweating like a heifer, she was rather 'nifty' and there was no Odorono in those days.

In the world of sport Steward, the Manchester United goal keeper, lived up the road but in those days City in the first division, claimed my allegiance. Among cricketers my mother had danced with A. C. Maclaren, while R. H. Spooner was the hero of elder brothers. But my contemporaries will remember: Makepeace, Hallows, Tyldesley (E) Watson .... opening the Lancashire batting and Tyldesley (R) and Parkin among the bowlers, Cecil Parkin who would put his foot down in such a way that the ball ran up his trouser leg into his hand.

My relations c. 1924. Jack Paterson, brother-in-law; Mrs Jessop Hulton, grandmother; Jessop Hulton, grandfather; myself in Eton Suit; my mother half-hidden; my father 'The Judge'; my sister Brada Paterson, just married. All in 'Sunday best' for Church.

CHAPTER 2

RPM's BROCKHURST

Church Stretton, with All Stretton to the North and Little Stretton to the South is an urban district of Shropshire situated on a low watershed in a narrow longitudinal valley 13 miles south of Shrewsbury between the Longmynd and the Caradoc ranges. Between them, abreast the Ragleth hill, Brockhurst School and its grounds lay on its own plateau above the Great Western Railway line still in service from Shrewsbury to Ludlow, Bristol and South Wales. On the other side, the western side of this valley, the road South, A49 curves round the Brockhurst hill from Church Stretton to Little Stretton. No longer the main road, after World War II a by-pass for all three Strettons was built running along the line of the old Roman road on the eastern side close to the railway.

On this 'hill of badgers' a Mr. A. H. Atkinson established his independent preparatory school in 1894 naming it Brockhurst perhaps because there were badgers there then. A record shows that 180 Old Brocks - boys not badgers - and eleven masters served in the 1914–18 war. Eighteen Old Brocks and three of the masters were killed or died of wounds. On the mole at Zeebrugge in April 1918 Lieutenant Commander Leyland-Harrison won a V.C. but died of his wounds. Over twenty other Old Brocks and masters won decorations during the 1914–18 war.

My parents were first attracted to this district of valleys, silver streams and wooded hills in 1903, taking short holidays at The Malt House, Little Stretton subsequently. In 1919 Atkinson sold his school to Reginald Philip Marshall, Repton and Keble College, Oxford born 1877, who had been a civilian master at the Royal Naval College, Osborne since 1905. Lunching with Mr. and Mrs. Marshall in December 1920, they were impressed; my mother's diary records, "Nice homely people with a boy of thirteen, two girls and a baby called Anthony; liked it all very much."

So on May 4 1921 her little Anthony aged 8½ went to Brockhurst, not by the nice steam train that left London Road Station, Manchester at 2.50 p.m. (change at Shrewsbury) but in our local Altrincham brown smelly Fiat taxi with my father and brother. My mother, critically ill with influenza and pneumonia, could not see me off from her sick bed and I was car sick at intervals.

There were then forty six boarders in the school, Hannah (called Bobbie) Norah and Barbara, the three Marshall children, being pupils too.

We were divided into five classes, the first and fifth each with about six, and the middle three each with about twelve. For competitive purposes half the school were Greeks and the other half Trojans. For good and bad work respectively, individuals were awarded stars (red) and stripes (blue) written out by masters from books the size of a cheque book, which the recipients handed in to the Headmaster, who recorded them in red and blue blobs on a large chart pinned to the dining room door. Three stripes in a term probably meant 'the swish' from R.P.M., as a caning was gleefully called by the boys. A swizz, not a swish, was that whereas stripes were stripes, the stars were printed in quarters, one quarter usually being awarded at a time.

We slept in five dormitories on the first and second floors of the bright and airy house, eight or nine boys to a dormitory each with a prefect in charge. That hot summer of 1921 - like those of 1940, 1959, 1976 and 1990 in Britain - will always be remembered. Slow to sleep in the heat, the sound of the trains running south to Marshbrook or chugging up the hill to Church Stretton still remain a memory. So too does a beastly boy called Bamford II, who kept order in our Blue dorm among us little boys with a slipper, or a sharp punch with a clenched fist on the muscle of either cheek of one's bum. One of the school rules on a printed card was 'Ask and keep on asking. I don't know will never be accepted as an excuse'. In the Blue dorm however the illuminated text said:

> *Question not but live and labour*
> *Till yon goal be won*
> *Helping every feeble neighbour*
> *Seeking help from none*

The contradiction being a pleasing example of those "Follies and nonsense, whims and inconsistencies" that diverted Elizabeth Bennet of *Pride and Prejudice* into laughter.

Brockhurst also had a motto, *Palma non sine pulvere*, which RPM, translating as 'No palm without dust', declared came from the Olympic games, where no runner could win his palm without kicking up a dust. Having represented Oxford at cross-country running when at Keble College, athletics were his subject the meaning of the motto boiling down to no prize without effort.

By degrees the staff and parents added a school flag, a mast and halliards, the flag being renovated by a parent Mrs. Doyne-Ditmas, in time for Sports Day 1980 at Marlston House, near Hermitage north of Newbury, the school having moved there in 1945.

For meals we fitted into one dining room looking Eastwards at Ragleth, the hill beyond the main playing field. RPM, with his wife – always 'Mater' never Mabel – opposite, presided at the largest table, with the first form seated on either side. Mademoiselle Junod, a Swiss lady endeavoured, regrettably with little success, to impose *Parlez francais* at another. Matron, Miss Gardener-Brown presided over the juniors, with masters at each end of the remaining two tables by the windows. Brockhurst food was good. Writing my Gradely Lancashire Chronicle, THE HULTON DIARIES in 1987, I came across Paul de Lacey Hulton-Harrop of Wellington who was at Mill Mead, Brockhurst's nearest rival (destroyed to improve the road out of Shrewsbury after the last war.) He has never forgotten the sausages he had for tea after matches at Brockhurst.

Close to the house there were a second playing field, a school yard, eight WCs and a gym with a carpentry shop on one end. Two grass tennis courts were close to the front door. Beyond it there was a superb rock garden with a gold fish pool that always looked its best for the midsummer half term. All these were on the first plateau as well as a vegetable garden beyond the main playing field.

From the school yard a steep path, passing a small classroom and a music room led to the Masters' cottage with bedrooms for four. The path continued upwards past some fine old oaks, good for climbing and an open space for a swimming pool, ending on a second plateau big enough for a boys' rugger field. Both were established later. The western side of the field falling sharply to the main road was all woods, with lots of bracken from which we built snug 'houses' for fun on summer Sunday afternoons. Sunday services had to be held in the dining room until on 25 June 1922 Brockhurst's own chapel, converted from an army hut on one side of the School yard, was consecrated by the Bishop of Hereford attended by many parents, who had helped to pay for it. Pleasantly panelled in wood, the altar window of stained glass was dedicated to the Marshalls' eldest child, Eleanor who had died when she was only about seventeen.

Sunday mornings in Eton suits writing letters home followed by Matins were tedious, but, back in shorts for lunch, Sunday afternoons walking up the Longmynd, climbing Ragleth or just throwing stones in the streams of Callow and Ashes Hollows were fun. Only the under 10s had to go with a master and there were occasional cars to spot en route with names like Crossley, De Dion Bouton, Willys-Overland and Trojan, now only to be seen in motor museums.

At Evensong after a good tea Mrs. Marshall pedalled prettily on the harmonium and RPM would unleash a good sermon suited to his favourite topic "The Modern Boy". In 1923 we learnt that Bonar Law who had been – I hardly need say – the Conservative Prime Minister was a saint; a belief I held firmly until I came across Kingsley Martin's *New Statesman* twenty years later. Prayers too were not just for saying in chapel or when kneeling by the bed. There were good reasons for prayer at work and play. There were indeed; we tried it repeatedly when two goals down to Mill Mead but it just didn't seem to work.

Licensed by the Bishop of Hereford as a Ruridecanal Lay Reader RPM took the services and by 1925 had produced a little red book of Brockhurst hymns not in Ancient and Modern. They included Bunyan – 'He who would valiant be', Milton – 'Let us with a gladsome mind' and 'Ye seraphs' to the tune of the old German national anthem now revived.

RPM of course liked Kipling and read aloud to us *Stalky & Co*, good manly stuff for the modern boy! Thus *The Children's Song, Land of our Birth, we pledge to thee* was also included in the Hymn book. For school boys the meanings of some of its verses are far from clear. For example: "Teach us to look in all our ends" is a little difficult starting with one's ears or nostrils without considering the ruder possibilities. And once, singing the previous verse, "Teach us to rule ourselves alway Controlled and cleanly night and day" there was a loud splutter from the front pew. The luckless Ba had wet herself and was led out. We boys frequently admonished by RPM, her father, as 'No better than the sons of coal heavers', assumed the look of little white hens who never laid away from home.

Our secular songs came mostly from Cecil Sharp's Song book. The school's music master was A. A. Lambert a University of Wales graduate, whose black hair liberally anointed with Anzora – the predecessor of Brylcream – protected him from smelly socks and halitosis. Kipling's imperialism was left at the post when two score Brock trebles sang loud and clear:-

> *Shoulder to shoulder we merrily march along*
> *Fair and square, never a care*
> *Singing a rousing song,*
> *Sons of Britain are we, ready on land or sea*
> *To fight for right and follow the flag*
> *of the Empire free*

It wasn't long since the free Empire had killed 400 Indians for unlawful assembly in Amritsar. And even ten years later Britain was about as unready on land sea or air as Ethelred himself. And how about this to mellifluous music?

> *The Spring is coming resolved to banish*
> *The King of the Ice with his turbulent train,*
> *With her fairy wand she bids them vanish*
> *And welcomes the sunshine to er- earth again.*
> *Then maidens forgo-o the wintry kirtle*
> *And lace every bodice with bright green string-ing*
> *And twine each lattice with wreaths of myrtle*
> *To honour the advent of joy-o-ful Spring.*

Even Wilhelmina Stitch, whose *Fragrant Minute* appeared almost daily for years in the *Daily Sketch* never contrived a lyric such as this.

Another master, Mr. Whittaker, occasionally plied the slipper in the fourth form as an aid to learning Latin from that infamous book *The Shorter Latin Primer*, the title being converted to Eating primer by every good student with two deft strokes of his pencil. But Mr. Whittaker, who had a little Charlie Chaplin moustache, lost face. After the Chapel, the next addition to our amenities had to be a swimming bath. Staff and boys did the digging, and parents - even rich uncles - coughed up in the holidays when nephews showed them a little yellow card headed *The Brockhurst Swimming Pool Fund*. At the opening in the summer of 1924, Mr. Whittaker took no aquatic part but was later seen when nobody was about on the end of an instructor's pole waving his arms and legs about like Mrs. Leo Hunter's Expiring Frog. In short Mr. Whittaker had never learnt to swim.

Spurred by the daily dip in the cold bath, we boys learnt quickly, though the pool, being open and unheated, made for a short season. In 1954 exactly thirty years later, after Brockhurst had been established at Marlston near Newbury, other modern boys started digging their own pool, 60 feet by 30 feet and 8 foot deep. It was opened in 1962 by Julian Critchley M.P. for Aldershot, an Old Brock who had recoiled in horror at RPM's Start-em-at-the-deep-end technique when he was at Church Stretton in 1942.

Our sports master was another Welshman, Thomas Llewellyn Harry, dark and swarthy, who must have taught somebody some subject besides games. Though normally pacific, I have an indelible memory of him facing a Latin class warming his backside on the anthracite stove, with a boy close to him attempting to translate some Latin sentences being hit hard with a slipper across the back of his legs. But in 1925 there arrived from Keble wearing the widest pair of grey flannel trousers - the then fashionable Oxford bags - a young, lanky master called Keith Tarling. Capable, easy going, loved by the boys, in 1931 he moved to Yarlet Hall, a preparatory school near Stafford that Brockhurst played at cricket and football. Keith became joint headmaster, marrying in 1934 Joy Harris, a niece of his co-head. From 1937 to 1970 he was head of Yarlet on his own; ninety nine terms in which not one candidate failed to pass Common Entrance. There was one son of the marriage, Nicolas, now a solicitor in London, but Joy died in 1967. Before retiring in 1970 he had a house built for himself near the school, marrying again in 1975 Margaret Woolf, a widow of an Old Yarlet boy. After a life surrounded by small boys, living to be over ninety seems to me to be a miracle. Keith Tarling will certainly be remembered as a dedicated and humane preparatory school headmaster.

Work and play at schools was often interrupted by infectious epidemics such as measles, mumps, chicken pox, rubella, scarlet fever, whooping cough. At Brockhurst scarlet fever struck in October 1921 and I was one of the seven victims. The masters' cottage was evacuated to become our isolated prison for months. Complications could be dangerous; to avoid them we were kept in bed for three weeks on a diet of milk, junket being an occasional treat. The skin then peeled and another five weeks followed

RPM, Old Boys' Day, 1935.

JUST A HOGG'S LIFE

before the patient was considered free of infection. Not until December 16 when I was given a carbolic bath and, almost too fat, pushed out through the window did I go home after a wasted term. Semi-isolated on our plateau away from the town, must have helped to keep the school free of epidemics during the next five years.

With no acceptable radio, and no television until after the 1939 war, schools made their own entertainments. At cricket and football we were usually beaten by Old Hall at Wellington and Kingsland Grange in Shrewsbury, each with half as many boys or more. Mill Mead and Yarlet Hall were more our match and when, after some years, fixtures were arranged with the Choir school at Tenbury we even won sometimes.

In the summers the Paters XI played the school with bats made narrower and when the school played the staff, Mlle Junod and Matron, in their normal clothes delighted the boys by running like riggers to hold spectacular catches on the boundary. Journeys to Away matches with half the team crammed into the Willys-Overland and RPM at the wheel, while the other half plus driver made a sardine tin of the Arrol-Johnson hired from the local garage, were very exciting. Far too exciting once, when a motor cyclist crashed head on down the Wellington Straight into RPM, miraculously without casualties.

There were outings too. Norah Marshall's birthday early in June was always celebrated with a school picnic in Ashes Valley where there was room for rounders and once, a demonstration of how to tickle trout by one of the boys. At half term boys with absent parents or invitations would be taken by RPM and Mater for a great tea at Chelmick. Each winter some of us would go to watch Shrewsbury School play the Corinthians, that great amateur soccer club in those days. Paid entertainers did the rounds of private and public schools, the most memorable being Frederick Chester at the piano with a song called, *The Phantom Regiment*, which vanished into the distance as "The Big Drum-Major fills the little boys with awe" and the accompaniment faded to *pianissimo*. RPM was at his best with *The Floral Dance*.* Though the correct name in Cornwall, he declared was 'Flurry'.

Come to think of it in 1923 there was my own solo, "I'm tickled to death I'm single." This was a number by Melville Gideon, one of the two pianists of *The Co-optimists*. Only a pierrot show, I had seen it in Manchester after a long run in London. Stanley Holloway, Davy Burnaby, Hermione Baddeley, Phyllis Monckton were the Stars. My sister had the song on the gramophone; at the age of eleven I didn't understand a word of it!

*Peter Dawson's EMI CD11 7-63107-2 sings it well among Twenty Favourites.

All these events were duly reported in *The Brock*, published at the end of each term in time for prize giving and revived in 1977 when the School had re-settled near Newbury. RPM's prizes for work were books bound in maroon leather with

BROCKHURST
PALMA - NON - SINE - PULVERE

on the front in gold letters. Since I cannot recollect in my entire life further prizes for work, I rather treasure the five I still have, each inscribed by RPM in his neat manly hand. The first was *The Pickwick Papers* Vol. 1, "Maths Prize Class IV July 1923". I was to read it to my wife in dim calor gas light by the shores of Loch Long during 1942. Next was *Peter Simple*, "Star Prize for general excellence December 1923". I think we must have beaten Mill Mead that term.

The Talisman, December 1924 was again a Star prize for general excellence. Next came Reid's *The Scalp Hunters*, lacking an inscription, due I fear to mental laziness by RPM. The fifth, *Westward Ho!* was a leaving prize in March 1926. Mental laziness was my besetting sin; the swish was applied to correct it. This was the only time I was beaten. By 1924 there must have been a little collusion between my father the Judge and the headmaster. In his bachelor days, when a guest in a Dreadnought, the Navy had given my father so many pink gins it could do no wrong. That, combined with RPM's enthusiasm for a cadet or two at Dartmouth among his scholarships, must have been why I went to stay with Lowther Grendon Tippet, a Brockhurst boy of my own age, whose own father was a retired Commander R.N living at Goring-on-Thames. He too had run a preparatory school, St. Prians in Maidenhead. On Saturday July 26, we made an early start for Alverstoke in the De Dion Bouton, the Commander at the wheel with his wife, and we two boys in the dickey, all invited to see the Naval Review on board the destroyer *Saumarez*.

I had hardly ever seen the sea. Admittedly our 1920 family holiday had been at Tenby and in preceding years at Llanbedr where the tide seemed to be permanently out beyond the Mochras sands. My chief Llanbedr recollection was of a passing tractor back-firing with a tremendous bang when I was six. Made sudden bang-shy for life, I was very apprehensive when told that a 21 gun royal salute would be fired at the review. Saluting guns fortunately were twelve pounders not 15 inch. The weather was misty; we could neither see nor hear the big ships lying a few miles eastwards at Spithead. In fact the only shooting came from two small boys firing cherry stones from a dickey at other cars in the queue going home.

A few days later crossing the Channel for the first time I found the sea was no friend of mine. My mother, a very bad sailor, lay down; my father – never sea sick – and I tucked into roast beef and pickles before going forward on deck to see the coast of France. "Look out", cried my father. I did; just in time to dodge a near miss from above as my own lunch landed on an unsuspecting passenger below.

With this background I must have had my doubts when RPM asked me if I'd like to join the Navy, adding that I was just the boy the Navy needed. So that was that. The immediate advantage was that during the summer evenings of 1925 we studied Euclid together in his study with an ample supply of Bourneville chocolate. After being a master at Osborne for fourteen years he certainly knew the ropes that candidates had to climb.

Osborne was now closed, Dartmouth being the one college taking the officer entry to the Royal Navy. A batch or 'term' of 45-50 cadets aged thirteen joined in January, May and September each year. Candidates had to undergo three tests in London: a medical, an interview and a written examination. My turn came early in February 1926. An anxious time for the family, my sister Brada living with her husband Jack Paterson in Markham Square had given birth to a daughter there after a Caesarean operation. Mother and child did well and so did I when I eventually went to sea because uncles dining in the gunroom are privileged – for reasons still unknown – to put their elbows on the table.

After dining at Simpsons in the Strand on their much over-rated roast beef and Yorkshire, my parents took me to Alice Delysia and Ernest Thesiger in *Still Dancing*, a cheery review. The following day my father left me at the Admiralty at 3pm for the medical to be followed by the interview. I remember first being asked to undress and climb a few feet up a rope. This it transpired was not a first exercise in getting to know the ropes, nor for any peculiar purpose readers might imagine. Just a routine check on no curvature of the spine!

The Dartmouth interview board was generally said to be composed of admirals but in fact there were only one or two, the others being schoolmasters. The most successful candidate was the boy who, when asked to name three admirals replied, "Nelson, Rodney and I didn't quite catch your name, Sir." There was later an Admiral-Chairman of a post-war selection board who told the Press, "The Navy only wants half wits; we'll put the other half there".

I forget what I was asked; my father having left to catch the 5.30 north from Euston one of its members escorted me back to Chelsea on top of a London bus. I often wondered whether that was still part of the interview. The two day written examination took place a month later at the Examination Rooms in Queen's Square, Bloomsbury. The papers were: English, History, Geography, Arithmetic, Algebra, Practical Geometry, Theoretical Geometry, French with oral exam and Latin. The Admiralty notified the parents of successful candidates a fortnight later before sending an alphabetical list to the Press.

Looking sixty five years later at all the subjects above, I cannot imagine how I was among them. I was not the first Brockhurst boy to go to Dartmouth. Frank Fletcher the second of two brothers from Boxmoor was two terms ahead of me. Later on there were L. G. Bloomer, A. R. (Tony) Marshall, RPM's son, J. C. Coldwell, G.P Blake and N. R. H. Rodney. Passing the Common Entrance exam without undue difficulty, most of RPM's boys went on to Public Schools. Rowley Hill, the middle brother of three whose father farmed at Marshbrook three miles down the line, became Head Boy of Shrewsbury, making a speech of welcome in Latin when the Prince of Wales paid a visit. Not that the Prince understood it! How do I know ? In later years I became acquainted with one of his tutors, Max Halliday a master at Eton, Epsom College and finally High Master at Eastbourne College. Max collected the Prince's written work, a surprising hobby since it was far from being a good advertisement for his tutor. All three Hills became clergymen, which was quite a testimonial to RPM's belief in manly Christianity and cold baths before breakfast. Now only Richard, the eldest, survives living quietly with his wife in Ludlow.

Another brotherly trio, whom I came to know in my wine trade 1950s, were Ken, Basil and Philip Kendall. Ken went to Shrewsbury from Mill Mead where he learnt to play cricket from the school coach, Neville Cardus, who became the celebrated music critic and cricket correspondent of the *Manchester Guardian*. Basil and Philip were at Brockhurst. These Kendalls were an Oporto family, associated with Croft and other port shippers, including Offley Forrester which Philip, my contemporary, joined after war service in the RAF. He died in 1991.

Their father A. C. Kendall was the leading light of the Oporto Cricket and Tennis club, attracting good sides, notably the Cryptics, to play cricket matches there between the wars. The Club's first such match had been Port v Pink Gin in 1863, their opponents being the Navy's Channel Squadron.

The three Hewat brothers, known as Yut 1, Yut 2 and Yut 3 came all the way from Putney, where their father lived while he was for many years Principal Medical Officer, Public Health Department of the London

County Council. Aubrey Middleton Hewat M.D retired to Bexhill reaching four score years and ten. Bamfords, Harleys, Kewleys, we had lots of brothers. Marris, I remember enthralled the Upper Green dorm after lights out with the Adventures of Tom, Dick and Harry which he solemnly swore he made up himself. But alas he never became a Sapper or a Dornford Yates; the Marris family turning the name round to Sirram, made their well known picnic baskets in Birmingham, where I fear our chum was required for duty.

A more successful *raconteur* was Don Gilchrist who returned to Brockhurst as a master in the middle Thirties and then wrote a book called *Seely-Bohm at School*, which was serialised in the *London Evening News* in 1939 just before the war. Seely Bohm was a likeable little boy always getting into trouble by accident or design. To any Old Brock it was obvious that Dr. Crump, the old fashioned headmaster was based on RPM. That Old Victorian was not amused, though few readers would have identified the book with any particular school. During the slump of the Thirties numbers at one time had dwindled from 47 to 25. Born in 1877 RPM was a Victorian, the same age as my mother incidentally. In 1919 when he took over Brockhurst he was already forty two. By 1942, gradually becoming deaf, he was a sad old man of sixty five unable to get staff for a run-down school with Britain very close to defeat in the Atlantic and the Germans occupying Europe from France to the Black Sea. And, as RPM might have said to the extra Latin class "To pile Ossa on Pelion the cruiser *Cornwall* has been sunk in the Indian Ocean by Japanese bombers and my son, Tony could be dead or their prisoner". *Dorsetshire* shared the same fate but happily Tony was among the 1,122 officers and men from the two cruisers picked up by our own ships after spending thirty hours in a shark-infested tropical sea.

By the end of the summer term when Brockhurst had been sold to St. Dunstans and the school was to close, a certain Mr. John Park appeared and said to the boys, "Do you want your school to close?" The answer was 'NO'. Thus, though the property went to St. Dunstans, RPM allowed John Park to find new premises for Brockhurst School. An agreement was made with Thompson of Broughton Hall School in Staffordshire, which allowed Brockhurst to share their hall, though operating separately. But the rival schoolboys had a pitched battle leading to litigation, and Park failed to win his case. The story reads rather like that farcical film *The Happiest Days of your Life* (1950) in which Alistair Sim, (Headmaster Boys) has to share with Margaret Rutherford (Headmistress Girls). Next in this unlikely tale two fairy godmothers, the Misses Harrison, offered Maer

RPM'S BROCKHURST

BROCKHURST SCHOOL – SUMMER 1921

Back row: Carmichael · Warren · Bather · Nicholl · Gilchrist · Kendall · Smith · Ditmas II · Tuke · Hall · Pritchard-Gordon
(M) Noel Newton (M) J. Whittaker
Pochin · Lloyd · Gardener · Milward · Ditmas I · Badger · (M) TII Harry · Buchanan · Meek · Toone · Pearson · Wills · Holland · Clegg-Hill
Seated: Mlle Junod · Kewley I · Barnaby · Bamford I · Marshall · (M)Gardener-Brown · Hepburn · Norah Marshall · RPM · Mrs Marshall (with Tony) · Bamford II · Sheppard · Bailey · Kewley II · (M) Miss Parkes
Front row: Tippet · Hogg · Cross · Beytagh · Marris · Hereford · Barbara Marshall · Harley · J.C. Fletcher · Davidson · Swinburne · Browne · Green
(M) = Master or Matron

Hall, their home some five miles away and Brockhurst was re-established there until 1945. With the war over it became possible to rent Marlston, a large 19th century house in the woods south east of Hermitage, a village north of Newbury. With willing help from John Park's sisters and others, Brockhurst continues to be a great success. There are now 150 boys at Marlston and 45 at the junior school.

After John Park died in June 1974, Nicolas Park, his nephew, and Jonathan Pudden, already his Co-headmaster, ran the school. John Park's eldest daughter married James Fleming, a regular in the Black Watch until he retired in 1947. He joined the staff as Bursar in 1976 after being a District Officer in Uganda for some years. Retiring in 1990 he is now busy making a record of Old Brocks from 1884 to the present day. Much of what I have written comes from his *Brockhurst Scrapbook 1884 to 1984*.

The Scrapbook ends with some old boys' opinions of RPM's Brockhurst. To R.H. Hill, my contemporary, he was a tall impressive figure, vigorous and energetic. Despite furious storms that blew up in Latin lessons reducing the victims to paralysed terror, he was a powerful influence for good and many boys remember him with gratitude and affection.

In Schools until the 1950s, with a few enlightened exceptions, corporal punishment was a matter of routine inflicted at will by masters and prefects. During the 1914-18 war in the Navy a Lieutenant finding fault with a midshipman on watch might hand him his signet ring. No instructions were necessary. The offender was required to take it to the Sub-Lieutenant in charge of the Gunroom returning it to the owner after, and not before, he had received six of the best.

After *Repton* and seven years association with the Navy at Osborne, RPM was bound to rely on the cane to maintain discipline, though I do not think he made excessive use of it during my time except once. Boys had to be trained to behave like little gentlemen. Filled with indignation over a boy reported to have farted in a prefect's face, RPM made an example of him in front of the first form. Disinclined to bend over, the victim received two or three across the back followed by six. This spectacle of a large man flogging a small boy for a childish offence remained a repugnant memory. When later in life I spent two years as Sub-Lieutenant of a battleship's Gunroom, having been at the receiving end often enough as a cadet, I regarded corporal punishment as an outworn shibboleth. Belatedly Europe has agreed with me. Julian Critchley, Conservative M.P. for Aldershot since 1974, found himself aged twelve at Brockhurst in 1942. His father, Macdonald Critchley, a distinguished neurologist of Bristol, naturally imagined that the heart of rural Shropshire would be safer for his little boy than remaining in a City frequently bombed by the *Luftwaffe*. Becoming a journalist later in life, Critchley has given his headmaster a stinking report. "The school was run as a penal institution. RPM would flog both privately and in public, with an abandon that today would have brought him before the courts. He combined a taste for punishment with a taste for piety."

His young pupil concedes they were well taught, not however in swimming, RPM's technique being to throw non-swimmers in at the deep end. To Critchley he gave this personal attention every Friday, his victim sinking like a stone, but when your initials are JC you are bound to bob up again. Relief came not from Nazi bombs but when kind and jolly Mr. J. F. Park took over and RPM retired to Devon.

We are not told whether the unfortunate Critchley, who describes himself as a nervous child, escaped the cane himself. Could he have been the boy to whom RPM was alleged to have said, "Don't stand there whimpering boy; you ought to stand up and say, 'Thank you sir, I think that's done me a great deal of good' " ?

The Marshalls were a nice family. Mabel was a Miss Trelawney-Hare. Expecting her to marry a blue-blooded aristocrat her own family were so toffee-nosed about schoolmasters that it was some years before they reluctantly accepted RPM. She ran the school well, played the harmonium and was kind to the boys. "I could not have had a better mother-in-law" said Helen, Bobby's American wife. Living with a deaf husband cannot be easy; perhaps she was the saint, not Bonar Law.

Hannah ("Bobby") the elder son had a successful advertising career in the U.S.A, returning to London and finally to Lavenham in Suffolk, where he died in October 1990. His American wife survives him. Norah born c1908 went from Brockhurst to the Godolphin School, Salisbury. Her first marriage to Lazonby ('Lal to his pals') soon ended in divorce. Attractive and good fun Norah's next husband Doug Winter owned the Boatyard in Salcombe. Together they messed about in boats from there to Spain and Portugal. There was a daughter of the first marriage who became Yvonne Dunne. Norah died in 1984. Catherine ('Ba') born c1914 won an Exhibition to Cheltenham Ladies College. After training to be a vet herself, she married one, Stafford Walter Beckett. They had two children John and Gay. John, a schoolmaster in Teignmouth, married in 1984, became a financial consultant. Though still in Teignmouth, he has an office in Torquay. 'Ba' became a magistrate and died of cancer in 1982.

A. C. (Tony) Marshall born 1918 was certainly well trained by his father for he not only made Dartmouth but became one of the two Chief Cadet

Captains. A survivor of the cruiser *Cornwall*, sunk by the Japanese in 1942, he served in submarines. The war over he became a London Stockbroker with Priors and married an actress. When she became seriously ill he nursed her devotedly and then died himself of a coronary. "He first deceased, she for a little tried, to live without him, liked it not and died." Jean Marshall, born 1926, is the last survivor and at sixty five looks like her father at forty, active and handsome. By 1942 she was a wartime bargee on the Grand Union Canal before joining that special section of the Wrens which ran boats during blitzes at our South coast ports. Becoming 'Jane' not 'Jean', for some reason when she married Pete Taylor, boats became their bread and butter with a business on the Hamble river called *The Ditty Box*.

When offered the chance of crewing a round-the-world yachting trip in 1953, they ended in New Zealand a year later with only a canvas bag and twenty dollars. Living rough with varied jobs, from dairy farming to establishing a successful bus company, they brought up a family of five children living by the sea at Russell in the North. Jane, one time skipper of the Paiha to Russell ferry was the P&O line's first woman captain. Starting a family was inspired by watching the birth of a calf. Distressed by cruelty to animals her house has long been a haven for dogs, injured birds and unwanted kittens. Kind to humans too – she has only just retired after ten years of driving the local ambulance for St. Johns.

A widow since 1989, Jane's supportive family descend at Christmas from different parts of the globe, while she still sails her own yacht on a coast that must remind her of Cornwall where her lively life first began. Address; Queens View, Oneroa Road, Russell, Bay of Islands, New Zealand.

RPM was not the only member of his family to become head of a boarding school. His sister, Mrs. Beatrice Burton Brown known as Beachie, was co-founder of Prior's Field, the girls' school still close to Charterhouse, near Godalming.

Prior's Field had been started in 1902 by Julia Huxley, married to Leonard with four children, Julian, Aldous, Trevenew, and Margaret. The pupils were six girls, aged between seven and a half and sixteen, plus Aldous aged eight and a staff of two. As one would expect of a granddaughter of Dr. Arnold of Rugby, Julia had her own plans and ideas, giving more freedom than was usual. By 1914 there were a hundred girls. Mrs. Burton-Brown, invited by Julia to join her, had been a partner since 1906. Not only a school, Prior's Field was the Huxley family's home, Margaret being a pupil while the three brothers returned from Eton for the holidays.

Early in 1908 Julia became ill. It fell to Beachie to tell her that she had cancer and on 29 November when only forty six Julia died and Beatrice took over the school alone. Aldous writes of his mother's death poignantly in *Antic Hay*.

By a curious coincidence my own parents spoke of meeting a charming Mrs. Burton Brown in June 1922 when on holiday in the Dolomites. Thirty years later coming with my wife to live in Chichester, we found that this great and much loved headmistress had retired and was our close neighbour; 'made for one another' as the television currently repeats nightly. She died on 4 October 1976.

Towards the end of the war the Brockhurst estate, sold by St. Dunstans, had become a Roman Catholic Training College for priests. There was little money and it was poorly maintained when I called in 1946. Disdaining an Anglican chapel, they worshipped in the gym, the chapel becoming some sort of a depository. For many years now the house has been flats, for elderly people mostly, so that the infamous swimming bath lies unused. Nowadays hundreds of people from Midland towns and cities get out and about these wooded Shropshire hills and valleys with their silver streams, while a few very Old Brocks remember nostalgically the Marshall's Sunday pies of bilberries, not found – like the grouse – south of the Longmynd.

Jane Taylor, youngest Marshall child, still active at Queen's View, Russell, New Zealand.

CHAPTER 3

GIEVES* ARRANGES EVERYTHING

The essential preparation for candidates was, *How to become a Naval Officer (Dartmouth)* written and published by Gieves, the naval tailors of 21 Old Bond Street, with branches at Portsmouth (The Hard), Chatham and some other naval ports.

Punctilious in keeping records they could then have told you Nelson's inside leg measurement and whether he dressed right or left. But these records were destroyed by a German bomb hitting No. 21 Bond Street in 1940 so that only Lady Hamilton can be said to have carried such intimate measurements to her grave. They have portraits of Captain Bligh of the *Bounty* and of the Duke of Wellington, whose waist increased by two inches about 1812, perhaps due to the first shipments of vintage port (matured in bottle not wood) to London clubs.

In 1913 operating as Gieve, Mathews and Seagrove Ltd., of 65 South Molton Street they first set up their fitting room for candidates in the Russell Hotel, Russell Square during the examinations, displaying 'A Sea Chest and Complete Outfit'. Mr. Robert Gieve, the present Vice-Chairman, calls these "Tea and Anxiety Sessions", the former a sedative for anxious parents. They continued into the 1930s. Learning that I was a 1926 Greynvile (G25 to be precise; like old lags at Dartmoor we each had our number) he lent me by return of post a copy of *How to become a Naval Officer*, and a 1935 List of Uniform, Hosiery and Sports Clothing with prices (6 sheets first quality 7 shillings) that was supplied to each cadet.

But the most impressive enclosure was an A to Z list of my 1926 Greynvile Term headed *Entered Dartmouth 47. Outfitted 47.* Gieves had no competitors at all where Dartmouth entry was concerned. Later, in my experience there was just one competitor. Finding Gieves rather expensive my mother suggested that a local tailor, Mr. Betteridge, in Epsom where we lived, could make me a reefer and trousers for much less. "After all", she said, "Mr. Betteridge has a son in the Merchant Navy and knows what to do". Accordingly, Mr. Betteridge, looking like Beatrix Potter's Tailor of Gloucester, went ahead drooling a little in his dimly lit room. "There"

---

*Like Jeeves.

said my mother, "It fits beautifully". We took it home and opened the parcel. In the daylight the suit was sky blue. I had it dyed; as the wearer I nearly died too, sweating in Malta with the dye running down my legs.

The two day written examinations took place in Queen's Square, Bloomsbury about six weeks before each of the terms that began in May, September and January. The results, published soon afterwards, gave Gieves about a month in which to make the clothing required, sending most of it with a trunk and a 'Gladstone' handbag to each cadet's home address. The rest he would find unpacked and stowed in his chest in the right dormitory at Dartmouth by stewards who were R.N. pensioners. The bill, £50 to £70, went to the cadets' parents who also paid the Admiralty about £50 a term for their offspring's education there.

One Mr. Gieve, so the story runs, when Chairman of the local Bench fined a Sub-Lieutenant £10 for reckless driving or some such offence. 'Put it down to my account Mr. Gieve' cried the impertinent young man, who was promptly fined a further fiver for contempt of court. In one of the big night air raids on Portsmouth in 1941, a Sub-Lieutenant and some ratings bravely saved No.21 The Hard from total destruction by putting out incendiary bombs on the roof as they fell. The Commander-in-Chief sent for him next day, adding after a formal commendation, 'When I think of all the Sub-Lieutenants with large unpaid accounts, you must be the most unpopular officer among your colleagues this morning'.

It is a fact however that in World Wars I and II and the Falklands 1982, Gieves never pressed for settlement any outstanding account of any customer killed in action. A gesture of which they must be proud and one of great help to the 1914—18 widows whose pensions were a disgrace.

Gieves little book rightly describes the Royal Navy as an honourable service and the first line of defence of the greatest Empire the world has ever seen. Conduct becoming an officer and a gentleman was essential to advancement up a ladder not made from the wrecked hopes of brother officers as in some other professions. This was sound comment, though any officer deciding to join the Engineering Branch might be inclined to put his spanner in the works of the Pall Mall United Service Club known as "The Senior", when he found only Executive Officers were regarded as 'gentlemen' eligible for membership. Free medical attention, adequate food partly paid for, duty free wines, beers and spirits when serving in H.M. Ships at sea and a pension on retirement in middle age were considerable advantages over civilian life.

As to the Empire few British people saw much of it until it had become the Commonwealth by the 1960s, when modern aircraft carried them above the weather in comfort rapidly around the world. In the inter-war years H.M Ships were on the China station, in the East and West Indies, and in South Africa so that naval officers not only saw the Empire but were entertained, made honorary members of the best clubs and played all manner of games with their hosts.

Based at Malta, the large Mediterranean fleet cruised regularly to Yugoslavia, Athens, the Greek Islands, Haifa, Alexandria, Oran, Tangier and Gibraltar, introducing the Ships' officers and men to the cradle of our civilisation. Roughly as large, the Atlantic or Home Fleet (the name changed in 1931) based itself on Gibraltar from January to March before a big war exercise took place with the Mediterranean Fleet in the Atlantic. This ended with both Fleets returning to Gibraltar for a week of analysing the exercise, inter-Fleet competitions, parties, 'runs ashore' and visiting other ships to have a gin with one's friends. A Ship's commission lasted two to two and a half years with long leave only on return to the home port. This was 42 days a year. For the men, whose state education had probably ended when they were boys of fourteen, a football match was more enjoyable than a guided tour of the Acropolis. The open mess tables and wooden benches, one along each side, had changed little since Nelson, while the officers' cabins with bunks, basins and piped hot water approached London club standards.

The Home Fleet returned to the Home Ports - Plymouth, Portsmouth and Chatham - to give leave throughout April, August and December, half of each Ship's Company taking fourteen days plus a week-end at a time. Seeing one's wife or family every three months was a tremendous advantage. There was until shortly before the war in 1939 no marriage allowance; in practice this meant that without private means few officers married much before they were thirty. There were, of course, a few ancient mariners said to be wedded to the Service, which may have meant that young ladies found them about as entertaining as the starboard watch of stokers.

The 'Med' Fleet did have one consolation; in Malta there was plenty of suitable accommodation for wives, sweethearts and 'The Fishing Fleet', those unattached young ladies who went out in the winter to stay with friends hoping to become attached by the spring.

The Home Fleet in May and June was preoccupied with practising for the Fleet Pulling Boat regatta held in Scapa Flow. Ships then dispersed to show the flag at English and Scottish resorts during July. The autumn cruise was to Rosyth and Invergordon exercising in the North Sea first on passage and then in the Moray Firth most weeks. After 1934 this routine was interrupted when in 1935 Mussolini invaded Abyssinia and in 1936 the Spanish Civil war began. After that came Hitler's aggressions leading to war in 1939.

How to become a Naval officer divides officers of the Royal Navy into military and non-military. the latter were the paymasters, surgeons, dental surgeons, instructors, constructors and chaplains, whose head was the Chaplain of the Fleet. The former were the Executives, from lowly cadets to captains and admirals in command of ships, squadrons and fleets and also officers with these same ranks, who chose to join the Engineering branch after the compulsory eight months training at sea as cadets.

In 1903 to train the military branch, Admiral Lord Fisher, the First Sea Lord, replaced the two old wooden hulks, *Britannia* and *Hindustan* moored together in the river Dart, with two new Colleges, Osborne on the Isle of Wight near Cowes, and Dartmouth in South Devon. A cadet spent his first two years at Osborne and his second at Dartmouth, where the new college designed by Sir Aston Webb (1884–1930) became H.M.S *Britannia*. (A leading British architect he later designed the new front to Buckingham Palace and the Admiralty arch at the other end of The Mall). Leaving Dartmouth aged seventeen the cadet would spend a further eight months at sea in a training ship before being made a midshipman. Osborne was closed in 1921 leaving Dartmouth alone to provide the general education in eleven terms. During the last three terms cadets went on weekly cruises in a Forres class sloop attached as a tender to H.M.S Britannia (the College) and finally, instead of another training ship, they were appointed to battleships or cruisers in the Fleet being made midshipmen after eight months if they behaved themselves. There was of course a written Passing-Out examination at Dartmouth, failed by one or two cadets occasionally, who lost three months seniority by having to sit the Exam again after an extra term. The midshipman spent a further two years and three months at sea before taking the Seamanship Examination for Lieutenant, a pass promoting him to Acting Sub Lieutenant.

After two terms at the Royal Naval College, Greenwich learning Mathematics, Physics, Applied Mechanics, Chemistry, French, English and Modern History, a further two terms were spent at Portsmouth for courses in Gunnery at Whale Island, Torpedoes and Electrics in H.M.S. *Vernon* and Navigation in H.M.S. *Dryad* all three shore establishments. Each of these five exams required 85 per cent for a First Class, 70 per cent for a Second Class and 60 per cent for a Third Class. With five firsts the holder was promoted to Lieutenant in nine months; with five thirds he had to wait three years.

All who passed were no longer 'Acting' but full Sub-Lieutenants with a single stripe of gold braid on each sleeve. The round jacket or 'bum freezer' and the dirk of a midshipman would now be replaced by a frock coat and sword and, with over a hundred young officers making the transition each year, Gieves must have been well pleased.

Summarising the way forward as the politicians are apt to say: promotion from Lieutenant to Lieutenant Commander was automatic after eight years. To Commander it was by selection from those between seniority of two years and seven years as Lieutenant Commanders.

From Commander to Captain it was again by selection, the zone being five to eight years as a Commander. From Captain to Rear-Admiral, to Vice-Admiral and to Admiral were then largely on seniority, those not promoted being retired. The highest rank Admiral of the Fleet was also by selection, usually confined to one, the First Sea Lord of the Admiralty. Besides Dartmouth, since 1913 there had been the 'Special' or 'Public School' entry at the age of seventeen. Numbers varied, being about forty a year in the Twenties. They were trained in the monitor H.M.S. *Erebus* moored in Plymouth before being sent to the Gunrooms of the Fleet. The two categories, 'Darts' and 'Pubs' met as Acting Sub-Lieutenants at the Royal Naval College, Greenwich for the course just described.

There were also opportunities, when a Lieutenant of two years seniority, to specialise in Gunnery, Torpedo, Navigation, Communications, Submarines, Anti-Submarine Warfare or the Fleet Air Arm. The attraction of *not* specialising was the likelihood of mainly small ship appointments, with a chance of a first command as a Lieutenant-Commander. A non-specialist remained a 'Salt Horse'.

CHAPTER 4

DARTMOUTH AT THE DOUBLE

THE TERMS

Chronological Order	*Admiral*	*Year of Birth*	*Dartmouth Order*
1	Greynvile	1541	1
2	Drake	1545	4
3	Blake	1599	3
4	Benbow	1653	9
5	Anson	1697	10
6	Hawke	1705	2
7	Rodney	1718	7
8	Hood	1724	8
9	Duncan	1731	6
10	St. Vincent	1735	5
11	Exmouth	1757	11

Each new term of cadets was required to join Dartmouth a day earlier than the others, the better to become acquainted with the College and its ways. We, the Summer 1926 Greynviles, should have assembled at Paddington to be escorted by Lieutenant-Commander H. W. McCall on Wednesday 5 May. On Monday 3 May with a general strike threatened, my mother and I went to London. Euston from Altrincham (Single Fare 22s. 8d, Lunch 4s.) having booked rooms at the Royal Court Hotel, Sloane Square. That evening my father received a telegram, 'Cadets should join Dartmouth forthwith'.

But on Tuesday May 4 there was not a bus, nor a tube, nor a train; Wednesday brought another Admiralty announcement on the wireless: 'All cadets to catch a train at 0915 from Paddington tomorrow'. But at 8 a.m on the morrow Cadet Hogg temporarily scared himself stiff finding he could not do up his Gieves stiff collar nor get to Paddington because taxis had all joined the strike.

Fortunately young Mr. Wilde, the son of the hotel's proprietor kindly drove my mother and me to Paddington. The train was crowded, the cadets' reserved coaches crammed. We novices squeezed into a corridor to squat on our Gieves 'Gladstone' handbags. Three bowler-hatted drivers were said to be on the foot plate, one a clergyman, which must have made his dog collar fit only for an old black retriever. At Newbury there was a long delay. I learnt later that my brother-in-law and his friend Dick Riviere were running the signal box, stopping all drivers to discover whether any were, like them, Old Etonians. Proceeding via Bristol all cadets disembarked at Newton Abbot late in the afternoon, but the buses for us had gone to Totnes, so it was back to the train. Towards dusk our bus passed some tennis courts. I could just see a notice that said *Speed Limit 15 knots*.

I don't recall having anything to eat or drink on this journey, not even my favourite tipple 'Champagne Ciderette'. It became my longest day until June 6 1944 off the Cherbourg peninsula protecting the American landings on *Utah* beach in the cruiser *Black Prince*. Straddled at dawn by a shore battery, by 6pm it was safe to abandon Action Stations and open the Wardroom bar.

On the train I had already met my first two Greynviles, J. C. M. Harman and C. B. Jelf, fellow squatters in the corridor. Now, over a very welcome tea awaiting us was P. W. Gretton. The war to end war had only ended eight years before; it was unbelievable that there could be another European war against the same enemy employing the same Starve Britain tactics at sea. Yet World War II is now history, and if any one man could be called the leader in defeating the U-boats in the Battle of the Atlantic it would be a Convoy Escort Commander who had become, before ill health forced his retirement, Vice-Admiral Sir Peter Gretton, KCB., DSO., OBE., DSC.

Facing south on its hill looking over Kingswear, with the town of Dartmouth hidden in its own hollow on the opposite side of the Dart, Sir Aston Webb's building is an impressive edifice.

From the main entrance under the big clock tower one can look South to the open sea beyond the Castle that has guarded the narrow harbour entrance since the days of Drake. A balustrade in front of the main entrance, with steps leading down to a large parade ground, forms the saluting base when cadets march past. And across the stone frontage of the College itself are the words in three foot lettering: *It is upon the Navy under the good providence of God that the safety honour and welfare of this realm do chiefly depend* – taken from Articles of War in the reign of Charles II.

The wardroom and dining room for staff officers, the galley and a large dining hall that fed the five senior terms occupied the South West corner.

At the South East corner was the chapel and the Captain's house. Indoors between these two corners stretched a long wide corridor passing the gunrooms of terms 8, 9, 10 and 11. At meal times each term fell in outside its gunroom charging ravenously for the dining hall on the order "Right Turn Double March". Likewise term 7 whose gunroom was tucked away at right angles in a position that overlooked the Headmaster's House and garden.

Terms 1 to 6, constituting the junior college, occupied 'D' block, added on the north side above the main building with its own dining hall and long corridor passing the six gunrooms of Terms formerly at Osborne.

Close to the main entrance was the Quarterdeck a fine rectangular space with a parquet floor, lined on each side by classrooms and surrounded up above by a gallery for spectators.

It was used as an indoor place of assembly for Evening Quarters with Prayers, monthly payments, dancing and occasionally theatricals. Each gunroom was furnished with three long tables, six benches and lockers, one for the books of each cadet. Our only recreation space, it could seat the whole term for prep or a harangue from the Term Officer.

The dormitories were on the three floors above the long corridor, each one with beds and sea chests for about thirty cadets. With terms of about forty five this left fifteen of one term to share with fifteen of another, which should have been no problem except that cadets were not allowed to speak to those of another term. For the juniors it would be cheeky, for the seniors the authorities would consider immorality to be imminent in this establishment where permission to converse even with a brother in another term had to be obtained.

The Admiralty view of human nature was quite simple. Where two persons were gathered together immorality would take place. Even a Term officer was not permitted to live locally with his wife during term time, for that would take his mind off his duties at the College.

Between the dormitories there were washrooms with baths, basins and a 'plunge', an expanse of cold salt water said to be run off from the swimming bath higher up, in which cadets were expected to plunge when a bugle sounded reveille. An unusual number of cadets had ear trouble resulting in the painful mastoid operation removing bone behind it, this stale sea water being a possible cause of the infection.

Between dormitories too there was a comfortable cabin large enough for Term officer Henry McCall to keep a dog, and a dog whip he deemed better than a service pattern cane for administering cuts.

Breaches of service or college customs were known as 'guff'.

Some examples: forgetting to salute a passing officer or master; entering the gunroom of any term but one's own; failing to double past the gunroom of any term senior to one's own; hands in pockets (mostly sewn up fortunately). In the dormitory, clothing not laid out on sea chests in the customary manner; chests not 'dressed' in a straight line; talking after lights out. In the manner of a traffic warden, the Cadet Captain (prefect) attached to each term would note infringements with a tick in his little book reporting them to the Term officer, the standard punishment then being three cuts in pyjamas after lights out.

The best advice for a new cadet in the Twenties and Thirties was that popular song *Run Rabbit Run*, which reminds me that yet another punishment was half an hour doubling up and down a roadway near the gym under the supervision of a P.T.I. (Physical Training Instructor). I had to do it once but I really cannot remember why.

This was the timetable for weekdays in Summer.

Time
0635 .... Call terms 8 to 11.
0700 .... Studies
0730 .... Call terms 1 to 7.
0750 .... Muster in Gun rooms
0755 .... Studies dismiss. BREAKFAST
0845 .... Senior College provide arms — Rifle Drill
0856 .... Divisions on parade ground. Prayers
0910 .... Studies
1005 .... Change Studies
1100 .... Stand Easy
1120 .... Studies.
1210 .... Change Studies
1305 .... Studies dismiss
1310 .... DINNER
1345 .... Medical muster in dormitories
1435 .... Sandquay classes fall in. March to Engineering workshops.
1445 .... Studies.
1535 .... Change studies.
1630 .... Studies dismiss. Tea in messroom. Shift into flannels.
1650 .... Clear college for recreation
1910 .... Return to College and Shift.
1920 .... SUPPER
1950–2035 .... PREP
2045 .... Junior College turn in
2120 .... Remainder turn in
2135 .... Rounds of dormitories

NOTES: Wednesday and Saturdays. Half days with recreation from 1355 to 1910. Dancing after Supper
Winter. Recreation from 1420 to 1600
Sundays - 0930 Divisions 0955 to 1100. Services and Divinity 1230 Dinner. 1300 to 1945 Cadets allowed out of College
2000 Evening Quarters. 2015 Church 2100 Turn in.

Scheme of Studies.
Class periods were allocated as follows:

Mathematics	6	
Science, with laboratory work	6	
Engineering	4	(2 in the first four terms)
French	4	
History and Naval History	2	
Geography	2	in the first 4 terms
*Scripture	2	
Seamanship	2	
Navigator and Pilotage	2 or 3	(in the last year)
Drill and Physical Training	2	
*General Lectures	1	(in first seven terms)

For different subjects each term was divided into three classes marks being given after examinations in the third, fifth and eight terms. One of the masters was assigned as a tutor to each cadet, a tutor set being held weekly, but the tutor played little or no part in his tuition or advancement.

Alpha Class Brain-child about 1928 of Eric Kempson, Headmaster, this group was selected from the ablest cadets in their last year to do more advanced work with more time for personal study. Some of their passing out papers were different.

Passing Out Examination. A First class advanced the date of promotion from Acting Sub-Lieutenant to Sub-Lieutenant by four months; a Second Class by two months.

The Teaching Staff.
The naval staff under Captain Dunbar-Nasmith VC, a submariner who had destroyed ninety six Turkish vessels in the Sea of Marmara during the war, ran the games, college discipline and the teaching of naval subjects. A Commander as executive officer ran the place. One Lieutenant

---
* Not part of Passing Out Examinations

JUST A HOGG'S LIFE

looked after two terms, a senior and a junior aiming to be like a Public School housemaster, guide, philosopher and friend to each of his cadets. The total number of officers in 1927 including an Engineer Commander with two Engineer Lieutenants, a Paymaster Commander with two Paymaster Lieutenants and several medical officers came to twenty eight.

The professional staff, counting the mortar boards in my 1927 staff photograph, came to thirty nine and, with few exceptions, a pretty dreary lot of old has-beens they were. There was PTH relating with sadistic pleasure the fate of some cadet who had displeased him - 'Did I report him, the first day? Did I report him the second day? No! I waited a week until he thought I had forgotten, then I reported him'. Geography, which was only taught for the first four terms, was in the hands of W. L. Bunting, a former Rugger international. In the Staff alphabetical list after ten years his name was still marked 'Temporary Addl:' which stood for additional not addled.

Permanently addled would have been apt for 'Mossy' Warner, whose one egg-stained blue serge suit, with celluloid collar achieved the strongest of all stinks in the laboratory. However I remember with pleasure some General Lectures by masters on their own subjects for which one volunteered. Mr. Grenfell an RNVR officer in the British monitor *Severn* had followed and destroyed the German raider Königsberg up the Rufigi river in East Africa. Mr. Ferguson imparted his enthusiasm for Gilbert and Sullivan with gramophone records. Mr. Piggott the deputy head and a fine organist, took us a stage further to Bach. And there was English from Mr. Brophy who, reading aloud J. C. Squire's poem *To a Bull-dog** reduced his class — at least temporarily - to weeping pacifists.

I also remember the youngest and most successful of the masters, because teaching us French only for a term, he and his wife asked me out to tea. Educated himself at Osborne, Dartmouth and King's College Cambridge, George Barnes taught French for three years before climbing swiftly up the BBC ladder from Director of Talks and Head of the Third Programme, to Director of Television in 1950. Knighted in 1953 he became Keele University's first Chancellor dying tragically, when still young.

Recreation
Facilities for recreation were excellent. From the back of 'D' block the rose walk led to the gymnasium and indoor swimming bath with squash courts close by. Halfway down the steps to Sandquay there was a racquet court.

---

*An Anthology of Modern Verse. Methuen 1934.

GREYNVILLE TERM 1926-1929 ON LEAVING IN DECEMBER

Baines Smeeton Cockburn-Mercer Moss Dobbs Bintley
Barstow   CPO Mitchelmore   Hogg
Nares   Fanshawe
Ruck-Keene
  Yorke   Hallwright Custance Rose Wheen Baker Ham
Kimpton Duff Jelf Gretton Harrel Finch Knox Robinson Lewin Cardew
Fisher Holford Harman Bonsey Groome Burton McKendrick Briggs Woodward
Champness Verner-Jeffreys McBarnet Woodhouse Carter Hankey Scott Stuart-Menteth
Lt. Cdr. Havers   Lieut E Nicholson

A path passing the Beagle Kennels led to one playing field large enough to take two games of cricket or football at a time, with another of similar size and a canteen on a higher level above. More extensive playing fields were at Norton, a mile from the College on the B3207 road. Tennis Courts and a rifle range completed the amenities.

For cricket and rugby there were three College teams, each with a fixture list: Junior, Colts and First all supported by cries of 'Ship' from the touch line, 'Britannia' sounding a bit wet, which meant silly. In the Easter term the games were soccer to keep in touch with the sailors, and hockey useful on hard grounds abroad. There was no polo but anybody could hunt with the beagles.

A different form of recreation appealing to those who disliked organised ball games was sailing on the Dart in cutters or whalers, or just taking a Blue boat and rowing. This could be done on Wednesday, Saturdays and Sundays with steam boats ready to rescue the novice or to tow the sailing boats to race outside the harbour in Summer. The celebrated sea-going ketch *Amaryllis* belonged to the college too. When as midshipmen in the fleet our primary duty would soon be taking charge of picket boats and launches, what better training could there be?

When the bugle sounded 'Clear College' after lunch, these exercises, whether on land or sea, qualified as 'a log' required of each cadet. In winter when the gales blew and the grounds were unfit for play, a log

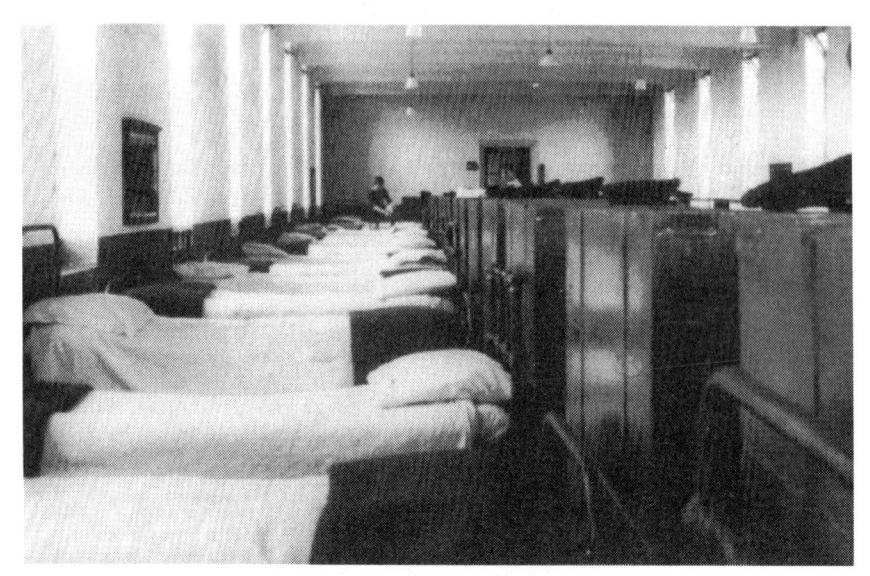

Troubridge dormitory 1930; note chests in line, caps on top.

needed a two mile run to Black Cottage on the Stoke Fleming road, and back. This too was training for the future for a very tiresome admiral called Arbuthnot had left the Fleet a trophy for a road race, craftily calculated to involve every man and boy from every ship annually in November.

After the sixth term when we Greynviles formed part of the Senior college, life became easier and more lively. Henry McCall left, making a place for himself in history in 1939 as the Captain who was Naval Attaché in Montevideo, where the German pocket battleship arrived after the action with the British cruisers, *Exeter*, *Ajax* and *Achilles*. In the film of *The Battle of the River Plate* he appears telephoning in uncoded English a demand for fuel that misled the Germans into the belief that more powerful British ships would be awaiting *Graf Spee* if she left Montevideo, a ruse that played its part in Captain Langsdorff's decision to scuttle his ship. After further distinguished war service mainly in the Mediterranean, he retired as a full Admiral in 1953. Two of the term incidentally played their parts too: E.D.G.Lewin as pilot of the *Ajax* aircraft reporting enemy movements and D. T. McBarnet wounded in *Exeter* when controlling her fire.

McCall's successor was A. A. Havers, Navy Rugby player and swimmer known as 'Pog'. Unmarried, he played a great part in the Term's activities walking most of us in turns on Sundays a prodigious distance for two eggs *and* an enormous Devonshire cream tea, which cost 1s. 6d. each.

There were several places nearer at hand for Sunday teas but at two shillings. I was in a group which patronised a Bed and Breakfast cottage some three miles away. By bolting our roast seagull at lunch, we could just reach The Sportsman's Arms in time for a pint before closing time at 1430. Nearly everybody smoked then - pipes were manly - but smoking was not allowed in the Navy when under 18. At the cottage of course, out came the pipes and the packets of Players, until one afternoon with the room full of smoke a young couple arrived to inquire about rooms. The visitor was Anthony Kimmins, another nice term officer, just married to Elizabeth Hodges, daughter of Admiral Sir Michael, soon to be Commander-in-Chief Atlantic Fleet.

Would he report us the first day or wait a week like PTH? Fortunately he pretended not to see us, more concerned perhaps that by having his wife so close to the College in term time he too was breaking the rules.

Anthony Kimmins, educated at Osborne and Dartmouth, had been a midshipman in The Grand Fleet during the war, and was one of the first Fleet Air Arm pilots after it. In 1932 he retired to become an Author,

Playwright, Film Producer and Director. His comedy in 1932 *While Parents Sleep* ran for years in London. But when war came in 1939 his many commentaries on naval operations, broadcast live for the BBC from ships as the bombs fell around them, were memorable. By 1945 he was Chief of Naval Information, British Pacific Fleet with the rank of Captain.

Although I doubt whether we Greynviles differed much from other terms, we were sufficiently high-spirited to earn a reputation of being, 'A bit bolshie', a word my mother always pronounced 'Bowl-she'. The Russian revolution had been over for nearly ten years yet it was still the subject of ignominy in popular taste.

In the *Daily Mirror*'s strip cartoon, characters such as Popski, the Russian dog and Wtzkoffski, a bewhiskered person dressed like Guy Fawkes, laid the foulest plots for Pip, Squeak and Wilfred. At Dartmouth two foremen of the Office of Works, who habitually marched round the grounds together looking rather scruffy, were known as Lenin and Trotsky and 'A bit bolshie' was universally applied to those not amenable to discipline.

Trouble arose when somebody complained to Havers that his term were not singing at Evensong. Probably it was an isolated case of not knowing the hymn tunes. However, Havers enlisted our co-operation suggesting

Senior Terms Messroom, 1931.

that we should cease to sing at all to demonstrate the true magnitude of our normal contribution. Only when we saw that Harry Piggott, a more lively player, was at the organ instead of Mr. Locke should we call off the strike. After a week or two Harry Piggott duly appeared when Havers and half the term were away in Forres, the training sloop. What a relief! Twenty four Greynviles opened up, singing to the Lord with cheerful voice. Pavarotti would have been proud of us. There were no further complaints.

During our last term two Greynviles were sentenced to an O.C. for the heinous crime of playing a radio during prep. O.C. stood for 'Official Caning', all the other canings to which we were subjected being unofficial! The punishment engendered the greatest awe and speculation. It was said that the sentence was executed in the gymnasium by a Sergeant-Major of the Royal Marines of phenomenal muscular power, that the recipient was tied across a box-horse and that the proceedings started when the Sergeant-Major reported to the Commander, who replied in a voice of great solemnity, "Do your duty Sergeant!" Furthermore that the Sergeant reported again after each cut and should the recipient unfortunately faint, the medical officer was present with sponge and cold water so that the job could be finished on a conscious cadet.

At the appointed time the Greynviles filled those dormitory windows that gave an excellent view of the rose walk leading down from the gymnasium to the main buildings. When at last the two malefactors emerged looking none the worse for their experience, a great cheer was raised. But it was soon evident from the tale they had to tell, that an 'O.C' was not what it was cracked up to be. The Executioner, far from being the redoubtable sergeant was in fact the fat and kindly old Commissioned Gunner, who could have been seen beforehand walking up the rose walk, rather breathlessly, carrying his canes wrapped up in brown paper hoping thereby to conceal his distasteful mission. Furthermore this was not the only paper involved in the affair, the material also makes good protective clothing inside the trousers. Learning the truth their term mates felt that the great cheer had perhaps been overdone.

The college authorities looked at the matter differently. The cheer was a pre-meditated collective act of insubordination and the Greynviles, after being addressed at length on the honour and tradition of the Service, to say nothing of common good manners, were deprived of a larger number of privileges for one month.

For dancing on the Quarterdeck the cadets formed their own band but more often the professional Royal Marine (Pensioners) orchestra performed. A versatile band of musicians, they blared out *Colonel Bogey* and *Blaze Away* on the parade ground in the morning and, more mellifluously, fiddled sweet dulcet tones of contemporary hits like *Tea for Two* and *Bye-Bye Blackbird* at night, though their tempo would have surprised Victor Sylvester as much as a cadet's idea of a reverse turn. We danced together because tradition decreed that sailors did. There were no girls so the only variation was approaching one's term officer, a blue chinned Navy XV forward as like as not, saying in a piercing treble, "May I have the pleasure of this dance, Sir?"

Sometime after the war the First Lieutenant was Ian Cox, a friend who like me lived in Chichester. The Captain sent for him one day and said,

"About this visit of the French training ship, you realise, Cox, that every Frenchman thinks every Englishman is a homosexual; what will they say if they see the cadets dancing together?"

'Well, Sir I had better cancel the dancing on the evening they are to be shown round the College', Ian replied.

'Certainly not, Cox! certainly not! Dancing is a naval tradition. Just change the time table so they don't see it'.

This was how a party of bewildered Frenchmen found themselves at dusk on the playing fields of Norton a mile out of the town.

Aerial view of the College, 1919.

The College choir composed of masters and cadets performed well in the chapel accompanied at times by the strings. After a voice trial when we joined, I was in fact a reserve, but I was so hoarse from shouting 'Come on Ship' the previous day that I had no voice at all. I still have however, the Carol Service programme of Sunday December 1938 to which I was invited, probably by Peter Gretton, then a Term officer. It includes the XVI century Italian carol, *Once as I remember at the time of Yule* and the Dutch *King Jesus hath a garden'*, 'Gibbo', a master, being to the fore on 'the tender soothing flute'. This latter carol returned to the King's College Cambridge service in 1990, but the former I do not remember ever hearing again.

Thomas Crick the Senior Chaplain, who later became Chaplain of the Fleet and Dean of Rochester, prepared us for Confirmation. This was entirely voluntary, a point he repeatedly made saying 'It's your pigeon, Greynviles', which always reminds me of the Frenchman who had no religion at all.

> *Il y avait un jeune homme de Dijon*
> *Qui n'avait point de religion*
> *Il disait 'Ma foi qu'l m'embête tous les trois,*
> *Le Père, le fils et le pigeon'*

I was among the ninety cadets confirmed on Sunday July 10 1927 by Lord William Cecil, Bishop of Exeter, a magnificent figure with a great big beard who might have been Abraham himself.

Attending Holy Communion at 8 a.m. on Sundays subsequently, had the disadvantage of finding, when we emerged for breakfast, that 'the heathen minority' had eaten all the marmalade.

The other Chaplain, William Anderson, frothing a little at the mouth, preached a sermon largely about a woman's body being the most beautiful thing in the world. Unacquainted with carnal knowledge so far, this was a novel subject to which we all listened with rapt attention. William Anderson was certainly a man of the world. He had already served in four services: (1) Army Sergeant Major 1911-16, (2) Royal Naval Air Service 1916-18, (3) Flight Lieutenant RAF 1918-19. (4) The Church, in which he finally became Bishop of Salisbury 1949-55, where I hope he found that wonderful spire even more inspiring than feminine heads, bodies and legs.

For cadets even to see a female it was necessary either to be ill in the hospital, where there was a matron and two sisters, one of them the attractive Sister James from Tarporley, Cheshire, or to visit the canteen where the serving ladies were known (pardon the breach of common good manners) as hags. From the seventh term dormitories we looked eagerly for a glimpse of the headmaster's daughter Rachel Kempson, but she was away at boarding school or learning how to be an actress from Cyril Maud, the famous actor who lived in retirement near Dartmouth.

At best we only saw her horse in the field as we marched down the steps to engineering at Sandquay. This animal was so seldom without an erection that it came to be regarded as a barometer, like the novelty toy summer house of the times with its little man or woman popping out. Wet weather when out; fine weather when in; just about right for the West Country!

For me games were the most enjoyable feature. Moderate at cricket I kept wicket for the term, usually dropping the ball amid confident cries of "How's that?" to the dismay of my team mates. At soccer I made the first XI in my ninth term. The best match, against Bradfield, never seemed to come off due to some epidemic. At rugger I was a centre or wing three quarter for the Colts but hopes of the first XV were dashed when I was carried off with a broken ankle half way through the last term.

Nowadays with a fractured fibula and tibia in plaster, the victim leads a normal life, but in 1929 it meant a month in hospital. I still recall my acute disappointment when not allowed out to watch the match against Downside. Public school boys approaching eighteen were apt to be heavier and to run faster than cadets, who left Dartmouth at seventeen. This time, hoping for a first win, we lost 10-9.

Work, that last term, was largely revision for the Passing Out exam. I had passed in about fifteenth in the term, steadily descending into the thirties as the syllabus gave more time to mathematics, science and engineering at the expense of the Humanities. To swot by oneself in hospital was not easy, the prospect of failing the exam and returning for another term when one's own term mates had gone to sea was the spur to scorn delights and live laborious days. The Alpha class had special treatment but for me the damaged, slowest ship of the Greynvile convoy there was only an exhortation to work harder from Percy T.H. Harrison. (PTH)

The broken ankle was not the only pain I was to suffer that last term. Early in December the Royal Navy XV played Devon, the match that year being at Torquay. Leave was given and a large number of cadets climbed through the woods in the train from Kingswear to Paignton. Arriving on the platform for the return journey, after a good tea at Dellers, somebody said that Fogg-Elliot, the Lieutenant in charge, had already gone back by an earlier train. It seemed safe to light our pipes. But this information was false; five of us Baker, Dobbs, Wheen,* Hogg and Jelf had our names taken.

With only ten days to go before the end of term Baker and Wheen being Cadet Captains were disrated. Dobbs, Hogg and Jelf were each awarded an O.C of six cuts. Havers refused to have any member of his term strapped. "They know how to bend over", he said. Dobbs kept a copy of the day's *Times* which I thought too risky. In the event one cut missed *The Times* making a completely different sound to the others much to the amusement of Havers and our two Cadet Captains, Duff and Harrel, who had to witness the punishment.

I like to tell people that an O.C. was usually awarded for acts of the grossest immorality. When they wait salaciously for some case of mistaken genders or an affair with a beagle, it is pleasing to say my act was just, "Did smoke pipe on Paignton platform".

---

*Obliged by poor eyesight, Wheen transferred at Dartmouth to the Supply branch, becoming a Rear-Admiral C.B. on retirement in 1966. Living at Chobhamwith his family, he remained active in local affairs and a very good golfer of the region.

H.M. Yacht Victoria and Albert *visits Dartmouth, July 22 1939.*

To celebrate our departure I arranged a term dinner at the *Isola Bella* in Frith Street. My parents kindly agreed to put up my friends Knox, Cockburn-Mercer and Jelf at Richmond House, Epsom into which we had recently moved. Leaving in good time to catch the last train from Waterloo we lost Knox in Piccadilly Circus and looking for him, the three of us missed the last train. What were we to do ? We had no money for a hotel. But Cockburn- Mercer had Pog's address in Kensington so we took a taxi.

Greatly ashamed, I was sick on the doorstep over my dinner jacket before being put to bed by Pog and his mother. In the morning a telephone call to Epsom revealed that about 2 a.m. Willie Knox had arrived in the care of a policeman. Later Willie was to describe how, feeling rather drunk he did not like to ask the police how to find Richmond House but eventually he did go to the police station.

It was bitterly cold when my father, the Judge, opened the front door without his false teeth and with his pyjamas rolled up to the knee, which for reasons unknown, was his custom. A good host, he said "You must be cold, have a whisky and soda". Poor Willie nearly passed out at the thought.

None the worse he slept till lunch time, while I, still in my revolting dinner jacket, faced the daylight journey home through London, suffering a new experience called a hang-over.

Some days later I was greatly relieved to find I had Passed Out of Dartmouth, last but two or, more accurately, five. Three members of the term having failed would have to return for the extra term. After Passing Out already on my term officer's doorstep, failure for me would have constituted a double.

CHAPTER 5

MIDSHIPMAN MOD

Soon after Christmas I received that famous letter its form probably unchanged since the days of Marryat's Peter Simple.

CW.   *By Command of the Commissioners*
for Executing the Office of Lord High
Admiral of the United Kingdom, ec.

To   *Mr. A. L. S. Hogg RN*
THE Lord Commissioners of the Admiralty hereby appoint you *Naval Cadet*
of His Majesty's Ship *"Rodney"*
and direct you to repair or board that Ship
at *Portsmouth* on *7th January 1930*
Your appointment is to take effect from that date.....
You are to acknowledge the receipt of this Appointment *forthwith*, addressing your letter to the Commanding Officer,
HMS *"Rodney"*
taking care to furnish your address.

By Command of their Lordships
O. Murray
Admiralty, S.W.1

   In this case obeying the command merely entailed catching a steam train from Waterloo to Portsmouth Harbour and taking a taxi to South Railway jetty, where Britain's latest battleship could be seen lying alongside with a large gangway to walk up.

   There was no likelihood of being made drunk like Peter Simple, then led to believe he had insulted his captain and finally finding himself fighting a duel. However uncertainties can arise. In the early months of the 1939-45 war a midshipman living in Gloucestershire was instructed to join a battleship at Scapa Flow forthwith.

   Deciding that 'forthwith' meant 'immediately', he took a taxi all the way to Wick, boarded a ferry and managed to join just before his ship sailed. His expenses claim, approved by the Captain, found its way to the Admiralty, where accountants deliberated for months as to whether it was reasonable. Had it not been for action generated by Dunkirk it might still be unpaid.

Nelson and *Rodney*, forming the second Battle Squadron were designed by Sir Eustace Tennyson d'Eyncourt with all nine 16 inch guns forward, a control tower aft of the guns known as Queen Anne's mansions and below the upper deck a belt of armour that projected as far aft as the engines. *Rodney* built at Birkenhead by Cammell Laird and launched by Princess Mary, Viscountess Lascelles in December 1925 commissioned in 1927. She was 710 feet long, 106 feet at her widest point, with a displacement of 35,000 tons drawing about 32 feet of water. Her secondary armament on either side aft were six 6 inch guns in three turrets (twelve guns in all) while on the boat deck above there was a battery of 4.7 inch anti-aircraft guns, augmented by Pom Poms Lewis guns and saluting guns. There were torpedoes too, 21 inch fired underwater from the bows.

Stowed on the boat deck in crutches and hoisted out with a main derrick were two 20 ton picket boats and two launches, each taking 120 liberty men. Two cutters, two whalers, two gigs and a Captain's motorboat were secured at davits along the upper deck ready for use when required.

Completed two years earlier, *Nelson* was the flagship of the Atlantic Fleet flying the flag of the Commander-in-Chief and accommodating most of the Fleet Staff officers. *Rodney* being a 'private' ship the Captain could live in the Admiral's spacious quarters aft with a dining cabin that could seat twenty people comfortably. The Commander – second in command – moved up one too but – if *Nelson* was refitting for example – the Admiral and his staff would move to *Rodney*, so the names above the doors were not changed. Thus, one cadet, unaware of these domestic matters, bearing a message for the Captain tapped on his W.C. door saying "Captain Sir" was rather shaken when a voice within replied, "No, no, my boy I'm quite alone."

We midshipmen and cadets were, if I remember rightly, "Bipeds of incredible stupidity used to convey messages of abuse between officers of unequal seniority".

"Mr. Hogg, go and tell the First Lieutenant that if he cannot get the picking-up rope to the buoy any quicker...!"

"Snotty, when you call the relief, kick Lieutenant Slocombe out of his bunk, otherwise he'll never turn out!"

"Put your wheel the other way, boy, and go astern on the port engine!"

Life would have been rather more difficult had we carried out our instructions to the letter! Fortunately perhaps, they were often only half heard, for words are apt to get lost if spoken, however loudly, into a 20-knot wind on a battleship's bridge or at a chugging picket boat from a quarterdeck twenty feet above.

HMS Rodney, Britain's new battleship. Algiers, February 1930.

JUST A HOGG'S LIFE

We messed in the gunroom and slept in a vast cabin 'flat'. Our hammocks were slung nightly near our chests and stowed away by boys of the ship's company who received the princely sum of one penny a day for their labour. I remember after two months, when my sheets looked as grey as the ship's side, asking my hammock boy if he had changed them. "Not this cruise, sir!" he replied in a voice of great astonishment and indignation.

At 0630 we would do P.T on the quarter deck - a customary but imprudent arrangement, for the deck was still being scrubbed.

Before 9 a.m. we had washed, shaved, run baths for our superior officers, the Sub-Lieutenants, done a 15-minute exercise in semaphore signalling, had breakfast and (when very junior) polished some brass work in the gunroom. For the rest of the day until 4 p.m. we were mostly "under instruction," a term embracing a variety of subjects from making a Double Mathew Walker (a knot, not a brand of spirits) to the study of heavenly bodies - which is concerned with navigation, not film stars.

These last, however, had their share in our lives. Ian Hay and Stephen King-Hall had followed their humorous play, *The Middle Watch* with *The Midshipmaid* and there was hardly a gunroom in the 1930s without a photograph of the entrancing Jane Baxter in the name part. The play was

Morning P.T. on board H.M.S. Rodney.

also the thing in HMS *Rodney*; I had hardly been on board a week before being summoned to the Wardroom for a voice trial. It was said that the Commander, Robert Burnett had written privately to the Commander at Dartmouth hoping that our batch of six would comprise two rugby footballers, two cricketers, one boxer and one cadet with a falsetto voice. My attempts in this role soon failed but my husky baritone was considered eminently suited to the female chorus of *District Visitors* destined later (as well it might!) to delight the combined Atlantic and Mediterranean fleets meeting for the annual spring "war".

The complement of *Rodney* was 1,300 officers and men. At Action Stations less than 5 per cent saw the 16 inch guns firing. The majority were below in medical parties, repair parties, communication parties, fire parties, control parties, with some two hundred in the boiler and engine rooms coaxing 23 knots out of the monster if needed. Also embarked was the detachment of Royal Marines, which provided that indispensable combination for entertainment and ceremonials on board or ashore, the Guard and Band.

The ship had spacious sick quarters with an X-ray department, six telephone exchanges, a post office, a reading room, a library, a book stall and a recreation place for showing films.

Contributing useful profits to the sports fund was the N.A.A.F.I dry canteen, virtually a good grocer and tobacconist. The initials stand for Navy, Army and Air Force Institute, a body more efficient than its nickname, No Aim, Ambition or F*****g Interest, implies.

On January 7, when the six of us joined, another new arrival was enjoying his forty seventh birthday. Captain Andrew Browne Cunningham D.S.O and Two Bars was reputed to be a strict martinet. Wedded so far to the twelve ships he had previously commanded, on December 21 he had married Nona Byatt, whose brother Sir Horace Byatt had just retired as Governor of Trinidad. He joked that she was his thirteenth successive command and the *Rodney*s all hoped that marriage would mellow him a little.

Becoming a cadet in *Britannia* in 1897, ABC, as he became known to the Navy, first saw land action when visiting the naval brigade in the Boer war. His first command, a Torpedo Boat, came in 1908. In 1915 another naval brigade landed in the Dardanelles, his destroyer *Scorpion* bombarding the Turks with such vigour that he won a DSO and was promoted to Commander.

Operations against the Germans in the Greek islands, by the Dover patrol across the Channel, and in the Baltic after the Armistice, brought him two bars to his DSO and promotion to Captain in 1920.

JUST A HOGG'S LIFE

A master in handling and manoeuvring small ships, Cunningham then became Captain D 6th Destroyer Flotilla in the Atlantic Fleet, sailing with a new flotilla leader *Wallace* in 1923 to take over the 1st flotilla in the Mediterranean.

With the Washington treaty limiting the size of navies, sea appointments for senior officers became scarce but after doing Inter-Service courses, Cunningham was appointed to captain the light cruiser *Calcutta*, flagship on the West Indies and North American station, the Commander-in-Chief being his old friend and admirer, Admiral Sir William Cowan. This was a new and fascinating experience largely showing the flag south from New York, round Cape Horn and up the Pacific coast as far as San Francisco. The base was Bermuda; the squadron consisting of several 5000 ton light cruisers, Cunningham's contemporaries wondered how he would handle all 35,000 tons of *Rodney*.

Aged forty three only five years younger than his captain, Robert Lindsay Burnett, the executive Commander was a fellow Scot, educated at Bedford School who, in 1911, had specialised in Physical Training being a fencer, boxer, footballer and cricketer. He too had commanded destroyers of the Grand Fleet in the 1914-18 war and he too was a martinet, particularly towards the Gunroom.

Known as 'Springers', specialists in P.T. were generally considered to be all brawn and no brains. Cunningham was fond of saying, "Springers keep their brains up their arses." Bob however was ambitious. He had a clever brother in the Army and confided to a friend, "If I had his brains, and he had my bull- shit, we'd both get to the top." In the event Bob picked a good staff and became an admiral on the latter alone.

Next in seniority came George Creasy, the First Lieutenant, by custom responsible for the mess decks and being in charge on the Cable deck. Promoted to Commander in June 1930 at the age of thirty five, he had an outstanding career during the last war retiring finally as Admiral Sir George, Commander-in-Chief, Portsmouth 1957.

The Gunnery officer in charge of the nine novel 16" guns was Geoffrey Oliver who, educated at Rugby, had gone to sea aged seventeen in 1915. Like everybody else he found Cunningham and Burnett, an intimidating pair. Cunningham usually believed that a job could be done in half the normal time and usually he was right. Then, having driven those responsible to distraction, he would say something so light hearted and kind that exasperation was transformed to admiration. Inspired perhaps by ABC, Oliver survived the worst of the Mediterranean as Captain of the cruiser *Hermione* 1940-42 ending a distinguished career as Admiral Sir Geoffrey CB., DSO., Commander-in-Chief East Indies 1950-52.

According to a guide book , the Paymaster Commander's Store would provide anything from a bar of soap to a cap ribbon. Among the items each cadet was required by their Lordships to possess was an S509:

JOURNAL
for the use of
MIDSHIPMEN
and
SEAGOING NAVAL CADETS

Regrettably the Paymaster could not supply one for me for three weeks. The opening words of my now invaluable antique, "I joined the ship about 1600 in a taxi" caused great mirth. In this heavily bound tome, 14 inches by 8, we recorded our observations on the ship, the fleet, people and places ashore, adding our own plans and sketches, Track charts, Plans of Anchorages etc.

The officer in charge of Junior officers, better known as the *Snotties' Nurse*, initialled all journals once a month and the Captain from time to time. Finally the journal had to be produced at the Seamanship Examination for the rank of Lieutenant when marks to a maximum of 50 (out of 1000) would be awarded.

On Saturday forenoons we would sit round the gunroom table recording the week's observations in language quite unsuited to Their Lordships wishes. Somehow a "bowdlerised" edition was committed to paper and gradually some journals became readable as well as legible. A poor draughtsman, I suppose clear handwriting earned me 44 marks out of that 50 maximum. In today's world of junk mail jargon and businessmen's clichés, the ability to write clearly and concisely may give the former bipeds of incredible stupidity a unique distinction. Punctuated occasionally with the signature "A. B. Cunningham," whose bust is in Trafalgar Square, perhaps I should take my journal to Sotheby's auction rooms one of these days.

HMS *Rodney*. The Gunroom, Spring 1930

Sub-Lieutenant A. B. Cole
Midshipmen.   Hood Term   C.E.R.Sharp, M.F. Andrew,
                                      F.R. Twiss, B. Walford,
                                      J.F. B. Brown
                       Rodney Term   G.C.MacKenzie, C.E. Fenwick,

Cadets	Public School Greynvile Term	G.A.L. Woods, E.G.P.B. Knapton, C.T.B. Tibbits, J. C. H. Price. R.T. Tripp, G.M.Wheadon, R.E.Topp W. Scott, F.P.Baker, C.F.S. Robinson, R.L.W. Moss, W.N.R.Knox, A.L.S.Hogg
Paymaster Midshipman	Public School	A. G. Davidson
Paymaster Cadet	Public School	R. H. Coleby

On that gusty afternoon of January 6 when we reported "Come on board to join, Sir" the quartermaster, observing our approach hurried away to fetch the Officer of the Watch, a handsome young Royal Marine Subaltern engaged at that moment in the lobby studying shirt patterns. These were of such startling colours that even a colour blind Commander could not have failed to notice them if passing through the lobby into the Wardroom. But the perspicacious Rex Madoc, aware of such a danger, had concealed them in the back of the Deck Log, a large canvas covered book in which little else than the force of the wind and the temperature of the air would be recorded each watch when alongside. As we passed down the ladder he made the epoch making entry "Joined ship 6 cadets." On the deck below, a Royal Marine sentry guarded the ship's key board issuing and recording keys drawn and returned. Theatre goers who had seen *The Middle Watch* knew him as Marine Ogg. Along the port side, passing through several heavy steel watertight doors, we came to a small wooden one marked *Gunroom*.

The shape of the room was largely governed by the 6 inch gun turrets, their cylindrical casings penetrating down to the bowels of the ship leaving irregular spaces in between for this mess of the so-called "young gentlemen." There were two tables for working and dining, long enough to seat thirty on a guest night and a comfortable corner with armchairs and a sofa for the senior group. A piano, a gramophone, a book case and some lockers fitted into odd corners. Three scuttles, known to land lubbers as port holes, were each just large enough for one young gentleman to plunge himself into the sea some fifteen feet below, an escapade never indulged in when sober. The principal supply of air came from the many ships' fans blowing a breath of old Wigan through *punkah louvres* in the trunking overhead with sufficient force to scatter any papers lying about.

After a cup of tea made with watered condensed milk, we retraced our steps aft to the ladder, descending to the space below the sentry, known as the After Cabin Flat, which led to Officers' cabins on each side. Some of us had our chests and slung our hammocks here. The Midshipmen's Chest Flat, known as Lenin's tomb, was one deck below, "fruity" with the smell of damp towels and rugger shirts long over due for the laundry. With Wardroom officers passing to and fro to their cabins, the After Cabin Flat had to be spick and span, but Lenin's tomb was happy chaos.

On Saturday mornings before Captain's rounds of the mess decks, a dozen juniors hurled boots, shoes, caps, drills, oilskins into the chests and for half an hour the tomb would look a credit to any garden of remembrance. Looking back I cannot think how we managed. Besides our uniform clothing, we needed plain clothes.

A suit in which to pay calls, a tweed jacket and grey flannel trousers, known as 'dog robbers', a dinner jacket for dances ashore and all the paraphernalia of games from golf clubs to tennis and squash racquets.

Besides the hammock boy we each had a servant. The duty of looking after the officers belonged to the Royal Marines who, unlike sailors, swore an oath of allegiance to the monarch on joining. A Royal Marine should therefore be the last man to mutiny and can be relied upon to stop officers' throats being cut or their gins being laced with deadly nightshade by recalcitrant tars. In fact I remember a question, said to be a possible in an exam, which was, "What officer is entitled to have a chamber pot in his cabin?" The answer, which I'm sure cannot be verified, was the Major of Marines because, in the event of mutiny the Detachment would rally outside his cabin in which he might therefore be confined for days. The idea was so pleasing that nobody even asked why he could not be escorted to the W.C. by such an overwhelming force.

Thus, in the Wardroom as well as Stewards, Royal Marines acted as attendants, and Bandsmen worked part-time between playing Colonel Bogey and a hymn for Divisions, and "My canary has circles under his eyes" then popular at social functions ashore.

The pay was ten shillings a month (50p today) for what was hardly a 'Jeeves' service. In fact even seeing one's bandsman once a month was quite an achievement.

❖ ❖ ❖

Stores for the Use of... Any doubt as to the existence of the Major's jerry was dispelled by Mrs. Oliver Mason of Wadhurst in a letter of September 7, 1990 to *The Times*.

Working in the Admiralty during World War II she found in an Admiralty list of naval stores:

1. Pots, chamber, crested, admirals for the use of.

JUST A HOGG'S LIFE

2. Pots, chamber, rubber, lunatics for the use of.

Keeping the pot boiling another correspondent declared he had met in an Army married quarter, "Pots, chamber, babies officer, handled with crest." When he and his wife left, a clerk noted "CBS" in his ledger, explaining that this meant, "Cracked but serviceable."

❖ ❖ ❖

Somewhere between the flats and the Gunroom was the Gunroom bathroom, a tiled space with three baths, a variety of valves mostly labelled "Steam" and some basins. In order to get hot water by 0700, it was necessary for the valves to be suitably manipulated at 0600, a task performed in turn by the six junior cadets. Having opened the valves, the duty cadet had to call the other cadets and midshipmen in time for them to do PT on the quarterdeck at 0640. A dozen or more of the young gentlemen climbed out of their hammocks, donned their shirts and shorts and ascended to greet the roseate hues of early dawn or the black bat night that hadn't flown.

From 0600 to 0700 it was the custom in H.M Ships to scrub and wash the upper deck, a work of such importance that the Commander himself appeared daily at 0600 in a mixture of pyjamas and uniform to say "Scrub and wash the upper Deck" in a commanding voice before going back to his bed or into his bath.

By 0640 the brushes and hoses were replaced by long-handled implements, called squeejees, which pushed away the surplus water so that slipping on the wet surface instead of tripping over the hoses became the principal hazard.

Exercise over, we would descend to the gunroom for a cup of tea to be joined by those who had been on watch or running boats the night before. They were entitled to lie in until 0645. The Duty Cadet meanwhile had returned immediately – and anxiously – either to a cloud of steam or a stone cold tank in the bathroom.

Hailed as a feckless crackpot by his mess mates he was liable to be beaten if unable to coax the infernal steam machine to provide hot water for the Sub-Lieutenant's bath by 0740. By 0750 we were all to be found, shaved and properly dressed, on the upper deck, pads and pencils in hand for a signal exercise.

In less than a decade short wave wireless was to make semaphore with hand flags or mechanical arms as obsolete as the cannon ball in theory. But during the war when W/T silence was in force or W/T apparatus damaged, inter-ship semaphore and flashing lamp morse code could be the only means of communication. In the thirties a square flag of Blue and White stripes flying at the flagship's yard arm indicated that a general message to the fleet was being made by semaphore. This would be read on a score of flag decks, revealing for example allocation of sports grounds for the week or arrangements for Lady Cholmondley's ball ashore. For those of us in charge of power boats it was as well to signal with the rapidity of a ticktack man in Tattersalls when, as frequently happened, they broke down. An Irish midshipman in a twin-screw picket boat delighted everybody with: "My starboard engine's broken down and its the only one that's running."

Breakfast for the ship's company was from 0700 to 0750 when they cleaned and polished guns and mess decks, while in the Gunroom we put away porridge, cereals, bacon and eggs until an immensely long bugle call announced Divisions. In *Rodney* those involved were Able Seamen, with some Leading Seamen and Petty officers, who were divided into Forecastle men; Topmen and Quarterdeck men these being equivalent to the Bows, the Middle and the Stern, respectively the parts of ship they looked after. Boys (under eighteen) and the Ordinary Seamen (over eighteen) formed separate divisions. A Lieutenant Commander or Lieutenant with several midshipmen to assist was in charge of each one.

After the Divisional officer had inspected and reported correct to the Commander we marched aft for Prayers and a hymn to exercise the Padré and the Band. Occasionally everybody would spread out for PT, before the proceedings ended with the Commander and the Chief Boatswain's Mate falling out this party and that for the morning's work.

In practice more men managed to escape than to attend Divisions. The technicians – Engine room Artificers, Electrical Artificers, Stokers – clad in overalls managed to be in the right place at the right time without bugle calls. "Both Watches fall in" was for Seamen only and many of them were excused, having jobs in remote corners of the ship. For example the Double Bottom party of seamen and stokers cleaned these nether regions inside; the Side party perpetually pottered round the waterline outside, painting the black boot topping. The Gunner's party were dispersed in obscure stores full of rifles, green webbing and Blanco. There were messmen in pantries belonging to the Officers', Chief Petty Officers' and Petty Officers' messes; others called Sweepers cleaned the flats. Traditionally, the painter, the plumber and the shipwright each has to have a mate.

Then there were the watchkeepers, working day on day off, such as that little trio of Quartermaster, Boatswain's mate and Side boy standing smartly at the top of the gangway embarrassing civilians coming on board unsure when to raise their hats to the quarterdeck. The boats' crews too worked the same day on, day off, routine.

After Divisions midshipmen and cadets departed to various forms of instruction, individual progress being recorded by their instructors as Exceptional, Superior, Satisfactory or Moderate, the subjects being Seamanship, Navigation and Pilotage, Gunnery, Torpedo and Electrical, and Engineering. Form E 190, a fourteen page booklet with a final page for recording detailed results of the Oral Examinations for Lieutenant was kept for every one of us. My own progress starts with a Moderate in every subject and, on the principle of give a Hogg a bad name, rarely rises above 'Satis'; though eventually I was to confound my instructors and utterly astonish myself by getting a 2nd class in the Seamanship exam for Lieutenant. Mod! Mod! Mod! Out of thirty two markings I have counted thirteen making Midshipman Mod a good title for this chapter.

The midday break for dinner was from Noon to 1315, afternoon work and instruction ending at 1540. The dog watches, First Dog from 1600 to 1800, Last from 1800 to 2000 could then be devoted to leave and recreation. *Rodney*'s long foc'sle was excellent for deck hockey, played with a ring of twisted tarred hemp known as a grommet instead of a ball and a walking stick shaped like a hockey stick.

A ship's company normally being divided into two watches, Port and Starboard for duty, the four hours from 1600 to 2000 were split to prevent each watch always having the same periods, the name Dog probably being a shortening of Dodge. In a four hour watch the ship's bell is struck every half hour from one to eight. 1830 however is denoted by one bell not five, because five bells was chosen as the signal to start the mutiny at the Nore in 1797.

In harbour leave would be given to the Port and Starboard watches alternately from 1600 to 2300, or to 0700 in places like the home ports where there was enough accommodation for a night ashore. Normal leave for midshipmen and cadets was until 1930 starting at 1300 on Saturdays and Sundays, which gave time for football or golf and a beer in the canteen or pub before the boat left for the ship at 1900. Then in what remained of the hour before dinner at 2000, Lenin's Tomb came to life. Boiled shirts, bow ties and "bum freezers" replaced blazers, muddy shirts and shorts bunged into the nearest drawer in time for Rounds at 2100.

Dinner usually began with soup, invariably Brown Windsor to match the chairs we sat on, followed by Fish, Joint and Savoury. It was not what The Wine and Food Society – soon to be founded in 1933 incidentally

– would call a memorable meal, though the cost is memorable enough in retrospect. We messed for 2s. 7d. a day each, 1s 6d. from the individual, the additional 1s.1d. being the Victualling allowance, a subsidy paid by the Admiralty, for every officer and man. Our wine bill of 15 shillings a month was sufficient for plenty of beer, occasional glasses of sherry at 2d. a glass and a choice from port, madeira or marsala when these three decanters were passed on a guest night for the loyal toast, drunk of course seated in H.M ships since that Georgian monarch banged his head on a beam. Spirits were forbidden to officers under twenty.

At 2100, when the Commander, or more often the Duty Lieutenant Commander of the Day went the rounds of the messdecks, we gunroom officers would be spread about the upper deck in pairs, ready with pads and pencils for a signal exercise, returning below twenty minutes later, the message having been flashed by one of the other ships present.

Two or three times a month there was a guest night when we dined in state off polished tables with the Royal Marine band playing seated in the gangway outside the gunroom door making entry or exit an acrobatic feat. The main course was often Blackcock removed from the ships cold storage and about as hard as the compartment's steel deck. After the loyal toast a chair was placed alongside Mr. President for the Bandmaster, invited to sit down and take a Bandmaster's glass, virtually a double.

Guest night at table was governed by many traditions. No mention of feminine christian names; not more than three words of a foreign language; no elbows to be rested on the table unless you were an uncle: usual penalty a fine of one or more glasses of port. Before the loyal toast the President should stopper the decanters the stoppers not being removed again as long as the President is sitting. This was to imply that the wine was provided solely for the loyal toast.

Towards the end of dinner the party might become more obstreperous spurred by the cry, "Dogs of War out Mr. X!" whereupon X would be unceremoniously thrown out, landing possibly minus his trousers in the midst of the Band. The worst customs had largely fallen into abeyance by the 1930s.

Fork in the Beam was derived from the old wooden ships with men of forty and midshipmen as young as eleven. When the conversation became bawdy the youngsters were required to leave, the last one probably being hauled back and *firked* or *cobbed*, terms which meant being beaten with a stocking filled with sand or half a bung stave of a cask, which blistered the poor boy's bottom.

JUST A HOGG'S LIFE

A milder form *Breadcrumbs* required junior members to stop their ears; *Fishbones* their eyes. The cry *Bumph* sent us hurtling in search of a piece of lavatory paper to be brought back signed by the Officer of the Watch. This I'm delighted to say, had its risks for the perpetrator. One wet night when gold braid was hidden by oilskins, a cadet mistook the Captain for the Officer of the Watch and that august person was not amused. The Sub-Lieutenant suffered a timely rebuke, better known as a 'bottle' or, more recently, 'a rocket' and though doubtless he caned the cadet it was unwise to repeat the practice.

Lift and Launch however gave the gunroom a chance to vent their feelings on any sadistic, despotic Sub-Lieutenant. When seated as President at the head of the table a concerted lift and launching of the table would pin him to the bulkhead behind his chair.

But the days of these gunroom 'games' were largely past and if occasionally they were in evidence it was without malice. The focal point after dinner was the gunroom piano, a remarkably well tempered clavichord considering the beer with which it was frequently lubricated. Surprising too that somebody could usually be found to strum it. And the repertoire? For the answer to where are the songs we sang I must refer you to a Sphere Original Paperback published in 1967 entitled, *Why was He Born So Beautiful and other Rugby Songs* collected by Michael Green. When his readers complained that their favourites had been omitted, *More Rugby Songs* appeared, adding another 150 to the first volume's 186. Even so I rather think I can detect at least one omission. Should you want to present a copy to your daughter now that girls' rugby is all the rage, rest assured astericks are substituted for the words she probably knows best already.

At work we cadets began as understudies either to the Officers of the Watch in harbour or to a midshipman in charge of a picket boat or launch. Since watch keeping in harbour largely consists of pacing up and down the Quarterdeck, instruction in the forenoons and afternoons took precedence. Practical experience in handling power boats, on the other hand, took precedence over instruction. Thus if the instruction was going to be dull, the crafty midshipman would escape by persuading the Quartermaster to appear soon after it began saying, "Picket boat called away, Sir. Rather a long trip I'm afraid." Playing games also provided an escape, particularly if the Gunroom team was playing another. In the lunch hour the Senior Midshipman would take the leave book to the Snotties' Nurse and the Commander for signature, timing his arrival to coincide with their pre-prandial pink gin in the Wardroom.

"It's your return match against the *Nelson* today isn't it? You've got a full team out, I suppose?" inquires Bob Burnett, the Commander.

"Yes Sir, except for Barnaby, who's running the 1st picket boat."

"But Good Heavens, boy, you can't play the Nelson's gunroom without Barnaby. Petty Officer Jackson's perfectly capable of running the boat for a couple of hours."

The Senior Midshipman would retire with signature, recalling the Snotties' Nurse's last talk on boats.

"No boat must ever go away without her midshipman."

And a month earlier from the Commander when the 1st picket boat had broken the quarterdeck gangway,

"That man Jackson isn't fit to play with himself, let alone a picket boat."

Our day ended when a Regulating Petty Officer appeared at 2230 to lock up the Gunroom. Soon after 2300 all was quiet and the lights dim in the After Cabin Flat; only the squeaky boots of Marine 'ogg and an occasional muttered oath from a Wardroom officer bending and groping under our hammocks on the way to his cabin broke the silence.

The Gunroom, HMS Rodney

Charles Robinson writing his journal in the Gunroom.

CHAPTER 6

At Sea with ABC

At 0730 on January 10 *Rodney* left Portsmouth for Portland arriving there about 1330. On the way Lieutenant Lawson, the second Gunnery officer explained my Action Station, which was working the Enemy Bearing Indicators (EBIs) one each side of the Compass Platform. Normally called the Bridge, this was where the ship was conned and what with the Captain, the Navigating Officer, the Officer of the Watch, the Chief Yeoman of Signals and a messenger or two, I thought there were quite enough people present without me.

However, there I was with two EBIs, each shaped like a pillar box four foot high with a gyro in the top. When I pointed the instrument at a target it continued to point at that target however much the ship altered course. Instructed to follow EBI the Fire Control Table operators in the bowels would bring the mighty 16" guns below us on to the target by a system of following pointers and aligning black with red.

The seamen spent the morning streaming and recovering paravanes, an exercise frequently practised by the big ships to see who could do it quickest. The paravanes, one Port and one Starboard, were underwater kites, which veered outwards when towed from the bows of the ship. One end of serrated steel towing wire was secured to the point of tow and the other end to the paravane. Any moored mine in the ship's path should have its mooring rope sawn through by the serrated steel wire or be passed along the wire into cutters on the paravane itself. Mines coming to the surface would then be sunk by small arms fire.

Each paravane was swung out, lowered and slipped from its own small davit close to the cable deck. When both paravanes were seen to be running correctly at short stay, the special shoe to which the serrated towing wires were shackled could be lowered on an endless chain from the bows to about the same depth as the ship's keel. Various back hauls held the shoe against the stem of the ship, while pendants and slips allowed the paravanes to run out to the full length of their towing wires. The shoe was lowered and hoisted by a wire led round the power operated capstan.

To recover the paravanes the shoe was hoisted to its up position on the cable deck. A recovery wire from each davit could then be slid down the

60

Operation of the paravane.

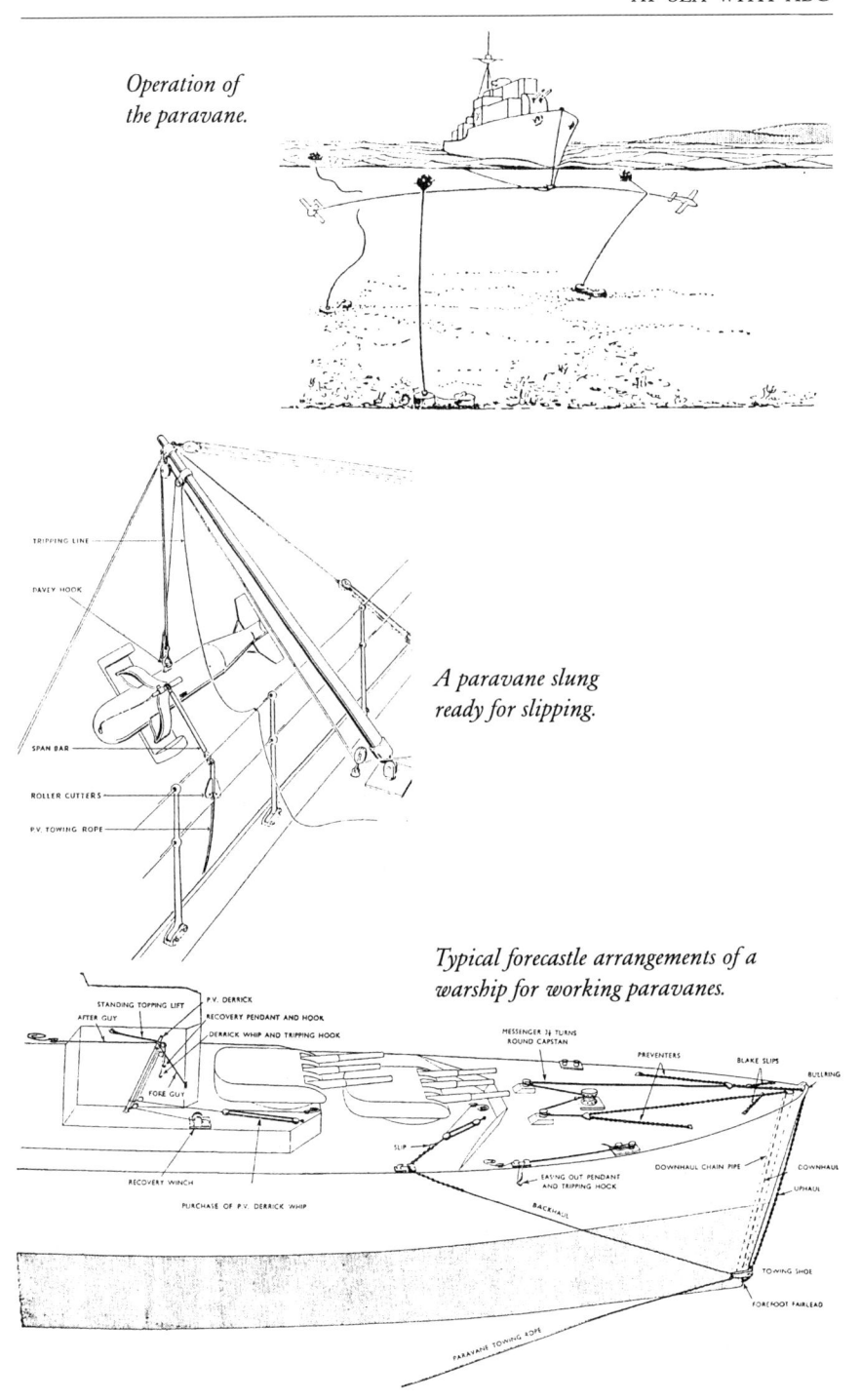

A paravane slung ready for slipping.

Typical forecastle arrangements of a warship for working paravanes.

towing wire to each paravane allowing it to be hoisted up, swung inboard, put on its trolley and returned to its stowage position on the upper deck. It all sounds very simple but if the paravane elected to run inwards it could foul the bilge keel or any other projection under the ship. When however the war came in 1939 the German mines which damaged the *Nelson* in Loch Ewe and sank shipping off our East coast were ground mines, shaped like bombs and laid mainly by aircraft. On November 22 two were dropped on the mud near Shoeburyness, which John Ouvry and Roger Lewis proceeded to make safe and remove to HMS *Vernon*. These proved to be magnetic mines which exploded when a ship passed over them. This was not unexpected; we had our own which worked on a slightly different principle. Possession of these German samples soon brought about the system called "degaussing", which reduced a ship's magnetic field to a safe level by passing a strong current through its full length.

I knew both Ouvry and Lewis well and was proud to be in HMS *Vernon* when King George VI presented them each with the Distinguished Service Order. Later, in 1944, I met Roger in Naples when he was at Staff Headquarters in the Palace at Caserta. He was driving an enormous German car which had belonged, he said, to Goering. "How on earth did you keep it?" I asked. "Quite simple", he said. "I put a large notice on the back Danger Unexploded Bomb and drove it here from Rome."

Back at Portland in 1930 a sixty mile an hour gale on Sunday 12 January blew a small cargo steamer on to the breakwater with *Rodney*'s searchlights illuminating as the crew scrambled to safety on to the breakwater itself. A greater disaster overtook the Admiralty tug *St. Genny* off Ushant. On passage to Gibraltar with the target-towing *Snapdragon* and another target-towing *St. Cyrus*, she was struck by a huge wave and sank, losing three officers and twenty men. Only five of the crew were picked up. The Fleet's departure was delayed until Tuesday 14th.

The night before most of the Gunroom were invited to the Wardroom for a voice trial. A Ship's show was clearly being planned.

The war game plan divided the Atlantic fleet into Red, defending Britain, and Blue based on Spain. But with force B1 in the English Channel and B2 off the North coast of Spain, Red's object was to prevent B1 and B2 joining each other. The early thirties were bad times for Britain with huge unemployment and great hardship. Even Fleet exercises had to be carried out at economical speed and few if any new ships were being built for the Navy. Except for *Nelson* and *Rodney* ships taking part were very old. The letters in brackets indicate: [b] battleship, [c] cruiser, [bc] battle cruiser, [ac] aircraft carrier, [ml] minelayer, [d] destroyer. [kn] speed allowed.

	RED		BLUE
R1	**R2**	**B1**	**B2**
[b] *Nelson* 13 kn	[b] *Emperor of India** 11 kn.	[bc] *Renown* 13kn	[b] *Barham* 12 kn
[b] *Rodney* 13 kn	[b] *Marlborough** 11kn.	[bc] *Repulse* 13kn	[b] *Malaya* 12 kn
[c] *Hawkins* 13kn	[c] *Centaur* 16 kn	[b] *Tiger* 13kn	6 Destroyers 16 kn
[c] *Frobisher* 13kn	[ml] *Adventure* 11kn	[ac] *Argus* 13kn	
[c] *Comus* 13 kn			
[c] *Canterbury* 16 kn			
[d] *Wallace* 16 kn			
[d] *Warwick* 16 kn			

* Representing battleships of the *Revenge* Class

The Red cruisers widely spaced formed a patrol between Ushant and the Scillies with *Nelson* and *Rodney* about eight miles to the westward. Stationed in the Channel to the eastward, R2 sighted B1; soon after that we, in R1 sighted B1 sinking all but *Repulse* and *Tiger,* which our cruisers were ordered to shadow throughout the night. Then at 1140 next day *Rodney* and *Nelson* having sunk *Repulse* and *Tiger,* the C-in-C cancelled the Exercise. Precisely how the calculations as to who sank who were made was never disclosed; left to destroyers, by throwing the dice in the wardroom probably, but for Fleet Commanders-in-Chief there was a Confidential Book on the conduct of Fleet Exercises. The Atlantic Fleet also had two flotillas of V and W class destroyers, good little ships completed towards the end of the war.

Days at sea were invariably eventful, particularly in rough weather. One of *Wallace*'s officers fell down a hatch. *Valhalla* and *Wallace* needed to lie under the lea of the Spanish Coast to transfer the latter's doctor. This was usually done by lowering a boat until the war when the two ships would steam close abreast, establishing a taut jackstay between each other on which men, mail, provisions etc., could be pulled across. A method used incidentally as long ago as 1810 to get Wellington across the Douro, which he himself may have learnt even earlier in India.

Good gunnery required trials to establish the effect of the ship rolling. Good ship handling required the Lieutenant-Commanders to take over Captain on the Compass Platform as opportunity offered. After dark, ships were darkened and navigation lights switched off, while the destroyers played hide and seek in order to attack the capital ships. Peering into the darkness with binoculars, the first to sight the outline of a destroyer would be the Captain, ABC, telling the rest of us that we must be blind. The 4.7 inch guns would then illuminate them with starshell, provided

JUST A HOGG'S LIFE

Cadet Hogg had trained his EBI correctly. There were searchlights too, controlled by midshipmen and cadets from abaft the Compass Platform, one either side. Torpedoes were not fired on these occasions though this was perfectly feasible. In peace time their warheads were replaced by collision heads filled with sand, carrying flares that burnt at the end of their run helping the destroyers' whalers to locate and take them back to the right destroyers.

After five days, average nine knots, we reached Gibraltar, *Nelson*, *Rodney*, *Malaya*, *Hawkins* in that order securing alongside the South Mole, with *Barham* and *Frobisher* at the detached mole. The cruisers were at buoys as were the destroyers, mostly in pairs. Ahead of *Nelson* lay the submarine depot ship Lucia with four submarines. One of them was the M2 which had a hangar for a small aircraft.

The Commander Bob Burnett soon announced that boxing training for a tournament would begin. Recording my disappointment, I was delighted that my ankle was still too swollen for me to participate after being broken at Dartmouth three months earlier. At Dartmouth I had once been cajoled into the ring against one, Berger, a civilised fellow in the red corner, who obviously had no wish to punch peoples' noses or knock out their front teeth. Like Agag we trod delicately for three rounds, my assessment in occasional light blows being Berger 25, Hogg 24. The Judge, one of the masters called Hodges, who usually bawled, "Red is the winner, good fight Blue!", merely said, "Extra round of three minutes, you haven't hit each other yet." The better tactician, I saw that Berger won.

It was always thought advisable to move at the double when the Commander or the Captain could be about, avoiding them if possible lest one should be asked some awkward question to which the only answer was, "I'll find out, Sir". Doubling to Divisions one wet morning, I slipped backwards on the upper deck coming to in the Sick Bay having knocked myself clean out. This at least prevented my taking part in a second rehearsal for a Ceremonial Landing Party's inspection and march past on the Gibraltar parade ground, for which the four battleships each landed a company. When next we met, all Burnett said was "So you've been trying to knock a hole in my deck, Mr. Hogg."

Besides the Boxing there were Fencing and Bayonet competitions, and a Tug of War in which each battleship entered two teams of Royal Marines and two of Seamen, Heavy and Light-Heavy. *Rodney*'s long foc'sle made an excellent practice ground for Tug of war and with Bob Burnett urging the teams to greater exertion *Rodney* swept the board. Another trophy that found its way into our cupboard without my assistance was the Squadron's

Boxing Cup. This was celebrated with a Gunroom Guest night at which we entertained Captain, Commander, Engineer Commander, First Lieutenant, Navigating, Gunnery and Signals Officers. The Fleet Engineer Officer, who was accommodated on board, was also a guest.

With better weather and the arrival of the Fleet's main aircraft carrier *Furious*, *Rodney*'s 4.7 guns occasionally fired a few rounds at a drogue target towed by one of the Fairy III F aircraft. Unexpectedly seven Australian midshipmen - Gale, Morrison, Bracegirdle, Rattigan, Haines, Power and Bowden - joined us one day to stay until *Ramillies* and *Royal Oak* of the Mediterranean fleet, to which they were appointed, arrived in March.

Mondays - not every Monday thank God - was the day for General Drill, described by Bob Whinney in his excellent book *The U-Boat Peril* as a harbour exercise universally loathed by all participants. The worthy object was to practise things that might have to be done as quickly as possible in an emergency, but the manner of doing them was often a case of more haste less speed. Some examples: Prepare to tow; Prepare to be taken in tow; Away all boats, lie off the ship; Fire in the galley or compartment named; Fire ashore, send fire engine; send almost anything to flagship. Some items were fun such as send fried egg to flagship. Once when the signal *Replace Gear* was made the flagship inadvertently sent back a poached egg, an error that had to be corrected.

General drill began about 0930 after Divisions, ending in time for everything to be correctly replaced before dinner at noon. "Midshipmen man the whaler!" "Cadets man the galley!" boomed Bob Burnett for a start on this particular Monday. The boats were already in the water secured to the mole, so thither we rushed our galley getting under way before the midshipmens' whaler, much to our satisfaction. *Rodney* had one gig and one galley which were similar, the galley being the boat the Captain liked to sail. And that is precisely what he did on this particular morning. We were called alongside the gangway and down came ABC bent on exercising six cadets. The crew had to sit in the bottom of the boat as far aft as possible. Knox and I were the two bow men. On the order 'Ready about' we had to dash forward to the bow, unhook the tack of the foresail, pass it round the foremast and then replace it. ABC, with the boyish complexion and piercing blue eyes was hard to please. Either I was that galumphing elephant who upset the trim of the boat or that slow and indolent cadet who didn't move fast enough. Later, in the summer sailing regatta we were to beat ABC, who liked to shine as a helmsman. Charles Robinson, in our group of six, had learnt his sailing on The Broads and was a very useful competitor.

JUST A HOGG'S LIFE

On 24th February we were at sea once again on some war game, heading out into the Atlantic closed up at action stations with the ship darkened, when suddenly on went the anchor light on the ship's jackstaff in full view for miles. Somebody had gone into the paint shop, switched it on by accident and departed locking the place up. After some minutes of shouting instructions by telephone and voice pipe from the Compass Platform, it was still on and the Commander had been sent for by the Captain. "Cut the wires Commander! Cut the wires!" shouted ABC. Rushing headlong for the ladders shouting, "Out of my way, boy, Out of my way", Bob Burnett knocks most of the midshipmen at the searchlight controls for six. Eventually the paint shop key is found.

The next morning *Rodney* did a 16 inch 'throw off' shoot at *Nelson* the range being about twelve miles. Each of the three turrets fired six rounds making eighteen in all. In this type of practice the turrets were trained off target a number of degrees sufficient for the shells to fall astern. 75 per cent were straddles according to the analysis in this one. Practice shells were of course sand – instead of explosive – filled. The alternative shoot was at a battle practice target made of wood towed by a tug or the special vessel called *Snapdragon* at the unrealistic speed of eight knots. Yet another target was the obsolete battleship *Centurion*, manned by a skeleton crew who transferred to her attendant destroyer shortly before the Open Fire signal was made, but were still able to control her course and speed by W/T. They could also haul up and down a flag signal. Not aware of this a liner in the vicinity was horrified when a flag signal was hauled down as great splashes fell around her. How could the Navy leave one poor man there!

From *Rodney*'s Compass Platform one looked ahead and downwards upon those nine 16 inch guns, each one almost as long as a cricket pitch and each turret a flat topped sheet of armour. Each shell, four feet seven inches long and weighing a ton, took half a minute to travel ten miles. The blast from a broadside of nine could have damaged the ship so salvoes of five guns and then four were adopted.

Whether 16 inch, or 15 inch as in the older capital ships, there is something awesome about these great guns trained towards a target miles away going up a little, then down, as the pointers are followed inside the turret. The Captain gives the order, 'Open fire'. Nerves tighten as in an aircraft about to land. The next few seconds seem an age. What can have gone wrong ? Then comes the ting-ting of the fire-gong, heard down a voicepipe from the Director Control Tower above, as a great explosion is followed by a withering sheet of flame from the muzzles and yellow tinted smoke that stinks of cordite passes through the Compass Platform blown aft by the ship's speed.

The fire gong rings at intervals. Spectators adjust their ear plugs or cotton wool; those with binoculars turn to look for splashes on the horizon until the danger flag is hauled down. The ship returns to normal, and the awning stanchions and other fittings, removed to avoid blast damage, can now be replaced.

Down in the Fire Control Room they have heard nothing, only a great shudder as *Rodney* reels with each salvo. In the turrets themselves the noise is of machinery not gunfire. Machinery that operates the hoists from shell room and magazine to turret. A telescopic ram pushes the ammunition into an open breech and a hydraulic press closes, turns and locks. Electricity trains the turret, fires the guns and powers the air blast that clears the bore of burning gas.

In the other battleships the four turrets were named A and B forward and X and Y aft. *Rodney*'s three A, B and X were all forward: later in the year we were to do firing trials to see how far X could train and elevate guns without blast damage to herself or her inmates. Those on the Compass Platform looked like being guinea pigs.

After acting as target for *Nelson*'s 6" throw off shoot and another by the cruiser Centaur, we steamed eastwards along the North African Coast for Algiers. Far from being uneventful, a Greek Steamer called *FoFo* sank after an explosion. Rescued by *Nelson*, the crew were transferred to *Tetrach*, a destroyer, thence to *Rodney*, to disembark them at Algiers. Our two cutters towed their boats and brought their luggage, which included one hen and one canary. In the crew of twenty two there were only two casualties, a burnt face and a damaged leg.

Rodney, firing a 21 gun salute, answered by the pier battery, arrived at Algiers at 0700 the next morning. A pilot who spoke no English and did not understand Bob Burnett's French gave ABC a nice opportunity to handle the ship himself. Going astern into the harbour he dropped both anchors, port and starboard, in the middle. Then paying out their cables *Rodney* dropped astern towards a jetty, lowering her two cutters when 25 yards away, each taking and securing a grass line to bollards on the jetty. These enabled the stern to be secured with three bridles of 3½ inch wire and three of 5½ inch on each quarter. Even these were not enough when a strong wind blew across the beam next day. Strain on wire made fast to the bollards on the quarterdeck tended to bend the deck itself upwards. The remedy was a 6-inch wire, passed around the nearest 6-inch turret with both ends secured to the towing slip on the quarterdeck, thus giving the turret all the weight.

ABC enjoyed his golf almost as much as his sailing. The game being encouraged, Baker, Robinson, Knox and I landed next day to play on the local 9-hole course which had greens of sand. Dusk approached as we played the last hole and since I was not a long hitter, I thought the couple ahead on the last green were well out of range. But like Betjeman in his poem *Seaside Golf*:

> *I played an iron sure and strong*
> *And clipped it out of sight*

Plain to see however was a puff of sand as the two figures on the green took abrupt avoiding action. They were ABC and Bob Burnett. Speculating whether this meant six cuts, leave stopped or both, I found them seated with a drink in the Club House and stammered an apology.

Those piercing blue eyes looked at me with great solemnity. Unknown to me the London Disarmament Conference with Italy, France, Japan and USA had just ended. The voice said, "The League of Nations are trying to do away with Senior Officers, there's no need for you to do the same."

ABC's capacity for saying something one never forgot was illustrated again some months later. We had been told to draw up a plan for getting the Atlantic Fleet in and out of Portsmouth. As taught at school I put my name 'Hogg' at the top right hand corner of the paper. It came back with, "You are not a Peer of the Realm."

Without doubt he must have been the admiral who, when greeted by a subordinate with a hearty "Good morning, Sir", replied "I didn't ask for a weather report thank you."

A week passed quickly. Cruising liners such as the *Empress of France* and the *Mauretania* looked in for a day. When the ship was open to visitors I showed round in quick succession two Dutch ladies, an odd collection of French girls and a French mistress with most of her girls school. At aperitif time French Officers called on the Wardroom and Gunroom, calls being duly returned. Dances were held on board both for the officers and the Ship's Company. There was a golf competition, ending for me in the dark with a near miss on the Captain of *Lucia*, the submarine depot ship, putting on that almost fatal last green.

The Atlantic Fleet next assembled at Pollensa Bay, that ample inlet on the North coast of Majorca then unknown to tourism. Although the usual exercises took place on passage, for *Rodney*'s Wardroom rehearsals of a Musical Extravaganza entitled *Prelate and Pirate* were high priority. The one performance, to which officers of both Atlantic and Mediterranean Fleets assembled in the Bay of Palma would be invited, was only a week away. The Gunroom was, of course, involved. Midshipmen F. R. Twiss and J. F. B. Brown played Kayanne and Chili, wards of the Bishop of Lee.

With three others I formed the *Folie Bargee* chorus of District Visitors. Though we sang in unison there was a unique harmony because Peter Baker, third from left could only sing on one note.

> *District Visitors always are ladies, are ladies*
> *Of our smile every sinner afraid is, afraid is*
> *But to the meritorious we,*
> *Dispense the savoury bread of charitee*

The Bishop – I hardly need say – was played by Robert Burnett whose ruddy complexion needed no make-up to recall Raymond Asquith's line, 'The sun like a bishop's bottom, rosy and round and hot'.

> *In me you see, The Bishop of Lee*
> *The flower of our episcopacy*
> *The drink refusing, though much amusing*
> *The quaintly, saintly Bishop of Lee.*

Inevitably, in *HMS Pinafore* style, the Bishop was really the Pirate Captain and vice versa.

The Verrey-Würst Male Choir rehearsing The Pirates chorus was captured for posterity by a *Times* Photographer who had joined us at Algiers. Captain J.J. Casement was the last survivor of the Pirates, while F. R. Twiss rose to be Admiral Sir Frank D.S.C. Second Sea Lord 1967-70, followed by Gentleman Usher of the Black Rod, House of Lords from 1970 to 1978.

When both fleets anchored off Palma, the stage was rigged on the quarterdeck in a day and the curtain went up that night in half a gale. For refreshment afterwards the starboard side of *Rodney*'s long foc'sle had been rigged like a petrol station where the guests helped themselves to gin or whisky from the pumps. *Rodney*'s boats plied far into the small hours taking officers back to the smaller ships in weather too rough for their own boats, while the shipwrights dismantled bars and stage. At 0900 when the Fleet sailed there was no outward sign of our revels; inwardly, as far as four District Visitors, unaccustomed to imbibing spirits were concerned, there was every sign.

In my half dozen sea appointments during the Thirties, there was hardly one without a Ship's concert party. And if duty free liquor played

JUST A HOGG'S LIFE

The Verrey-Wurst Male Choir.

Prelate and Pirate. *A quartet of District Visitors. Left to right: Midshipmen M.F. Andrew, A.S. Hogg, F.P. Baker and R.E. Topp.*

Prelate and Pirate
*Kayenne and Chile, wards of the Bishop of Lee.
Left to right: Midshipmen F.R. Twiss and J.F.B. Brown.*

70

a small part in their inspiration and execution, it undoubtedly played the lead as an inducement to the rest of the Fleet to fill the house.

The extra work however caused by the Officers' theatricals was not always popular with the Ship's Company. Stephen King-Hall and Ian Hay delighted London audiences with the opening scene of The Midshipmaid, where a sailor was washing paint work prior to some show.

"And the ships' Company?" said a Cabinet minister being shown round by the Commander, "I suppose they play a part in all this." "Oh, of course, Sir! They enter fully into the spirit of the thing." The sailor, played by A. W. Bascombe, turned towards the audience. He said nothing; his expression was enough to bring the house down.

The Atlantic fleet now went in one direction and the Mediterranean Fleet in another, prior to the main exercise intended to investigate the pros and cons of fleet actions at night. Sir Ernle Chatfield, our Commander-in-Chief who had been Beatty's Flag Captain at Jutland, believed that a well trained fleet could repel night attacks by destroyers and was determined to try out new tactics. In this he was supported by the Hon. Reginald Aylmer Ranfurly Plunkett-Ernle-Erle-Drax, Rear Admiral of the 1st Battle Squadron, in the *Barham*, who will appear in these pages in due course as Commander-in-Chief Plymouth. After being shown round the *Rodney*, he had turned to ABC and said, "On no account, Cunningham allow yourself to become entangled in the technicalities of this great ship."

The Commander-in-Chief Mediterranean Fleet however thought engagements between capital ships at night should be avoided at all costs. This he did so well that the fleets never met, so we all returned to Gibraltar after two nights of "war", for a week of discussions, social intercourse and games.

Heading for home and leave, it was decided off Cape St. Vincent that *Rodney* should practise towing *Nelson*. Having won all the cups with our tug of war teams, I suppose this was meant to be just another big pull for heavyweights. Assuming the ship to be towed is broken down without power, the towing ship passes close enough to fire a small rocket and line. On its end is a larger line, then a grass hawser which will float and finally a large steel wire hawser 6 inches thick in this case. If able, the ship to be towed provides all this, the tow-er hauling in on its after capstan until the eye of the towing hawser appears. The tow-er then secures it to a towing slip on his quarterdeck, or possibly to a large steel wire around the after gun turret. Meanwhile the towed ship has secured its end of the towing hawser to the outer end of her chain cable, which is now veered for one or more shackles.

In *Nelson* and *Rodney* even one link of chain cable would be too heavy to lift by hand so that the sheer weight dangling under water between the two ships would take the strain off the towing hawser. All this went very well, speed being increased slowly to 8 knots. However, when the order to slip was given, in *Rodney* we held on temporarily to our end of the hawser to make it easier for *Nelson* to heave in. But her chain cable snapped at the sixth shackle, leaving us in the middle of the Atlantic with 450 feet of her heavy cable at the end of another 900 feet of 6 inch wire hawser.

ABC wrote in his memoirs, "If anyone wants a good exercise in seamanship, let him try to recover cable weighing forty to fifty tons hanging from right aft when the only machinery capable of dealing with that weight, the capstan, is right forward."

The towing had begun around 1430 and ended about dusk. We shackled on our 6 inch wire to *Nelson*'s, leading it forward some 700 feet to the capstan. Purchases had to be put on to save fouling the superstructure when going round corners. At 2030 having buckled our 6 inch we had to substitute the 6½ inch. At 2300 *Nelson*'s cable came in sight but jammed in the fairlead. A cable clench and strop were then rigged to take its weight while a 5½ inch wire was shackled to it and led to the after capstan. By pulling gingerly on both capstans it was hoped to bring the cable through the fairlead. But in fact the sheer weight of seven shackles of dangling cable was too great. *Nelson*' 6 inch hawser parted on our forward capstan and so did our 5 inch on the after capstan.

Heavy wires parting can be lethal as they whip round. ABC continues: "We had six links of *Nelson*'s cable on the quarterdeck. Then the *Nelson*'s wire parted on the capstan and we lost the lot. It was an exciting moment to see the heavy wire surging from side to side as it rushed aft. Fortunately every one sprang clear and not a man was hurt."

All this happened on the port side. At the outset a similar towing hawser and lengths of cable had been connected on the starboard side making a two bridle tow. This one had been slipped and recovered first without difficulty. *Malaya* had also towed *Barham* and *Tiger* had towed *Repulse*.

The next day we began a full power trial at 0830 which ended at 1230. After the usual economical 12 knots, 21 knots was quite a thrill, allowed only two or three times a year to test the machinery. And so at the end of March, rolling 12° through the Bay of Biscay in wet West Country weather, *Rodney* reached her home port Devonport at the end of her first commission.

THE SECOND COMMISSION

After a 14-day leave period the last of the old commission marched into the naval barracks and the following day April 16 in spring-like sunshine the best part of 1000 officers and men marched out to recommission *Rodney*. I say the best part because total personnel in the Navy was being reduced by about 2000 a year reaching 91340 by 1932, the lowest figure since 1877, consequently drafting departments in the three manning ports could not meet requirements fully.

Among the officers few had done the whole commission so there were few changes. The Commander, Bob Burnett addressed the new Ship's Company showing them *Rodney*'s trophies specially placed on deck beside him. The new arrivals included Lieutenant G. M. Sladen, an England centre three quarter, and a very large 'Schooly', Instructor Lieutenant-Commander C. R. Benstead, author of *Retreat: A Story of 1918*, which had not been too kind about Padres. The Wardroom wondered how he would get on with the new Chaplain the Rev. G. St. L. Hyde Gosselin, a positive bearded figure.

On April 26 we sailed for Invergordon, calling at Portsmouth to embark and hoist the flag of the Commander-in-Chief, Sir Ernle Chatfield, which allowed *Nelson* to finish docking and then embark, the new Commander-in-Chief, Sir Michael Hodges. When *Nelson* arrived three weeks later, Sir Ernle departed to take command of the Mediterranean Fleet. He was pulled ashore from *Rodney* in a cutter manned by fourteen Lieutenants with the Commander at the helm, while the Ship's Company manned the side to give the customary three cheers.

As now, the Royal Tournament took place at Olympia each May and the *Rodney*'s victorious tug-of-war teams were with their coach, Mr. A. F. Vickery, Gunner Royal Marines. Comparable to David Leadbetter, the international golf coach to whom the great men go to change their swing, Mr. Vickery was a tug-of-war genius. After training teams for thirty years he was master of the 247 points to be observed by all those who lie on ropes in an almost horizontal posture. On *Rodney*'s fo'c'sle out of working hours, he had exhorted his teams for a year before launching them triumphantly against the so called invincible Dockyard Police.

At Olympia his 'Lights' and 'Heavies' defeated all their opponents whether Army, Navy or RAF. And what pleased him most was that the trophies, for the first time, had been won by a real ship, *Rodney*, not just a Barracks or other shore establishment, commonly called a *stone frigate*.

At Invergordon that same month, practice twice daily in cutters, whalers, gigs, galleys and even skiffs was in full swing for the annual Pulling Regattas at Scapa Flow, the main one being that of the heavy ships, due to take place on Tuesday and Wednesday June 3 and 4. Pulling in heavy sea-worthy boats bears little relation to river rowing in eights, fours etc., where the seats slide and it is necessary to tread delicately to avoid putting a foot through the canvas. Otherwise the toil and sweat must be the same, with blood too from one's bottom doing the sliding over a hard thwart. With over twenty races every department had at least a gig or whaler's crew in training; the larger ones, such as the Seaman, Stokers and Marines, each entered a cutter and a whaler.

Usually at sea firing guns or torpedoes in mid-week, at weekends Invergordon had enough football grounds for inter-ship matches. There was golf too on the sheep-maintained course at Nigg with a Scottish tea of scones and flap jacks afterwards. Opposite Cromarty, five miles along the Firth from Invergordon, Nigg assembles oil rigs nowadays, and looks like a shipbuilder's yard, but the pier, the club house and the course are still there.

Tug-of-war. Mr A.F. Vickery coaching Rodney's invincible team.

On May 31 the big ships were at sea for a forenoon rendezvous with *Nelson*, looking particularly smart flying the flag of Sir Michael Hodges the new Commander-in-Chief, who proceeded to lead his fleet into Scapa Flow, where the anchorage was soon alive with Admirals' barges paying their calls on him.

Tuesday June 3 being the King's birthday, all the heavy ships fired a royal salute at 0800, after which hands piped down and the regatta began at 0900. The course was little more than two miles long each ship towing her boats to the start. The crews pulled to a finish amid cheers as they passed between the two lines of heavy ships, which were *Nelson*, *Rodney*, *Barham*, *Malaya*, *Renown*, *Repulse*, and *Tiger*. Probably for the first time, a Tote was run on board each of them, possibly a mixed blessing should backers develop a financial interest in crews of another ship winning rather than their own.

Though we had trained two Gunroom crews there was only one race for Subordinate officers in which *Rodney*'s gig was third. In fact *Rodney* only gained two firsts, a Marines' Whaler and a Boys' Cutter. The winner was *Malaya*, another Devonport manned ship that had been in commission much longer. *Nelson* was second and *Rodney* third. Like Cup winners at Wembley, *Malaya*'s 'Chucking- up party' holding the Cock did a lap of honour round the Flow.

The Fleet now dispersed for individual ships to show the flag at different resorts, *Rodney* anchoring off Portrush just as I had been placed in the Officers' Sick Cabin with measles, which another cadet fresh from Dartmouth had brought with him. For several days we rolled so much at anchor in an Atlantic swell that boats could not be lowered, which combined with measles I found most unpleasant. Leave was impossible and the sailors were furious when the *Londonderry Sentinel* reported they were all being seasick. Furious too with frustration were the scores of whores said to have come up from Dublin to entertain them.

One day in May after Divisions there was Physical Training. Terence Robinson, Lieutenant of the Training Division, turned to me saying, "I expect you know the Activity Exercises Hogg, just jump up on B turret and take the men from there."

I was indeed acquainted with the little Blue book of Activity Exercises, "Knees bend," "Arms stretch," Press ups and so on, but unfortunately Pog Havers our Dartmouth Term officer, had taught us another one, all his own called 'Chicken Breathing.' Nervous perhaps looking down on a sea of expectant faces, I cried out, "First Activity Exercise Chicken Breathing". Those faces changed to utter astonishment and scarcely concealed laughter; Out of the corner of my left eye I could see the Captain and Commander saying something like "Good God the boy's mad!" The exercise consisted of bending one's arms across one's chest horizontally, with elbows sideways, and then flapping them up and down taking a deep breath with each flap in the manner of a demented fowl. I had them all doing it until somebody quickly called PT a day. Nothing however was said to me, perhaps they decided that the boy had power of command. Nevertheless I was known as "Chicken Breathing" for some weeks.

Our next mission was to embark a Parliamentary delegation at Rothesay and take them to Iceland for the millenary of the Icelandic *Althing*, believed to be the oldest parliament in the world. Its members were Lord Lamington, Lord Newton and Lord Marks, Sir Robert Hamilton, the Liberal MP for Orkney and Shetland and Mr. Rhys Davies, Labour MP for West Houghton. Captain Taprell Dorling, DSO, who wrote many naval books under the pseudonym *Taffrail*, and Mr. Warhurst a very good Times photographer came too. Last, and perhaps the most interesting, was a special *Manchester Guardian* correspondent, Mr. Kingsley Martin who would become editor of the *New Statesman and Nation* the following year until he retired in 1962.

Sailing at 1300 on Saturday 21 June, some of us saw our first whales before anchoring in the Bay of Reykjavik at 1000 on Tuesday 24th, close to the new French cruiser *Suffren*, the first warship to arrive. Having saluted Iceland with 21 guns Captain Cunningham next called on *Suffren*'s captain, who returned the call within the hour. The British Consul-General came at 1100 departing with a salute of 13 guns at 1400. Next came the Prime Minister of Iceland with 19 guns when he left at 1630. International etiquette as laid down in King's Regulations and Admiralty Instructions, was carefully observed.

A dance in *Suffren* gave the *Rodney*s attending a chance to look at the 10,000 cruiser similar to our London class. Eight 8 inch guns, eight 2.9 inch AA guns, six 21.7 inch torpedoes, two seaplanes between the funnels and a speed of 33 knots were impressive, but the greater attraction was the Wardroom, which had papered walls.

New arrivals were the *Tordenskgold* a Norwegian Coastal Defence battleship and two R. N. Fishery Protection vessels, *Rosemary* and *Boyne*.

The next day there were royal salutes for the King and Queen of Iceland and Denmark, arriving in the Danish battleship *Niels Juel* and the Crown Prince of Sweden in the Swedish battleship *Oscar II*. Liners appeared bringing American, Canadian, British and Scandanavian tourists and students, said to have swelled the population from 107,000 people to over 130,000.

After ABC had paid his call, King Christian visited *Rodney* in Danish naval uniform though being an Honorary Admiral of the Royal Navy and a Knight of the Garter he could have worn ours. An invitation to walk round the Ship's Company fallen in at Divisions in our No.1s. was accepted as can be seen from the photograph on page 94. The Crownprince preferred to chat to ABC.

The celebrations, which lasted four days were held on the huge plain of Thingvellir, thirty miles from Reykjavik along the worst possible road, drivers going at hair-raising speeds in and (usually) out of pot holes. Surrounded by great mountains, some being extinct volcanoes, the lush grass watered by streams and a lake of icy blue water made the plain a beauty spot, with geysers in the distance blowing vapours skywards.

Here in 930 AD a Parliament of forty two Vikings was formed, meeting regularly until 1798. Its members now appeared as of old in corselets and cloaks with twin-horned helmets and big beards. Adopting Christianity in 1000 AD, duelling was abolished soon afterwards. But alas this did not prevent a battle in the Althing itself some years later, nor did they escape civil war in Lutheran times. For centuries Norway threatened their independence, taking over in 1262 until she herself fell to Denmark. Finally in 1904 Denmark granted Home Rule and 1918 brought sovereign independence under King Christian.

The fifteen 'nations' represented included the Faroes and the Isle of Man, whose representative claimed his own island's Parliament was older. ABC found the lunches, dinners and particularly the speeches in a Nordic language, only allowed him one free day for fishing. The best speech came from an American, the twentieth of the evening. He swayed, beamed, said "Gentlemen" and then passed out to sympathetic applause. ABC decided that in June, with daylight day and night, the islanders never went to bed, making up their lost sleep in winter by a long hibernation. The British however were impressed by the Icelanders' enthusiasm for all things English except motor cars. They either spoke good grammatical English or were keen to do so. Kingsley Martin described later in the *Manchester Guardian* how a student suddenly interrupted a conversation he was having with another Englishman outside a hotel. The student complained that he had *split an infinitive*, saying he was upset because it was not grammar and not logical.

In Reykjavik thousands of people gathered in the main square to hear *Rodney*'s Royal Marine band play for almost two hours, looking exceedingly smart in their white and scarlet caps and blue uniforms. For libertymen a trip ashore was less attractive; Iceland was not wholly dry but the weak local beer was not enticing and I seem to remember that a special licence was necessary to drink spirits. Moreover on the four days of the celebration the shops all closed as their owners and staff departed for their tents at Thingvellir.

20,000 to 30,000 people were said to be there each day but how they got there with no railway and only 300 cars and buses on the entire island remains a mystery. 4200 tents were provided; with pony racing, folk dancing, part-singing, historical plays, gymnastics, wrestling, speeches and mountain climbing going on far into the night that did not exist.

Lunch will be provided. This emphatic statement was often the cause of confusion at Combined Services Staff Colleges when visiting other establishments. The Army took their own sandwiches while the Navy thought it meant the host establishment would provide.

At Thingvellir the authorities kept a table decorated with Union Jacks and a gorgeous gastronomic spread for the British navy which mysteriously never came. They looked in vain for a British uniform among the crowds. Only on the last day was it realised that officers were there, but in plain clothes that being our custom. C. R. Benstead described the gargantuan repast which began with salmon, followed by a team of delectable waitresses bringing course after course of delectable steaming meats. His party had begun the meal at the wrong end.

All Iceland and all the delegates from the nations flocked on board for *Rodney*'s afternoon reception. One old Icelandic lady, speaking lovely English, of course, congratulated her hosts on the exceptional quality of their Kia Ora lemonade, so much better than the bottle she bought ashore. Nobody could think of a reason, except that adding ship's distilled water, which is tasteless, made it better than Icelandic geyser.

In Reykjavik dried cod was everywhere in stacks, flattened, filleted, salted, to be washed scraped or cured. With us we had brought a cup from the Hull Fishing Vessel Owners' Association for Captain Cunningham to present as a Challenge trophy to the Icelandic Steam Trawler Association. Mr. Ofalgu Thors, who accepted the cup explained that a thousand years went by before Icelanders realised the value of the fishing around them. As recently as the turn of the century Britain had provided them with their first steam trawler. While the festivities ashore were in full swing, *Oscar II* challenged *Rodney* to a boat race. There were in fact three races. The Midshipmen, pulled in *Rodney*'s gig and galley which were identical. The Seamen pulled first in *Rodney*'s two cutters and then in two similar

AT SEA WITH ABC

Swedish boats. It mattered little which boats we were in, we lost all three races. These Viking descendants, rowing round the Bay, looked as if they could go on like Tennyson's brook for ever. And, judging by the reception given to the losing crews in *Oscar II*, the Swedes trained on Schnapps.

One day at Reykjavik a fishing trawler inside the harbour caught fire. *Rodney*'s launch, with a fire party and a fire engine, got away quickly with Bob Burnett in charge. The distance to go from *Rodney* was two miles but the Reykjavik Fire Brigade, first on the scene, had put it out.

Corporal Faull, one of the crew of an RAF flying boat, was stricken with a perforated duodenal ulcer, flying a thousand feet above the Bay. The pilot immediately landed on salt water. Delivered quickly to *Rodney*'s sick bay three medical officers operated in time to save his life.

It was still daylight at 2230 on Tuesday July 1 when we fired a 21 gun farewell salute and sailed for Holyhead. Exhausted by lack of sleep ABC at least had the consolation of another medal on his chest; by Royal Proclamation he was a Knight Commander of the Icelandic Falcon. On passage the spare pair of paravanes got more of a testing than was intended. The preventer chain parted and away they went to be lost in the deep like *Nelson*'s cable.

In spite of fog, *Rodney* anchored off the pier at Holyhead at 0400 on Saturday July 5th. By 1130 the guests had gone and with thirty one bags of mail on board we departed for the Scilly Islands on what had become a glorious summer day.

The Scillies, twenty five miles West by South of Land's End comprise about forty islands of which only five are inhabited. St. Mary's is the main island with Hugh Town, both capital and port, where the *Scillonian* berths most days bringing supplies from Penzance and taking back bulbs, early spring vegetables and flowers, destined for mainland markets. The other inhabited islands are Tresco, Bryher, St. Agnes and St. Martin's.

With strong tides, reefs, shoals and shallow patches of under four fathoms, *Rodney* approached St. Mary's with considerable care before anchoring in eight fathoms half a mile off Hugh Town's pier.

It was not my first visit to the Scillies; the previous summer half my Greynvile term at a time had been there from Dartmouth during our week's sea training in the *Forres*. In company with us on this fine Sunday morning was *Carstairs*, another sloop-cum- minesweeper of the same class, doing the same job for Public School entry cadets based in HMS *Erebus* at Plymouth.

My abiding memory of that *Forres* cruise is an invention called the *Seajoy Plaster*, which my mother had sent by post so that her little boy would be saved from seasickness. Roughly ten inches by five, I stuck it on my tummy for the duration of the cruise. Fortunately the sea remaining calm all week, was the joy. The plaster was of course useless; Hyoscine tablets appearing a few years later were the first real remedy.

With the Atlantic Fleet's sailing regatta at Falmouth only five days away, ABC's priority was vigorous practice for all, so that *Rodney* would do well. First, being Monday morning, there was no escaping General Drill which started with, "Aft all booms, Down all davits". But after several deaths – drowning from the former and crowning from the latter – had been narrowly averted, this evolution was stopped. Play continued with the Marines getting out a collision mat, the Cable party bringing the Sheet anchor to the centre line capstan, one part of ship passing a spring (a heavy wire rope used for securing to a jetty) and another rigging both 120 foot motor launches for sailing.

At cricket Cadet Hogg contributed one run and actually stumped a Scillonian batsman in which St. Mary's beat *Rodney* by five runs. We played them too at golf on St. Mary's sporting 9-hole course. There was bathing, ashore and from the ship, in the amazingly warm water due to the Gulf stream.

The one omission seems to have been a trip to Tresco, 20-30 minutes by motor launch, to see the famous sub-tropical gardens, close to the Victorian Castle-style house built and owned by the Dorrien-Smiths. The occupant then was Major Dorrien-Smith whose son was an Anson Term cadet about to leave Dartmouth. The Major had taken a lease of Tresco when the Duchy of Cornwall took over the rest of the Scillies on the death of his father.

Fifty eight years had passed when on Wednesday April 13 1988 my friend Margot Simon and I caught the 1600 Penzance helicopter to Tresco landing in less than thirty minutes in a field near the gardens. This flight was part of the regular service to St. Mary's and to Tresco. The weather in Southern England had been sunny and warm for some days. A long open truck towed by a tractor took the passengers along the one road that ends after a mile or so at the Island Hotel where we had booked.

The following morning, Thursday, we awoke to rain, drizzle, a strong West wind, visibility a hundred yards and the helicopters grounded at Penzance. The 1025 tractor took us to the gardens whose twenty acres with enormous trees might have been a tropical rain forest. Flocks of sea birds, the islands' other attraction, were sheltering unseen.

Tresco's communication with St. Mary's is by open launch which we took at 1400 on Friday from a pier near the Island Hotel. Another passenger was Mrs. Anne Phillimore, née Dorrien-Smith staying with her husband and daughter at the castle. She had to go to the dentist and hoped to catch the same launch back at 1630. To be weather-bound with tooth-ache on Tresco would be very unpleasant.

On Saturday optimistic talk about helicopters came to nothing so with many others we went once more by the open launch to catch a crowded *Scillonian III*, which sailed at 1645 and reached Penzance at 1920.

In 1991 John and Wendy Pyatt completed extensions and improvements to their excellent Island Hotel which I strongly recommend. If fully booked there is now a new hotel on St. Martin's and a smaller one on Bryhers Hell Bay.

In 1930, weather for the Fleet's sailing regatta was wet and windy. We anchored in Falmouth's spacious harbour about noon on Friday 11 July after a morning of manoeuvres. While cutters, whalers and gigs raced during the afternoon, the two picket boats were made to sweep some dummy mines. These 20-ton steamboats were the Fleet's maids of all work, each with a mounting for one 12-pounder saluting gun that could be used to support a landing party. With their raked-back funnels and polished bright work they looked smart and carried a crew of five: a Midshipman, a Coxswain, a Bowman, a Sternsheets man and the Stoker, not meant to be seen wearing a white cap cover poking his head out of the engine room when coming alongside. The cabin aft seated about ten people with room for more outside in the open and on the casing. A pain in the neck for the engineers they frequently broke down; a pain in the arse for any midshipman whose speed created a wash that swamped another ship's side party as he sped past. If the ship signalled a complaint, six cuts was a probability. Accidents sometimes happened. A spectacular way of going alongside a ship's starboard gangway was to approach almost at right angles, putting the wheel over to starboard at the last moment and going hard astern on the engine, which caused the stern to swing inwards alongside the bottom of the gangway. There was however the tale of the midshipman who didn't quite bring it off. His passenger was some tremendous big-wig. The Admiral of the squadron, the Flag Captain, with Guard and Band paraded, waited on the quarterdeck to greet him. The Commander stood on the top of the gangway

JUST A HOGG'S LIFE

watching the approaching picket boat with increasing anxiety. Sensing disaster he waved his telescope frantically warning the boat not to come alongside.

But it was too late. The picket boat crashed into the bottom of the ladder bows on. The V.I.P was a bad case of concussion, the stoker broke his nose and the Commander, still clasping his telescope fell twenty feet into the sea below.

The Sailing Regatta proved to be a triumph for *Rodney* with 30 points to 8 apiece for *Nelson* and *Malaya*, *Barham* being disqualified after her whaler had capsized during the Midshipmen's race. This was won by Midshipman Fenwick in spite of Hogg being in the crew and ABC, the chief fan, shouting encouragement through a megaphone from his motorboat. In a handicap race for cutters, whalers and gigs, he had broken his main mast sailing his galley*. But by rigging his foremast amidships to carry the mainsail he finished the course and scored points. Ahead of him in the gig, Cadet Robinson finished second in conditions that were much easier for the heavier boats.

Rodney's Torpedomen acquitted themselves well by winning a devilish thing for cutters called the Obstacle race. Over a two mile course the cutters starting under sail were next pulled after taking down mast and sails, finally sailing again after re-stepping masts and re-hoisting sails. By a well trained crew each of these changes took about fifteen seconds.

Winners of other races were Lieutenant-Commander G. N. Oliver the Gunnery Officer, Lieutenant-Commander Halahan, Lieutenant-Commander P.S. Smith and Commander R. L. Burnett. Cricket Result: Falmouth 164 for 6 declared. *Rodney XI* 36 and 81 for 8. Hogg 33.

This was also the week in which two batches of senior midshipmen, one from *Rodney* the other from *Malaya* did their oral Seamanship exam for Sub-Lieutenant. Our five, C. E. R. Sharp, M. F. Andrew, F. R. Twiss, B. R. Walford and J. F. B. Brown, examined by a panel in *Renown*, returned with four firsts and one second; quite an achievement compared with *Malaya*'s seven (names not recorded) examined in *Barham* with six seconds and one third.

These early Thirties were a distressing time for Britain. Unemployment was so great that Sir Oswald Mosley, a member of Ramsay Macdonald's Labour government resigned. Not only men, but ships were unemployed, laid up to rust in harbours such as Falmouth and Dartmouth for want of cargoes. And with the big yachts *Cambria* and *White Heather* of the

---

* A gig becomes a galley when provided for the use of a Captain, much as a picket boat becomes a barge when provided and embellished for an Admiral.

Royal Yacht Squadron also visiting Falmouth, the contrast between rich and poor was demonstrated for all to see.

Rodney moved on, anchoring for a long week-end off Lyme Regis with a lost Sunday too rough for boats to run. But, as always when showing the flag, the ship was open to visitors on at least one afternoon, among them my parents who had motored from Epsom. Saturday's programme of cricket, water polo and a bus trip to Dartmoor for the boys, ended with dances on board and ashore.

Briefed I dare say, as to what the Captain liked best, the Mayor, Mr. Baker, presented a cup, which was duly won by ABC sailing his galley, with Cadet Robinson and our crew of cadets hard on his tail.

Sailing at 0400 we anchored in Cawsand Bay near the Plymouth breakwater at 1130 in time for the hands to be piped to dinner before proceeding up harbour on the afternoon tide at 1400. Returning to the Home Port for leave was always a happy occasion with the band playing on the Quarterdeck and most of the Ship's Company fallen in, smartly dressed on the upper deck facing outboard.

A 90° turn to port is needed round Drake's Island as the spectators wave from the Hoe. Beyond Millbay the channel narrows to a few hundred yards abreast Stonehouse, with another 90° turn to starboard into the Hamoaze. We are now passing Admiralty House Devonport; the bugler, standing with the Commander on B turret, sounds the Attention and in all probability the Commander-in-Chief Plymouth himself will return the salute standing in the shelter at the bottom of his garden. Next comes the Torpoint ferry, the dockyard then occupying nearly a mile and a half of frontage on our starboard side.

Two tugs accompany *Rodney*, helping to turn her before berthing alongside, the whole journey taking the best part of two hours. The public had a close view from Devonport but I do not recall any documents being necessary to enter the Dockyard. Relatives and friends would merely satisfy the Dockyard police at the gate.

The difficulty for the authorities as regards leave periods for the Gunroom was that if we were required back on board after a fortnight's leave how were we to be gainfully employed for the next fortnight? There were no boats to run, watchkeeping was barely necessary and instruction, whether on board or in Shore establishments, was difficult to arrange when half their staff were on leave too. In April we had had only the regulation fortnight because the ship was re-commissioning. This time we were allowed from 24 July to August 19.

Tarantella

Do you remember an Inn, Miranda ?
 Do you remember an Inn
And the tedding and the spreading
Of the straw for a bedding,
And the fleas that tease in the High Pyrenees,
And the wine that tasted of the tar ?

Hilaire Belloc

My parents usually took a May holiday to Venice, Florence or the Italian lakes. Their only French holiday had been with the family in August 1924 when my father, seeing an advertisement in *The Times* had booked rooms for us in the Hotel Fronton, which was 'the local' of Itxassou, a Basque village fifteen miles inland from Bayonne. My mother's first impression was smelly but nice.

The smell came not from Basque cattle but English-owned dogs. Our fellow residents were a Mr. and Mrs. Feuerheerd, who were breeding from about forty Pekes and West Highlanders. They were in their thirties I suppose, Jock tall and handsome, Jane with flaming red hair breaking the silence one night with a piercing, "Jock, Jock, the Highland bitch has gone!" Within two days my mother and I, covered with flea bites, were scratching like the dogs. I still believe that the Feuerheerds and their favourite dogs had vacated our rooms when they knew our arrival was imminent. But to be fair to the dogs we caught Spanish fleas staying at Tolosa and my mother, greatly to her indignation, caught one in Bayonne Cathedral. My sister and brother were similarly bitten; my father and Jack Paterson, my sister's husband, were never touched. The gastronomic taste of *Pulex irritans* remains a mystery; unless - like American vine roots to the phylloxera bug - some men are too thick-skinned for a flea. There were no efficient insecticides then; we sprinkled pyrethum powder hopefully to little avail.

Sixteen years later, when I had almost forgotten Jock, I was to meet Claire, another Feuerheerd, who described him as the black sheep of the family whom she was never allowed to meet. He was not married; the redheaded Jane was believed to be one of the painter Augustus John's many natural children. Emigrating from Hamburg to Oporto C.1750 the Feuerheerds started as general merchants, Claire's father, Albert becoming such an Anglophile that he declared his children would be educated in the best English Public Houses. Feuerheerd also became a small port shipper, Albert's best business deal being to buy Quinta de la Rosa on the right bank of the Douro just below Pinhão.

After Sutherland rain 1925, Windermere rain 1926 and staff who were difficult when my father rented The Vicarage at Bray-on-Thames in 1927, we had gone back successfully to France in 1928, with a month in the rented Manoir d'Armor at Le Richardais, a village inland from Dinard. Though it survived the war, the Manoir had to be bull-dozed to make way for the road that now crosses the river Rance tidal barrage.

In August 1930 the holiday plan was to motor in three cars south to Cannes. Now seventeen, I had a licence to drive a car after having one only for motorcycles since I was fifteen. My uncle 'Sandy' Hogg had given my mother our first car, an Austin 12, in 1925 as a forty eighth birthday present. Aided by his chauffeur and her own determination, she learned to drive without serious accident for 25 years.

My father the Judge, the least mechanically minded of men then fifty five, was apt to drive with the hand brake on until half asphyxiated by smoke. A stickler for being punctual for meals, being a few minutes late himself one day for lunch he drove smartly into the dining room. Though unhurt he gave up; after all he had a wife, seven years younger, who would oblige as *chauffeuse*.

By Friday August 1 1930 when we left Epsom for Newhaven, the Austin tourer had been exchanged for an Essex saloon, which I drove most of the way through France. There were no car ferries then. Cars were hoisted into a cargo ship that preceded the cross channel steamer. In theory they should have been unloaded waiting on the quay at Dieppe when their owners disembarked from the steamer,. In practice there was usually a wait.

Considering my father needed an 11 a.m. stop for beer and another to 'pump ship' soon afterwards; while my mother liked to stop for afternoon tea, we did well to reach Auxerre about 6 p.m. after lunching at Versailles. The distance from Dieppe was 210 miles. My brother Martin, with Isobel Grant a family friend, arrived next in one 14 h.p. Delage, followed in another by my sister and her husband, Jack Paterson. Both vehicles were second hand, open sports cars each with four bucket seats.

The second day Sunday took us 250 miles down the N6 to Valence, the beer stop being at Saulieu with lunch at Chalons-sur-Saône where Jack's Delage broke an axle. The third day we reached Cannes by 8 p.m. after a long luncheon stop at Avignon with 140 miles still to go. How pleasant it was motoring in France then! The long straight roads were more than adequate for the relatively few vehicles using them. No need to book rooms in advance; though stopping by 6 p.m. was advisable. No white lines, and petrol about one shilling and twopence a gallon roughly six pence today.

Following the Rhône valley along N6, a different route back could prove to be very different. Leonard Woolf, the author, planned to return with Virginia up the middle of France quite unaware that the Massif Central existed. In March 1928 they had climbed into a great snow storm with punctures every twenty five miles for the last 500 miles to Dieppe. Indeed, it was not until the 1950s, when Freda White wrote *Three Rivers of France*, that the delights of the Tarn, the Lot, the Dordogne, the Creuse, the Indre etc., became widely known.

The parents had a ground floor room overlooking the garden in the Victoria Hotel only two hundred yards from the beach. Pension terms were four guineas a week. Still in the Michelin guide sixty years on, a bedroom for one night is now £50. Isobel, Martin and I each had a room in an overflow hotel close by. Though he said nothing, my father was clearly unhappy that his son-in-law and daughter were paying twelve pounds just for their bedroom in the posh Mirimar hotel.

John Sidney ("Jack") Paterson born 1899, educated at Eton and Royal Military College, Sandhurst, had left the Army in 1920 with a commission in the Grenadier Guards intending to make a career in the Diplomatic Corps. At Sandhurst he had achieved a very rare double by winning the Sword of Honour for the best 'Gentleman Cadet' and 'The Saddle' as the best equestrian. His maternal grandmother, widow of a Mr. Mason of Michigan, after inheriting his fortune in copper mines, brought her four daughters to Europe where they all married well; his mother 'Orchie' to Sidney Paterson, who ended a career in the Egyptian police as a Colonel. He was one of ten children brought up at Colonnade House Blackheath when their father was a Sheriff of the Corporation of London. After Sidney's death in 1921, his widow Orchie, with her daughter Phyllis aged seventeen, took to spending her life – and her fortune – staying in Europe's best hotels as she felt inclined, with her son Jack at her beck and call.

Marrying my sister Brada in 1924 he was working as one of several partners in Norman Paterson, a company they had created to sell ice flasks and other gadgets in those days before domestic refrigerators. Fluctuating, with more downs than ups, it ended after the General Strike of 1926 with one partner called Rampton suing all the others for fraud and then avoiding paying damages by going bankrupt when he lost the case. Not only had my father put up money for the business, but as a County Court Judge having to appear as a witness in such a shoddy case embarrassed him.

By the end of 1926 Jack, with a salary of £500 p.a., was managing a Haulage Works in Harrow in which my parents' friend, Francis Scott of the Provincial Insurance Company in Kendal, had an interest. By 1930 they had two children, both girls, each requiring a Caesarean operation that added greatly to expenses.

Apart from inability to live within his means, largely due to his mother's example, Jack had become a valued cosmopolitan addition to our provincial family. He could do anything with his hands from assembling a wireless set to a motorcar, the latter learnt at Eton he said. His faultless good manners upheld the Etonian reputation and he enjoyed relieving my mother of housekeeping and marketing during our summer holidays, speaking French or Italian adequately for this purpose.

This holiday was largely spent in and around the Casino swimming pool at Palm Beach. Phyllis Paterson, married in November 1926 to the Belgian Count Philip de Ste Aldegonde de Marnix appeared with him from Brussels. Jack's cousin Donough O'Brien, who had become the 16th Baron Inchiquin in 1929 was there too. Two years older than Jack, from 1916 to 1918 he had seen war service in the Rifle Brigade becoming A.D.C. to the Viceroy of India, Lord Chelmsford after it and marrying his second daughter the Hon. Ann Thesiger. These names, sufficing for a social columnist to reach for his Kodak, a picture of the Baron, the Countess, my sister and Miss Grant duly appeared in *The Tatler*.

August 15, my parent's twenty ninth wedding anniversary was celebrated with a ten shillings a head dinner at the Malmaison, a smart restaurant. The bill, which my father paid, was £6 for ten people including a champagne cup, table wine, liqueurs and coffee.

To rejoin *Rodney* I departed on Sunday afternoon at 1600 with a carriage to myself chugging along the Côte d'Azur 2nd class in a so called Express that stopped at every station.

But after Toulon and Marseille the carriage became packed, four a side in sweltering heat with no means of getting a drink. I have never been able to sleep sitting, I need to lie down. This has some advantages; as Officer of the Watch at sea one is less likely to ram the next ahead. But an all night hot train to Paris, with the lighting too dim to read and no refreshment, was as miserable as Wigan on a wet Sunday. The only entertainment came from a fat Frenchman sitting opposite who, judging by whispers of "Assez, assez, mon ami" from time to time was masturbating his poëlu friend in the next seat.

Back in *Rodney* various courses had been arranged for us. First a week on the Trevol range doing a pistol and rifle shooting course, with instruc-

JUST A HOGG'S LIFE

tion in Lewis and Vickers quick-firing guns. Each of the three Home Ports – Chatham, Portsmouth, Devonport – had its Naval Barracks, with a Gunnery School and a Parade ground for Field Training. Our second week was at the Gunnery school with five periods of Field Training in the forenoons, returning after lunch in our own gunroom, to lectures and practical work on the 4.7 inch High Angle gun. Marching up and down a parade ground doing rifle drill and sword drill is tedious at the best of times, but for us it coincided with a 90° heatwave.

The third week began on Monday 1 September with our group of six cadets falling in on the Quarterdeck to be officially promoted midshipmen by the Commander, Robert Lindsay Burnett.

Our instruction ended with three days at the Torpedo School housed in the old wooden ship *Defiance* moored on the Cornish side of the Hamoaze.

These courses held little attraction for me. In mechanical matters I was a complete duffer. I had tried once to decarbonise the engine of my 250 cc Raleigh motorcycle. Having got the cylinder off and then the piston rings I could not get them back again. My mother came to help and together we broke two of the rings. Eventually I tied all the parts to the machine pushing it two miles to a garage, whose bill, paid reluctantly by my father, was £13, £37.00 being the bicycle's price when new.

Neither Officers nor the Petty Officer instructors received any training in how to teach, nor did anybody explain that knowledge of these subjects gained now, could lead to higher marks in our examinations for Sub-Lieutenant three years hence. And had anybody told me that eight years hence I should be the Officer in charge of this Barracks' (HMS Drake) guard, waving my sword in salute at ceremonials on the Hoe, I should have regarded him as a case for the RN looney bin.

Still alongside on Sunday 7 September (a date that would be my wedding day ten years hence) I went ashore after the usual (then compulsory) Divine Service on the quarterdeck to play golf at Mountbatten with two other older midshipmen, Roderick Tripp and Terence Tibbits. On the high ground East of Plymouth Sound the course was in poor condition with trippers sitting on most of the greens. We were glad to reach the cosy bar of Lockyers, – a little hotel close to Derry's Clock that even survived the *Blitz*, – when it opened on Sunday at 7 p.m. Delayed a little, first by the lovable Dolly with her chipped front tooth and then by an excellent mixed grill, it must have been after 8.30 p.m. when leaving the bus, we walked back through the dockyard to the *Rodney*.

Unfortunately the Commander was also returning to the ship in his car, physically fortified by his own golf at Yelverton and spiritually uplifted by Evensong in the village church no doubt. "Could it be possible that the three young gentlemen he passed were breaking their leave? Daily he signed the leave book, surely no times after the usual 7.30 p.m. had been requested. He would order the Officer of the Watch to investigate".

The following morning the three of us were ushered into the Commander's cabin by the Sub-Lieutenant. The penalty for a sailor overstaying his leave was one day's pay, one day's leave stopped and although the highest standards were expected of officers, an hour adrift was not a great offence. Roderick and Terence were about twenty; not yet eighteen, I hoped I would be treated as one led astray.

Bob Burnett sat at a large roll top desk his chair swinging round towards us standing to attention. Above him was a piece of brown board inscribed with, "Don't worry it may never happen". I don't remember if he even asked for an explanation as to why we had overstayed our leave.

"I cannot tolerate ill-disciplined conduct of this sort" he said. "You young gentlemen will be given extra work in the dog watches, you will go to the masthead from time to time when I think fit, and, as long as I remain in the ship, you will have no more leave. So young gentlemen you may pray for my speedy departure". "As for you Mr. Hogg, the offence is doubly bad. Only last week promoting you to midshipman, I counselled you not to feel the weight of your patches. Within a week you flagrantly choose to disregard my advice. In addition to these punishments the Sub-Lieutenant – and here he beamed at the Sub who looked as if he too was about to come under fire – will doubtless have much pleasure in giving you a round dozen with the cane".

As the party filed out of the cabin, the boom of his tirade crashed to the floor "Don't worry it may never happen". Outside the Sub-Lieutenant turned to me and said. "You've had quite enough, take the cuts as being administered". He was Bob Whinney whose book, *The U-boat peril, An Anti-Submarine Commander's War** not published until 1986 I have already praised.

Whinney, a Greynvile leaving Dartmouth as we were joining, had already found Gunroom life in the battleship *Resolution* one of 'constant confusion, fear and bewilderment'. Hoping to gain real sea experience in a small ship as a Sub-Lieutenant, he found himself back in a battleship, because his father's friend at the Admiralty thought he would do well under Captain Cunningham. In *Rodney* of the Gunroom he writes that he was expected to maintain discipline in an unacceptably harsh manner. For the Commander he was to be sure that all its members played games

---

* Blandford Press Poole Dorset £9.95

and moreover won them. These included rugby football, ship's cross country and hockey teams, a compunction distasteful to Whinney, who longed only for the right kind of pony and a polo stick.

Disenchanted with the Cunningham/Burnett regime, he applied to join the Fleet Air Arm. But the former, whose first flight was not until 1929, refused to forward the application. Cunningham certainly belittled the Fleet Air Arm and underrated air power generally, but this probably saved Whinney's life, for flying casualties were high in training and very high during the war. Besides, since Cunningham had taken over *Rodney*, one Sub- Lieutenant, A. B. Cole had left, followed by his successor Alan Black, who was to become a Fleet Air Arm pilot. Had Whinney waited another two months when Cunningham was required to take up a new appointment, being famous for his war exploits in command of small ships, he could hardly have refused to help Whinney to follow in his own footsteps.

The main mast being rather unpractical as a long stay parking place, I went up to the High Angle Control Tower above the Compass Platform, where my sympathetic messmates brought me lunch. After a few wasted hours by which time Bob Burnett had forgotten my existence, the Officer of the Watch obtained my release. Stoppage of leave was less depressing than expected because games being part of Burnett's muscular Christianity didn't count as leave. At Invergordon there were no other attractions and, later in Portsmouth, I remember making a quick change in a Gaumont or Odeon Cinema's Gents from football shirt and shorts to Dog Robbers, the naval term for grey flannel trousers and a tweed jacket.

On September 9 the whole Atlantic Fleet, assembled from Plymouth and Portsmouth South of the Isle of Wight bombarding Cowes when not being attacked itself by sixty land based aircraft. The object of this exercise, the largest of its kind to date, was to assess air capability against warships and The *Times* special correspondent gave it two long columns. *Nelson* and *Rodney* led the way accompanied by *Norfolk*, a 10,000 ton cruiser, *Centaur*, older and smaller, the minelayer *Adventure* and a flotilla of destroyers. Taking us by surprise nine Flycatchers dived out of the clouds, another six straffed the guns' crews of the cruisers. Then came eighteen, ancient and obsolete Dart torpedo bombers, dropping real torpedoes with collision heads substituted for warheads, at a range of about half a mile. Those that hit would have dented heads on recovery. From these and records kept in the ships they attacked, the conclusion was that 40 per cent would have hit within five minutes of the two battleships opening fire on Cowes. Six shore-based Fairy III Fs, the bomber used by the Fleet Air Arm then, attacked the old battleships *Marlborough* and *Emperor of India* successfully; others attending to *Barham*, *Malaya* and *Warspite*, recently refitted in Portsmouth.

The Times correspondent concluded that while air power cannot save the civilian population, it can reduce the severity of a bombardment by heavy ships and might even make such an attack too risky.

The speed of these aircraft was around 100 mph. The following year Britain won the Schneider Trophy with a Supermarine reaching 340 mph sponsored incidentally by Lady Houston "the richest woman in Britain" because the Government would not allow the RAF to enter an aircraft during the financial crisis.

In 1939 when the war began the Fairy III F in the Fleet Air Arm had been replaced by a bi-plane already obsolete called a *Swordfish*, its speed little better than its predecessor. In 1918 on April Fool's Day the Royal Naval Air Service had been amalgamated with the Royal Fly Corps to form a new third service, the Royal Air Force. Five thousand naval officers and men, 2500 aircraft and about a hundred air fields world wide passed over to the RAF and the Navy lost all control of all research and development of naval aircraft. By 1938 when the Navy took back its Fleet Air Arm, British industry was concentrating desperately on producing Hurricanes and Spitfires. Not until after the United States had entered the war was the Fleet Air Arm equipped with modern aircraft under Lease-Lend.

Meanwhile fighting at sea and supporting the RAF against the *Luftwaffe*, the Stringbag – as the air crews called the Swordfish – had played a vital part paying a heavy price in lives and aircraft lost.

It was a torpedo from a Swordfish that struck the rudder of the *Bismarck*, reducing her speed, which enabled superior British forces to sink her next day. Had this great battleship joined forces with *Scharnhorst* and *Gneisenau* at Brest, this fast heavy squadron attacking North Atlantic convoys would have been well nigh invincible.

In the Mediterranean the attack on Taranto in November 1940 by twenty Swordfish from the carrier *Illustrious*, armed with torpedoes or bombs, crippled three battleships and kept the Italian fleet in harbour for the rest of the war.

JUST A HOGG'S LIFE

Until the day – if ever – when the battle flags are furled, *War in a Stringbag* by Commander Charles Lamb, DSO, DSC., who flew through it all and endured twenty seven operations as a result, ought to remain in print; not only as a saga of heroism among the air crews, but as a dreadful example of sending men into battle with inadequate equipment.

Dangling cables and parting pendants in the *Nelson* and *Rodney* towing affair, should be quite enough about anchor work for this book. But during our fortnight at Invergordon, some night exercises completed we anchored at 0130 in Dornoch Firth rather hurriedly, after sighting some destroyers unexpectedly anchored ahead.

In the Merchant Navy they stop the ship first, then drop the anchor going sedately astern paying out the cable. In the Royal Navy a fleet anchoring must be precise and it is smarter to drop the anchor while still going ahead and then to go astern on the engines. Going a little too fast our cable parted at the tenth shackle, sending 10 X 25 yards = 250 yards to the bottom. Marking the spot with buoys, we returned when weather permitted lowering boats which dragged grapnels across the seabed, sending down divers and dragging our own anchors across it too. On the second day an anchor made contact and all ten shackles were recovered eventually.

Returning to Portsmouth on 30th September we started to work up to full power at 0800 for a trial that lasted two hours from 0930 to 1130, with a similar work down at the end. *Rodney*'s 47000 horsepower achieved 22 knots and it was a revelation to be off Cromer by 2130 the same evening.

Next came the occasion described in Oliver Warner's biography, *Cunningham of Hyndhope* when ABC told G. N. Oliver, the Gunnery Officer, that de-ammunitioning before going into dry dock was to be done in a day. The derricks were in fact rigged passing Beachy Head before anchoring at Spithead at 1615 on 1 October. At 0900 the next morning *Rodney* went up harbour berthing at North Railway jetty. While marines and stokers secured the ship to the jetty and hoisted out boats on the main derrick; the seamen made a flying start with de-ammunitioning and had finished by 2300. If this sounds miraculous, I should explain that 16" and 6" projectiles remained on board, material disembarked being 4.7 inch projectiles, all cases of cordite and small arms ammunition.

Rodney docked in 'C' lock on Monday 6 October as the newspapers told how Britain's Airship R 101 had crashed near Beauvais in France the

Note. Before 1949 1 shackle = 12½ fathoms = 25 yards.

day before, killing forty six people out of the fifty four on board. Among them were Lord Thomson Air Minister, Air Vice Marshal Sir Sefton Brancker, Director of Civil Aviation, and Wing Commander Colmore, Director of Airship Developments.

This annual bottom scrape took until November 17. There was no dock at Devonport large enough for *Rodney*, which was hard on a Devonport-manned Ship's Company with sweethearts and wives living there.

We midshipmen were sent off daily for a week to do a gas course at Tipner, an area of waste land with a rifle range where the 275 motorway now runs in to Portsmouth's North End. A staff of three - Superintendent, First Lieutenant and Surgeon Commander - lectured on different types of gases used in chemical warfare while Petty Officers taught us respirator drill. It was customary to wear respirators for a minute or two in a hut filled with chlorine and finally to run a quarter of a mile race in them. They told us of a Royal Marine, who was so keen to win this race that he cut away with scissors the rubber exhaust flap of his respirator. Unaware of the chlorine test, he went out like a light when it was introduced into the hut.

For us the Superintendent had a different surprise. He said "I'm sure you would like first to try Caparsine, a mild form of DM, one of the nerve-sneezing gases. Don't bother to put on your respirators they will be quite useless". A few seconds later everybody was coughing fit to burst and some were beating on the door to get out. It was most unpleasant.

Afterwards the Surgeon Commander said, "You were a bit unlucky to have the Superintendent in charge, he can hold his breath for so long. When the little fat gunner is on duty, you get out much sooner".

Believe it or not the following September at Plymouth we were despatched to do the same course at the Trevol Chemical Warfare School. Chlorine, 440 yards and one extra race, through smoke and other obstructions, across a No Mans Land! No wonder the following was a popular song done with motions on Guest nights:

> *We don't want to march like the infantry*
> *Ride like the cavalry*
> *Shoot like the artillery*
> *We don't want to fly over Germany*
> *We are the Royal Navee!*

In Portsmouth having re-ammunitioned in double quick time *Rodney* carried out Blast Trials south east of the Isle of Wight. The object was to determine the effects on personnel in exposed positions when X turret fired on after bearings and at high elevations. I can only remember now that standing on the Compass Platform looking a yard or two down the barrel of a 16 inch gun was quite enough. The galaxy of Gunnery officers decreed that X turret should not train abaft a certain point, the Compass Platform assembly being left to grin and bear it.

Back at Devonport on 1 December, Commander R. L. Burnett left the ship, with the band playing and the Ship's Company raising a cheer. The tune - though Bob Burnett was unaware of it - was, said the sailors, "He won't come back no more". His relief was Commander C. M. R. Schwerdt.

Relieved by Captain R. M. Bellairs, who had been Director of Plans at the Admiralty, ABC also departed, his year being up. After some surgery in Edinburgh he had time to relax at Rowlands Castle before becoming Commodore of the Royal Naval Barracks Chatham in July.

The midshipmen's leave period was from December 4 to January 2.

Reykjavik, June 1930. Bob Burnett leads the way as King Christian of Norway and ABC walk round Divisions. Lieut. J.J. Casement salutes.

Cadet Peter Baker takes Rodney's launch into Reykjavik (ships' boats flew the White Ensign in foreign ports).

Millenary of Althing. Celebrations on the plain of Thingvellir.

CHAPTER 7

Westward Ho!

1931. On return we learnt that *Nelson, Rodney, Hawkins* an old cruiser, *Norfolk* and *Dorsetshire* new 10,000 County class cruisers, *York* another of 8000 tons and the minelayer *Adventure* would form Force A of the Atlantic Fleet, spending the next two months showing the flag in the West Indies. The remainder, Force B, would go to Gibraltar, rejoining Force A for the annual battle with the Mediterranean Fleet late in March.

Rodney proceeded to the Sound to paint ship, officers invading Gieves in George Street to buy tropical white uniform. Conveniently close to Gieves was "The Sawdust Club", a long bar with great barrels of beers, sherries and ports along one side and a man who made, while you waited, a variety of delectable sandwiches on the other. A great loss to Plymouth, this spacious rendez-vous closed when the lease ended just before the war, that wiped out George Street altogether.

So in *Rodney* 1178 officers and men, augmented by Captain Totton MC., and Mr. S. L. Stammwitz, his assistant from the Natural History Section of the British Museum, sailed on 8 January Westward Ho! some 4000 miles for Trinidad, a 14-day voyage at 12 knots. Attacked by submarines and destroyers for the first two days, the latter took our mails to Lisbon, while in Force A beyond the Azores we ran into very bad weather indeed. A whaler and the Captain's motorboat were badly damaged by a 30 foot wave which penetrated the galley and some of the mess decks.

The heavy seas lifted 35,000 tons of *Rodney* like a cork. Living below became oppressively hot and uncomfortable adding to post-typhoid injection misery. A cargo-carrying aircraft Trade Wind attempting a trans-Atlantic flight was never heard of again.

Not until Saturday 17 January, entering the Tropics nine days out from Plymouth, were we ordered to change our blue reefers and trousers for white.

The Gulf of Paria, that almost land-locked water west of Trinidad and north of South America, is silted from the mud that flows out of the Orinoco river, consequently *Rodney* had to anchor three miles from the capital Port of Spain. This it seems makes it a breeding ground for the *Stomalophus* jelly fish. Captain Totton, the Natural historian was delighted to collect specimens in a bucket. Engineer Commander Simpson foreseeing a choked condenser-intake was not amused. The Fleet's Wesleyan chaplain, living on board, declared that one or two persistently turned up in the wash-basin of his cabin.

Three of us went ashore aiming to write our names in the Governor's book. On the way we passed the prison where the coloured warders seemed to welcome visitors, so we found ourselves on a conducted tour of workshops, bakeries, kitchens, rows of cells and finally the execution gallery. A really gruesome native officer went into details, showing us three trap doors with a ring over each. The prisoner stands on one with the rope round his neck and the end made fast to the ring. He then suffers an awful moment when the bolt is drawn away to open the trap door. Some did not die at once but groaned and shrieked for a few minutes. However they were all left hanging for an hour before being cut down.

Looking back, this macabre person would have been a fine recruiting officer for The Howard League of Penal Reform! At seventeen my knowledge of capital punishment had not progressed beyond Ko Ko and his

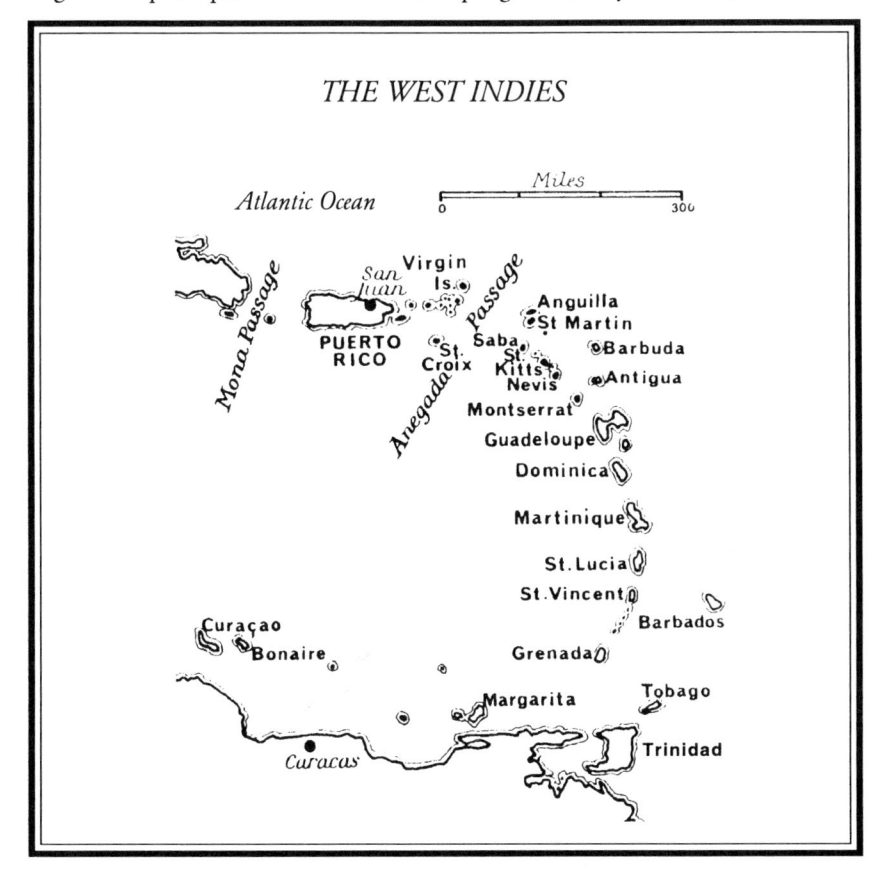

JUST A HOGG'S LIFE

Snickersnee. Enlightened by *The New Statesman* during the war, I joined the League soon after it.

The first day *Rodney* was open to vistors, I was running the 2nd Launch – capacity about a hundred who had to stand. Inshore a large crowd was waiting. A large steamboat took them off by degrees but did not seem so keen to bring them back. It was customary when in charge of a launch or picket boat for a midshipman to wear his dirk. This was the only time I remember that I – or any other midshipman – stood with dirk drawn, like Horatio on the bridge, to repel boarders.

With trips to see the famous pitch lake, dances at the pleasantly sited Queen's Park Hotel, at the Marine Club and on board *Hawkins* as well as *Rodney*, sixteen days passed quickly. The high spot of *Rodney*'s revue that packed the Empire Theatre was *Morris Chevrolet*, alias Lieutenant-Commander Hayter whose imitations of Maurice Chevalier were highly professional.

At Tobago, 26 miles long by 6½ miles wide, the weather was too bad to land at Scarborough, the capital. At Plymouth, on the other side, the launch had to tow a whaler in order to land dry shod on a white sand beach. With a few "planks" added, over a hundred leading residents and guests were able to follow Mr. Meadow the Warden of Tobago, to a tea party and a film on board, the latter being a rare entertainment for them. And the following day when we put in to Man-of-War Bay, a beauty spot at the north west corner, more black people than white re- appeared out of the forests to join us in a last bathe.

Next morning, Friday 13 February, *Rodney* anchored about half a mile off Kingstown, St. Vincent, a pleasant change from the three miles at Port of Spain. This island 26 miles long by 11 miles wide has a backbone of wooded volcanic hills and valleys surmounted by its volcano Soufière (3500 feet) which had not erupted since 1902. Driven through the bush by their host, a Wardroom party reached the crater parched and brown with dust to be told that the island had plenty of water but it all lay at the bottom of the volcano. However, later than expected, the boy with the cold beer appeared, bearing also the juice of freshly squeezed limes, a mixture promptly relished by the quart. To complete the cooling process they were next bundled into a water fall. The population of this island was about 45,000, including Kingstown's 4000. The small British community were most hospitable. *Rodney* replied by taking 2000 Boy Scouts and children round the ship and giving a dance for 250 guests. The concert party performed ashore, the £60 proceeds going to local charities, while *Adventure* joined *Rodney* in a searchlight display.

After ten days we moved north east from the Windward Islands to Montserrat and Antigua of the Leeward group. Only 11 miles by 7, and twenty seven miles south west of Antigua, a brief look into the harbour, another Plymouth, with a friendly waggle of our 16 inch guns sufficed for Montserrat, the home of lime juice.

The date now was Monday February 23 as we anchored 2½ miles from Antigua's capital St. John's for a nine day visit. Pronounced 'Anteega', the island, 54 miles in circumference is proud to be Britain's oldest colony dating from 1663, with only a short break when taken by the French temporarily in 1666. Unlike St. Vincent and Martinique it has no mountains and the 30,000 inhabitants (80,000 in 1988) have suffered from frequent drought and fresh water shortage.

At the local club Davidson, our Paymaster Midshipman and I were introduced to a Mr. Henzell owner of a big sugar factory. His son had been at Dartmouth in the same term as J. W. Forrest, who would become an England XV cap and the Navy's rugby selector later on in my career, as well as Wood, also a Navy player and a sprinter, who was to tell me in 1937 that I would not be good enough to play for the Navy.

Mr. Henzell, who had many good stories about Dartmouth, kindly showed us his factory and dined with us on board after entertaining seven members of the Gunroom for two days on his island just off the mainland.

Entertainments and hospitality proceeded as usual. Unusual however was an afternoon in which Lieutenant Q. P. Whitford, the second Torpedo officer, went away in the launch to exercise the Demolition Party, which was supposed to be done by fitting and firing charges once a quarter. An area had been buoyed and ground bait laid to attract the fish. It was hoped some interesting specimens would be stunned and collected for Captain Totton.

These charges varied from 16 to 48 lbs; a whaler was manned to help recover the fish. The first charge brought a quantity of grey and red mullet, garfish, bream and some nameless specimens. The second brought nothing. The third brought a variety, including some blue flatfish with a sting on each side and one nameless beauty speckled brown and white. After the last one – a 32 pounder – it was sometime before we noticed a large fish floating on the surface.

Unable to hand it over the gunwhale of the launch, the whaler's crew caught hold as the mighty fish came to life, slipping over the side. We thought it had got away but they managed to haul it up. Its grim looking teeth indicated a barracouta of 30- 40lbs and taking no chances the bow man, looking like a blacksmith at his anvil, despatched it with blows from a stretcher.

With a wide choice of pretty, many coloured fish still afloat, we thought Captain Totton would have been excited. Not a bit of it! only one, the most miserable specimen, small and ugly, was wanted for the British Museum.

My only regret on leaving Antigua was that no arrangements were made to visit English harbour at the southern end of the island about twelve miles from St. John's. This was where *Nelson* was stationed for three years when Captain of the *Boreas*, his first command, doing his best to stop corruption in the Dockyard. He used it again to refit and provision his fleet during the great hunt for Villeneuve, which ended in the battle of Trafalgar. But it became neglected until after World War II when the Governor Sir Kenneth Blackburne, achieved a restoration so successful that it now looks much as it did in *Nelson*'s time.

Force A, assembled once more, headed East for Madeira at 13 knots. *Nelson* the flagship had been to Jamaica and on to Panama for Sir Michael Hodges, the Commander-in-Chief to pay courtesy visits to the United States fleet at both ends of the canal.

With three exceptions, Tripp, Topp and Wheadon, public school men about to take their exams, our group of midshipmen had been the seniors since January, while another ten cadets had joined from Dartmouth.

Forgetting the heavenly bodies that had excited us on West Indian sands, we now had to observe seriously, with sextants and the Admiralty Manual of Navigation vol. 1., those in the firmament on high. The Certificate, which miraculously found its way into my record book, signed by the Instructor Officer, the Captain and the Fleet Education Officer certified that Mr. A.L.S. Hogg had completed and worked out ten different altitudes of celestial bodies to find the ship's position by drawing position lines. It was just as well he did, and kept his Dartmouth Navigation note book too, because as a Sub-Lieutenant he would find himself Navigator on a Royal cruise. There was one Sub-Lieutenant on a submarine, who took an altitude of the sun alright with his sextant but could not remember how to use the tables. They were in the North Sea and his kindly Captain said he'd see what he could do. Ten minutes later he summoned the Sub, "Take off your cap, Sub", he said, "We are now in York Minster!".

By day fixing the ship by sun sights – provided it was visible – was relatively easy, the technique being to bring an image of the sun down to the horizon by moving the arm of the sextant and reading the angle in degrees and minutes on the engraved scale. But with the moon, a star or a planet this could only be done at dusk and dawn when a horizon was visible. At sea far from land, the navigating officer would fix his ship at dawn, noon and dusk, choosing his stars from a star globe. Observation of one celestial body produced one position line; with three intersecting at one point he knew he wasn't in York Minster.

There was always plenty of activity among HM Ships at sea. Man overboard was often rehearsed at Evening Quarters, life buoys being dropped for cutters or whalers, specially rigged as sea boats, to pick up. By day the Gunnery Officer supervised Inclination Exercises and sub-calibre shoots that fired small ammunition from the big guns. Paravanes were run and respirators worn and inspected at Divisions. By night ships played 'hide and seek' using star shell and searchlights. In our two years in *Rodney* the Record of Instruction and Progress declares we spent forty seven days in the Engineering Department. I suppose we must have studied Air Pumps, Feed Pumps, Circulating Pumps, turbines, gearing and many other aspects of Marine Engineering, but I now remember only Boiler Cleaning. *Rodney* had eight Boilers, made by Yarrow. Oil fuel replacing coal had reduced Staff enormously; from 320 to 42 in the big liner *Aquitania* for example and from thirty to twelve in the latest destroyers.

Each boiler had one large steam drum and two smaller water drums below it. The big steam drum was connected to each of the water drums by a series of inclined generating tubes numbering over a thousand. Pumped into the steam drum, feed water descended through the tubes most remote from the fire and rose through the tubes nearest the fire being converted into steam, which passed on through piping via a superheater to the engine rooms, which in the *Nelson* class were forward of the boiler room to make smoke less likely to interfere with fighting the ship.

These boilers had to be cleaned after twenty one steaming days. In practice steam was only raised in all eight boilers together for a full power trial, which produced 45,000 horsepower and maximum speed of 23.5 knots. The method of cleaning was for two Stokers to lie inside the steam drum each pushing his brush down each tube. The brushes had hinges at intervals like those of a chimney sweep. It is difficult to conceive a more monotonous job nor of a more cramped position. Finally the Chief Petty Officer Stoker handed them a bag of ball bearings with instructions to drop one down each tube to prove that it was clear. Cleaning a boiler took ten days. Concentrating on doing it well myself, my lusty push scored a near miss on the eye of a diligent Engineer Lieutenant looking up the same tube to see how we were doing.

In *Rodney* - and in most ships I imagine - all this essential work was done by one Boiler Cleaning Party of stokers whose Divisional officer must have changed individuals from time to time.

The mighty Red (Atlantic) fleet now concentrated near Madeira to do battle with the mighty Blue (Mediterranean) fleet emerging from the Straits of Gibraltar. The war began at 1800 on Saturday March 14 but after two nights at Cruising stations with Action Stations at dawn, followed by numerous sighting reports flowing in, the two fleets had failed to sight each other so we called it a day and headed for that annual meeting of old acquaintance under the Rock.

Nelson alongside the South Mole converted the coal sheds into a spacious theatre for *Between the Bollards*. The popular tune of the moment *All the King's horses and the King's men,* becoming Med warships and Med men, we heard :

They've got their dicers,*
They've got their wives,
They settle down in Malta living quiet peaceful lives,
All the Med warships, And the Med men.

Two days later *Queen Elizabeth*, the Mediterranean Flagship also alongside the South Mole staged, *The Curate's Egg* including a neat riposte:

They've got the Baltic
They've got the Spanish Main,
And yet they have to make a mess in our backyard again
All Mike's† warships,
And Mike's men.

Rodney being a private ship and therefore junior to a flagship was anchored in the Bay outside the Mole. *Nelson*'s 'At Home' after the show had been a little too much for our colleague Willie Knox, who some of us managed to escort back to *Rodney* in one of her boats. The problem then was to get him up the gangway and down below, unseen by the Officer of the Day, who happened to be Lovell, the Snotties' nurse. Fortunately he and the OOW were occupied on the other side of the Quarterdeck, checking the sobriety of returning sailors.

---

*Phonetic spelling of *Dghaisa*, the smaller Maltese version of the Venetian Gondola.
†Admiral Sir Michael Hodges, Commander-in-Chief, Atlantic Fleet.

WESTWARD HO!

But next morning at 0630 there was Willie, as hearty as Bob Burnett leaping over a gymnasium box horse, totally oblivious of our heroic rescue that saved him from stoppage of leave for life or whatever!

Our anchored position in this bay was nearer to Algeciras than to Gibraltar giving a chance to land there and wander through its old cobbled streets. Those who did were impressed by the air of prosperity and the fine modern road that went up the coast to Malaga. Burnt down several years before, the *Reina Christina* Hotel had been rebuilt.

The British Consul was so agreeable that a *thé dansant* was held on board for him and the local British community. It seems incredible that within five years Spain would tear itself apart by Civil War. The Bay of Biscay reminds me of A. A. Milne's Jonathan Joe whose wheelbarrow was full of surprises. This time about 0700 on a Sunday morning we ran into a fog so thick that even the jackstaff could not be seen from *Rodney*'s Compass Platform. Usually battleships proceed in line ahead, distance apart two and a half cables, which meant 270 yards between *Nelson*'s stern and *Rodney*'s stem. In fog *Nelson* would stream and tow a small fog buoy which we would keep in sight. About 0750 out of this fog came a 3,000 ton collier called *West Wales* heading for *Nelson*. In spite of blasts on sirens and hasty avoiding action by the battleships she bumped into *Nelson*. Apart from a flooded fore peak this intruder was undamaged and by early afternoon when the fog lifted the two ships were able to go their separate ways. It must have been about the same time, 0750, that *Nelson* was damaged by a German magnetic mine on December 4, 1939 entering Loch Ewe. It was after breakfast and the explosion broke many lavatory pans on which men were sitting. Casualties were sixty eight including three killed. A well kept secret, *Nelson* returned unaided to Portsmouth.

With sand banks close to the buoyed channel in and out of Portsmouth harbour, the safe passage of big ships, particularly with a cross wind, is not exactly plain sailing. There was another occasion after the war when *Nelson* became firmly stuck close to South Parade Pier on a sand bank called (Lady) Hamilton to the delight of Pompey bystanders.

Attacked by submarines, *Tiger*, the battle cruiser *Renown* and *Rodney* all came home to Plymouth with a cheer for the old *Tiger* as she went up harbour for the last time. Before departing on three weeks leave the Gunroom had to hold a guest night, primarily for those who had coached our three ex-Public schoolboys Tripp, Topp and Wheadon, each awarded a 2nd in their Seamanship exam. A delightful trio as messmates!

Roderick Tripp was a big fellow always pleased to say he had been educated 'under the shadow of the great Cathedral', which meant King's

School Canterbury. They certainly taught him to adorn his journal with exceptionally good drawings, particularly charts of Scapa Flow, the Windward Islands and the other places where the ship had been. After Sub-Lieutenants' courses, he found his metier in the Surveying Service, that small body of British naval officers forming part of the Admiralty Hydrographic Department, which surveys 'the oceans' – largely from small boats with lead and line in those days before Echo sounding – their work forming the basic material for Admiralty charts.

This Hydrographic Department was established in 1795; in 1931 it comprised roughly, the hydrographer, 15 naval assistants, 23 chief cartographers and cartographers, 57 draughtsmen and 38 clerical staff. Admiralty charts are published to meet the needs of seamen world wide, fulfilling those great lines in the naval prayer "that we may be a security for such as pass on the seas upon their lawful occasions;" Most maritime nations now have their own hydrographic departments, information passing freely between them. Long may it be so!

Robin Topp, a Lieutenant in the battleship *Resolution* in 1934, was a good Rugby full back, who went on to specialise in Torpedoes. After the war he was Commander of *Defiance*, the Devonport Torpedo School, but much to the disappointment of his Captain G. C. Blundell was never promoted to captain himself.

Max Wheadon joined the Navy from Cheltenham College. A very good athlete, I remember him best playing rugby for United Services Portsmouth against Richmond at the Old Deer Park in March 1934. We won this match, Max side stepping down the right wing to score a spectacular try. The following year he played for the Navy. Some years later a bad bout of malaria led to an extraordinary affliction called narcolapsy, the victim just falling asleep anywhere all of a sudden. Inevitably he was invalided in the 1940s controlling the disease to some extent and working for a paint business in Newcastle. Max died in 1981; his wife Marguerite ('Bay') survives him. With the departure of Tripp, Topp and Wheadon the Senior Gunroom group became; F.P. Baker, C. F. S. Robinson, R. L. W. Moss, W. N. R. Knox, W. Scott and A.L.S. Hogg. Next followed a batch of seven Ansons six months younger: O. N. Bailey, M. Buist, P. N. Medd, A. H. Nicholls, K. R. S. Leadley, F. A. B. Fasson and A. R. E. Evans. And after them six Benbow cadets: J. H. Walwyn, J. S. Dalglish, J. N. Kennard, N.E. Ward, J.A.V. Hickley and R. N. Everett. Followed now by four Hood cadets: M. N. Tufnell, C. L.Gruning, B. S. McEwen and E. H. Player. There were also the Paymasters: Midshipman R.H. Coleby and Cadets A. N. Ashby, C. E. Smith and K. H. Farnhill.

From the Royal Naval Reserve (RNR) and Royal Naval Volunteer Reserve (RNVR) others came for periods of training giving rise to the saying the RNR are seamen but not gentlemen; the RNVR are gentlemen but not seamen; so the RN can't bloody well be either.

You're from Antig - u - a ... I can tell it by your fig - u - a. (Revue number, 1930s).

CHAPTER 8

Has anybody here seen Kelly?

After three weeks leave in April, it was back to Invergordon once again with practice for the Pulling regatta all through May. Aircraft attacks on the fleet now became a more prominent feature of the Exercise programme. It was thought that Torpedo bombers, having to approach on a steady course at 20 feet above the sea for a whole minute before releasing their torpedo, would be easily destroyed. The airmen argued that in war the planes would be faster, descending from the clouds at great speed. Alas, as you have read in Chapter 6, for the Fleet Air Arm such aircraft never appeared until 1945. Indeed even this might never have happened but for one man.

Richard Smeeton, a member of our Greynvile term, lost no time in joining the Fleet Air Arm as a pilot when our courses for Lieutenant were over. By 1941 he had become Assistant Naval Attaché (Air) in Washington

*Admiral Sir John Kelly.
(Courtesy of the Royal Naval Museum, Portsmouth.)*

D. C. Under Lease-Lend the Americans were prepared to supply suitable aircraft to Britain for the Fleet Air Arm. Proposals had been sent to the Admiralty but, in spite of reminders, no replies had reached Washington when the Committee met to take the final decisions. For Lieutenant Smeeton it was now or never; courageously he chose to order a few million pounds worth of Avenger aircraft.

Commanded to report in person to the Admiralty, he received a formidable rebuke, telling me I remember that the Civil Servants were the most outraged. However, his promotion to Commander soon followed, with an appointment in 1943-44 to the Staff of Admiral Nimitz USN, the great Pacific Commander-in-Chief. Moreover when the British Pacific Fleet reached Sydney in 1945, with four carriers full of Avenger aircraft, it was Richard Smeeton who became Air Plans Officer on the Staff of Sir Philip Vian in command of them, supporting the Americans in the capture of Okinawa.

He retired at his own request in 1965 as Vice-Admiral Sir Richard CB MBE. After being Flag Officer Naval Air Command, he was wanted as Director and Chief Executive of the Society of British Aerospace companies. He died in March 1992 survived by his wife Betty.

Of the Summer Cruise 1931, apart from steaming over the centre of an earthquake there is little worth recording. The result, in points, of the Pulling regatta had been: *Nelson* 513, *Malaya* 362, *Rodney* 336, *Repulse* 321, *Renown* 262, *Valiant* 234. Our only winners were the Seamen's whaler and the Ordnance and Electrical Artificers' gig. *Nelson* won practically all the other races, a great triumph for the Fleet flagship .

June was a bad month with rain on land and fog at sea. Sailing South off Flamborough in fog, *Rodney* was suddenly uplifted. Was it a shallow patch ? Why did the engines suddenly race and the whole ship vibrate ? The answer came in the Press next day; the seismologists declared an earthquake centred off the Humber. *Rodney* now spent a month in Portland harbour firing torpedoes in conjunction with the Torpedo depot at Bincleaves to discover why some shots made a nose dive into the bottom. For us, given plenty of "Make & Mends" (known as a half day off in civilian life) the shots were on the Came Down golf course, Willie Knox having acquired an ancient M.G. midget into which we somehow crammed four golfers with four bags of clubs.

The summer cruise ended with the Sailing regatta held in Torbay in which *Rodney* relinquished most of the cups won the previous year.

JUST A HOGG'S LIFE

However from the Gunroom Midshipman Medd won a cutters' race to retain at least one trophy.

The leave period was from Saturday July 25 to Sunday August 23. Navy Week when ships at the three Home Ports were open to visitors was an annual event in August raising money for naval charities. This year at Devonport *Rodney, Eagle, Furious, Dorsetshire,* and *Norfolk* were open. *Revenge* too could be seen in the floating dock. A Tea dance, a Life-saving display, a Fun fair and a Dance band were all part of the show.

One of *Rodney*'s sailors on leave in Bristol boarded a motor coach for a mystery tour, the destination being part of the mystery. A few hours later he found himself in the dockyard alongside *Rodney,* invited to pay one shilling to go on board his own ship. On August 24 Ramsay Macdonald resigned as Prime Minister of the first Labour Government. The next day the King suggested that he should form a National Government, which he did immediately. But that did not solve the crisis, which was much the same as we are having now, sixty years later: appalling unemployment with reduction in purchasing power of the pound. The Government's remedy was to reduce the Dole by ten per cent with the same reduction for Civil Servants, the Road Fund and upkeep of the Armed Forces.

In accordance with normal practice, on 5 September our group of six went in pairs to different destroyers of the Atlantic Fleet for three months small ship experience. Moss and I were lucky, we had only to walk across the basin to reach HMS *Vidette*. The others departed to Chatham-manned ships. In *Vidette* our accommodation was one single cabin on the port side below the bridge. Moss slept in the bunk; I slept under it; with a change round agreed for 'half time'.

Ross Leonard William Moss had joined Dartmouth as a Blake two terms above us Greynviles. A football injury to his spine involving surgery had put him out of action for six months before he was appointed to *Rodney* to join us. A big fellow and a useful cricketer, he had enough money to own a decent car and as a giver of lifts he was very kind.

The officers of *Vidette* were: Lieutenant-Commander A. D. Nicoll, Captain, Lieutenant L. A. K. Tyrwhitt, First Lieutenant, Lieutenant H. W. Falcon-Steward, Cable Officer and Anti-Submarine Officer, Sub-Lieutenant A. G. B. Tulloch, Engineer Lieutenant J. A. Ruddy and Gunner W. E. Hayward.

My job was to be a "Tanky", a naval nickname for Navigator's assistant, the Navigator of *Vidette* being the Sub-Lieutenant; Moss was to assist the First Lieutenant, who in a destroyer was both Executive and Gunnery officer.

On September 7/8 the Atlantic Fleet assembled off the Isle of Wight for passage to Invergordon for the big ships and to Rosyth for the destroyers. The big County Class cruiser *Norfolk* now had an aircraft that crashed into the sea when being catapulted. Miraculously both pilot and observer were unhurt. In *Vidette* we made a dash for the RN Hospital Haslar, securing to buoys bow and stern almost on the mud of Haslar Creek; to land an urgent cot case from *Norfolk*.

Between 2000 and midnight the destroyers searched for and attacked 'enemy' battleships, my role changing from twiddling Enemy Bearing Indicators on *Rodney*'s Compass Platform to *Vidette*'s chart house below the bridge, plotting our ship's course and speed and enemy reports when received. The room was fuggy and with plenty of movement on the ship I felt seasick.

There were two destroyer flotillas in the Atlantic Fleet, some of the V class begun in 1916, others of the later W class. These 1000/1500 ton ships had a maximum speed of 35/36 knots, their main armament being six 21 inch torpedoes. They also had four 4 inch guns, two forward and two aft; some had an additional 3 inch anti-aircraft gun, others a pair of Pom Pom anti-aircraft guns. Asdic's (Anti Submarine Detection Investigation Committee) were becoming more efficient and depth charges could be kept unprimed safely on the Upper Deck.

Each of these flotillas was led by a Captain (D) in a leader, a slightly larger ship which could accommodate the flotilla's staff officers. On arrival at Rosyth it took an hour to berth all these ships alongside in the dockyard which was unacceptably slow.

In the air the current event was the Schneider Trophy. As Italy and France had scratched from the race, Britain had only to fly one of her S6B seaplanes over the Spithead/Solent course once to retain the trophy. Over this 100 kilometre closed circuit Flight Lieutenant Boothman averaged 340 mph, capped by Flight Lieutenant Staniforth the following day with 379 m.p.h. Within a month he increased this to 408 m.p.h., then a world record.

The Great Western Railway too was breaking records. 77.75 miles from Swindon to Paddington in 59.5 minutes, average 78.5 m.p.h. made this the fastest start to stop Express in the world.

Monday 14 September was the prelude to the Invergordon mutiny. At Rosyth all destroyer captains cleared lower deck to explain the Government's pay reductions, saying that men who felt they would be unable to make ends meet should see their Captain so that steps could be taken to alleviate hardships.

JUST A HOGG'S LIFE

On Tuesday 15th rumours reached us that large numbers of men in the big ships at Invergordon had refused to work until something was done about the reductions. On Wednesday 16th this was confirmed in the newspapers. By evening an Admiralty message had ordered all ships of the Atlantic fleet to return to their Home Ports, where Commanders-in-Chief would go into cases of hardship resulting from these cuts.

In *Vidette* few of the ship's company welcomed this, because returning home now would not help them to save money for the Christmas leave period. Furthermore there were many more football grounds available at Rosyth than at Devonport.

By Saturday 19th *Rodney*, *Vidette* and other Devonport manned ships were back there and I walked to *Rodney* to find out what had really happened at Invergordon.

The refusal to work was on quite a large scale organised ashore in the canteen there. *Nelson* had remained in Portsmouth because the Commander-in-Chief Admiral Sir Michael Hodges was temporarily on the sick list. Thus the meeting chose *Rodney* to be the ring-leader, a part this largely West and North country crew agreed to play only reluctantly, but, having done so, they became determined not to quit. Great care was taken to see that officers were not inconvenienced, that boats were run normally with the normal watchkeeping staff on the Quarterdeck. Nevertheless *Rodney* got a bad name. As at Rosyth Captain Bellairs and Commander Schwerdt addressed the Ship's Company reading out an Admiralty letter which spoke of pay cuts without specifying precisely what they were. The truth was that the pay of a Leading Seaman, an Able Seaman and an Ordinary Seaman would be reduced by twenty five per cent causing great hardship, particularly to those who were married. In these circumstances however any man hesitates to risk being noted as a disgruntled person, while both officers and Petty officers, however sympathetic, cannot associate themselves with those who refuse duty.

It was unfortunate for Whinney that he was still the Sub-Lieutenant and closely involved as an Officer of the Watch at this time. Worried that the men's behaviour might worsen, he told the Commander that in spite of his and the Captain's talks, they did not know what the cuts were and what action would be taken.

Four months later reporting to the Admiralty after leaving *Rodney* he was informed that an adverse report had been received about him. Yet not a word had been said to him as required by the regulations. Moreover the Admiralty refused to tell him what this said or who made it. Instead he would be placed under Special report; two of these if satisfactory would end the matter; one, if unsatisfactory, would mean discharge from the Service.

Regarding this outspoken Sub-Lieutenant as insubordinate, Commander Schwerdt must have drafted the report, presumably signed by the Captain, Roger Bellairs. The former was relieved within six weeks of the mutiny; the latter remained the Captain until the end of his second commission in April 1932. Neither officer received further promotion. Though not to blame for the pay cuts, having been in command of a ship's company that neither trusted nor obeyed them did for them both. Whinney gives a more detailed account in his book *The U-Boat Peril: An Anti-Submarine Commander's War*. Among the first to qualify as an anti-submarine specialist, he became a successful hunter of U-boats awarded a DSC and two Bars in command of destroyers. The book is rightly commended in a brief foreword by Vice-Admiral Sir Peter Gretton KCB, DSO and two bars, OBE, DSC.

ABC, who had just become the Commodore of the Royal Naval Barracks Chatham, blamed everyone in responsible positions – including himself – for being insufficiently aware of the conditions under which those in their charge lived. He invited immediately any rating in the Barracks to come to him and state his case; over five hundred did so.

My own observation, writing almost exactly sixty years later, is that if Mrs. Thatcher's Government had studied what happened then, she might have refrained from launching the ill considered Poll Tax.

The cuts were reduced to a maximum of 10 per cent. Atlantic Fleet was re-named The Home Fleet and since Admiral Hodges was still not fit, Admiral Sir John Kelly was appointed its Commander-in-Chief. Sir John, then aged sixty-one and about to retire, was a 'salt horse' more interested in the welfare of men than in material matters. He was a real character able to speak to them in a language they understood. His younger brother, Howard was also an admiral then in the Mediterranean, but they had little in common.

After nearly three weeks alongside at Devonport, which I spent mainly playing rugger, either for the destroyers or the *Rodney*, with some golf at Yelverton or Tavistock, we sailed once more to a rendez-vous off Sandown Isle of Wight, Sir John flying his flag in *Nelson* for the first time. In a night exercise off the Scottish coast destroyers actually fired twenty nine torpedoes spending three hours until midnight trying to find them. Twenty five only were recovered.

Sir John anchored his capital ships below the Forth Bridge, destroyers berthing in the piers of Rosyth dockyard as before. After visiting and addressing the ship's companies of the big ships, he came to the dockyard where destroyer officers and about a hundred men had foregathered on the pontoon abreast the cruiser *Centaur*, flagship of the Commodore (D). Walking round every rank took about an hour, then came his speech which my journal describes as a masterpiece. This huge man with a great jowl began: "Take a look at me - I know I am no oil painting - but take a good look, so that when we see each other ashore you won't say, "Who's that funny old bugger over there?"

He could make men laugh but he could also make them feel ashamed. As to recognition, when walking round the playing fields he would of course be in plain clothes. One day he met a youngster, who was still in civilian clothes because it took several days to kit up new recruits.

"How long have you been in the Service ?", asked the great man.

"Two days", replied the lad "How long have you ?"

"Forty five years", said Sir John a trifle astonished.

"My, they've taken a f******g long time to kit you up", said the boy, even more astonished.

At the end of his speech he received four cheers, one more than the customary three the extra one being spontaneous. However, his debunking did not mean that he tolerated slack behaviour; ships and ship's companies were required to be smart and efficient. At general drill one evolution was "Send Royal Marine band to flagship." *Rodney*'s arriving first, proceeded to play *Has anybody here seen Kelly?* Later at Admiralty House, Portsmouth when Commander-in-Chief he had a book for visitors to sign; one young officer decided to do so having finished a game of squash in a court near by. Kelly caught him in shirt and shorts with racquet in hand. There was hell to pay.

Among many incidents I like the one in which he was about to go down the gangway of *Nelson* into his barge as C-in-C Home Fleet to pay some official call. Guard and Band were paraded, the Flag Captain, the Commander of *Nelson*, the Officer of the Watch all saluted as he was piped over the side. The only word he spoke was to the Royal Marine Corporal fallen in by the gangway with the Boatswain's Mate.

When he had gone the Commander said, "What did the Commander-in-Chief say to you, Corporal?"

Much embarrassed the Corporal said it was private and something he could not repeat.

"But I really must know," said the Commander testily.

"Well, sir" said the Corporal, "He looked down at his left hand cupped by his side and giving it a wave in your direction he said, 'Did you think any of them f—g bastards here can see I've got a cigarette in me 'and?'"

When last mentioned A. L. Bonsey, a likeable impish Greynvile cadet, was doing an extra term at Dartmouth after failing to pass out. Since then he had become a midshipman in the *Nelson*'s Gunroom illustrating his journal with excellent drawings, including a caricature of the new Commander-in-Chief. Seeing this the snotties' nurse, thinking that to caricature so great a person might be lese-majesty, took it to the Commander, who took it to the Captain, who declared the Admiral himself should handle such a matter.

Summoned to the presence the diminutive Lionel must have wondered whether his fate would be death from a knock out blow by this former heavy weight boxing champion. He need not have worried. "Not bad, not at all bad! Can you do a couple more, one for my wife and one for me", said Joe Kelly, looking up from Lionel's journal.

This of course created a bond between them and a little later when Lionel Bonsey was found to be colour blind, an edict signed by the Commander-in-Chief no less went forth to say he should not run boats after dark. Later he was able to transfer to the Supply branch becoming a Lieutenant (S), formerly called a Paymaster Lieutenant. He managed to get two books published and died on 5 February 1989, survived by his widow Mary Norton, the author of childrens' books, who lived on in Hartland village, N. Devon until her death on 3rd September 1992. Her four children and twelve grand children survived.

In restoring morale Sir John Kelly, GCB, KCB, CB had combined conspicuous understanding with firmness and fun, but he had worn himself out visiting and inspecting his ships with all the climbing up and down ladders that this entails and was glad of a comparative rest as C-in-C Portsmouth from 1934 to 1936. On the penultimate day of active service he was promoted to Admiral of the Fleet and the Union Jack flew over Admiralty House. He died on 4 November 1936. His wife Mary, whom he had married in 1915, survived him for one more year. His epitaph might have been the signal sent when ships were over doing preparation for a royal visit.

Pro Bono Publico
No Ruddy Panico

A fatal accident.
On Monday 19 October the Sixth flotilla sailed for exercises beginning with some sub-calibre practice, firing at a small target which any destroyer could stow on deck, hoist out and tow. Although warned not to cross the guard rails on to the target, which was about to be slipped and streamed, Able Seaman Emery of *Vidette* did so and accidentally fell into the sea to the cry of 'Man Overboard'.

Dashing down from the bridge, I found the whaler was already manned with Moss in charge. Within thirty seconds of the accident it had been slipped, *Vidette*'s engines having been put to full astern. But the wind and the sea along this northern coast of the Firth were coming from astern of *Vidette*, the whaler having to pull through rough water to reach Emery. From the upper deck he could be seen about forty yards away on the starboard side. Able Seaman Phelan dived to the rescue followed by Sub-Lieutenant Tulloch swimming out with a rope. Phelan actually reached Emery but once the air in his clothing had gone, he disappeared, the whaler arriving two minutes too late.

Had the wind and sea been from any other direction, or with hindsight, had the slipping of the whaler been delayed until the ship was near to Emery, he would have been saved. A Court of Inquiry was convened but no adverse report was made. As was the custom, an auction of the dead man's kit took place, with much of it put back to be sold again. Donations from *Vidette* officers and from other ships increased the fund, which was raised for his dependants.

On 27 October there was a General Election. In the flotilla we were at sea. I suppose officers and men eligible voted by post but I do not recall any Wardroom talk about it. Ten years later, war time R.N.V.R. Officers were being told by a lecturer on "Mess Customs" that three subjects were never mentioned : *Politics, Women, Religion*. One of these officers, Paul Wilson, was the Senior Engineer of *Black Prince* in 1943 when I was the Torpedo Officer. He used to say with a grin, "I suppose that lecturer was right, but we've never talked about anything else this commission have we ?"

Paul, a Socialist, subsequently became Lord Lieutenant of Westmorland and a Life Peer as Lord Wilson of High Wray. Staying with him and his wife Val, in their house in Kendal he appeared for breakfast one morning in full Lord Lieutenant's regalia.

"What on earth!...", I said.

"I am going to sing sea chanties to the W.I.," was the reply.

Thinking this was a joke we laughed. The Lord Lieutenant was not amused.

In October 1931, the results with two still awaited, as recorded in my journal were:

For the National Government	Conservatives	470
	Liberal National	35
	National	2
	Liberal	33
	National Labour	13
		553
Opposition		
	Labour	53
	Independent Liberals	4
	Independent	3
		60

For my nineteenth birthday on November 6 my father sent me £10 by Registered Post. More than a month's pay it was stolen from our cabin. I recorded this theft because it was the only one I experienced in twenty eight years ashore and afloat in the Royal Navy. Only now, writing about 1931, has it dawned on me that the thief must have been a desperate victim of those pay cuts.

Tuesday 10 November was a tremendous skylark. For exercise purposes Rosyth and environs were South American territory. Our 6th flotilla sailors became a band of highly trained insurgents attempting to capture a guano factory in the north west corner of the dockyard. The exercise began at dawn. Inverkeithing was in a state of Civil War. Great Britain sent the 5th flotilla to protect British subjects and interests. The cruiser *Centaur* in support was due to arrive at 0930.

Our sailors, delighted with the role, dressed up as insurgents with a few in drag as prostitutes, to whom they could give chase. Our sagacious Lieutenant Thew, normally Captain of the flotilla's XV, forging a signature or two captured two lorries (representing armoured cars) which were earmarked for the British. These made a detour round Dunfermline to launch a surprise attack from the western side.

JUST A HOGG'S LIFE

I was attached to 'A' Company's Headquarters with the Company Commander, Lieutenant-Commander Rodgers, a jovial fat man known as *Haleeb* which is Maltese for milk. This I imagined was what he carried in his water bottle, for we were dressed with webbing equipment and pistols in holsters as for war. At the height of the battle we retired to a quiet corner behind a shed. *Haleeb* took a swig and handed me the bottle. Neither water nor milk, it was a well prepared horse's neck (brandy and ginger ale).

Some of the insurgents, armed with sand bags, took up a strategic position half way up the large dockyard crane. These they dropped as the platoon of Royal Marines landing from *Centaur* marched by underneath en route to end the revolution. One sand bag scored a direct hit on one Royal Marine laying him clean out. Discretion being the better part of valour, the umpires brought the Civil War to a close.

The same afternoon for midshipmen there was an oral examination in *Walpole* on Seamanship, Gunnery, Torpedo and Navigation in destroyers. All went well with me until it came to Gunnery. "Gunnery is a noisy bore", said my examiner, a young Lieutenant, "Lets have a glass of port". A few minutes later the glasses were as empty as his marking sheet. I had been awarded a mere 19 per cent. They doubled this figure in the official results sent back to *Rodney*, but it was hardly adequate, for we had always understood that marks would be made 'respectable'.

> *With the sports that we practise and games that we play,*
> *We keep ourselves fit in a wonderful way*
> *And our chief recreation is healthy indeed*
> *For those who have shares in Saccone and Speed.*

Saccone and Speed and Stokes and Harvey were virtually the sole suppliers of duty free wines and spirits to H.M.Ships. Far from making rapid profits they had to fill the Wardroom wine store first, being paid by the Wine Caterer, usually the medical officer or the paymaster, in instalments as the contents were consumed and mess bills paid.

As Midshipmen our fifteen shillings a month wine bill rose to five pounds as a lieutenant in the Wardroom and with gin at tuppence and sherry fourpence a glass, the verse is a fair summary of naval life in the Thirties. There were however some destroyers in which the *chief recreation* was far more healthy for the shareholders than the participants. In harbour the gin sessions could last from noon to 1500 and in *Vivien*, the ship often alongside *Vidette*, when the First Lieutenant and *the Chief* (Engineer officer) sat down on the fender and ordered their first glass of port it was said the Navigator went to put the chronometer right. He knew it was four o'clock precisely.

But at sea in destroyers and other small ships there was practically no drinking. Captain the Hon. Hermon-Hodge of *Versatile* (Fifth flotilla) used to be brought a large whisky and soda on the bridge at sunset by his coxswain; but then, being an Hon., in Mitford mythology he was entitled to be a rebel.

Our Captain Angus Nicholl's contribution to morale was what he called a *Funny Party* and after rehearsals for a month The Sixth Destroyer Flotilla FUNNY PARTY was staged in the R. N. canteen at Rosyth on Saturday 14 November. Advertised as 100% Talking, 105% Shrieking and 324% Tripe, it played to a full house.

Only the finale, the great Battle Scene from Gasolini's famous opera *L'Appreziazione della Situazione* need be recorded here for posterity. It was composed at the Staff College Greenwich in 1928, when the idea of Staff Officers seemed quite absurd to old diehards at sea. The producer Angus Nicholl could have been Gasolini himself. While I committed the words and the tunes to memory, I cannot remember who played the parts, except that R. L. W. Moss was the Flag Lieutenant.

A Rear-Admiral, Angus Nicholl CB, CBE, DSO became Defence Correspondent of the BBC External Services Defence in the 1950s. It is surprising the work has been overlooked by the BBC. In the days of *Let's Face the Music*, produced by Walter Todds, a short interlude with Joyce Grenfell (Admiral ?) Bernard Levin and Richard Baker would have been fun.

Born in 1896 Angus Nicholl joined the Navy as a Special Entry Cadet from Brighton College in 1914. His DSO and CBE stemmed from being in command of the cruiser *Penelope,* damaged and lying alongside in Malta in 1942. Attacked by wave after wave of German bombers the crew managed to make their ship sufficiently seaworthy to slip away unseen at night. The epic story of how Angus Nicholl maintained morale was told in a book called *The Pepperpot.*

On our last Sunday in *Vidette* Commander Henry McCall, a bag of golf clubs substituted for the dog whip, took Robinson, Baker and me in his car to Gleneagles. The weather was perfect, blue sky and an autumn sun. A quick sandwich lunch enabled two rounds to be played, Peter Baker and I losing both to Henry McCall and Charles Robinson. The next day Moss and I bade our farewells. We had enjoyed destroyers, the weather being

JUST A HOGG'S LIFE

kind when we were at sea and I had played more Rugby football than in any previous three months. At one moment a terrible smell had pervaded our shared single cabin. From my humble berth under the bunk I asked Moss if he had been sea-sick. He replied in a firm negative waving a playful toe in my face. That was the smell – toe rot!

Nine years later, on May 10 1940 at Imjuiden in Holland, I found myself alone in the identical cabin below the bridge of the destroyer *Whitshed*. The smell this time was burnt cordite. I was in charge of a demolition party taken from Dover in the *Whitshed* to destroy harbour installations before the German invaders marched in. Bombed by waves of enemy aircraft, one near miss ignited a cordite case, which went up in a sheet of flame under X gun where I was standing. My face and hands were badly burnt and I was blinded temporarily. The full story forms part of my last chapter and of Sam Lombard Hobson's *A Sailor's War**. Lieutenant Colin Madden, subsequently Rear Admiral CB, CBE, DSC** who took my place, recorded on tape for the Imperial War Museum how the harbour was blocked and how the Dutch royal family and the demolishers escaped.

In 1931 *Rodney* brought us back to Plymouth on Friday 20th November. Bearing in mind that 38 per cent for Gunnery, I did not relish my report reaching Commander G.C. Cooke, the new Commander who had relieved Schwerdt.

The following Saturday, after a week of deammunitioning, our group was staggered at breakfast to learn that we were appointed from *Rodney* to the old battle-cruiser *Repulse*, a Chatham ship that being too large to berth there, swung round a buoy in the Medway tideway off Sheerness throughout the leave period. It seemed a dismal, retrograde step until a midshipman called Williams, who had just left *Repulse*, told us what a splendid ship she was and that we were very lucky. A trip to Dartmouth, where the Gunroom lost 6 – 3 to the College, a pub crawl and a Guest night, with Sing-Song in the Wardroom, ended our two year stay. On December 1 the Officer of the Watch was highly entertained by a meleé of midshipmen shouldering their trunks over the gangway. Not a very dignified departure, but we revealed our power of command by keeping the Cornish Riviera waiting two minutes!

*Orbus Publishing 1983.

CHAPTER 9

Bold Gendarmes in Barbados

Baker, Hogg, Moss, Robinson and Scott duly joined *Repulse* at Sheerness on the last evening of 1931. Willie Knox, having spent the winter having a cartilage removed from his knee, followed by sick leave, had missed his destroyer training and was now about to do it. In his place another member of our Greynvile term, Donald McBarnet appeared from somewhere to join the bridge players.

Cadet Langton, youngest officer in the ship, duly struck the ship's bell sixteen times at midnight, eight for the old and eight for the new being the custom.

Originally the great Lord Fisher intended battle-cruisers to be fast, lightly armoured 'Scouts' able to knock out cruisers that protected battleships. But after Jutland where three of Beatty's battle-cruisers, *Indefatigable*, *Queen Mary* and *Invincible*, blew up when plunging shells penetrated their armour, new ones were to be as big and powerful as battleships but with greater speed. Completed in 1916, *Repulse* and *Renown* had been built on the Clyde by John Brown and Fairfield respectively. Statistics: Displacement 32,000 tons. Overall length 794 feet. Beam 102 feet. Draught 32 feet. Armament: Six 15 inch guns in three turrets, A, B and Y. Four 4 inch guns Anti-Aircraft. Four 3-pounders. Five Machine guns. Speed: 33 knots using 1400 tons of oil fuel a day at this speed; 180 tons at economical 13 knots. Cost of Building £2,627,401. Complement 1250

Hood, 42,000 tons and 860 feet long also built by John Brown and launched on 22 August 1918 was Britain's largest warship. For various reasons not made public, the magazines of the two after 15 inch turrets and of the 5.5 inch secondary armament were above their own shell rooms. Forward the original design had been changed, but not aft, an omission that led to Hood's destruction and the death of her 1400 officers and men in her twenty-second year.

Her first Captain was Wilfred Tomkinson, who took the £6,025,000 ship round to Rosyth dockyard and by 15 May 1920 she was ready for service. With Rear-Admiral Sir Roger Keyes flying his flag (as A.C.Q.Admiral Commanding Q for Battle-cruisers), the first commission went well, Sir Roger and Tomkinson having already worked together in the Zeebrugge raid of 1918.

JUST A HOGG'S LIFE

The second commission, with Rear-Admiral Sir Walter Cowan, who had already been involved with three mutinies and Captain Geoffrey Mackworth, an unpopular, ill-tempered martinet, was unhappy.

Our 1931 trip to the West Indies was not the first time *Hood* and *Repulse* had sailed together. Leaving Britain on 28 November 1923 on what the sailors called the Matelots' World Booze, escorted by six D class cruisers, this Special Service Squadron returned ten months later, *Hood* having steamed 38,153 miles and received 752,049 visitors (1,936,717 all ships). South Africa, Ceylon, Malaya, Singapore, five Australian ports, Auckland, Honolulu, San Francisco, Vancouver, Panama Canal, Halifax, Quebec and Newfoundland summarises this voyage. The strain of combining duties on board with continuous social events ashore over so long a period can be imagined. Admiral Sir Frederick Field and his Flag Captain John *ImThurn* fortunately stood it well.

On 5 January 1932 *Repulse* left Sheerness for a rendez-vous with Hood off the Isle of Wight, but next morning with a south westerly in the Channel having already reached gale force, Home Fleet exercises were cancelled. *Hood* and *Repulse* were ordered to proceed to Fayal, capital of Horta, the main island of the Azores. For us this was to be the first stop to Port of Spain, then on to Grenada, St. Vincent and Barbados.

For the first four days the gale blew non-stop. In the Gunroom of *Repulse*, only about six feet above the water line, life was most unpleasant. The scuttles had to be kept closed in practically any sea. Even so water found its way into the Gunroom and the after cabin flats. The shipwrights were busy all day stopping up the holes; my journal remarks that for the sake of the inmates no attempt should ever be made to make *Repulse* gas tight. Normal instruction was quite impossible, in water six inches deep we paddled around and played Bridge in sea boots.

Speed down the Channel was reduced to six knots but the worst of the storm came on Sunday, when about 0400 a huge wave struck one of the cutters rigged as sea boats. The slings carried away, the bow crashed into the sea, and for a moment the boat poised vertically before dropping to a watery grave.

The chest flats and cabin flats became a nocturnal battlefield. Chests overturned, No.1 suits floated about, Sunday divisions and Church were postponed until the Dog watches when the worst was over. We arrived at Horta about 1800 two days late to find the cruiser squadron, *Dorsetshire*, *Norfolk*, *York* and *Exeter* already there, accompanied by the Auxiliary Fleet oiler, *Appleleaf*.

The next day in sunshine while we oiled, the inhabitants, mainly of Portuguese origin, pleased to see six warships of their oldest ally, circled round us in their motorboats. For our part we looked south east across the ten mile channel to the larger island of Pico, named after its 7600 foot peak conspicuous for miles around.

The group we casually call the Azores actually extends over 400 miles. San Miguel, main island of the eastern group, is 780 nautical miles from Lisbon and 2,300 miles from New York. Fayal, Pico, San Jorge, Terceira and Graciosa form the western group. But the famous 'Flores in the Azores where Sir Richard Grenville lay' is as much as 140 miles West North West of Horta.

Another five days largely of throw off practice shoots between *Hood* and *Repulse*, with a Dog watch Deck hockey knock-out for any team – officers or men – that cared to enter, brought us to Dress of the Day, Officers 8B Men No.5. For the former this still meant long white trousers and a white tunic buttoned up to the neck. Real tropical dress – shorts and shirt – may have been permissible East of Suez but not in the Mediterranean, nor on short spring visits to the West Indies.

Four more days largely occupied painting ship, brought *Repulse* to Port of Spain where we anchored five miles off the town's landing place, which meant forty minutes for me when running the launch. Unlike last year the bay was no longer a sea of jellyfish and two unlighted buoys had been removed.

The Captain Edward Cochrane, son of an admiral, was an H.M.S.*Britannia* entry now aged fifty, who specialised in Gunnery and had already commanded the light cruiser *Cairo* on the East Indies station. Retired as a Rear-Admiral in 1933, he was at sea again in the 1939-45 war as a Convoy Commodore. He and his wife Mary (née George) had a daughter and a son, who was killed in the Tunisian campaign. He died aged ninety one on 27 January 1972.

The Commander, Anthony Morse, eleven years younger than his Captain, was just a Lieutenant when war had broken out in 1914. Mentioned twice in Despatches and with a DSO in the Dardanelles campaign, his promotion to Commander came in 1927 and to Captain in 1934, soon after *Repulse* had paid off for a long refit.

The 1939-45 war brought him a CB, CBE and finally KBE. Praised by ABC (Cunningham) he was the Naval officer in charge during the 1941 evacuation of Crete. Sharing a headquarters in a cave with the New Zealand General Freyburg, they got 6000 troops back to Alexandria without loss among Admiral King's rescuing ships on May 29/30, the last night of the evacuation. He lost a son too, in the Battle of the River Plate in 1939.

This pleasant easy going combination made *Repulse* a happy ship. At sea the Captain, whose last appointment had been Director of Training and Staff Duties at the Admiralty, invented imaginary situations that could arise in war time or that might lead to war, for his officers to appreciate, forming syndicates on Staff College lines to study and decide the best courses of action. Knowing that *Repulse* would pay off for a long refit at the end of this cruise did of course make for a relaxed atmosphere.

Anthony Morse, always calm, cool and collected, liked young people and got the best from them. Sitting one day in the Wardroom in weather too rough to do much else, he taught me a simple game with fifteen matches. Arrange them into three piles of seven, five and three. Moving alternately as in chess, the object is to leave your opponent to take the last match. In any move, you can take, one, two or more matches – even the lot – *but only from one pile*. Anthony Morse always won. So can you! But serious study is recommended before taking on your children or grandchildren.

Next in seniority and therefore First Lieutenant was the Torpedo Officer, John Ouvry. A quiet man but perfectly good at his job he was passed over for promotion and remained a Lieutenant-Commander. When war broke out in 1939 he was working in the Mining Department of HMS *Vernon* giving special attention to magnetic mines. Thus as already related, he rendered safe the first German magnetic ground mine winning a DSO, with another for his colleague Roger Lewis.

John enjoyed nothing more than a childrens' party and thanks to him there were few better childrens' parties, with all sorts of gadgetry, than the one given by HMS *Vernon* each year.

The Gunnery Officer D. M. ("Bunny") Lees did have a face rather like a rabbit, a fierce rabbit at times as I was to discover in 1943 when he became my Commanding Officer as Captain of the cruiser *Black Prince*.

The next Lieutenant Commander was Casper S. B. Swinley, our Snotties' Nurse. This job was usually given to a Lieutenant and certainly would not help his promotion much. Exploiting his real talent to the full, he and a tall Lieutenant R.N.V.R. named Sanders, who had come for the cruise, devised a musical comedy called *A Sail for a Sale* for the entertainment of West Indians such as cared to attend. After rehearsals on board and a final one in the Port of Spain's Empire Theatre, the Trinidad performance at 8.30 p.m on Thursday 28 January went well.

Swinley, besides being General Manager, played the leading part of the Rt. Hon. Sir Bullyon Blunt KCB, MP on board the s.s. *Repulse* in 1952. Supported by a real mixture of officers, sailors and stokers all from the ship, the only female part was Marion, Blunt's daughter played by Mr. C. T. Gaughran, a muscular Warrant Engineer. Bullyon Blunt was a sort of *Pinafore* Sir Joseph Porter; the show's music however came from *The White Horse Inn,* then in full spate at London's Coliseum.

But the sensation of the show was a number called Operatic Motoring in which a car – an Austin 7 – made its first on-stage appearance in the West Indies. Anthony Morse, invited me to be his partner in a duet. As garage proprietor and mechanic, we sang topical verses to the tune of Offenbach's bold Gendarmes, running 'em in right, left and centre. What the verses were or why we were received in Barbados like Callas at Covent Garden, I cannot remember. But this is not surprising when one thinks of all those rum cocktails.

HMS Repulse. Operatic motoring in Barbados. R.L.W. Moss the owner, E.T. Larken at the wheel, singing mechanics J.A.V. Morse and (r) A.S. Hogg.

On Saturday 23 January the cruiser *York*, sister ship to the *Exeter*, was placed in quarantine after reporting a case of spotted fever (inflammation of the cover of the brain). By Wednesday 27th a plane had brought a serum from Porto Rico and *York* sailed for home at maximum speed. To no avail the victim, Stoker Halligan, died on Saturday 30th.

A greater tragedy on Wednesday 27 was the loss of the submarine M2 off Portland with all hands. At least ten British submarines had been lost since the war ended.

Running the launch every other day and rehearsing new ideas for the theatricals did not leave much time for shore leave. But on the last day in our ten at Port of Spain, three of us went bathing at Macquerite Bay up the coast with a Mrs. Knaggs and her two daughters, staying for supper and singing plantation songs round the piano afterwards. As yet few people in Trinidad had radio sets and many of the English speaking women played the piano. Quite a crowd bade goodbye to the last boat at midnight singing "For they are jolly good fellows" to which we responded with "Goodnight sweetheart" hit tune of the moment.

Grenada, southernmost of the Windward Islands, lies only 85 miles from Trinidad and 140 from Barbados. 21 miles long and 12 wide, it is said to be the prettiest of this group. Mount Catherine, 2750 feet, is the highest point and in the centre, 1750 feet above sea level, lies the Grand Etang, a lake of thirteen acres. Two of us tried to go there but a twenty five shilling taxi fare was not for five shilling a day midshipmen so we went up St. George's hill to find a magnificent view of the Carenage, the town and ships out at sea. Higher up the old fort, guarding the entrance to the Carenage, had become Police head-quarters.

The Governor of the Windwards had his residence at Georgetown, the capital, with a population of 5000 out of 70,000 in the whole island. Grenada seemed happy, with some education and exports of cocoa, nutmegs and cotton.

Columbus discovered Grenada in 1498. The French, with the native Caribs, occupied it until, captured by the British in 1762, it remained British by treaty in 1783. Of course there had been the Battle of Grenada in 1779, but we do not read much about it because Admiral the Hon. John Byron known as "Foul- weather Jack", was outnumbered by D'Estaing's twenty one ships and failed to dislodge the French from the island.

Slavery ended in 1837. Since 1974 Grenada has been an Associated State with the Queen its Head, a Governor-General and a bicameral Parliament. On March 13 1979 this was overthrown and replaced by a People's Revolutionary Government. Disagreements within it led to violence and the death of its leader, Maurice Bishop. Smelling a red rat, the Americans intervened with further force. Since 1984 elections have taken place, and with democracy restored the Americans withdrew.

Fourteen people were convicted of being involved in the murder of the Prime Minister on evidence that a British attorney- general condemned as an appalling miscarriage of justice. All were sentenced to death including Bernard Coard, a former Prime Minister, and his wife Phyllis. This act of barbarism was committed to life imprisonment at the last moment on 15 August 1991. An unnecessary demonstration that capital punishment upholds capitalism has thus been avoided, but the whole case should be re-opened.

After five days at Grenada we spent another five at Kingstown, St. Vincent joined by the *Hood* which allowed A.C.Q. Vice-Admiral Tomkinson to inspect the ship's company of *Repulse* and the two ships to compete at General Drill and boat sailing. The *Hood* was never a satisfactory ship; her bows plunged under water in heavy seas, and her quarterdeck during the recent gale had been continuously underwater. Even my journal describes the Gunroom as hot and unpleasant with daylight entering through one miserable skylight. Paying them a social call, our *Repulse* party thought being offered only one beer in half an hour was by far the worst feature of all.

On Friday 12 February, after a poor 15 inch full calibre throw off shoot of three rounds per gun at *Hood*, *Repulse* moored (two anchors) in Carlisle Bay, the one good anchorage of Barbados. Known as 'Little England' Barbados has never flown any flag but the British. Only the size of the Isle of Wight and as pro- British, it is said that in 1914 with war probable, the British Prime Minister received a cable, "Go ahead Britain, Barbados is behind you".

From Mount Hillaby (1,100 feet) in the middle, the land on all sides falls gently to the sea and all the lovely white sand beaches. The first settlers were Royalists escaping from the Civil War; with sugar plantations introduced soon afterwards the Barbados population had grown to 170,000 by 1932, which meant over a thousand people to the square mile with one white to about nine blacks. Having had enough of tropical scenery, the view from our anchorage, reminiscent of the Sussex coast from the Channel, was as refreshing – but happily less intoxicating – as the island's rum and fresh lime drinks.

Walter Scott, our senior midshipman – apt to be referred to as Mr. Bloody Bloody but not on this occasion – invited me to spend 48 hours staying at Enmore, the home of his cousins Mr. and Mrs. Austin, a family prominent among MCC, I Zingari and Free Forester cricketers. George Hurry, a lively Lieutenant in *Repulse* and a number of officers from the cruiser *Dorsetshire* also with us, arrived for dinner before we moved on to a dance at the Yacht Club to meet the élite. Ending at 0215 this was followed by a large bacon and egg party in the kitchen at Enmore, the cooks being Anthony Morse, Lieutenant Taylor,K. Hurry, and E. T. Larken augmented by L. A. K. Boswell, Gunnery Officer of the *Dorsetshire*, who was to settle into Funtington House, Chichester in 1950, as a Captain RN turned fruit farmer. Inevitably the party burst into song before it broke up about 0330.

> *The first thing I saw on waking this morning was a large green lizard hopping about the bedside table. It made me scratch my head a bit until I saw it was a real one.*

This is the entry in my journal for the morning after. The object of the journal being to train 'the young gentlemen' in a) the power of observation and b) the power of expression, it does at least deserve a mark for observation in difficult circumstances. The day's social engagement was a tennis party at Ilaro, the palatial Italianate home of Lady Gilbert Carter, widow of a former Barbados Governor. A bad tennis player, I found myself on what appeared to be 'the centre court' under close lorgnette scrutiny by Lady C, with a pretty partner who looked as if centre courts were just her line. To my consternation, she explained she had just arrived in a cruise liner and, recovering from flu, was not really fit. That indeed was an understatement; hardly scoring a point I was glad to retreat into the palatial swimming bath.

Mr Austin showed us round his sugar factories; his daughter Cloe paddled us about in her canoe. *Repulse* gave a thé dansant, after which the Austins took a large party of officers in five cars on a bathing picnic. Returning on board at 0130 was an early night in Barbados. Next *Repulse* opened for visitors and half the island tried to board my launch.

A Sail for a Sale played to a full house but we gendarmes, surprised by the ovation, had no encore ready other than a repetition of our last verse. After the show the hospitable Lady Carter laid on bacon and eggs, champagne and beer at 'Ilaro' for the cast, the party lasting till 2am.

For childrens' parties capital ships are ideal. In *Repulse* hooked to the purchase of the main derrick a large wooden box holding half a dozen children at a time hoisted them up and swung them around. A chair running down on a taut wire from the Flag deck to the Boat deck was popular. From the Captain's deck down to the Quarterdeck, there was a wooden slide. No casualties; only three were tea sick; not bad really in a party lasting from 4pm to 6.30.

Our visit wound up the same evening with the second performance of *A Sail for a Sale*. This time the gendarmes, after local research, had a good supply of topical verses, which greatly amused the natives. After the finale bunches of flowers and other souvenirs were lavished upon us and once more it was 2 a.m. before the party ended at the Aquatic Club.

After almost a fortnight *Hood* and the cruisers reappeared off the island as if to drag us reluctantly away. The British West Indies was then a depressed area, the 1931 and 1932 squadrons being sent to raise the islanders' morale. Hopefully we succeeded; indubitably their hospitality and kindness, outstanding in Barbados, did us a power of good. Rum cocktails and Planter's Punch played their part. My journal refers to these refreshments as 'long cooling drinks'; the truth - 'Returned on board sloshed after a session at the Aquatic Club' though showing commendable power of expression was best not recorded by those under twenty who, on board, were not even permitted to drink spirits.

This rum that combined so well with ice and the juice of fresh limes was white rum, odourless and colourless unlike the dark, heavy-bodied rum then being issued daily to the men of the Royal Navy, but not to the officers. We were only entitled to a free tot on the order 'Splice the Main Brace', a dangerous task in sailing ships, given on Royal occasions or after great victories. Diluted with water in 1740, halved in 1824 and reduced to 2½oz (1/8 pint) in 1850, the ration was finally replaced by cans of beer for the men and commercial spirits for Chief and Petty officers on 1 August 1970.

On passage once more to Fayal, we successfully towed *Hood* for two hours at a speed of 8 knots using revolutions for 12. To begin, *Hood* lowered a cutter to secure a grass line to a buoy *Repulse* had paid out astern, a somewhat leisurely proceeding compared to firing a Schermuly rocket, which had string on the end, from one cable deck to the other. But then, in those days, nobody envisaged a capital ship being disabled by aircraft with torpedoes and bombs, least of all the Gunnery specialists who predominated. However, replacing gear without accident we were at least one up on *Nelson* and Rodney.

After two years at sea my first journal was full and I have had to begin a second. At Fayal the weather forced all ships to hoist their boats while only my launch continued to distribute mail and correspondence to them. Steering devious courses because it was unsafe to get broadside on, I suppose there must have been something on which to hold on, standing in the stern the tiller between my legs. Without the fresh air I should have been sea-sick like my poor stoker, sitting by my feet at the engine. *Repulse* received a pat-on-the-back signal from A.C.Q. for our endeavours.

Ashore in Horta next day I remember buying a bottle of Pico red wine. On its own it was quite repulsive and sampled with hot ship's cocoa in the middle watch showed no improvement.

With the ship due to pay off and refit in June, the Wardroom dined the Gunroom, Caspar Swinley making one of his celebrated funny speeches in which there was not one word of sense. Occupied on this cruise wholly with Entertainment, we never discovered what his ship's duties really were; any absence from about Thursday to Tuesday however became known as a Swinley week-end.

Leaving Fayal on March 8 we carried out a full power trial from 1700 to 1900 with an average speed of 28.6 knots. In the Gunroom and Chest Flats the vibration and noise were so frightful that I spent the time on deck. On the port side a small piece of the bilge was torn away; when the weather worsened next day the hole grew larger and we reduced to 8 knots, taking no further part in the Red v Blue war that was going on. After inspection by divers at Plymouth we continued to Sheerness.

Toasts have long been part of the naval tradition; in *Nelson*'s time there was one for every day of the week when at sea. *Monday*, Our ships. *Tuesday* Our men. *Wednesday.* Ourselves. *Thursday.* A bloody war. *Friday.* A willing foe and sea-room. *Saturday.* Sweethearts and wives. *Sunday.* Absent friends.

The first four had long fallen into abeyance. Absent friends ceased because on Sunday, a running supper, probably followed by a film, became usual. As a child at home for Sunday lunch after Matins, my parents always drank to 'Absent friends' with dessert, after passing the port.

Dining at sea on suitable Saturdays however, the youngest officer present was expected to reply to 'Sweethearts and wives – may they never meet!". So let it be recorded that in the Gunroom of HMS *Repulse* on Saturday March 12 1932, Cadet L. E. D. Walthall made an excellent and amusing speech. Specialising as a Fleet Air Arm pilot he survives on his farm near Cirencester as Captain Walthall CBE., DSC., retd.

There must have been other such Saturday nights at sea during my time as Sub-Lieutenant in *Royal Sovereign* but the one I remember was in the carrier *Glorious* in 1937 by the Marquess of Milford Haven, an eighteen year old midshipman quoting 'There's a divinity that shapes our ends, Rough-hew them how we will', in relation to some of his mess mates' erotic activities in the nocturnal haunts of Valletta.

Back at Sheerness in time for a Swinley weekend, young Trelawney, who had been a first rate pianist in our show, went with me to Norway House in Trafalgar Square to dine with Lieutenant Sanders RNVR at his club on the top floor. The other guests were Commander Morse, Surgeon Commander Tozer, and Lieutenant Larken. We went on to an RNVR musical in HMS *President*, headquarters of the London Division, moored on the Thames embankment then as now.

Home at Epsom for the weekend, my father had good seats for Twickenham (easy to get in those days) where England beat Scotland in an exciting match. A whole month's leave from March 22 to April 21 followed.

Wedded to the Service was the expression used to describe the keen naval officer. Reading my journal throughout the summer of 1932 we appear to have been completely wedded to golf. The first weekend back in *Repulse*, given a lift each day by Moss, four of us played forty holes at Belmont, near Faversham on Saturday, while 93,000 people watched Newcastle beat Arsenal at Wembley in the Cup-Tie final. Dropped there again on Sunday, after Matins on board, it was fifty two holes.

Arriving at Portsmouth in *Repulse* on 27 April in time to watch the Home Fleet sailing yet again for Invergordon, our quartet Baker, Knox, Robinson, Hogg bought a communal 1926 Morris Cowley for £15, its main purpose being to convey us to golf courses, primarily Hayling Island.

Given weekend leave we headed for my home at Epsom, where Robinson took a train to London while Baker and the car went on to Cobham, Kent, his family home and links. On Sunday night we met at Epsom for the return to Portsmouth.

To play at Hayling, leaving the car at the end of the Eastern Esplanade, one crossed the Langstone Channel in the motorboat ferry to begin at the 14th hole. Clubs then were very kind to service people offering them temporary membership at a reduced rate. We were fortunate to know Engineer Commander "Jock" MacKenzie, a distinguished Hayling member with a low handicap. A former Scottish Rugby International he had coached us at Dartmouth and was next appointed to the Royal Yacht *Victoria and Albert*. The yacht rarely put to sea; just by chance of course, cricketers and footballers likely to be needed by the Navy at Lords or Twickenham found themselves appointed for a spell in the *V and A*.

How nice and simple golf was in those days! Just a bag over the shoulder holding a driver, a brassie, a mid-iron, a mashie, a niblick and a putter. No lefthand glove, no spiked shoes, just a jacket or a pullover; and a cap to raise to the quarterdeck on return. A single or a foursome took under two hours; tea or a pint of shandy and we were off again.

With neither time nor money for lessons, one improved slowly just by playing. By 1934 I had a handicap of 16 with a consistency that won me a 36 hole trophy at Tyrrells Wood. Our best player in the Gunroom was F. P. Baker, already in single figures. On June 2 the entire Gunroom of *Repulse* was to move to *Renown*, due to recommission on June 9 after her refit. Meanwhile our group of Midshipmen was lent to HMS *St. Vincent*, the boys' training establishment across the harbour at Gosport, while *Repulse* sent working parties daily to clean up *Renown*.

CAPTAIN CASPER SWINLEY

Captain Casper Swinley, DSO, DSC, who died on September 3 at the age of 84, had a distinguished naval career embracing both world wars, and was Chief of Naval Information, Admiralty from 1947 to 1948.

Casper Siles Balfour Swinley was born on October 28, 1898 and educated at Epsom College from where he joined the Royal Navy with a special entry cadetship in 1916 in time to serve in the First World War as a midshipman and sublieutenant in HMS New Zealand. In the aftermath of the war he was in HMS Ceres when the ship stood by at the evacuation of White forces from Odessa during the Russian civil war.

After a short course at Queen's College, Cambridge and a period as Private Secretary to Sir Charles O'Brien, Governor of Barbados, in 1921-22 he found himself involved in another evacuation, that of Smyrna in the Greco-Turkish war. In this he was serving in HMS Curaçoa.

Between the wars his appointments took him to the West Indies and the Africa Station and he commanded HMS Express during the Abyssinian crisis.

Among his wartime duties was the conveying of King George VI and Winston Churchill to France in the "Phoney War" period and he joined the French destroyer Brestois for liaison duties during the evacuation of Namsos in the Norwegian campaign of 1940. In 1940 he also commanded the demolition party at Calais, sent ashore to deprive the Germans of use of the harbour facilities there, after the embarkation of the remnants of the British Expeditionary Force. He was awarded his DSC in 1940 for his services in these operations.

Further wartime active service included command of HMS Isis in the North Sea and Mediterranean where he was awarded his DSO in the Crete operations. From 1943 to 1945 he was Director of Service Conditions, Admiralty.

Postwar appointments included those of Chief of Naval Information, 1947-48 and Captain-in-Charge, Captain Superintendent and King's Harbourmaster, Portland, 1949-51, in which year he was also ADC to the King.

After his retirement he was Commodore and Chief of Staff, Royal Pakistan Navy 1953-54 and Senior Whale Fishery Inspector, South Georgia 1959-60.

He married, in 1928, Sylvia Jocosa, a daughter of Canon W. H. Carnegie. They had two sons and two daughters.

I do not remember ever meeting Caspar Swinley again but reading The Times *on September 8 1983 it was pleasing to read this obituary, which reveals why we were feted at Barbados.*

CHAPTER 10

Battle Wagon with a Squash Court

On a glorious Wednesday, the First of June, Gunroom officers left *Repulse* marching a short distance across Portsmouth Dockyard to join *Renown*, her sister ship. On the quarterdeck we met our new Captain, T. F. P. Calvert DSO, the Commander, Daniel de Pass, Lieutenant George C. Colville, our 'Snotties Nurse' and G. C. M. Falla, the Sub-Lieutenant, a *Rodney* term cadet two years above us at Dartmouth, where we had admired his boxing, cricket and Rugby football. Attached to the Foc'sle division, I also met Lieutenant-Commander R. M. Spencer, who belonged to that lucky age group, sent at Admiralty expense in 1919 to complete their education at Cambridge.

An urgent request found me keeping wicket by early afternoon on the United Services ground near the Guildhall in a match v Gosport R.A.F. Both sides however adjourned to listen to the Derby on the club house radio. To wide astonishment the winner was *April the Fifth*, an outsider owned by actor/manager Tom Walls, who lived at Ewell a mile from my home, the horse being trained in an Epsom stable. Tom Walls, Ralph Lynn and Yvonne Arnaud were the principals in a whole series of Ben Travers Aldwych farces.

Friday June 3 was George V's sixty seventh birthday, so for us that meant week-end leave. On June 9 *Renown* recommissioned with her new ship's company, suitably greeted by Captain Calvert with a short speech. Then after exercising Fire and Collision stations, night leave was given. Ammunitioning took three days, followed by trials in the Channel, engine trouble leaving the great ship stationary for some hours.

Portland has always been a harbour where newly commissioned ships work up to maximum efficiency. While Holmes and Sutcliffe were making 555 runs, a new record for a first wicket partnership, we fired our guns and torpedoes, recovering the latter with difficulty when they nose-dived into the mud. Painting ship came last in sunny weather so that by 6 July looking very smart we proudly took station astern of *Hood* before the Home Fleet anchored in Weymouth Bay.

During *Renown*'s work-up our group of senior midshipmen had been sent for two days with the Mine Sweeping Flotilla composed of five *Forres* class sloops. There were only two ways of sweeping moored mines, the 'A' sweep and the Oropesa. In the former the ships formed line abreast, towing the sweep wires after each had passed the end of its sweep wire to be secured to the next in line, i.e. A to B, B to C etc.

Greatly superior, a Double Orepesa enabled each ship to sweep effectively by itself in similar fashion to a paravane. A multi plane kite-otter took the outer end of the sweep wide out on the quarter of the minesweeper, and a float with flag secured to the kite-otter showed where it was for station keeping purposes. 300 fathoms of sweep wire were usually veered using a depressor, similar to the kite-otter secured to it, to determine the depth of the sweep.

At Weymouth on Monday 11 July 1932 the Royal Yacht Victoria and Albert anchored ahead of *Hood* and between *Nelson* and *Warspite* at 1730 after approaching between the lines of ships' companies manning ship at the guard rails to give three cheers for Their Majesties. The *V & A* wearing the Admiralty flag at the fore, the Royal Standard at the main and the Union Flag (Admiral of the Fleet) at the mizzen made an impressive scene.

Quite a week too for VIPs! The Commander-in-Chief, Sir John Kelly himself, had paid *Renown* a call the previous day, recognising a staggering number of former shipmates as he inspected Divisions. One of five midshipmen invited to lunch by Captain Calvert, I felt a bit of a VIP myself.

About 1830 on Tuesday 12th the Prince of Wales and Prince George, his youngest brother, came on board *Renown*. They stayed for forty minutes possibly to see if the squash racquets court was still there! It was, and in use. The Prince of Wales had sailed in *Renown* on his Canadian and USA tour from August 1919 to December 1919. Off again in March 1920 to Australia, New Zealand and the West Indies, via the Panama Canal, a second tour took seven months. Fitted into a corner of the boat deck for Royal use at sea, nobody ordered the Court to be removed and a unique asset it remained.

On Thursday 14th led by the *V&A*, the Fleet put to sea in ideal weather. Submarines in line ahead dived and surfaced. The 2nd Destroyer flotilla attacked the heavy ships with torpedoes scoring two hits. Promptly at 1115 *Warspite*, *Nelson* and *Rodney*, with the first named controlling, opened fire at a Battle Practice target 18,000 yards (nine nautical miles) away, straddling with the third salvo and wrecking the target thereafter. The cruisers carried out a High Angle shoot at a drogue towed by aircraft from *Courageous*.

BATTLE WAGON WITH A SQUASH COURT

HMS Renown c.1933.   National Maritime Museum, Greenwich

Gunroom Deck Hockey at sea c1930. Foreground left, Hogg, Woods (in striped shirt); Foreground right: Ryan (who was lost in submarine Thetis, May 1939).

Usually on these occasions there are delays; a fault in a turret, trouble with the tow, line of fire not clear are examples. This time every item in the display was carried out successfully at precisely the scheduled time. It was most impressive; the Royal Yacht flying the signal *Splice the Main Brace* for the first time since the Armistice in 1918 as she steamed once again between the lines amid cheers from a Home Fleet taking pride in itself once more. During the four day visit, the King had been pulled over to *Nelson* in his state cutter and spent half a day in *Courageous* with the two Princes. The Prince of Wales flying in one of the planes transmitted a message from the King to the Fleet. The King also managed to inspect a representative body of men from battle-cruisers, cruisers and destroyers assembled on *Hood's* upper deck for the purpose. A sailing regatta was held on Monday 12th, a model of Nelson's *Victory* also sailing to advertise the forthcoming *Navy Week*.

Hood and *Renown* next paid a four day visit to Sandown Bay where ACQ, still Vice-Admiral Tomkinson CB, MVO, carried out his last inspection before being relieved in August. This he had learnt by chance on the radio on the way to the West Indies. At Fayal, though promoted Vice-Admiral, a censorious letter from Their Lordships blamed him for indecisive action to prevent the Invergordon mutiny. This 'passing the buck' after the First Sea Lord had congratulated him verbally, I find despicable. While it was best to make a clean slate by relieving senior officers closely involved, it was Their Lordships who should have resigned in protest to the pay cuts. Not one of them did. A feature of these inspections required one or two men in each division to lay out their kits. The Flag Lieutenant, given the list, picked the names at random. I remember one who picked the worst with uncanny accuracy. After that inspection I asked him how he did it. "Very simple", he replied, "I just choose the Irish names".

Admiral Tomkinson's last inspection lasted two days starting with Divisions in Sunday best. Mess decks and Storerooms followed, all looking spick and span. The second day began at 0900 with Action Stations, the Admiral and his staff visiting many quarters imposing numerous breakdowns. Finally there was General Drill with all boats pulling round the *Hood* as orders were given in rapid succession to "Rig hand capstan" "Work the starboard cable by hand", "Fire a gun", "Out Fire Engine" and "Land Royal Marine emergency platoon".

Completing these by 1300, Tomkinson congratulated the ship's company in a farewell speech. In spite of his misfortunes he served as C-in-C Bristol Channel during the war and lived to be ninety three,

The *Times* obituary receiving many letters defending his conduct at Invergordon.

Securing once again on 21 July to our Sheerness buoy, the leave period began on Friday 26th and ended on Thursday August 25th each Watch having a fortnight. With our seamanship exam due in November Baker, Knox, McBarnet and I were given the job of keeping Officer of the Watch throughout the second leave period. Apart from a weekend when the ship was open to the public, with a thousand visitors mainly from Southend taking advantage of it, things were quiet. One afternoon I took a train to Canterbury to visit my godfather Hewlett Johnson, who had been moved from Manchester as Dean soon after his wife, Mary, had died tragically of cancer in 1931. He was just back from a long visit to China investigating famine relief after the terrible floods of 1931. I explored the Cathedral noting the tomb of the Black Prince unaware that a cruiser so named would take me from Murmansk to Melbourne one day. I also saw the Deanery tucked away behind the Cathedral with its fine garden and portraits of former Deans along its walls.

For golf we went to Cobham, Peter Baker's home course to be joined and entertained by his father, a Gravesend Solicitor, who, for reasons of economy presumably, wore a safety pin in place of a tie pin. Gunroom golfers now included, G.H. Culme-Seymour, whose father, a retired Commander, lived in Edinburgh and took us to Rugby at Murrayfield. Charles Kennaway, was another, who had learnt to play well with his father on the Merrow (Guildford) course. His father was stone deaf from the war; Charles and his sister communicated with their hands. Perhaps I should also include John Willis, a Gunnery officer to be, who was going round the Weymouth Municipal Course in steady eights when he came to the sixth hole of 183 yards. Determined to reach the Green he drove with unerring aim, the ball passing between two men, who were still putting on it, into the hole. In those days such singular achievements were generously rewarded by makers of whisky, jerkins, razors and such like to whom one sent a properly signed card in the post.

Five of our colleagues in the Gunroom: Harrison, Bateman, Mountifield, Troughton and Sutton left to join the cruiser *Emerald* in the East Indies being replaced by five cadets from Dartmouth: Goodhart, Kirke, Stacey, Hobart, and Hankey, making a total strength in the mess of about twenty. The Autumn cruise began on 31 August with an immensely long voyage all of seven miles to Southend, where we were joined by *Hood*, both ships opening to visitors during a week's stay. The most important visitor however, who came on board *Renown* on Sunday 4 September was the new A.C.Q. Rear-Admiral Sir William James. Grandson of Sir John Millais, the painter, as a child he had been the model for 'Bubbles', a famous Pears' soap advertisement and 'Bubbles' James he became for life. A commander of the battleship *Benbow* at Jutland he had since been captain of battleships *Royal Sovereign* and *Royal Oak* after being head of the Staff College at Greenwich. Pleasant and able, he ended by being a full Admiral, Commander-in-Chief Portsmouth. Omitted from his *Who's Who* entry is '*Recreation.* Golf'; he was, I fancy, a member of the Royal and Ancient with a single figure handicap. The autumn cruise might have been planned for him. After a week at Whitby and ten days in mid- October at Invergordon, it had been 'Golf galore' from Rosyth by the time we returned to Home Ports, on 18 November.

The other outstanding personality in Hood was her newly joined Commander Rory O'Connor. He told the ship's company on joining that *Hood* would be the smartest ship in the world and win every possible award within a year. They laughed derisively but this is precisely what they did. He was worshipped by the men, of whom it was said that they'd paint the coal on the jetty white if he asked them.

His book *How to run a Big Ship on Ten Commandments* was read eagerly, particularly by the younger officers because he regarded midshipmen as responsible young people needing experience, declaring that a picket boat smashed, might one day mean a battleship saved. On the other hand in 1935 when Captain Pridham took over the *Hood*, he found surfaces had been painted over dirt and rust, storerooms neglected and discipline lax, for which he blamed O'Connor's policy. Rory O'Connor was lost as Captain of the cruiser *Neptune* when she was sunk by an Italian mine off Malta on 19 December 1941 with only one survivor.

In *Renown*, to us young officers, our Captain Thomas Frederick Parker Calvert, a big man with a monocle, seemed the epitome of an old eccentric sea dog. Son of a Southsea parson, rising fifty in 1932 he had gone to sea from Haileybury winning a DSO with a Mention in Despatches during the 1914-18 war. Evidently a forward-looking officer he had been in charge of the Air Section of the Naval Staff 1924-26, Captain of the cruiser Frobisher 1926-28 and Director of the Naval Staff College Greenwich 1930 to 32. As with Cunningham in *Rodney*, he had been given a capital ship to command for one year, post Captains far outnumbering the ships themselves. We on board of course, were not aware of his previous career.

During the refit *Renown*'s Compass Platform, formerly open to the elements, had been covered in with a flat roof of one inch armour-plating as a protection against low flying aircraft. This seemed to irritate Tom Calvert; he liked to see at night that the fore steaming light on the foremast above was burning. The plating prevented this; neither was it visible leaning out sideways and looking upwards.

So a hole about the width of a champagne cork was drilled in the armour-plating directly under the steaming light so that the Captain, cocking his monocled eye under it, could verify personally that all was well. This gave him much satisfaction; he turned to an RNR newcomer keeping watch for the first time saying, in his rather slow but deliberate way, "Officer of the Watch have you seen my hole?" Not knowing what to say, the OOW was astonished to see where it was and indeed its purpose.

His admonishment surprised one midshipman: "Speak up boy, speak up! Don't you realise that when you've been in the service thirty years like I have, you'll be a bit gun deaf: you foolish bugger!" And Midshipman Mountifield, who became a Gunnery specialist, recalls how Calvert pushed his head out from the Compass Platform to be sure he heard fully the sound of a 15 inch gun salvo about to be fired.

Then there was a sunset report we had to make when on watch at sea of items mostly kept in the ship's log on the Compass Platform, but almost long enough to include what the Chief Yeoman of Signals had for breakfast.

Guy Falla, the Sub-Lieutenant, put in charge of the ship's boxing team, covered himself with glory for the Navy against the Police in a London tournament. When in charge of *Renown*'s drifter, which made trips to and from the shore with libertymen or stores, his big hairy face coming in to berth on the port quarter would lean out of the wheelhouse window. Usually he gave no orders: the coxswain and the man in the bows with a heaving line knew precisely what to do.

But if, as often happened, the Captain and Commander were pacing the quarterdeck together, he would shout, "Haul away forrard" or something of the kind, loud and clear. One could almost see the Captain saying, "Very lucky with our Sub, Commander; good boxer, excellent power of command!".

Inspecting the Gunroom Wine Accounts one day the Captain sent for Falla. "What is this column Cocktails?" he asked, "The midshipmen are nearly all under twenty and they are not allowed spirits". "No sir of course not. These cocktails are very weak, sir; just a little sherry and fruit juices", said Falla. "But I have never heard of any cocktail that was not full of spirits Falla, have you ? I think there will have to be a separate column for this extraordinary beverage. You should clearly name it *Sherry Shakes*".

JUST A HOGG'S LIFE

The mess accounts unfortunately were not Falla's *forte*. After we left the *Renown* in December it was found that over £100 was owing to the messman. Falla was dismissed the Service SNLR. (Services No Longer Required). But *we* had to pay, about £10 each, much to the disgust of our parents.

A few years later he was found fighting in an All In Wrestling show in Plymouth. I last met him, shortly before the war.

"Doing well", he said, "They've made me the Treasurer!".

Whether he learnt to live within his means I do not know. But I often thought Guy was the sort of fellow, who would be the first to land on some Normandy beach. He probably was; the death of G. M. Falla, M.C. appeared in *The Times* some years after the war.

It was as well that after jollification in the West Indies we still had three months to prepare for the Seamanship exam for Lieutenant. As soon as *Renown* left Sheerness Daniel de Pass, the Commander set up a panel for a practice Oral thus:

Organisation: Commander D. de Pass
Rule of the Road and Rigging: Lieutenant Commander Wavish, the Navigator
Anchors and Cables: Lieutenant Commander Drage, First Lieutenant
Duties of Officer of the Watch: Lieutenant George Colville

The results were far from brilliant.

Ship contruction was a written paper, Instructor Lieutenant Porter doing his best to instruct us. Even the Fleet Constructor Officer himself honoured us with a talk. Make a drawing of your ship's Midship Section was almost certain to be a question. The details of decks and plating being so difficult to remember, it was customary for candidates to practise when seated on a lavatory seat after breakfast each morning making the drawings on service brown paper. Loud protests from the waiting queue outside however made serious concentration rather difficult.

In peacetime, naval life being primarily training for war, there was certainly a new spirit in the Home Fleet trying to make the job more interesting. Sailing from Whitby to Rosyth the Commander took over Captain, Colville became Cable Officer and we midshipmen manned the chains. These were two small projecting platforms on the upper deck from which soundings were taken with a lead and line. Heaving the 10/14lbs lead on the end of the 25 fathom line was quite an art; like bowling in cricket it could be done underarm or over the head. The fathoms were marked from 2 to 20 by strips of leather and different coloured pieces of bunting. Fathoms not marked were called deeps so that the leadsman

BATTLE WAGON WITH A SQUASH COURT

called out, loud enough to be heard on the Compass Platform above, "Deep 6" or "Deep 8", or "By the mark 5" or "By the mark 7".

Of course, usually on the deck above, there was a Kelvin Sounding Machine with a similar, 300 fathoms of fine wire on a drum, an automatic brake and a dial with a pointer. The apparatus needed its own boom with guys and a topping lift to carry the wire and sinker outboard. Fairly new, Echo Sounders were also being fitted in the chart house or on the bridge. But all these could be destroyed in action and when entering or leaving harbour only a leadsman could be the first to report the ship's movement ahead or astern, or ceasing to move, simply by holding his line still and vertical.

Besides the two battle-cruisers, *Nelson*, *Rodney*, *Malaya*, *Warspite*, and *Courageous*, the carrier, anchored at different times below the Forth Bridge made overnight leave and the amenities of Edinburgh available to the ships' companies, helped by plenty of buses from South Queensferry.

Admiral James expressed himself well satisfied with the battle-cruisers' gunnery and gave a talk to junior officers entitled "The Golden Moment". This might have been his 78 for *Hood* v *Renown* on the Barnton golf course, but turned out to be about Britain's admirals. By November our golfing gunroom had played on many Edinburgh courses, even hiring a car, which we could ill afford, for a Sunday at Muirfield, where we devoured roast beef and the last four eggs left in the Club House.

A month before our exam we were given another 'dummy run' with the Captain heading the panel. I recorded it as an invaluable five round, twenty minutes a round contest, in which I was repeatedly 'floored'. But one also learnt the best way to convince an examiner that one did know what one was talking about. The terrifying aspect of the actual exam was that in *Queries in Seamanship*, our guide, there were over 1200 questions to which one should know the answer. Published by Gieves I still have my 1928 copy.

Relations between the Wardroom and Gunroom were particularly pleasant and they dined us all the night before we returned to Sheerness. On 30 November seven midshipmen returned from Chatham with four First Class Certificates (over 85%) and three Second Class (over 70%). Scott, Robinson, Baker and Moss gained the former; Knox, McBarnet and Hogg the latter. Captain Bevan, Commander F. C. Baker and Commander R. M. McGregor had been our examiners.

Back in *Renown* our mentors were beside themselves with delight at these results. It was really rather touching; my own success as Midshipman Mod with 263 marks being acclaimed.

> *And still they gaz'd, and still the wonder grew,*
> *That one small head could carry all he knew*

❖ ❖ ❖

Promoted Rear-Admiral, Calvert became Chief of Staff Home Fleet 1933-35 and commanded the 2nd Cruiser Squadron 1936-38. His death on 1 July 1938 was unexpected.

Daniel de Pass as a Captain commanded the Tribal class destroyer, *Cossack* until poor eyesight restricted him to shore service. When I met him once more in the 1950s, living near Denmead, he had become a collector of very good modern paintings. He died in 1963, aged seventy one.

George Colville greeted me on board the *Duke of York* in November 1943 when we were both guests of Bruce Fraser, the Commander-in-Chief Home Fleet. Commanding destroyers successfully during the war, he died in 1985.

HMS Hood *in 1925.* *National Maritime Museum Greenwich*

CHAPTER 11

The Greenwich Night Pageant

Needing a break from housekeeping, servants, grandchildren and rheumatism my mother found Tyrrell's Wood Golf Club in the woods South of Epsom Downs, the Club House being a mansion occupied some years before by Sir Edward Hulton, the first Press Baron and his family. The Club being only too pleased to let its large bedrooms on the first floor, my parents let Richmond House Epsom, becoming resident members for the 1932-3 winter and I, taking up my own residence at the Royal Naval College Greenwich on January 4, 1933, was delighted to have at weekends bed, meals, golf and a particularly good Amontillado sherry at ten pence a glass.

The Greenwich Hospital had become the Royal Naval College in 1863, but ignorant of the visual arts it was sometime before most of us realised that we were living in one of the world's architectural gems. Every Sub-Lieutenant had a cabin, night or day there were no watches to keep, we walked sedately from one classroom to another and were free every weekend; indeed free nightly from about 1600 to 0900. But the rise from a Midshipman's 5 shillings a day to an Acting Sub-Lieutenant's 7s. 8d. hardly took one to the Ritz or a night-club, particularly as better messing ashore cost more. Wines and spirits were no longer duty free, so that a £2 wine bill maximum in place of 15 shillings permitted no great increase in consumption.

Eight miles south east of Central London on a great bend of the Thames between Deptford and Woolwich, with the Isle of Dogs on the other bank, Greenwich has been associated with shipping since Danish traders came up the Thames before the Norman conquest in 1066. Looking south east from the river over the Queen's House the ground rises through woods to Blackheath. In 1427 on the higher ground a watch tower was built to look out for revolting Kentish peasants or even foreign foes. Lower down by the Thames a Royal palace was erected, which was much improved by the Tudors and called Placentia.

With gardens, real tennis courts and a Royal Park, Henry VIII spent much time here, establishing dockyards to build warships, the biggest being the *Great Harry*. Edward VI died in the Placentia, Mary and Elizabeth were born in it; and it remained the house of the Court when the Stuart Kings, James I and Charles I, were on the throne. Wanting a smaller residence as a gift to his French Queen Henrietta Maria, Charles commissioned Inigo Jones, who completed the Queen's House for her in 1635. It remains the first example of the Classical style in England, designed in the manner of Palladio, by an architect fresh from his travels on the Continent.

After the King's Execution in 1649 to the restoration of the monarchy in 1660, the Palace of Placentia and its works of art were neglected being sold finally in 1652. Charles II, greeted by the people at Blackheath in 1660, was delighted to find the Queen's House good enough for him while he arranged for a new King's house to be built. Distressed at his royal master's execution, Inigo Jones had died in 1651, but Webb, his nephew and understudy, achieved the present King Charles block on the north western side by the river before the money ran out.

These were the days of Newton, and Charles II, scientifically minded himself, founded the Royal Society in 1660 before employing Wren to build The Royal Observatory to replace that old Watch Tower in 1665. This was the year of the Great Plague bringing refugees out of London including Samuel Pepys, Secretary of the Navy who set up the Victualling Yard at Deptford. Leaving a time ball to drop at noon for passing shipping, the Observatory moved out to Hurstmonceaux, Sussex in 1860 and now the building forms part of the Maritime Museum.

It was not until 1688 when Charles II had died and James II had gone into exile that talk of a hospital for old sailors, like the one at Chelsea for old soldiers, became a project in the hands of Sir Christopher Wren, then at the top of his fame. His team included Hawksmoor (Greenwich Parish Church) and Vanburgh(Blenheim Palace). The first forty two pensioners were accommodated in 1705 with completion about 1720. Endowment came from many sources.

Looking south east from the Thames towards the Queen's House, the four blocks are: North east Queen Anne. South east (with tower and chapel) Queen Mary. South west (with tower and Painted Hall) King William. North west King Charles.

Tenants of the Queen's House for some years were the Rangers of Greenwich Park, Governors of Greenwich Hospital and once the wife of a Prime Minister. After 1780 it became a Smuggling Centre, while the Park was an Asylum for Rioters and a Receptacle for Whores and Rogues. Since 1933 it has been part of the National Maritime Museum.

A separate infirmary close to the West gate, rebuilt in 1811 and enlarged after a fire, was leased to the Seamen's Hospital Society in 1873. In 1946 it became a National Health Service Hospital. Of the two globes on the West gate itself, one is a celestial sphere and the other the track of Anson's 1740-44 circumnavigation.

By 1860 decades of peace and declining defensive expenditure had greatly reduced the number of pensioners, leading to the final closure of Greenwich Hospital in 1873. Much to their credit an *avant garde* Admiralty declared it was to become a Royal Naval College providing higher education for naval officers under a Director of Studies, with Professors of Mathematics, Physical Science, Chemistry, Applied Mechanics and Fortification, not presumably a misprint for Fornication nor a study in passing the port. A course primarily for Royal Marines and perhaps Gunnery specialists.

Officers eligible for the College certainly included Royal Marines, Naval Instructors, Dockyard Apprentices and selected foreigners. *The Naval Review*, still published quarterly for members only, was founded in 1912, a year after Winston Churchill, joining the Admiralty as First Lord, deplored that no book on naval war was compulsory reading and that the one work on Sea Power was by an American, Alfred Mahan (1840-1914) Rear Admiral, entitled *The Influence of Sea Power on History*.

The Staff College became part of the whole College in 1919. The need to write clear and concise English on matters such as Naval History soon brought about another department, with Sir Geoffrey Callender, author of *Sea Kings of Britain* taking the Chair. A Royal Naval Medical School was set up in 1912, and in 1921 Sub- Lieutenants received a 6-months General Education course, while the Royal Corps of Naval Constructors was given a Professor. Fortifications however were abandoned.

Thus Wren's masterpiece became the Naval University with an Admiral President, a Captain and a Commander, each with their separate married quarters furnished with period furniture. This was roughly the position when we Dartmouth Greynviles of 1926-29 met on January 4, joined by our former Public School contemporaries trained in *HMS Erebus*. Knowing nothing of architecture the College history was unknown to us and The Painted Hall just a name we never saw because it was then a museum full of pictures which could not be seen for dust. The Refectory, called the Pensioners' Dining Hall was underneath it.

Another addition to our ranks was Gordon Gray, the son of a clergyman who had joined the Navy from the Nautical College Pangbourne in 1929 and in 1930 at Haifa was found to be missing from his ship, *Queen Elizabeth*, flagship of the Mediterranean Fleet no less.

After some weeks he re-appeared saying that he had joined the French

JUST A HOGG'S LIFE

Foreign Legion at Beirut because flagship life with its ceremonial and watch keeping lacked adventure. But the Legion had proved to be worse so he returned. A Court-Martial charged with desertion seemed probable but the Commander-in-Chief intervened, saying that the act showed courage and loss of three months seniority was imposed. Subsequently Gray was frequently mentioned in despatches ending his career as a Rear Admiral C.B., D.S.C. From 1951 to 1953 he was Executive Officer of the cruiser *Glasgow* the Mediterranean Fleet flagship.

One evening Lord Louis Mountbatten, the C-in-C returned on board saying he had asked twenty VIPs to dinner at 8 on the Quarterdeck. This required the table to be brought up from his cabin laid with lamps, lit etc., at very short notice.

The Electrical Storekeeper was ashore and the key could not be found. Eventually when the guests were all seated, the sailors were still crawling on all fours under the table, plugging in the lighting circuits. Ceremonial and adventure had combined at last on board the fleet flagship.

PUBLIC SCHOOL SUB-LIEUTENANTS.
HMS EREBUS/COLLINGWOOD TERM 1929

There were thirty nine in all, one Nitya Sukum was a Siamese, fifteen had become Engineer officers and twelve Paymasters, thus leaving eleven at RNC Greenwich in January 1933.

Name	*Final Rank or Fate*
Philip Bekenn	Lieutenant-Commander retd.
Anthony Godwin	Lieutenant-Commander retd.
P. Goldsmid	Sub-Lieutenant removed from list 1934
K. J. Harper	Lieutenant. Killed in action HM S/M *Thistle* 14 April 1940
Ian Hogg	Vice Admiral Sir Ian Hogg KCB, DSC* retd.
Horace Law	Admiral Sir Horace Law GCB, OBE, DSC retd.
Peter Milburn	Commander Died August 1981
J. W. T. Milton	Lieutenant. Medically unfit. Retd 1936. Died 1937 of obscure tropical disease.
P. L. Roberts	Lieutenant. Killed in action. HMS *Daring* 18 February 1940
Paul Whatley	Lieutenant-Commander retd.
Philip Yonge	Commander DSC retd.
Nitya Sukum	Major-General. Thai Water Police. Died 1985 (See Ch.12)

The subjects we Sub-Lieutenants studied, with their individual importance and my own miserable marks in the Sciences are now exposed for posterity.

Subject	Full Marks	Marks Awarded
Mathematics	200	100
Applied Mechanics	200	49
Physics	200	130
General Chemistry	100	60
History	125	89
English	75	61
French	100	59
Total	*1000*	548

3rd Class Certificate Sgd. Barry Domvile
President
RN College Greenwich

Professor Jimmy Searle, who looked like de Valera, the Irish Prime Minister, spoke little but filled black boards with the symbols of physics faster than we could copy them into our notebooks. A fast all rounder it seems certain from the evidence of a chosen few that he kept a night-club in London as well. A popular story was that when the Admiralty had a tricky problem he was locked in a room with the problem and a bottle of whisky. Unlocked next morning the former was solved, the latter empty and the Professor flaked out on the floor.

Since I have yet to discover what exactly *are* Applied Mechanics and who applies them, I suppose 49 marks out of 200 was pretty good. Our Professor, E. "Bert" Chappell, middle aged and portly, sporting watch and chain in his waistcoat pockets, paced up and down the small classroom as if it was a Quarterdeck. "You need a pencil sharpener", I can hear him say, "A penknife should be confined to removing superfluous timber".

In chemistry I think it was Professor Tothill who advised us most earnestly never to drink water from unknown sources, which greatly amused a class of committed beer drinkers avoiding H_2O at all costs.

For History and English we were in three classes, Geoffrey Callender taking the first, John B. Bullocke the second and William Tunstall, the third, all three being excellent and highly qualified. Tunstall took us through the 1914-18 war on land and sea, writing many books when at Greenwich from 1925 to 1937 and later as Senior Lecturer in International Relations at the London School of Economics.

Finally there was French with Monsieur Harrault. Being rather insular little Brits in those days, few of us really tried to understand the language as spoken by French people. When I joined Peter Dominic some twenty years later - a company founded and run by Paul Dauthieu, whose parents were French - I regretted my inadequacy.

The College ran Rugby and hockey teams that Easter term with home grounds in Greenwich Park. At Rugger we could not match the top clubs like Blackheath or the Harlequins, but there was a second class club in the fixture list called The Wasps. They beat us 50-0. It might be 150 today. After those Saturday games I would go home for golf on Sunday but there was one Sunday I spent in the College. The bar did not open till noon and in a short space of time before lunch I had drunk eleven sherries.

After lunch Wren's buildings went round and round like the music - the popular tune of the day. This was most alarming. My parents had just sailed from Venice to Alexandria to visit their son-in-law Bimbashie (Police Officer) Paterson, my sister Brada and their two little girls, all settled in a small house out at Ramleh.. The parents' new Essex saloon car had been placed in my care and I was supposed to arrive in Denham Bucks in time for tea and Bridge with Bobbie and Bertie de Klé, who was Colonel of The Blues. I jumped vigorously first into hot, then into cold baths. Setting out when I could delay no longer, 'Knocked 'em in the Old Kent Road' seemed a distinct probability. However South East London settled down and I even played Bridge without revoking.

These early thirties were dreadful years for the poor. Two and a half million people were unemployed in 1930 and Baldwin's Government introduced the Means Test which made them poorer in many cases. The General Election of 1929 had returned a Labour Government under Ramsay MacDonald, in which Sir Oswald Mosley was a member. Resigning a year later over unemployment policy, he formed the New Party in 1931 when the Labour government fell. Britain then went off the Gold Standard and a National Government was formed, Ramsay MacDonald accepting the leadership to the disgust of the Left.

By 1933 Mosley's party had become Fascists, with a body guard of men in black shirts, whenever he held meetings. Coming to Lewisham Herbert Morrison's Socialist stronghold, a few Sub-Lieutenants keen to take part in a rough house soon beat a rapid retreat when confronted with the merry wives of Lewisham brandishing razor blades firmly secured to the ends of large thick pencils.

Such was the slump that in America the employment reached thirteen million, with Bing Crosby, a new type of singer called 'a crooner' making a hit with a touching little song, 'Buddy can you spare a dime?' 1933 was the year Franklin D. Roosevelt became President ushering in the New Deal. Prohibition also ended. It had lasted thirteen years producing gangsters galore, who opened their own breweries with their own transport, bribing the police and, in the new talking films on our cinema screens, spoke a strange language. I still remember:

"Stick around a while the boss wants to see yer. Go along to room 28 you'll find the guys there"
"But say, these guys are ex-cons."
"Sure they're ex-cons"
"Will they pull a rod? Will they croak?"
"Will they pull a rod? Will they croak? These guys are on parole, they daren't even speak loud"

In London musical comedies and revues were "the thing" and we were still playing on our gramophones absurdities by Leslie Henson and Sidney Howard from *Funny Face*, a show in which Fred Astaire danced divinely with his sister Adele, later to become Lady Cavendish. Charles B Cochran (and his young ladies) followed Charlot as the leading *impresario*, with *One Damn Thing after Another*, *This Year of Grace* (1928) full of Noel Coward's tunes and lyrics – *Room with a View, Dance little Lady, Try to learn to love a little bit* – still remembered. In 1929 his operetta *Bitter Sweet* so enchanted my father that he never ceased to tell me to go and see it. But he never offered to pay, so it was not until the 1980s that I finally made the revival.

Most of the principals are dead, but there was one I remember, possibly still tap dancing and singing:

> *Lets creep away from the day*
> *For the party's over now*

in another Noel Coward hit *Words and Music*. His name? Sir John Mills.

In 1931 Cochran also brought The 4 Marx Brothers – and Margaret Dumont too – in person to London after *The Cocoanuts* and *Animal Crackers*, their first two films, had been shown over here.

Charles Robinson, who sailed boats so well against ABC, was among their first disciples easily converting me. I like to think he saw most of their other films in the Thirties, before being killed in action on June 8 1940 off Trondheim, when the German battle cruisers *Scharnhorst* and *Gneisenau* sank our aircraft carrier *Glorious* and her two escorting destroyers, first *Ardent* and then *Acasta*. Alone against hopeless odds, *Acasta*, firing guns and torpedoes, damaged *Scharnhorst* with one torpedo before she sank.

An account appears in Volume I of Winston Churchill's *The Second World War*. Charles Robinson was *Acasta*'s First Lieutenant. We picked up only one survivor; five others were recovered becoming prisoners of war in Germany.

GREENWICH NIGHT PAGEANT
Of all the entertainments mentioned so far, this was the most original. Conceived by Vice-Admiral Barry Domvile, the President of the Royal Naval College, who was born there when his father, Admiral Sir Compton Domvile was the President half a century before, the Mayor of Greenwich became an enthusiastic Vice- President of the venture. Mr. Arthur Bryant, (later Sir Arthur) author and historian, agreed to produce, while Mrs. Domvile became an enthusiastic honorary Secretary.

As a stand to hold 10,000 people began to be erected between King Charles and Queen Anne, the two buildings nearest the river, Professor Chappell (Applied Mechanics) was quite certain it would collapse, a foreboding supported by Professor Callender (History) who unearthed such a mishap a few centuries back and felt sure history would repeat itself.

A formidable undertaking, the pageant between 10pm and midnight, was to re-enact episodes of naval history that took place at Greenwich. 2500 performers would be required, proceeds being given to naval charities. Music, lighting, effects, seating, advertising, all needed attention; the performers would be recruited locally and more volunteers would be needed to make costumes, stage properties and to do clerical work. Rehearsals would have to take place after normal working hours and tents with refreshments in the college grounds would be necessary.

For clothing there were in fact seven work rooms in the district, besides some in the college itself. Some fourteen miles of hessian and perhaps seven of casement cloth were needed for the costumes. The bathroom of the Admiral's chauffeur was used for dying them. Dresses had to be stencilled; banners and head gear fashioned and decorated. The whole job took over four months.

The following gave their services: Officers of the College; NCO's and men of the Royal Artillery from Woolwich; Staff of the RAF stores Depot, Kidbrook. Officers of The Queens Own regiment in London; Officers of the 302nd Anti-Aircraft Searchlight Company R.E.

THE GREENWICH NIGHT PAGEANT

Members of:- The Special Constabulary, St. John's Ambulance Corps, South Metropolitan Gas Company, British Sailors Society, Hay's Wharf Social and Athletic Association, Charlton Stadium Company, the South Metropolitan Electric Light and Gas Company in association with the County of London Electric Supply Co., which presented the whole cost of the electrical installation, lighting and effects.

The band was the Royal Marines, Chatham Barracks, choristers and shanty singers came from several different local churches and choral societies, dancers from the local branches of the English Folk Dance Society and school of Ballet dancing.

The stage was the green sward between the Chapel and the Painted Hall which extends as far back as the railings to Romney Road, with the Queen's House beyond. The stage lighting was mounted above the colonnades on either side. When electric light was first fitted into HM Ships in Queen Victoria's days, the Paymaster was responsible because candles, the previous lighting came under him. Now, Electrics belonged to the Torpedo Branch, and the Long Course, beginning their theory at Greenwich, manned the stage lights. Looking down from the wings, others could join them by invitation on payment of one bottle of beer. The row of empties along the colonnade soon became almost as long as the Royal Guard of Pikemen about fifty strong. This guard, composed of volunteer Sub-Lieutenants, had to slope and present Pikes when the occasion demanded, with the precision of H.M. Foot Guards Trooping the Colour. With all these bars about when rehearsing after 10 p.m., one or more Pikemen usually had a terrible time lag causing the exasperated Arthur Bryant to tear his hair like Sir Ralph the Rover.

But all was well on the night. A *Times* correspondent wrote:

"I had the privilege of watching part of one performance from behind the scenes, and it was a sight not easily forgotten. Inside the colonnades Elizabethan yeomen of the guard mingled with Roundhead pikemen and cavaliers, blue Greenwich Hospital pensioners with Wolfe's red-coated soldiery and Nelson's seamen. A very convincing Henry VIII rubbed shoulders with his subjects, and in a small inner courtyard kings and queens, noblemen and their ladies, seamen, soldiers, townspeople, ballet dancers, Spanish ladies, trumpeters, heralds, prelates and priests, not to mention civic dignitaries, dressed in the costumes of every period, were mixed in gay profusion. They were a happy throng. Even at close quarters it was difficult to realize that their gorgeous apparel was nothing more than dyed hessian, casement cloth and gold and silver tinsel.

> *It was interesting also to watch the team working the novel and ingenious apparatus designed by Professor B.P.Haigh, whereby pictures and silhouettes of moving ships were thrown upon the huge back screen."*

The first night was on Friday June 16, thence nightly except Sundays to Monday 26th, which was an extra largely for King Feisal and his wife, who were on a state visit. The Princess Royal (Countess of Harewood) occupied the Royal Box on June 20, Prince George on June 21 and Edward, Prince of Wales on his birthday, June 23. On June 21 the Admiralty Board brought their guests, the Army and Air Councils, by water; while the following night the Lord Mayor of London, the Chairman of the London County Council, and the Port of London Authority were guests of the Mayor of Greenwich, Colonel H. A. H. Newington.

An increasing number of ticket holders also came by water and there was an attempt to revive whitebait dinners at the "Ship". An annual banquet for cabinet ministers, the whitebait dinners had ceased in 1894 after a long run, graced by Pitt in Georgian times.

On the second night, Saturday, at 1135, the Epilogue was relayed live from the College on the National 1554m wavelength. Entitled "The Freedom of the Seas", this opened with seamen singing sea shanties. Then came Holst's Marching Song and the mobilisation of the Naval Reserves on August 2 1914, signature tune "Nancy Lee". In the next phase "Admirals All", the Ghosts of Drake and Nelson appeared in the hour of England's need to "Drake's Drum" and "Twas in Trafalgar's Bay". Finally a march past of all performers and the passing of the Grand Fleet took place to a fantasy of British sea songs. Captain P. S. G. O'Donnell conducted the Royal Marine Chatham band supported by an orchestra under Mr. Edgar R. Wilby.

The programme of 24 pages, each 11 inches by 7, probably written by Arthur Bryant, has a Prelude and Epilogue with four Acts between them, each divided into two, sometimes three, scenes all acted by different groups.

Act 1 Gloriana
The first scene, shows the christening of future Queen Elizabeth in 1533 with pealing bells and singing choristers chanting the Te Deum, followed by a company of London citizens and dignitaries. Then came the Privy Council, Peers and Prelates in their robes and lastly, beneath a canopy of gold, the Dowager Duchess of Norfolk holding the royal infant. While this procession marches above the roadway, another of common people,

many in rags, march the same way along the road just below them. As the noise dies away, the Announcer, Henry Ainley, makes a short oration.

Then to rolling drums, out of the darkness at the back of the stage, came the Yeomen of the Guard, with gentlemen-at-arms bringing gifts and finally to blaring trumpets the King strides forth bearing the babe. Sounds of music and revelry came from within the colonnades where the crowds have gathered. Cranmer, Bishop of London with his retinue cross the stage where he sits to survey the scene as the night darkens and the Announcer has a last word.

Scene 2. 1581. *The Golden Hind* arrives at Greenwich on Apri 4. The crowds welcome Drake's vessel and cheer the Queen, who emerges from the Palace to knight Sir Francis on board his own ship. Raleigh of course is there to drop his coat on a muddy spot.

Scene 3. 1588. The Announcer recites the first verse of Macaulay's, "Attend all those who list to hear..." Great waves, flashes of lightning, beacons burning and sounds of battle, leave no doubt that the Spanish Armada is being scattered. There are cheers for the Queen, who replies with the oft quoted "Ye may well have a greater prince, but ye shall never have a more loving prince".

Act II The Makers of the Palace
Scene 1. 1633-1649 depicts King Charles I and his Queen out and about, the Court being entertained by a Masque with Prospero and Tempest ballet music. Scene 2 depicts Charles II, the restored Monarch being greeted at Blackheath on 29 May, 1660; his wife being Catherine of Braganza, that northern Trás-os-Montes town of Portugal, that I know well. The theme tune of this scene is the march Braganza; also popular, I was soon to discover, with the drum and pipe party that cleared out the latrines of the Gunnery school on Whale Island.

With the King riding bare-headed towards London to the strains of a Lancashire Morris Dance followed by "When the King enjoys his own again" and "Here's a health unto His Majesty", this was great pageantry.

Act III Pudding Time
The Announcer begins Act III, The Landing of George I at Greenwich with this Vicar of Bray verse:

> *"When George in pudding-time came o'er,*
> *"And moderate men looked big, Sir,*
> *"My politics I changed once more*

JUST A HOGG'S LIFE

> *"And so became a Whig, Sir;*
> *"And thus preferment I procured*
> *"From our new faith's defender;*
> *"And almost every day abjured*
> *"The Pope and the Pretender."*

And of course at 6 p.m. on the evening of 10 September 1714 the noblemen of England, with all the ships in the river firing salutes, turned out to show allegiance, the Whig Dukes dominating, with the Duke of Marlborough, as an old comrade in arms, receiving the warmest of royal greetings. The music was Purcell's Trumpet Voluntary, since credited to Jeremiah Clarke (c1670-1707) organist of St. Paul's Cathedral. Three groups are needed for the Fête Galante that celebrates the King's birthday in 1728. Though there are fireworks, the accompaniment is Handel's Water Music.

Act III Interlude – Wolfe 1759

It is February 1759; but for a few figures the stage is empty. Two are conspicuous; old Mr. Wolfe of Blackheath is talking with his son, General James Wolfe, a Westerham man partly educated at Greenwich. A small crowd gather to say Goodbye. The date is now 13 September 1759. Wolfe with some 9000 troops are before Quebec on the Heights of Abraham.

After some preliminary movements a double line of red English infantry can be seen drawn up in the half light of dawn facing the blue coated French. Aware of their superior musketry, the English can afford to wait, firing a tremendous volley at ten yards range. Montcalm lost the battle but the price of victory was the death of Wolfe. Shot by a sniper's musket ball, he dies in the arms of his officers. The light holds the little group before rising to reveal, above the Queen Mary Block, the Flag of British Canada.

Act IV. Nelson Goes Home, 1806

Scene 1 shows the good humoured Cockney crowd at 11 a.m. on Sunday 5 January milling around outside The Painted Hall waiting to get a glimpse of Nelson's body where it had laid for some weeks. In the Chapel opposite, the organ can be heard as Matins end, the doors open and the respectable congregation emerges. When an official opens the Painted Hall the crowd, now impatient make a wild rush. Men are knocked over, women faint. Order is restored and the procession of mourners continues until evening.

THE GREENWICH NIGHT PAGEANT

Scene 2 shows the funeral procession on Wednesday January 8. A great silent crowd forms an avenue from the Painted Hall to the centre of the stage, and thence to the river gates, where silver bargemen wait, their long oars draped in black. The trumpets sound as the Dead March in Saul begins on the great Chapel organ. Now the heralds of the Funeral Procession appear, with pipes and drums; pensioners follow the Royal Standard borne before. Next a company of sailors are led by a Captain and two Lieutenants in full uniform, with black waistcoats, breeches and stockings and crepe around their hats and arms. Other officers follow bearing the Shield, Sword, Helm and Crest of Nelson, his great banner borne by Captain Moorsom and two Lieutenants. Then, as the draped coffin, borne by men of the *Victory* emerges, every head in that silent crowd is bared and many too in the audience. The lights go out. When the lights shine again only the backs of the crowd at the riverside can be seen, as the barges proceed upstream to St. Paul's and the Tower guns can be heard sounding their greeting.

Fearing that if I became a pikeman, rehearsal time would decrease my chances of passing the exam, I had a minor role superintending in the car park across the main road around the Queen's House. Except for some difficulty with Nelson, a one-eyed and rather grumpy gentleman-volunteer from Blackheath, all went well.

To the stirring strains of appropriate music the pageant was an entertainment of great beauty, variety and movement, with an underlying motive that attracted huge audiences little short of 100,000.

The proceeds were divided between the Seaman's Hospital Society, which administered the Dreadnought Hospital at Greenwich and five other branches; the Miller General Hospital at Greenwich, the Blackheath and Charlton Hospital and St. John's Hospital at Lewisham.

Besides those already named the following deserve mention: Organising Secretary, Captain Edwin Clarke. Assistant Producers, Elizabeth Addison and Winifrede Thorne. Musical Director, Dr. Malcolm Sargent. Dress Designer, Maisie Marshall. Costume Manager, Peggy Church. Lighting Director, Nancy Newins. Assistant Engineer, T. S. Robertson B.Sc., Silhouette Designer, Sylvia Bryant. Sound Effect Manager, Lt. Cdr. Cuthbert. Property Managers, R. T. Ellis and T. H. Arundell. Organist, John Meux. Accompanist, Molly Blandford.

Cynics declared that the purpose of the Pageant was to obtain a knighthood to please Lady Domvile, Alexandrina, daughter of a Mr. Von der Heydt. Well deserved, it duly came the following year, with promotion

JUST A HOGG'S LIFE

to full Admiral on retirement in 1936. Sad to relate by 1940 the Admiral had become so pro-German that, with Oswald Mosley, it was thought necessary to intern him; and in 1941 their only son was killed in action.

Royal Naval College looking south east to the Queen's House; from the painting by Canaletto in the National Maritime Museum.

The Painted Hall looking West, College dining hall since 1939.

CHAPTER 12

Sub-Lieutenant Third Class to Malta

For my journeys to and from Epsom to Greenwich, I had bought a 12 H.P Morris 2-seater saloon for £15. It even took me north to Cheshire and back, the floor boards lifting six inches over 50 mph. Due to continue our courses in Portsmouth in September, I persuaded my father to lend me £70 towards a better car. For this I went to Henley's show room in Piccadilly to be taken 'round the houses' by a smooth salesman in an open Wolseley Hornet 2-seater newly painted cream with sky blue wings; the sort of model known in coarse circles as a tart trap. Inexperienced, I had exchanged cars for £70, discovering later that the spare wheel in the Wolseley boot was black, its original colour evidently. The cylinders were so worn that the plugs often oiled up on starting the engine, needing to be removed and cleaned before setting out. Ali Baba and the forty Garage Proprietors! The moral is stick to your local garage. Fortunately in Epsom Mr. Norman's Woodcote Motor Company was just down the road, serving me well in the future. Between leaving Greenwich on July 27 there was time before joining HMS *Excellent*, the Gunnery School at Portsmouth, for a fishing holiday with my brother, Martin, who was making Radiac shirts in Manchester with McIntyre Hogg, Marsh and Co., called Hogg, Bogg and Slosh by my ribald naval friends. After previous family holidays at Tomdoun, off the road to the Isles, and in the Culag Hotel at Lochinver, we now headed further North for Durness, a dozen miles from Cape Wrath. This north west corner of Scotland that looks on the map to have more lochs than dry land was advertised as the land of the big brown trout. Up to fifteen pounds weight they were caught by rowing slowly across a loch trolling astern a daddy long legs that dipped and hopped, a technique known as dapping. The Keoldale Hotel, still there shining white on the shores of the Kyle of Durness, wrote saying that they supplied the special rods and tackle but in fact they did not. However my brother caught two nice grilse in the river Dionard that flows into the Kyle and I had another in my hand at a time when I had lost my net. Two Anglo-Indian colonels on the other side shouted endlessly "Keep your rod point up" as I slowly played the fish. In vain I suggested that if they sent their ghillie across the nearby foot bridge with a net all would be well; inevitably it was the one that got away.

H.M.S. EXCELLENT, THE GUNNERY SCHOOL

Whale Island, named HMS *Excellent*, at the northern end of Portsmouth harbour had been developed as the Royal Navy's principal Gunnery school since Victorian times. During the Thirties 300 officers and 2000 men qualified in various courses annually. As Sub-Lieutenants our course for Lieutenant lasted from September 1 to early November. Above us were about a dozen Lieutenants, volunteers who had been selected for the Long Course, which would qualify them as specialists in Gunnery.

Divided into classes of twelve to fifteen under an already qualified Lieutenant (G), assisted by various Petty Officers who were Gunner's mates, we Sub-Lieutenants marched our platoons or companies into one another with gay abandon when learning "Field Training" on the Parade Ground. Another place of torment was West battery, devoted to gun drill and stripping, which meant taking to pieces a variety of ordnance and, hopefully, assembling them again. Under instruction we had to stand at (so called) ease round the ironmongery, laying the foundation of varicose veins for the surgeons of Haslar hospital to strip later. After the war the psychologists recommended a more relaxing posture, sitting on a bench. One visiting diehard told the Commander (G), head of instruction, that to his horror he had seen a class seated with hands in pockets. "That's terrible", said the Commander "The drill permits only the left hand".

No easy job teaching and taking charge of young people, better educated than the instructor, the Gunner's Mates did it well. I only remember one who suffered from terrible halitosis. "Pay attention, gentlemen, pay attention", he cried. "What's the good of me wasting good breath on you?" Poor man, he never understood why the class laughed!

Whether officers, or men qualifying for Seaman Gunner, Gunlayer, Director Layer or Range finder, the punishment for misbehaviour for the class was to double march round the island; no joke in boots, gaiters, with bayonets fixed and rifles at the slope. Moreover the Instructor, not wishing to punish himself, was entitled to walk, ordering the class to turn about whenever it was about to disappear ahead of him.

The smallest class on the island was certainly the funniest. The two Siamese Sub-Lieutenants, marching about the place took it in turn to be in charge, one shouting "Keep silence in the ranks" at the other. Returning to Siam in 1937 as a qualified Torpedo officer, Nitya Sukum had to train with the Japanese in a formerly British submarine, much to his distaste. However, he became a close adviser of the King. His widow sent a book about him to Paul Whatley. The officers' block facing East across the spacious playing field, with the Parade Ground lower down out of sight beyond, was a pleasant and peaceful place in which to live - at least until 0750 in the morning. This was the time when a Drum and Fife Band preceded the latrine party, which marched round, removing the buckets in "The Heads" to the tune, Lilliburlero. Rather disconcerting if you happened to be seated there. There were no water closets on the island until September 22 1937. By way of celebration the Devonport Barracks Gunnery School presented Whaley with a first plug and chain.

With no marriage allowance few officers married before promotion to Lieutenant-Commander when about thirty. The Wardroom was therefore full of boisterous life and *bonhomie* becoming a bit rough on Guest Nights with *Stripping the Willow, Billiard-Fives*, and *Field Gun*, a competitive race through the anterooms in Olympia's Royal Tournament style, dismantling bed-steads instead of field guns. Highly amusing of course, unless you returned from shore after midnight to find no bed in your cabin because they had failed to replace gear.

On most nights there was early supper for those who wished to go ashore in plain cloths to local entertainments. 1933 was a great year for films: *Gold Diggers of 1933, Flying Down to Rio*, in which Fred Astaire and Ginger Rogers stole the show dancing the Carioca; Charlie Chaplin's *City Lights* still doing the rounds of the Odeons; the great ape *King Kong* doing them too until banned by Surrey County Council. Bands - those of Duke Ellington and Cab Callaway among them - filled the music halls. Then there were the pubs, The Goat and The Bush in King's Road Southsea being our principal 'locals'. Every building along this short road leading eastwards into Elm Grove was destroyed by German bombers on the night of Friday 10 January 1941, the George Hotel and other buildings in Old Portsmouth likewise.

Four months married I was on duty in the Dockyard that night with FPK71 my wife's beloved Austin 7, parked in a garage under the railway bridge by the main gate of H.M.S. *Vernon*. Walking down The Hard next morning everything seemed a smouldering wreck; there could be no hope for FPK71. I shall never forget how utter gloom suddenly became elation; there she was with no more than a brick sitting on her canvas roof. Repaired by Vernon's sailmaker this paragon of reliability took us both up to Loch Long for my next job and back again. Paid off when the petrol ration ceased in 1943, she was recommissioned in October 1945 with a boy called Adam aged two making our complement of three.

JUST A HOGG'S LIFE

In that autumn of 1933 on Whale Island I'm sure my mind frequently wandered away from West battery to the United Services Rugby ground by the Guildhall, where it still is. There had been a trial, interrupted from time to time by a great bellow from a voice in the stand, "Take that man's number, I like that man". This, it transpired, was Captain Robert Lindsay Burnett, now the Navy's Senior "Springer" and a Team Selector. To our astonishment Terence Harrel and Anthony Hogg, term mates at Dartmouth, became the pair of centre three-quarters alongside Lieutenant 'Wally' Elliot, England's fly half.

United Services Portsmouth was a first class club then playing Harlequins, Richmond, Blackheath, London Scottish, the two universities, Oxford and Cambridge and other top teams each year. In October we had beaten Oxford at Iffley Road 15-12 on a wet muddy ground. At the end of November we were at home to Cambridge. I had hurt my shoulder but thought it would somehow be all right on the day.

Our two opposing three quarters were Freshmen. In my first tackle I hurt my shoulder badly. No substitutes were allowed then. Down at half time our Captain said I had better mark the other centre; he would not be so good. We were beaten 27-3. The first centre was Wilfred Wooller, the second R.C.S. Dick, who got as many caps for Scotland as Wooller did for Wales. Relegated to the third team, the lesson I learnt was never to play when not fully fit. Only twenty three then, Wally Elliot was a modest, unpretentious person, said to have forgotten once to take his boots to Dublin for an international. But with Burland (Bristol) and Gerrard (Bath) too, England had a formidable defensive trio. Specialising in Naval Aviation Wally won a D.S.C. in the war and when retired as a Captain R. N. became M.P for Carshalton and Banstead.

At the end of the Gunnery course, Sub-Lieutenants often celebrated, staging some boyish form of demonstration on the island. I never quite believed the one about an elephant until I found it confirmed in John Wells's excellent *Whaley The Story of HMS Excellent 1830 to 1980*.

It was April 1, 1955 when the officer on the Footbridge saw an elephant with mounted mahout dressed as a Sub-Lieutenant, escorted by four more Sub-Lieutenants, approaching across the narrow bridge from Portsmouth. This he reported by telephone to the Lieutenant of the Island who, having been made an April fool once that morning, dismissed the hoax and replied 'Let it pass'.

Concealed behind the drill shed during the march past the elephantine procession wheeling out to join it behind the last class, was spotted by the Captain at the saluting base. Determined not to return the salute of a masquerading mahout on an elephant, he said, "Remove that elephant Commander". "Remove that elephant", said the Commander to Commander (G) who passed it on to the Parade Training officer, who passed it on to the Chief Gunner's mate, who deflected it in the nick of time up a side road. While the Admiralty made a Trunk call to the Captain and the whole Navy loved the joke, I fancy the Sub Lieutenants' leave was stopped for some days for making a mockery of the parade.

My Third Class certificate reads:

	Subject	Full Marks	Marks Obtained
A	Field Training	120	81
	Musketry	10	4
	Section Leading	20	15
	Gun Drill	100	75
	General Gunnery	75	64
	Total	**325**	**239**
B	Fire Control (Paper)	100	56
	Fire Control (Oral)	20	10
	H.A. Control (Paper)	50	30
B	H.A. Control (Oral)	20	15
	Director & Sighting (Paper)	60	39
	Director & Sighting (Oral)	25	13
	Rangefinder	30	22
	Firings	30	21
	Total	**335**	**206**
C	Stripping	75	42
	Machine Gun	25	14
	Ammunition	60	38
	Hydraulics	100	50
	Note Books	30	23
	Total	**290**	**167**
	Grand Total	**950**	**612**

1st Class Certificate 800 marks and above. 2nd Class 700 marks and above. 3rd Class 550 marks

H.M.S. VERNON, THE TORPEDO SCHOOL

For our next course, in Torpedoes, Electrics and Mining, we continued to live at Whaley going daily to HMS *Vernon*, an establishment between Portsmouth Harbour Station and the Isle of Wight Ferry Terminal with its own pier and creek where tenders berthed. Neither HMS *Excellent* nor

HMS *Vernon* existed solely for training men to handle weapons. They were also responsible that those weapons were safe and suitable for use at sea. This entailed their experimental departments working closely with the designers through all the development stages, providing ships and men for their trials and carrying out final acceptance trials themselves on behalf of the Admiralty.

Established ashore since October 1923 *Vernon* had three experimental departments: Whitehead (producer of the first self-propelling torpedo in 1862), Mining (including Mine Sweeping) and Electrical (High and Low Power). All these needed experimental areas at Spithead and in Stokes Bay, as well as a Vernon flotilla of destroyers and smaller mining vessels the size of a drifter. As on Whale Island, the Captain had a house, the officers a Wardroom block with cabins and several blocks of accommodation for the men. In short a normal naval shore establishment, with more blocks and stores containing electrical equipment found at sea, from dynamos to fire control tables and telephones. Vernon's distinguishing mark, seen from afar and still there, is the round mining tank the size of an old gasometer, with a corrugated rectangular hat on its top. Built to note the behaviour of moored mines through its glass port holes, its floor can be moved up and down varying the depth. And since *Vernon* took over Diving after the war, it has become of wider use.

Begun about 6 November – my 21st birthday – and ending on 21 December, Acting Sub-Lieutenant Mod was pretty hot at Torpedo Control, which was a geometrical matter, but 75 per cent on the nuts, bolts and volts of Whitehead and Electrics was quite beyond him.

EXAMINATION IN TORPEDO SCHOOL

Subject	Full Marks	Marks Awarded
Whitehead Paper	150	73
Whitehead Oral	50	34
Torpedo Control Paper	150	135
Torpedo Control Oral	100	80
Electrical Paper	150	88
Electrical Oral	100	72
Mining	100	68
Total	800	550

Award 3rd Class Certificate

Note: 1st Class Certificate 680 marks. 2nd Class Certificate 600 marks. 3rd Class Certificate 480 marks

1933 was the year in which Hitler became the German Chancellor, to be voted Führer (Leader) by Plebiscite a year later. In Britain a Frenchman called André Simon founded *The Wine and Food Society*. For thirty one years he had run the London office of Pommery, the Champagne house of Reims, finding time to write and lecture on wine to people in the Trade. He had also written in English *A History of the Wine Trade in England from the Roman occupation to the end of the Seventeenth Century*, a scholarly collector's piece in three volumes. More concerned with the recession, the Board in Reims closed the London office without a word of appreciation to him.

André was a firm believer in management by Committee, provided there were not more than two members, of which one should be in hospital or on holiday. The second in this case was A. J. A. Symons, definitely a live wire, who had written a best seller in *Quest for Corvo*.

An Advisory Council of formidable imbibers was however formed, which included Marcel Boulestin first T.V. Chef, Sir Frances Colchester Wemyss; Ambrose Heath; Maurice Healy; Elizabeth Craig; Vyvyan Holland; G. B. Stern and Sir Jack Squire, nearly all of whom were writers on wine or food.

Mentioned first among the acknowledgements in André's *A Concise Encyclopedia of Gastronomy*, published in 1952 is my grandmother Blanche Hulton, who was a founder member and contributor to the Quarterly. Their friendship was to prove useful when I retired from the Navy in 1955 and was looking for a job in the wine trade. I had already contributed some articles to the *Wine and Food Society's Quarterly* enabling André to tell his friend and fellow Frenchman, Paul Dauthieu at Horsham that I might be useful to his 12-branch company Peter Dominic.

1934 HMS *DRYAD*, THE NAVIGATION SCHOOL

After fourteen days Christmas leave we joined *Dryad* on 7 January 1934, where there was room for us all. This fine building in the residential area of the Dockyard is only 250 yards from the main gate. There was of course a Captain, but it was said that the man really in charge was Mr. Wilson, the Wardroom messman. Offend him and you'd be failed in your navigation course! I remember as a midshipman, first meeting Mr. Wilson when, walking along The Hard, a luxurious limousine drew up, the driver offering us a lift. "Thank you, Sir", we said, to which he modestly introduced himself as "Your messman, gentlemen, when you come to *Dryad*". A very good amateur conjuror too, he reigned until about 1938, dismissed by Colin Madden and Gerald Cobb, whose family made Cockburn's port.

Other than playing rugger and usually going home in my Wolseley Hornet at weekends I have no record of how this winter passed other than the Pilotage Certificate dated 18 February 1934.

PILOTAGE CERTIFICATE
HM Navigation School, Portsmouth

Subject		Maximum Marks	Marks Obtained
I	Magnetic Compass and Terrestrial Magnetism	150	103
II	Astronomical Navigation (RN College)	250	173
III	Practical Chart Work	50	35
IV	Meteorology and Tides	150	85
V	Ship and Fleet Work	150	112
VI	General Navigation and Pilotage	250	160
	Total	1000	668

Award 3rd Class Certificate

Note: 1st Class 80%; 2nd Class 70%; 3rd Class 60%.

At least two of our Greynviles were involved in road incidents. One, arrested for being drunk in charge of a bicycle, told the Court that he was a quiet, pacific person who did not fight. When the policeman who had arrested him appeared with a large black eye, "Drunky" - for that was already his nick name for life - looked quite astonished.

A dockyard worker narrowly missed by a Sub-Lieutenant's car, thrust his head into the window and said, "Ain't you got a horn?" Looking down at his trousers, the offending driver merely replied, "Not at the moment, have you ?". Bert and Bill two dockyard mateys, sat munching sandwiches, Bert complaining of a terrible belly ache. "Why don't you go to the toilet, Bert ? said Bill. "What in me dinner hour! " cried Bert aghast at the suggestion.

By the end of February, courses completed, we dispersed on leave to await appointments. Nothing had come for me by early April when the Royal Navy and Royal Marines Golfing Society held its annual meeting at St. George's Hill, Weybridge. On the last day there was a Greensome Flag competition with a draw for partners. The previous night I dreamt that I, a mere rabbit handicap 16, would play with Commander Sheffield, a scratch golfer who had won the Navy championship the day before. One glance at the noticeboard showed my dream to be a fact, but an unnerving prospect, since he was said to be a nasty man.

However the nasty man was a different Sheffield. My partner, Hugh from Cooden Beach Bexhill, was great fun. Aided by his straight long drives and my sixteen strokes, we stuck our flag in on the 21st green, winning first prize, a small silver salver. Playing with us was Alan Black, former Sub-Lieutenant of Rodney's gunroom, who had become some sort of civilian aviator until recalled to naval aviation in 1939.

April and May passed pleasantly mainly on links round Epsom. The two courses at Walton Heath were much as they are now. Lord Riddell, proprietor of *The News of the World*, the sensational Sunday paper, was God there and the professional James Braid in his seventies, would still get down in two within a hundred yards of any green. Green fees were high, likewise the heather; my visits could only be occasional.

Rough and ready, playable except in Derby week, the Epsom Downs course is on the slopes below Tattenham corner and the Grand Stand, the terrain falling sharply down to Epsom College and the town itself a mile below it. I first played here in 1930 with my father the Judge, who already had a bad heart at the age of sixty. When I drove into one of several spinneys, a male person holding his trousers up with one hand emerged, protesting indignantly that he and his girl friend were busy in there and a third ball was neither welcome nor necessary. Another of my shots hit a car moving along one of the many roads that intersect on this slope and finally at the 17th or thereabouts a magnificent slice struck a big white house out of bounds. Sweating profusely at the prospect of at least two plaintiffs claiming damages, my father, retired to what turned out to be the world's most hospitable Club house. To escape without drinking five pink gins was as impossible as paying for a round oneself. At the annual dance my future brother-in-law, Michael Powell declared he had seen a stock-broking gentleman being sick with a cigar in his mouth and that the whole proceedings were much enlivened by a member 'in his cups' telephoning for the Fire Brigade.

Our next door neighbour, Willie Thompson the tea-taster, always wearing his pink Leander tie, introduced me to Leatherhead. Still much the same today with a club house surrounded by new roads, here is golf among the trees with a particularly fine short sixteenth (now the twelfth). I was rather puzzled by the frequency with which, the barman, formerly Chief Sick Berth Petty Officer Allright R.N. gave me free drinks. The professional, a former James Braid pupil at Walton was Alf Perry, whom Allright also supported.

Finding that the bar profits, if any, were far less than expected, the Committee dismissed Chief Sick Berth Petty Officer Allright, who reappeared as the petrol pump attendant at the Woodcote Motor Co's garage in Church Street, Epsom. Whether Alf concentrated better on his game as an abstainer we cannot tell, but he proceeded to win the British Open at Muirfield in 1935 with a 283, as low a winning score as any achieved before. Nowadays, he would have been a millionaire: then, he just returned to his pokey little shed across the car park, close to where the roads divide, left for Esher, right for Kingston. When in May 1940 I was carried into Deal hospital, burnt and temporarily blinded at the hands of the Hun, who should be there dispensing stimulants but Chief Sick Berth Petty Officer Allright.

The course I came to know best was Tyrells Wood. A treat for a mountain goat, originally the 16th hole ended in front of the club house, so that rather than go 300 yards down the steep hill to the road and up to the clubhouse again, many friendly matches ended there. Though the numbers of the holes have been re- arranged since the war, it can still be claimed that nowhere can a level stance be found except on the tees at Tyrrell's Wood.

Besides local people such as the Kidstons a jolly crowd of London members appeared at week-ends. I remember Jack Sands a banker and his wife Norah, Gervase Bailey an architect, with daughter known as Grown Up Girlie, a handsome young Aubrey Lawrence from Hammersmith and the two Earl brothers Sebastian and Austin. No longer able to play, my father behind his Times became a fount of local gossip, the paper usually being upside down declared the members. One day somebody brought Kaye Don, the usually-leading racing motorist. He partnered me in a four ball with the terrifying stake of 10/- corners. I made sure we won!

Everybody appeared to smoke then and in golf clubs Churchman's No.1 cigarettes did a roaring trade. Each packet of ten contained one card with a picture and description of one hole on the Old Course at St. Andrews. Playing a full round were three different golfers; Mr. Tiger, handicap scratch, Mr. Average handicap 9 and Mr. Rabbit, handicap 18. Individual scores at each hole were printed on the cigarette cards, three players and eighteen holes making a pack of fifty four different cards. To receive a silver medal spoon one had to collect eighteen cards that totalled par, or bogey as it was called then.

David Meredith, the Secretary and his wife moved to Saunton in 1936 when the Saunton Sands hotel, owned by John Christie of Glyndebourne, had just been built making for more competitive golf at the Club.

SUB-LIEUTENANT THIRD CLASS TO MALTA

Stationed in Plymouth later, I enjoyed one or two week-ends with them in the Secretary's house above the links. David died of cancer some years after the war in which the courses were taken over by the Army. It was not until 1976 that a second 18 hole course was ready again, that incredibly hot dry summer being a disaster for its fairways.

Finally at Epsom the nearest golf course was the Woodcote, part of the RAC Country Club, where the swimming pool open to non- members was popular in the Summer.

By June my father, concerned that I had received no appointment from the Admiralty, wrote to Commander Sir Archibald Richard James Southby, Epsom's MP but, more to his satisfaction than to mine, my appointment to the battleship *Royal Sovereign* in the Mediterranean arrived on June 4. Two days earlier my mother, thinking it was time her younger son met some nice girls took me to a cocktail party at the Headmaster's house at Epsom College where Arnold Powell was the headmaster. The two families first met because my sister Brada and their daughter Joan, had at different times, been to Miss Penrose's finishing school in Florence. Joan and her friend Audrey Hills, looked attractive and jolly dispensing the drinks and their conversation sounded bawdy, so I found myself in suitable company reluctant to depart for Malta.

Passage orders from the Marine Department, Board of Trade requiring me to sail from Southampton at 11.15 on June 20 in s.s. Jervis Bay of the Aberdeen and Commonwealth Line, I caught the 0815 (steam) train from Waterloo and was very glad to see the familiar face of R. C. ("Tom") Burton on board the ship. He had been appointed to the battleship *Resolution*. Ships of this line plied regularly between Britain and Australia. We passed Gibraltar about 6p.m. on the Saturday and at 0800 the following Tuesday on a perfect cloudless day with the sea as calm as a mill pond, a flat fairy tale island rose slowly out of the mist. Though I was soon to hear various derogatory descriptions of Malta – such as 'hell's bells and smells' and 'a septic piece of grit' – this is the one that still lingers in the memory.

Anchoring in Grand Harbour about 1000 we were impressed to see among the mêlée of small craft, both *Royal Sovereign*'s and *Resolution*'s picket boats, which took us to our destinations as soon as the luggage had been found.

While these two battleships were to survive the war, it was the gallant *Jervis Bay* that made history. Converted into an armed merchant cruiser, she was escorting an Atlantic convoy of thirty seven ships in November 1939 when the German pocket battleship *Sheer* appeared. About 1700,

JUST A HOGG'S LIFE

Captain Fogarty Fegen R.N., commanding *Jervis Bay*, hoping that as darkness approached to gain time for ships of the convoy to disperse, engaged the *Sheer* at full speed with his old 6-inch guns. The one-sided fight lasted until 1800 when the *Jervis Bay* was on fire, sinking at 2000 with the loss of over two hundred officers and men. Captain Fegen, awarded the Victoria Cross posthumously, was among them. His aim had been partially achieved. Delayed, *Sheer* only had time to sink five ships of the convoy before retiring to Germany now that her position was known.

H.M.S. Jervis Bay. *National Maritime Museum, Greenwich.*

CHAPTER 13

The Tiddly Quid

Arriving on board the *Tiddly Quid*, for that was what the Ship's Company called HMS *Royal Sovereign*, I was led down to the Gunroom, which appeared to be a sardine tin in which the sardines were imbibing gin. A party was in progress to which I was welcomed. Soon however I was taken to meet the Commander Leonard Hammersley Bell, who explained that Brian Gallie had just got his second stripe and that I was to relieve him as Sub-Lieutenant in charge of the Gunroom.

My cabin, where I climbed into uniform for the first time since March 16, was just below the quarterdeck close to the Commander's, but inboard with no scuttle.

Members of the Gunroom were:

Midshipmen: Peek, Cody and Collins, Australians due to leave in August for courses in Britain.

Brewster, Skottowe, Gordon, Australians a year or so junior to those above.

Midshipmen: Phillips, Ellsworth, Bruce, Westmacott, Phillpotts, Williams, six Dartmouth Drakes temporarily away doing their time in destroyers.

Midshipmen: Brownrigg, Langridge, Benians, three Public School entries who had joined in January 1934.

Pay Midshipmen: Carter, Clements and (no relation) Clements.

From them I learned that this Gunroom was in every way quite the best on the station. Next I met my Divisional Officer Lieutenant Commander "Tatters" Drawbridge, who told me that his Forecastle men were quite the best Division in the ship, winning all the games and all the cups. We paced up and down as he outlined my duties as his assistant, stressing at short intervals the 100 per cent efficiency of my predecessor, Maitland-Makgill-Crichton.

Sailing next day for the First Summer Cruise, this my first night was a Gunroom guest night, three of the Midshipmen temporarily in destroyers being the principal guests. The food was good and the Maltese stewards excellent. The Gunnery Officer Patrick McLaughlin invited me to the Wardroom, expecting to meet my namesake Ian Hogg. McLaughlin

JUST A HOGG'S LIFE

had been doing the Staff Course at Greenwich when we were there as Sub-Lieutenants. Always jolly and good company, he was soon promoted, commanding the cruisers *Spartan* and *Swiftsure* during the war and retiring finally as a Rear-Admiral CB, D.S.O. after being Captain of HMS *Excellent* 1947-49.

Inevitably pulling regatta practice was now in full swing and at 0630 I found myself on trial in the Wardroom crew. Due to guest night liqueur brandy my mouth was so dry that after five minutes I could not speak. At 0930 feeling far from my best I was presented to Captain B. H. (Bertie) Ramsay, who wished me to continue running the Gunroom as Gallie had done, keeping the bills fairly low.

"Judging by last night – this will be difficult", I wrote in my journal. Yes, another journal! To my own astonishment I had drawn another S519 *Journal for the use of Midshipmen* determined to record what I actually did and thought and not what one was expected to do and think. It covers my time in the *Royal Sovereign* from June 1934 to March 1935, page after page of legible hand writing without erasures or blots. While I have written books since, from mines to wines, I have never been able to do this again. Can it be the Biro replacing the fountain pen or just early senility setting in?

Commander L.H. Bell   *Captain B.H. Ramsay*

THE TIDDLY QUID

Most of the Mediterranean Fleet comprising *Queen Elizabeth* (flagship) *Resolution* and *Royal Sovereign*, the 3rd Cruiser Squadron and three Destroyer flotillas headed East on Wednesday June 27. *Furious*, the aircraft carrier, was also in company, one of her planes 'ditching' near the tug *St. Issey* which recovered the crew and the damaged aircraft. In the Cyclades, the island group that includes Náxos, the Fleet split up, our destination being Syra among the smallest.

I am one of five Officers of the Watch in harbour, the others being Lieutenants Cunningham, Gallie, Bennett, Lieutenant Boothby of the Royal Marines making the fifth. Since a 24 hour day requires two of the five to keep alternate watches, this was almost a one day on, one day off routine.

Lieutenant-Commanders and the Senior Lieutenants formed the Officer of the Day's "Union" requiring one to be on board daily and he usually eased our burden by keeping the Morning Watch (0400 to 0800). In the Middle Watch (0000-0400) when nobody was about, a deck chair was permissible, but being responsible for order and safety, going the rounds occasionally was necessary.

We arrived at our next port of call Rhodes one fine morning at 0700. The island was then Italian. The Captain called on the Governor, the British Consul, the Italian Rear-Admiral and the Captain of the Port, salutes being fired. As Officer of the forenoon watch (0800-1200) the only other power boat at my disposal, required to bring off the Consul, broke down. The Captain of the Port arrived in an Italian boat with two Italian lieutenants, there being much bowing, heel clicking and shaking hands in a haze of perfume before they sat down in the Wardroom sipping Vermouths. The Consul, dear old man, his consular flag flying arrived in the canteen boat and his flag took some finding before he left The Captain calls on the Governor, who returns the call accompanied by an escort of the Captain of the Port and the two aforesaid Lieutenants.

My First watch (2000-0000) was enlivened just before midnight by the arrival of seven Italians and one of our stokers, who was very drunk. All but one of the Italians brought the stoker up to the Quarterdeck explaining simultaneously with much gesticulation what had occurred. One was the Chief of Police, the other his boy friend acting as liaison officer. It appeared that Stoker Basher had fought most of the town, raising several bars to the ground. Other bashers were still ashore.

We had now been joined on the Quarterdeck by Roberts-West, Officer of the Day, a Royal Marine escort (for the stoker), a Maltese messman to interpret and Gallie my relief. Having been taken to the ship's cells

JUST A HOGG'S LIFE

by the escort, where one of them would remain as sentry, the parlé began in earnest, no one stopping to draw breath. Finally we turned out a patrol of one Warrant officer, one Petty officer and twelve men, sending them ashore to bring off all the other offenders. All however was peace; only Captain Bass, in charge of the Royal Marine detachment on board, and our second medical officer, Surgeon Lieutenant, F.G.Y. Scovell were to be found on the jetty having missed the last boat.

Before going on a tour of the old town with its museum related to the Knights of St. John, we were shown new developments by the Fascists. These included a hospice where those with internal troubles bathed in or drank the waters. The effect was such that a house of a thousand latrines, 1st, 2nd and 3rd classes had been built fifty yards away. Quite a step in such circumstances we thought! We sipped the waters with caution, reflecting that one of the Fascists' tortures was to over-dose those they arrested with castor oil.

Our next port of call recalls James Elroy Flecker's 'old ships sailing like swans asleep...' "For Famagusta and the hidden sun, That rings black Cyprus with a lake of fire". The Captain's reaction to the chief port of Cyprus was to escape for two days to stay in the Governor's Summer Palace up in the cool of the Trudos mountains. Drawbridge announced that he would be off for four days and would I look out for his duties. "Guns" decided that 'A' Company, comprising No.1, 2 and 3 platoons should be landed on the hottest stretch of sand that he could find. Once there my No.1 Platoon and No. 2 were to attack No.3, which had taken up an impregnable position in some dunes. After advancing 300 yards over rough ground I was asked what my plan had been. A difficult question; I couldn't really say to change my religion to Quaker as soon as possible. So we all jumped in the sea and continued to jump when, back on board, Aquatic Sports began.

Five days later at 0830, earlier than expected, the Commander-in-Chief Admiral Sir William Fisher arrived with his wife and guests in the steam yacht *Bryony* which was provided for his use. Ideally the Officer of the Guard should have called immediately but Lieutenant Price R.M. needed time to dry a clean tunic. I then saw for the first time, and by no means the last, a Leonard Hammersley Bell tantrum. His face went black with rage and he proceeded to beat his right thigh with his telescope. It was astonishing to see an otherwise rather pleasant character make such an exhibition of himself. Perhaps he was suffering from stress; promotions to Captain were made twice yearly and he only had two more chances, on 31 December and 30 June the following year. This lack of self control could hardly have been overlooked in his confidential report written by his Captain and he was in fact passed over. Commanders, declares my journal, should be fitted with mirrors and in this particular case Price reached the yacht before she had secured alongside in the port.

The war however came to the rescue of many passed over Lieutenant Commanders and Commanders, who were promoted after being recalled to the colours. Bell, the son of a clergyman, eventually retired as a Captain CBE, living at Pyrton, Watlington where he died on 24 November 1985 in his ninety fourth year.

While we were at Famagusta, the cruiser *Devonshire* was visiting Sámos, the Greek island only a mile from the Turkish mainland. Unaware of any danger, three officers in a skiff were fired on by Turkish sentries, wounding one and killing the dentist, Surgeon Lieutenant Robinson. A first rate fellow he had captained the United Services second XV in Portsmouth and I knew him well. Our next port of call was Alexandria where I was greatly looking forward to seeing my sister and brother-in-law Jack Paterson, who was a Bimbashi (Captain) in the Egyptian Police Force. This visit was postponed; instead *Queen Elizabeth* arrived at midnight to embark the C-in-C and together we sailed for Samos at 17 knots. Arriving about 0630 on 17 June the *Queen Elizabeth* joined other units of the Fleet now on the far side of the island while we remained on the other.

In the afternoon when I was Officer of the Watch, our Royal Marine Postman told me he was going to the far side of the island with fleet mail, riding a donkey if necessary to cross the ten miles through the hills.

"I give him full marks" said Commander Bell, "That man would deliver the mail even if we were in the middle of the Sahara".

About 6 p.m. his mate returned saying he might be a bit late on the donkey but will flash a lamp or come in the canteen boat if it is inshore waiting. The Commander seemed pleased. But at 8pm a signal tells us to join the other ships at 0700 next morning. At 9pm, required on the quarterdeck, I was the cause of Tantrum No.2.

"What in heaven's name did I think I was doing allowing the postman to go ashore? How did I think he was going to get back in daylight? What boat was there to bring him off?. Did I think at all?"

The last question was answered by the questioner in the negative.

Next for a similar reprimand was the Paymaster Midshipman who in the absence of Joe Britton, the Captain's Secretary had approved the Postman's trip and finally Britton himself was harangued for allowing a call of nature to interfere with his duties.

JUST A HOGG'S LIFE

Keeping the middle watch I confess to feeling worried lest the worthy Marine had run into some trigger happy smuggler as in Bizet's Carmen, but fortunately at 1am *Queen Elizabeth* signalled his safe arrival at midnight.

The Foreign Office now decreed that no demonstration of force by the Fleet should take place. The Turkish sentries themselves could not be blamed; any boat could be regarded as a smuggler. Diplomacy assured that three days later a memorial service, with a Turkish destroyer joining *Queen Elizabeth* and *Devonshire*, was held where the accident occurred and the Turks paid £2000 to Robinson's relatives.

Alexandria was cancelled; instead, accompanied by the 3rd Destroyer flotilla, the recently built A class, we went North to Mudros, the port of the island of Lemnos, close to the entrance to the Dardanelles. Sixty miles from Gallipoli this had been the fleet's base in the Dardanelles campaign. The anchorage, surrounded by barren land, without a blade of grass, was stuffy and hot. To be sure of a cool night's sleep I jumped naked and alone off the gangway at midnight making sure the Commander had turned in. It was customary when in harbour in the heat of the Mediterranean summer to spread the fo'c'sle awning as well as the quarterdeck awning. There were also side screens over the officers' cabins aft and the Sick Bay forward. In principle they were like the blinds with which shops shield their windows from the sun, though with booms, martingales and topping lifts to manipulate, they were rather tricky to handle. The Commander, who had now become a serious case of promotionitis, decided that in addition to lowering ladders and getting out booms for boats, the two big awnings and the side screens should be spread at the drop of the anchor when we arrived at Milos, back in the Cyclades. Stokers, who were not seamen, had to be lent to help, the Engineer Commander co-operating with the Executive Commander. But as most tourists know, there is apt to be a strong wind in the Aegean in June and July. This one was on the beam and the Fo'c'sle awning was first torn on a cleat and then, ballooning, was torn up one seam. In his rage L.H. Bell stood on the quarterdeck watching a proper tangle with his back to the ladder, not noticing the little Greek contractor, who now tapped him on the shoulder. Turning round swinging his telescope fit to decapitate the intruder, the little man ducked and said, "Nice leetle ship you haff here, Commander!". It would have made a good H. M. Bateman cartoon.

Summoned by the Captain I found him - not unexpectedly - with the Gunroom Wine Book, observing that one midshipman had seventeen bottles of beer down to him on 26th June. "I can't think how they get it into their stomachs" he said. This was on the Guest night of my arrival when the culprit had two guests; seventeen glasses between them seemed modest drinking to me in midsummer Malta boxed up in a giant Esse cooker. However, I imposed weekly limits aiming to spread the fifteen shilling allowance more evenly from one end of the month to the other.

It is curious that while so many British warships are named from Greek mythology we never received any instruction in this subject so that Vice Admiral Forbes, our Divisional admiral flying his flag in *Resolution*, might have begun his two and a half day inspection by asking "Have you seen the Venus of Milo?" A serious Gunnery specialist, who later avowed that anti- aircraft guns would deal adequately with aircraft attacking the Fleet, he stuck to his subject. Fortunately all went well, with a pause for laughter when the Maltese were sent to pull a boat and one of the crew - no Etonian - tried to do it with his loom instead of the blade on the feather, the swing swing being anything but together.

The Venus - to save any reader looking it up as I have done - is the best statue of Aphrodite, found on the island in 1820 among the ruins of the theatre and destined for the Louvre. Three pleasant days remained for picnics and bathing, while the Commander led a few Wardroom and Gunroom stalwarts up the local mountain and down again in double quick time.

NAZI OCCUPATION

Ten years later, in October, 1944, I was to find myself at Milos once more in very different circumstances. Serving in the anti-aircraft cruiser *Black Prince* as Torpedo Officer we had done a Russian convoy, fought a night action off Brittany, formed part of the otherwise all American bombarding force off Utah beach for the first ten days of the Normandy invasion, dashed to the Mediterranean to support the South of France landings in August ending finally at Alexandria to help liberate Athens. This had been done on September 15, the Germans now being in retreat except for garrisons holding out in some of the islands.

At Milos a British officer made contact with the Garrison Commander, who agreed to surrender to a landing party of 200-300 men of the cruiser *Aurora* then en route from Alexandria. Reporting his intention to the German H.Q. at Salönika, resulted in the arrival, by seaplane, of a Nazi SS man to relieve the Commander, forty eight hours before the Aurora was due. That put an end to any surrender.

Stationed out of sight on the South side of the island, Aurora spent a week trying to destroy the Germans' batteries, well protected by concrete, on the North side. We spent another week, with aircraft from a small carrier spotting.

"Friday 3 November. Extract from my letter home.
We have sat at anchor since Monday close inshore, except yesterday when we put to sea and fuelled from the carrier Emperor, 'Guns' has had a marvellous week continually bombarding and is in a trance with it all. No.1 target, the six inch battery, is still in order despite our efforts. Possibly two of its four guns are out of action. The other battery 88mm is constantly reported deserted by the aircraft and in action by the military. The Germans take cover until they are certain aircraft are not about and then fire a few rounds. Our landing parties were to have taken this battery on each of the last few nights, but the Greek Commander didn't agree with the British. A few heavy bombers would do the trick but the authorities do not want to kill Greeks as well as Germans.

We have two German prisoners on board, who were members of the 88mm battery's crew. They slunk away, giving themselves up after their N.C.O. had threatened them with a pistol for wanting to surrender. One says his wife and children live in Wilhelmshaven, bombed out with one child killed.

After two cruisers had each expended an outfit of ammunition to no purpose, it was decided to withdraw. I kept the Middle Watch, the vigil improved by my friend, Paul Wilson the Senior Engineer, appearing on the bridge with a bottle of stout, its colour in the moonlight looking like cocoa. As well the Captain did not appear, calling for a 'cupper'.

After weeks of blood, toil, tears and sweat, the first named from sliding our bottoms over wooden thwarts, three battleships, one aircraft carrier, three County class cruisers, five light cruisers, a Submarine depot ship and various destroyers assembled at Navarino on August 10 and 11 for the Fleet Pulling Regatta. This bay, West of Cape Matapan the southern most point of the Greek mainland, lies where the coast turns North, near the town of Pylos. Completely sheltered it is semi circular and about four miles long, ideal for this regatta. Though *Royal Sovereign* won six of the twenty three races, with four seconds, *Queen Elizabeth*, the Fleet flagship won The Cock on points, with *Furious* second and *Royal Sovereign* third.

The First Summer Cruise now ended with the Fleet returning to Malta. From various ships a score of Sub-Lieutenants and Midshipmen, including me, selected for the 14 day Short Air Course took passage in the

THE TIDDLY QUID

Furious. There were no spare cabins so, most degrading, it was back to a chest and a hammock. But before entering Grand Harbour, pilots flew off their aircraft to Halfar, the aerodrome six miles away from Valletta on the south coast, vacating cabins which made us comfortable. The course began with an amusing lecture on Photography from a Senior Observer, Lieutenant Commander Camidge; weighing nearly twenty stone we wondered how he fitted into any Fairy III F. Bobby Burton was among those doing the course so together we climbed into the Observer's and Telegraphist's positions behind the pilot, a small RAF chap who said, "No funny business!", before giving us a fifty minute flight round the island. The Mess accommodating the pilots was a delightful stone building beautifully cool, with a grand view out to sea. The food too was excellent.

The next day I was alone in a Torpedo bomber, except for the pilot, Lieutenant Skene, Royal Marines carrying out a torpedo attack on a destroyer. It took us forty minutes to climb to 12,000 feet and about forty seconds to dive down to 15 feet and drop our torpedo. I was advised beforehand that in bumpy weather diving was so unpleasant that I might jump out – others had done so before! Hastily I attached to my person the small wire pendant provided, but the need to hold one's nose and blow down it to equalise the pressure on both sides of the ear drums was rather a trial. During our next flight back again in a III F. we were to take photographs with a camera worth £250 thrust into my hands. Leaning out pointing this thing at ships and such like was a precarious business, one 'Hank' Rotherham, in charge of the course, writing cryptic comments on the back of my endeavours such as: *Too too terrible. Will send you a better one of a wing if you like* and *Am not fond of it*.

After lunch Boothby, Royal Sovereign's Royal Marine Subaltern and I were to go up and find the wind force and direction. "To hell with that", said the Flight Commander on the airfield, "I must show you how to put on your safety belts. You're going to need 'em". Once airborne he began with stalls, turns, dives, spins and I do not know what else. Everything from sky to earth went round and round until I just had to keep looking inside the cockpit, to avoid passing out. His landing too was spectacular; side-slipping in and the machine rolling from side to side all over the place.

The following day Burton and I volunteered for another III F flight, the alternative in an Osprey sounding the more unpleasant. Again our pilot was the same fellow known generally as Rastus. My safety belt firmly secured and the £250 camera forgotten lest it should fall out, we dived from 1000 to 10 feet, flying flat out round the island at that height. But this Rastus landing was docile – like that of a novice. With a nonchalant gesture he explained that he'd been a bit rough and some of the controls had come to pieces in his hand, leaving him with only his knees to manipulate the stick. I think my pen was still shaking when, two days later, we completed the course with an essay declaring whether we might be joining the Fleet Air Arm. Cole Porter currently supplied my answer:

> *I get no kick in a plane*
> *Flying so high with Rastus in the sky*
> *Is my idea of wind up the flue.*

Three years later serving in the carrier *Glorious*, Lieutenant-Commander Rastus Carnduff fell out with his superiors, the Wing Commander and the Captain, Bruce Fraser, who was the kindest of men. He was not recommended for promotion to Commander, though after the war began, he did make it to Commander under a war service concession.

During this course *Royal Sovereign*'s three senior Australian midshipmen had taken their exams for Lieutenant with Peek gaining a first class, Cody and Collins each a second. By way of celebration they took me for my first 'run ashore' in Malta. A popular place for junior officers was Captain Caruana's bar, though what he captained I cannot imagine unless it was a dghaisa. Next came a mixed grill at the Great Britain Hotel and then a film at the Manoel Theatre. After that there was a three fold choice of night spots, so close together in the Strada Stretta that calling on all three was not unusual.

The most exclusive was *Rexford*'s with lots of girls, a band playing dance tunes and stacks of sherry glasses full up on the bar counter awaiting consumption. These were coloured water, price ten pence a glass, which the girls chose if offered a drink, so they at any rate stayed sober. We all drank beer, preferably British, the local Farson's brews being relatively poor.

The *Moulin Rouge* was much the same with a number of persons equipped with musical instruments termed a band by the management. They did not seem to mind turns by the customers such as Bobby Burton, his shipmate Bertie Lyddon and a chorus of *Resolution* midshipmen singing "Dinah", "The Birth of the Blues", "Wagon Wheels" and "Home on the Range".

The third spot much smaller was *Jazz Varieties* better known as *Aunties*. It was Drawbridge who told me Auntie's story. After giving me supper in the Wardroom one night, he sat down at the piano when the mess was deserted. Having a sister ten years older than myself, I knew most of the tunes of the Twenties which he reeled off one after the other. "Swanee", Japanese Sandman", "Hot Lips", "I'm just wild about Harry".... you name it, Tatters Drawbridge would play it.

Auntie and her sister Patsy were the Lavender sisters in a touring company which came out to Malta. When it broke up, passage money home was offered but the two sisters, deciding to stay, set up a dance hall. During the boom years of the early Twenties, Auntie ran "The Pavilion" in Strada Reale, the main street and no visitor however distinguished failed to pay her a call. An ordinary pub up to closing time at 10 p.m., it then became a night club until the small hours with profits reaped by day and night.

A gradely lady from Lancashire, she made the one mistake of marrying an R.N. Warrant Telegraphist, who was a real rotter. There were two children both deformed; one with a withered arm now grown up, the other Sonny, fourteen with a deformed hip and a limp. The Warrant Telegraphist, a bigamist, married again, this third child also having a deformity.

With Auntie presiding behind her little bar, always wearing a summer hat reminiscent of a herbaceous border, anybody could do anything they pleased within reason. Luigi the pianist would play anything over three months old. You could lean against the bar smoking the foulest of pipes, without compulsion to buy drinks for resident staff and prices were not exorbitant - not even for 'sherries' or 'sticky green' waters that pretended to be *Crème de menthe*.

There were at this time only three artists. Hazel married to an Engine Room Artificer could tap dance and put over a song. Babs a huge blonde who should have been more at home as an animal trainer in a circus, and "Turkish", no oil painting but compulsive viewing in her extra special belly dance that required a double jointed navel to shoot in and out like a recoiling gun.

Auntie's two Hungarian girls, Betty and Annie had just been deported after some officers in hospital had attributed their venereal disease to sleeping with the former. Auntie would deny this possibility showing her patrons duplicate copies of health certificates signed by leading doctors in Malta, which she kept in an old cigar box.

Most of the girls in these places, some of whom were very attractive, declared they were of aristocratic Hungarian families. Their husbands had been brutal or unfaithful, forcing them to go abroad. Following the Fleet presumably, they were to be found in 'the joints' of Alexandria, Malta, Oran and Gibraltar.

JUST A HOGG'S LIFE

The air course, which had been enjoyable and instructive, ended on Friday August 24th with only five days to go before our departure on the Second Summer Cruise. The three remaining Australians, Skottowe, Gordon and Brewster, left to do their destroyer time in *Boadicea* and other 'B' class destroyers. Brian Gallie departed home in the cruiser *Shropshire* in September. To my regret we never met again, but surviving the 1939-45 war, he retired and settled in Portugal with his wife and children.

The family bought a convent in the Minho near Barcelos converting it into a fine house, where his widow, his son Piers with his wife and children still live. It is now one of the ancient manors that accept paying guests under a Government scheme. The Portuguese Tourist office, 1-5 New Bond Street, London W1Y ODB - 071-493-3873 can supply the latest information.

Another change was the arrival of David MacPhail to relieve Roberts-West as Lieutenant (G). After being Hon. Secretary of the United Services Rugby Club in Portsmouth, his masterly control of the ship's 6 inch armament, with my invaluable assistance, would shortly win a competitive shoot as I shall relate.

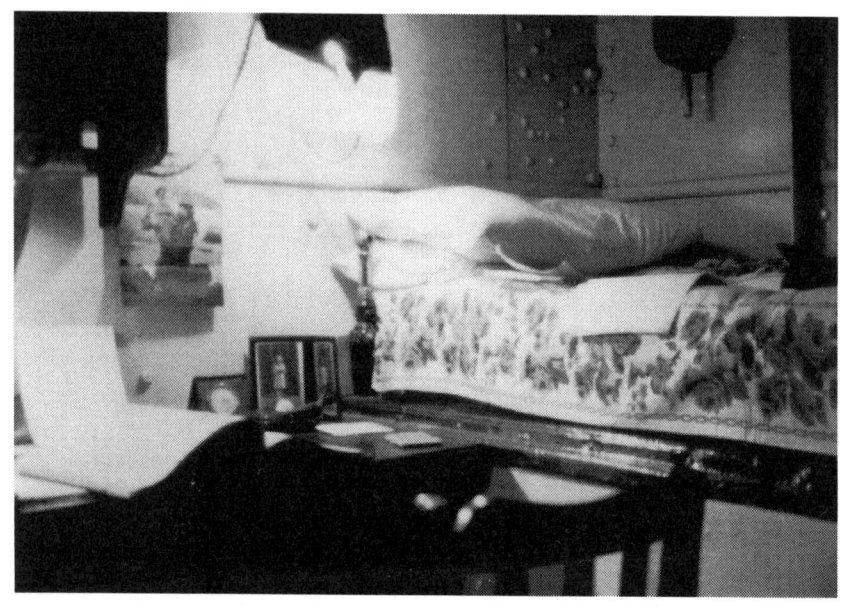

The author's cabin on board HMS Royal Sovereign.

THE TIDDLY QUID

Auntie (with stick), proprietor of Malta's Jazz Varieties, *on holiday in the English Lake District with her sister Patsy.*

The Tiddly Quid, modelled in wafers by the Captain's Cook, Christmas 1934.

CHAPTER 14

AN IMPOTENT SCENE SHIFTER

Place	*Arrive*	*Depart*
Malta		29 August
Susak	1 September	10 September
Brioni	10 September	19 September
Olib	19 September	24 September
Makarska	25 September	1 October
Gulf of Drin	2 October	12 October
Kotor	12 October	22 October
Malta	25 October	

This was *Royal Sovereign*'s programme for the Second Summer Cruise and we reached Susak on the afternoon of Saturday September 1. On the coast at the North end of the Gulf of Quarnero (Kvarner on later maps) Susak was in Croatia, separated by a small river and its bridge, from Fiume, the Italian frontier town. Bristling with customs officers and other officers from both countries, we were unable, without passports, to cross the bridge to see Fiume.

But being only eighty miles from Zagreb, the Croat capital and University town, fifty members of the English speaking club came to see *Royal Sovereign* and imbibe either tea or cocktails (some pretty potent White Ladies) on the Quarterdeck. Among them was the British Consul, who was only too pleased to supply British passports for £1 each to those who had already acquired the necessary photographs from P.O. Stamp, the ship's photographer.

Though the ship's football team lost a close match with Susak F.C., the local beer was repulsive and we were glad to move on to the island of Brioni (off Istria close to Pola then Italian territory) about sixty miles from Susak. With its lovely pine woods and really green grass, not to be seen in Malta, the island looked enchanting. Captain D3 in *Codrington*, departing with half his flotilla, signalled that they had enjoyed a grand time as the other half - *Active, Acasta, Achates* and *Anthony* arrived to take their place.

A walk ashore with Ripley, a Captain in the Cheshire regiment at Malta who had joined us for the cruise, showed Brioni's three attractions to be the hotel on the water's edge with an unusual gambling machine, the golf course, (green fee 10 lire a day [3s 4d] with its own club house) and an excellent soccer pitch.

The "big pots" from Pola came to call the first morning, the Mayor leading up the gangway in a terrific black hat which could have doubled as a lampshade. Next the local General, whose coloured uniform contrasted strongly with the civilians, was followed by a gentleman in a black shirt, black plus-fours, black stockings, black shoes complete with black Hitler-type moustache. The remainder were naval officers with one in morning dress mistaking Brioni for Ascot it seemed.

Three times the band played *Garb of old Gaul*, the tune laid down for civilian dignitaries, followed each time by *Gioveneza*, the national song Mussolini had laid down for Fascist Youth, the entire procedure being repeated when they departed. All this to the delight of Leading Seaman Ruffell, the ship's caricaturist who captured the scene for the main noticeboard.

At golf the Navy lost by one match to Brioni, whose team included three ladies all winning their matches. Perhaps Brioni was something of a women's world. Playing a soccer trial game our sailors were surprised

The hotel at Brioni.

JUST A HOGG'S LIFE

when they had to stop and give way for a Ladies Polo match. Becoming spectators their remarks on what was indeed a real cake and arse party – the latter mainly to the fore – were a joy to hear.

Another sporting activity was a Round the Island Bicycle Race between the *Royal Sovereign*'s midshipmen and those in the four destroyers. It sounded about as straight as Siena's celebrated *Il Palio* horse race. The destroyers' men won, having arrived first to pick the best cycles, while most of the competitors seem to have arrived back at the start within ten minutes of leaving it.

With beer at 1s.6d a glass and fresh milk from a cow 3d, rumours that the hotel's prices were high proved to be untrue. Apart from the weather, which was mainly overcast and sometimes wet, our genial week at Brioni was memorable, never to be repeated, because Istria became Yugo-Slav territory after the war; Marshal Tito, the country's dictator, using the whole island for his own private enjoyment.

An annual feature in the Fleet had long been the Midshipmens' Crash Cutter Race, but this year, with fewer midshipmen a Crash Whaler Race was decreed. Asked by the Commander to coach, I had chosen the crew and taken them away once so far. Whalers were to start at anchor with 25 fathoms of grapnel inboard and the 20 fathom mark stopped forward of the tack hook. The awning was to be spread with the crew laying on their oars. Then at the Order 'Go' :-

1. Boat oars, weigh anchor, furl awning and sail to line BB about 1000 yards away.

Makarska.

2. At BB down mast and sails, out oars and pull to line CC about 600 yards.
3. At CC boat oars and sail to line DD about 1000 yards.
4. At DD down mast and sails, spread awning and pull to the finish about 600 yards. Total distance about two nautical miles.

Having one whaler but no cutters, this Obstacle race was always a feature of destroyers' sailing regattas. Their officers however, were not going to give away any hints on the best tactics, because there were enough midshipmen training in destroyers to form at least one entry. Commander L. H. Bell however asked Mr. Bawler, the Boatswain to interest himself in the matter so together we – mostly he! – devised a cunning combination of a Wire pendant and some halliards, which on the order 'Down mast and sails' caused the mast to slacken the pendant allowing the sail to slide down. When getting up mast and sails the reverse happened. Tried out, it worked a treat. The crew as selected was: Clements G. (bow) Westmacott, Clements F, Phillpotts, Phillips (Stroke) Bruce (Coxswain).

Within a week Bruce had dropped a 6 inch shell on his hand when practising loading drill so he was out. Next F. Clements crushed a finger between the whaler and a cutter during practice and he was out. Brownrigg, a big fellow took his place and Langridge I selected as coxswain 'although he will never have the slightest ability to take charge of a crew!'

From Brioni the ship went south along the Dalmatian coast, joined by Captain D3 in *Codrington* with the other four destroyers of his flotilla at Olib, a small island South of Rab, a better known resort. Our next stop was Makarska, the resort on the mainland thirty miles south of Split. Attractive with white houses among the green pine trees, the mountains rose steeply to 4000 feet behind them. Out of sight the 6000 foot peak said to be the highest in Yugo-Slavia lay further inland.

The Commander was in excellent form. After a colossal tantrum about a picket boat, in which "Odd's blood!" was heard several times as he stamped his feet and belaboured himself with the telescope, he went a-climbing next morning taking with him Martin Price (Royal Marine Officer No. 2) "Wiggie" Bennett and a Lieutenant Commander Moore, recently joined. Not only did they climb the 4000 footer but the 6000 as well.

In these last ten days of September, boats had been sailed to prepare for a sailing regatta at Split, while the Crash Whaler's crew seemed to be trained to the satisfaction of the Commander, not to mention those fictitious characters, Sir Charles, me and the Boatswain. When the fleet assembled at Split on October 1 we were confident, but there was no wind

JUST A HOGG'S LIFE

and no sailing on the second day. On the third day "Fierce raged the tempest", *Resolution* winning two team races with *Royal Sovereign* last.

On Thursday October 4 even rougher weather caused the Crash whaler race to be postponed. Instead, at short notice, the midshipmen raced for the Beresford Cup in gigs, galleys, and whalers, which in the case of *Royal Sovereign* were not lowered and rigged before 0830, so that some of their crews had not even reached the starting line when the race began at 0900.

At 1300 came a signal confirming that the Crash Whaler race would start at 1530, Course X. Nobody seemed to know where and what course X was. After sailing all morning the whaler had been hoisted full of water with all gear wet. Ready by 1500 the Picket Boat, with Captain, Commander and myself in the stern sheets, together with the whalers' crew trying to keep warm, towed it for about half an hour to the starting line away to windward.

Near the start *London*'s towing boat had broken down so *London*'s whaler, with its crew, secured itself to ours. Two competing boats were missing, nor was there any sign of a starter or judge. He arrived at 1600 by which time we were all cold and miserable. He went round the boats declaring that it was too deep to anchor and that when he fired a rocket they should cast to starboard. The depth in fact was only thirteen fathoms.

As each coxswain held up his flag to indicate 'Ready', London's whaler was still secured to ours, its Cox oblivious of our shouts to let go. At this point the Captain noticed the wind was on our starboard bow, ensuring that our whaler would be cast to port by the wind. Before this could be corrected the rocket was fired.

The start was as ridiculous as it was sudden; no attempt had been made to get the whalers into line and ours was still made fast to the Picket Boat. As the Captain had foreseen our whaler paid off to port. The sail tended to be blown on to the block of the halliards and, sure enough, the bight became caught up in the block. Easy to clear in practice but not in half a gale. There was a delay before the mainsail was set, the Captain not improving matters with, "Didn't I say so" and "I knew it would happen". The coxswain, Langridge, doing his best to ship his mizzen mast, looked as if he and the mizzen might be blown over the side together. Meanwhile, with nobody holding the tiller the whaler sped at a terrific pace 120° off course. Last but one, the crew derived some satisfaction from the destroyer's whaler, in which the Australians, Gordon, Skottowe and Brewster, who had looked pleased with themselves at the start, were clearly going to be last. The winners were the cruiser *Devonshire* with *Queen Elizabeth* second, a crew that in practice had looked inferior to ours.

Surveying the scene in general the Captain declared, "This is the most disgraceful exhibition I have ever seen". Had he been referring to the efforts of the organisers I should have agreed heartily, but it seemed quite clear he was not. Phillips, Phillpotts and Elsworth signalled congratulations to the victors, their message being A & M Hymn numbers which, when decoded, revealed first lines such as, *Fierce raged the tempest oe'r the deep,* and *All things are thine, no gift have we.*

My own feelings were that my elders and betters with previous experience of Mediterranean weather might have advised me to practise for tempest as well as for calm, dispensing with the Boatswain's special pendant and halliards for the former. As well for Mr. Bawler that he was not present with us in the picket boat. He might never have received all the recommends that brought him finally to be Master Rigger of Portsmouth dockyard.

Next day the weather had moderated for the Commander-in-Chief's cup won by the first boat to finish, a gig sailed - as you might have guessed - by A. B. Cunningham now Rear-Admiral (D) flying his flag in the cruiser *Coventry*.

Between whiles there was plenty of inter-ship visiting by Wardroom and Gunroom officers. My namesake Ian Hogg brought the golf champion Hugh Sheffield over for a gin; Gordon ("Wullie") McKendrick paid me a call from his destroyer *Boadicea*. Throughout our time at Dartmouth he had always been top of our term, and then gained five good Firsts as a Sub-Lieutenant. Starting school at Edinburgh Academy, he always said he learnt nothing at Dartmouth until his fifth term.

Back at Dartmouth in 1937 as a House (formerly Term) officer he developed a brain tumour and was not fit for sea service until 1942. Commanding destroyers in the Home Fleet, he married in 1944 Hilda, widow of Walter Starkie, A. B. Cunningham's Flag Lieutenant in the first years of the war, who had been killed off Crete in 1941 when his destroyer *Juno* was sunk by bombs.

They had a son, who became a Doctor and a daughter. All seemed well when he retired as a Commander in 1958, but the tumour returned. He lost his voice and his hearing; nursed by a devoted wife, he died on 31 December 1978.

On Tuesday 9 October, when we were at Stari Grad, an island South of Dubrovnik, we heard that King Alexander of Yugo-Slavia had been assassinated in Marseille, together with the French Foreign Minister M. Barthou. The King had arrived in the British-built Yugo-Slav flotilla leader *Dubrovnik* and the two men were in a procession of cars going at walking pace through the streets to a function, watched by large crowds, before leaving for talks in Paris. The assassin, breaking through the crowd, mounted the running board of their car firing shots at point blank range killing the King immediately. M. Barthou died a few hours later. The King's son Peter, aged eleven, then at a Surrey preparatory school, succeeded to the throne.

Further news revealed that the murderer was a Croat, born in Zagreb. His automatic pistol also killed a Press photographer and wounded others in the crowd. Mauled by the crowd the murderer died of sabre wounds. While our Commander-in-Chief Sir William Fisher went in *Achates* to Split to offer the Fleet's sympathy, his battleships were practising their anti-aircraft High Angle fire before Furious departed for England. *Royal Sovereign* won the trophy, a pleasing present to mark the day, 11 October, the ship had commissioned two years before.

On Sunday 14th the Fleet, including four battleships, anchored off Split fired a 21 gun salute at minute intervals while the *Dubrovnik* bearing the King's coffin steamed slowly into the harbour followed by the ancient cruiser, *Dalmatia* and smaller craft. Yugo-Slav planes flew overhead trailing black streamers. Two French Tourville class cruisers escorting *Dubrovnik*, anchored ahead of us. British officers and men were fallen in on deck as for Sunday divisions from 0600 to 0730.

At 0700 a second 21 gun salute was fired as the coffin was disembarked for the people to file past until 1000. Four senior officers from each of our ships landed to join them. After 1000 and a last 21 minute gun salute, the coffin was taken in a special train to Belgrade.

At 1130 our Battle Squadron departed in spectacular fashion steaming in line ahead parallel to the coast line before turning 90° seawards in succession; though with every door shut in the streets and every blind down, there must have been few spectators. Returning on board our own officers estimated that fifty thousand people had been present, all dressed in black with every fourth man or woman in tears.

We fell in once more for another 21 minute gun salute at 1000 on Thursday 18th during the King's funeral in Belgrade. Attending the funeral the tall distinguished figure of Sir William Fisher - known in the Fleet as The Great Agrippa - made a great impression; his welcome, we were given to understand, exceeded that given to Goering, the Nazi Field Marshal to his ill- unconcealed displeasure.

Writing this in December 1991 when the Serbian army, pounding the Croats, has failed to obey Cease Fire after Cease Fire, agreed by politicians on both sides, I am appalled that the strong American and British naval forces in the Mediterranean have not even been offered to the United Nations. A carrier strike should have stopped the Serbs in their tracks; possibly a mere presence off the Dalmation coast would have been enough.

Exercises on the way back to Malta began with a night destroyer attack on the battle squadron. I had taken to wondering whether their purpose was to cram as many officers on to the Bridge as possible. 'Guns' was there telling the Principal Control officers what to do. 'Torps' was there telling me, the Searchlight Control officer what to do, though he really had a full time job thinking up technically worded excuses for the short comings of the searchlights to offer the Captain. When war came, in night action switching them on gave away a ship's position. Firing star shell did not.

One afternoon the C-in-C ordered: "Officer of the Watch manoeuvres, turning in succession with precision." Opportunities for young officers to handle big ships were rare and I was glad when the Captain selected Macphail, another Lieutenant and myself. I did three turns one of 90°, two of 180° with commendable precision but getting back into line ahead was not so easy. *Revenge* had already missed us by a biscuit's toss.

Full Power trials came next in which the four 'battle-wagons' thundered along at about twenty knots. *Queen Elizabeth* and *Revenge* went ahead slightly, while we claimed a twenty five foot win in a tussle with *Resolution*.

Royal Sovereign had been fitted with a catapult and crane right aft from which a seaplane was flown off and recovered on completion of its mission. Our pilot was Lieutenant Simon Borrett, a quiet but likeable character, who now flew off to Halfar for the last time in this commission, since the Mediterranean in winter was unsuitable for seaplane recovery. He re-appears as a Lieutenant Commander commanding a Swordfish squadron in *Courageous* when she was torpedoed and sunk by the U-boat on Sunday 17 March 1939. Charles Lamb, one of that squadron's pilots, describes in his *War in a Stringbag* how he and others pulled Simon, almost drowned, on board the destroyer *Impulsive*. And, moreover, how Simon recovered to re-form and train another Swordfish squadron. His life ended peacefully on 1 February 1992, aged 87.

Thursday 25 October was devoted to St. Barbara – the patron saint of Gunnery. After hoisting out our boats off Grand Harbour early, we went out to sea again for 15 inch and 6 inch competitive shooting, the former at two Battle Practice targets, the latter at one. Ammunition allowed; 15 inch – 10 rounds per turret, 6 inch – 10 rounds per gun. Order of Firing (drawn for) *Revenge, Royal Sovereign, Resolution, Queen Elizabeth*. We ex-

JUST A HOGG'S LIFE

pected to win the 15 inch, having straddled the target about seven times out of ten. But our 6 inch shoot was not so good. The results, announced a week later, gave *Queen Elizabeth* the 15 inch because our A turret had failed to fire two rounds and Y turret one. Having been the most accurate, this caused some ill feeling, mitigated however by being awarded first in the 6 inch. Perched somewhere above the bridge Macphail and I controlled this shoot. Half way through he said to me "Rate wants opening". By the time I had figured out what I was supposed to do ammunition had been expended. Analysis showed the rate did not want opening. Hogg's time-lag had won the prize!

From November when the rains came, to February when the C-in-C usually wanted a little rough shooting (shot guns not 15 inch) the Fleet stayed at Malta refitting the ships, with plenty of recreation for the ships' companies. There were competitive soccer, rugger and hockey matches, the rain made golf and racing feasible at the Marsa and the Malta Amateur Dramatic Club came to life. On board the ships themselves thanks largely to the efforts of Lord Louis Mountbatten, the Royal Naval Film Corporation supplied better films, shown and exchanged for others week by week. No wireless set (radio) was any good inside a ship but the Gunroom

Battle Squadron competitive shoot won by Royal Sovereign. *Photo by HMS* Chrysanthemum, *towing the targets.*

gramophone kept us up to date with London musicals. Records of *Streamline*, C. B. Cochran's latest, sent us by Midshipman Hunter RNVR were awaiting our return. The libretto by A.P. Herbert included a skit on Gilbert and Sullivan with music as charming as Sullivan's by Ronald Jeans. Hunter a great asset to the mess, had gone home from Brioni, hoping to start his career at the Bar preferably in Scotland.

In mid November I went down with some sort of fever usually known as Malta Dog. The PMO (Principal Medical Officer) prescribed a 50/50 mixture of castor oil and brandy and after a few days in bed my temperature was back to normal. Dashing to WC's frequently was not funny because the ship was in the floating dock its WCs being at the bottom of innumerable iron ladders. To be avoided at all costs was being sent to Bighi, the naval hospital, where they took test after test eliminating possibilities until the complaint had probably died a natural death. My complaint said the PMO was a mild attack of Para- Typhoid, not unlikely with the pollution that ships created in the tideless, innermost sea.

Thursday November 28 was declared a special Make and Mend to mark the wedding in Westminster Abbey of Prince George, youngest son of King George and Queen Mary to Princess Marina of Greece. The broadcast of the service came over well on the set in the Warrant Officers' Mess and ships in Grand Harbour were illuminated that night. The Royal Navy was often called the best club in the world and in Malta it had two excellent meeting places, the Union Club in Valletta's main street and the Sliema Club with good bathing off the rocks. A fine spacious old building, the Union Club had a big lower bar, an ample dining room above it and a number of chambers that could be booked for a night or two. Most Wardroom and Gunroom officers were members, paying a monthly subscription related to rank and charged on mess bills. Lady guests could be entertained in a set of separate rooms known as 'The Snakepit'. Among those I met in the lower bar were Eddie Baines, Exmouth - Destroyer *Antelope*, 'Jock' Gray, Anson - who joined the cruiser *Devonshire* on 3 December and Peter Gretton , Greynvile - joining the old cruiser *Durban* after a spell in the Royal yacht *Victoria & Albert* in Portsmouth. Life there he described as a month on leave and a fortnight on board, which did not preclude the occasional day visit to London. His duties on Sunday were particularly onerous - two rounds at Hayling in a foursome comprising his shipmates: Engineer Commander Jock MacKenzie, Lieutenant Commander D. P. Evans, formerly both popular Dartmouth Staff officers, Engineer Lieutenant-Commander Bachie Rebbeck and Lieutenant P.

JUST A HOGG'S LIFE

W. Gretton. Practising for the Navy v Army golf match no doubt, their respective handicaps were 3, 4, 5 and 6.

A jolly and unusual week for me began at 0545 on Monday December 10. Wearing black gaiters with a walking stick I was second in command of a Company of sailors going by boat to the Ricasoli Pistol Range at the North East corner of Grand Harbour, where I was to be in charge during a week of Pistol shooting practices. With Gunners' Mates to assist me I had little to do but to say "Carry on" and practise myself whenever there was a spare place. A best score of 188 out of 210 seemed satisfactory. The second half of the week we switched to the Rifle range. On the last day Tom Dimmock, our Torpedo Gunner took over the range while lots of officers appeared to do the course. To score 31 out of a possible 40 in a rapid firing test of ten rounds seemed good, but my 69 out of 100 in the main event was disappointing.

On Wednesday December 12 The *Times* announced the engagement of R.A.W. Dobbs (Bill) to Ann Stoker of Seaview, Isle of Wight, the first of our Greynvile term to become engaged. The *Times of Malta* announced the arrival of David MacPhail's fiancée. But the social event of the year was an invitation I received to dine with The Governor and Lady Campbell at San Antonio Palace, their residence outside Valletta. Baffled, I had no idea why I had been asked. The satirical Gunroom said quite obviously that I was the best looking Sub-Lieutenant in the Fleet. Donning my civilian dinner jacket just back from the cleaners in time, a taxi-driver going like Jehu got me to the Palace on time to be greeted by H.E., Lady Campbell and Jean their daughter. A dull dame, several military men with their wives, the old Maltese Baroness Inguanez and Mark Matthews the Governor's A.D.C, completed the party. After some rather unusual thick white cocktails I had Jean on my left at dinner and the dull dame on my right. The food and the wines were excellent but I did have an unfortunate mishap when helping myself to a delicious ice pudding. Half of it skidded into the dull lady's lap just as H. E. was asking how was her squash – the game not the pudding. From my left the lovely Jean said I was just the sort of person they needed in the Malta Amateur Dramatic Club; I would join wouldn't I ? The thought of playing Romeo to her Juliet being irresistible; of course I joined, finding myself in due course carrying a huge sofa, too big to lift through the trap door of the stage, round Valletta's very large opera house with fellow scene shifter 'Closet' Moss, who had a laugh that sounded like one.

When the ladies had left the table H.E.'s talk turned to horses, which was only to be expected as he had won the Grand National in his day.

AN IMPOTENT SCENE-SHIFTER

It took sometime to discover that my grandmother, Blanche Hulton, had been his friend, so she had written to him saying she had a grandson in the *Royal Sovereign*. A great one for writing, her bold hand using a conspicuous mauve ink established firm friendships with golfers, croquet players, Double Gloucester cheese enthusiasts and competitors in The *Observer*'s Sunday acrostic puzzles. Conversation was less successful; she became very deaf and was apt to reply 'Don't insult the Prince of Wales!' when you had merely said, "Have another small whisky, Granny ?"

After dinner we all went to see Elisabeth Bergner in the film *Catherine the Great*, occupying two boxes at the Manoel theatre, where the seats were as hard as a steel deck. Seeing Mark politely taking the hardest, I felt sure I would never make a good A.D.C.

In my twenty five years between leaving Dartmouth and retiring at my own request, I was lucky to spend only six Christmases away from home. This one in 1934 was the first. The others were 1936 H.M.S. *Glorious* at Malta, 1943 H.M.S. *Black Prince* at Scapa, 1944 H.M.S.*Black Prince* at Trincomalee, 1948 and 1949 H.M.S. *Birmingham* at Trincomalee.

Escorted by Peterson and Wiggie Bennett the Commander went ashore on Christmas Eve to buy presents. Peterson was a genial Lieutenant Commander, whose hair had gone sheet white having seen something nasty in the wood shed along the Yangtse so it was believed. Being in charge of a 15 inch turret, he and a Gunner's mate drew the keys daily to inspect the turret's magazine and shell room. On one occasion the Gunner's mate thinking Peterson had completed the inspection and left these compartments, locked up and departed himself returning the keys to the keyboard sentry. Poor Petersen beat upon the bulkhead at frequent intervals, hoping that a stoker perhaps would be working in the compartment on the other side. Not until next morning did this happen. The stoker went up to the Engineer's office to report a mysterious tapping. The Senior Engineer went down with the stoker to investigate; there was not a sound. A second time fortunately did coincide with Peterson's tapping leading to his release.

All Bennetts are "Wiggie" just as all Clarks are "Nobby". Our delightful character had risen from the ranks i.e., Boy, Ordinary Seaman, Able Seaman, to be a Mate (equal to a Sub- Lieutenant). Having left school at fourteen, this was no sinecure, with examinations to pass, both educational and professional. Later in 1940 when he had become the Torpedo Officer in the destroyer *Cossack* , commanded by the redoubtable Captain

Philip Vian, he would relate how one day, when Officer of the Watch at sea, he piped "Dawn Action Stations" which was the normal routine.

"But", said Wiggie, "It was a very peculiar morning; within a few minutes, when Philip Vian chose to arrive on the bridge, it had got dark again."

"What on earth is this?" exploded Vian, "It's pitch dark".

"Well, Sir, it was light a few minutes ago, it must be a false dawn", replied Wiggie.

"Bloody fool! you must be mad, never heard of such a thing. Fall out Action Stations."

Vian was furious. Later when in harbour, Wiggie reading a Wild West magazine in the Wardroom, came across "Destry rode into a false dawn". Unabashed he dashed down to the Captain's cabin saying

"There you are, Sir, I told you so".

To last more than a month on Vian's staff was considered a miracle. Wiggie's relief appeared in less time than that.

Then there was the story of the Pacific Fleet assembled in Tokyo Bay in August 1945 to witness the Japanese surrender. In the Cruiser *Swiftsure* to keep the crew amused while they waited, the ship's company were informed that a Japanese admiral would come on board to sign the surrender. As expected, he came up the gangway on time, greeted by the Captain with the Guard and Band paraded and the whole ship's company watching. The Japanese admiral of course was Wiggie, who being only about 5 foot 4 inches played the part to perfection. Apart from the Captain, in on the act, all were taken in.

The Commander's presents, bought in Malta's toy shops went down well; the First Lieutenant in charge of the mess decks receiving a clockwork housemaid with clockwork snakes going to one or two randy Lieutenants. Church, compulsory on the Quarterdeck at 0930, was graced by the ship's choir formed at the suggestion of Captain Ramsay, in which 'Torps', known as flat-face Harper and I sang lustily. Traditionally officers and wives, whose presence tended to keep the party clean, trooped round the messdecks. Having saved their tots, a large number of the men were rather drunk while others were just talkative and some dressed up as funny men, which undoubtedly they were not. The ship's commission of two and a half years had begun at Portsmouth in October 1932 making this the third Christmas away from home for most of the ship's company. With opportunities to specialise and the need to gain experience in large ships and small, officers' lives were peripatetic and less monotonous. After the messdecks the procession proceeded to imbibe champagne in the Wardroom and then the Gunroom, ending in the Warrant Officers' mess, changing to gin in the interests of economy. The best part of my day was at the Manoel theatre featuring Jessie Matthews in the film of the musical *Evergreen*.

The Captain and Mrs. Ramsay were very dutiful in inviting officers to dine at their home in Sliema. After being such a guest, I found it easier to obtain a basic rise of five shillings a head for the Gunroom's December wine bills. The excess was mainly due to the midshipmen giving away beers to their boat's crews and others who deserved a Christmas present such as the Maltese stewards.

My New Year's Eve was more of an ordeal than Christmas. I went along with the Warrant Officers to a Ship's Company Smoking Concert in an up to date cinema, the *Rialto*. C.P.O. Glasspool wandering about looking quite absurd in a multi-coloured school boy's cap was the Master of Ceremonies and Bill Bailey, Gunner of the *Tiddly Quid* was the star turn. The boxing ring and the rugger field had completely flattened his enormous nose giving him a frightful face, which not even the whole staff of Elizabeth Arden could put right. When he had finished C.P.O. Glasspool, to renewed cheers announced that Mr. Hogg would oblige. Mr. Hogg had an excellent repertoire of Smoke room songs and stories but through the smoke he could only see more sailors' wives and girl friends than sailors. However there was no escape and he gave an excellent rendering of: "Come sit down, drinks all round" a lyric which even the publishers of Rugger Songs overlooked. Though it contains not one four letter word, the room appeared to be entirely empty of all female relatives when he had finished.

World Events
1934. Hitler and Mussolini met at Venice. A German plebiscite voted Hitler as Führer. Churchill warned the World of German Air Force strength. Naval Disarmament Conference in London failed.

1935. The year began with two memorable films at the Manoel theatre which still delight television viewers today. The first was *Flying Down to Rio* with Fred Astaire and Ginger Rogers dancing the Carioca supported by a chorus of girls dancing on the wings of aeroplanes. And the other, Clark Gable and the entrancing Claudette Colbert sharing a tent demurely in what today would be renamed *It* didn't *happen one night*.

JUST A HOGG'S LIFE

Greeted as the only Sub-Lieutenant on the station he did not know, I paid a call on Mr. Tonner, local head of Saccone & Speed. Originating in Gibraltar, at a guess they must have supplied over 60 per cent of wines and spirits drunk by officers' messes, with Stokes and Harvey the other 40 per cent. Sitting in his office he kept open house in those days. That they, and I too, should be absorbed into International Distillers and Vintners, a consortium of the 1960s, would have seemed about as likely then as Jonah and the whale.

With two carriers, *Furious* and *Courageous* available, the Fleet sailed northwards towards Corfu on January 10. This was when I was called "A most impotent young fellow", not by any lady in Rexfords, a possibility from excessive imbibing, but on the Bridge by my captain. I had put the ship several degrees ahead of the required bearing, largely because the Navigator kept pushing me away from the compass while he took bearings of every vessel in sight. Altogether an impotent evening; Martin Price, Royal Marine No. 2 fired a starshell on a wrong bearing and everybody in sight was blamed because the black disc covering the compass case had vanished, being found eventually under a pile of books in the chart house. Anchored at Port Deprano for the weekend in wind and rain, the shoot-

Lieut. Martin Price RM, now Colonel DSO OBE RM retd, ready for the shooting party.

ing party shot little, while half-wild sheep dogs looked as if they might devour them.

Three days of attacks by carrier aircraft firing torpedoes followed until bad weather intervened. Instead, *Revenge* was ordered to tow *Royal Sovereign*. We provided the gear and making contact with Schermuly rockets within half an hour we were being towed at 8-10 knots, casting off the tow and replacing gear without a hitch.

A last exercise in which all the destroyers were to fire their "fish" at the Battle Squadron had to be cancelled because rough weather would have prevented boats recovering their torpedoes, so we were back in Grand Harbour on Friday January 25. Furthermore bad weather also prevented firings planned at sea during the next few weeks.

The M.A.D.C (Malta Amateur Dramatic Club) now opened its season with *There's Always Juliet* by John van Druten at the Club's headquarters. In the cast of four, Captain Chandos Hoskyns (Rifle Brigade) played the American in love with the heroine Jean Campbell, who revealed a pretty talent. Buchanan-Dunlop (Dartmouth St. Vincent) was excellent as the young, Bertie Wooster-ish extrovert and Kay Warren was good as the maid. Altogether an entertaining evening.

The two Warren sisters Ella and Kay, both unmarried, were the core of the M.A.D.C. Daughters of a naval officer who never introduced them to any others below the rank of Commander, Cupid passed them by. Courageously throughout the 1939-1945 war they stayed in Malta, dreaming about Noel Coward as a distraction from the blitz, and the day they met him visiting the island was the biggest thrill of their lives.

Throughout the first fortnight of February rehearsals of *Service*, a 3 Act play by C. L. Anthony (Dodie Smith) preceded the real run of three nights and a matineé on 15th, 17th, 22nd and 23rd. Stalls 5s., Boxes 30s, Seats (Unreserved) 1s. The Stage Manager, Henry Pasley-Tyler (Dartmouth St. Vincent) was also an excellent Ralph Lynne in Ben Travers farces. Chandos Hoskyns was the producer. There were good parts for him, Christopher Phillpotts, May and Phyllis Camozzi, Richard Fyffe (Rifle Brigade), Jean Campbell, Diana Moore-Gwyn, Hope Slessor and her husband Paul among some thirty characters in the play.

What with rehearsals that lasted from 9 p.m. to 1 a.m., occasional excursions to sea and various Rugby trials to select the Navy's team to play the combined Army and RAF XV, February was a busy month. The Rugby match, which we won 18 - 8 (only three points for a try in those days) was a good one for me, but with the last night of *Service* afterwards, my place was in the Opera House, not at the post Rugby dinner. This was the big night, with the Governor present and the house full. To stage a play of three acts and eleven different scenes with only eight stage hands (including me) was indeed a daring effort.

Few of the cast are alive today. Lieutenant Colonel Chandos Hoskyns commanding a battalion of the Rifle Brigade in the garrison ordered to defend Calais to the last man in May 1940 died of his wounds. Christopher Phillpotts was the son of an admiral, otherwise he might have chosen to join his sister Ambrosine on the stage. After mentions in despatches, when his R. N. career ended in 1943 through ill health, he was very successful with another in the Foreign office before he died in 1985. His wife Vivien lives in Brighton and their son, Simon, now married, is a Director of Simpson of Piccadilly selling Daks in the Far East. Richard Fyffe married Diana Moore-Gwyn, daughter of another soldier in Malta. On duty with the Rifle Brigade in N. Africa and Italy from 1942 to 1945, he retired as Lieutenant General Sir Richard in 1971 and died in 1972. survived by three daughters and his wife Lady Diana now living near Aylesbury. Paul Slessor, the senior Observer in H.M.S. *Glorious* was killed when the carrier was sunk by the German battle-cruiser *Gneisenau* off Norway on 8 June 1940. Jean Campbell married Mark Matthews, her father's A.D.C. Tragically she became an alcoholic and died young. Henry Pasley-Tyler and David Buchanan Dunlop survived the war but have died recently as have Ella and Kathleen Warren.

Joan Powell, the Epsom College headmaster's daughter to whom I had been writing quite often, was lucky to have an uncle, Carleton Walker whose asthma was the better for a spring cruise in warmer and drier weather than at his home in Sefton Park, Liverpool. Thus Uncle Carleton with his niece to keep him company, arrived one fine February morning on the P&O *Viceroy of India* anchoring in Grand Harbour for the day.

When I went on board about 1000, "Uncle Ritz" – as I liked to call this cultured coal owner – had gone ashore to meet Stewart Perowne, Secretary to Sir Harry Luke the Deputy Governor. A middle-aged bachelor he was apt to disapprove of the younger generation's drinking, lip-stick and such like, so Joan and I, consuming cold English beer in the ship's bar were a little late in collecting the car I had reserved from Mr. Zazu. In fact the only one left was an old crock, which conked out at Mosta after only five miles. The driver suggested we should visit the church while he dismantled the carburettor.

Built between 1833 and 1871 Mosta's great church was said to have the third largest dome in the world, which I thought would interest Joan, the devoted pupil and godchild of Miss Penrose in Florence. But by now, with bursting bladders, we could have filled that dome had it been the right way up. While I found a more conventional alternative, Joan dashed into what proved to be a hotel. Returning after some minutes with the proprietor, she did not disclose that he would find a full chamber pot in a first floor bedroom.

With our old crock still impotent, some passing tourists gave us a lift back to Valletta where, lunching in 'the Snakepit', we found Stewart Perowne and 'Uncle Ritz', who gave me a very disapproving look when told about the car.

Thus the four of us toured the island, with Stewart at the wheel of his open Sunbeam tourer and the coldest of winds freezing us along the coast road. From Rabat we entered Mdina, the old city on the 200 metre hill where stands the Cathedral Church of Malta. Though he had only been in Malta a few months, Stewart had found himself a charming small house with many books and a fine view south across the coast. The tea was better still.

Back in Valletta by 5.30 pm, the Viceroy sailed about six heading for Monte Carlo, where the baccarat table was for 'Uncle Ritz' a thing of beauty and a joy for ever – except presumably when he lost.

Orientalist and Historian Stewart Perowne then thirty four, married Freya Stark in 1947. Travelling and exploring the Middle East, besides working for international causes, he became a leading authority writing many books on this tumultuous region. He died in 1989 aged eighty eight. Dame Freya, a similarly authoritative author, survives him.

Royal Sovereign's last cruise of the commission was expected to be:

Arrive		**Depart**
–	Malta	March 4
March 7	Limasol (Cyprus)	March 15
March 15	Famagusta (Cyprus)	March 22
April 5	Haifa	April 1
April 23	Portsmouth.	

Before leaving, the Manoel Theatre showed us all four Marx Brothers in *Duck Soup*, a prophetic satire indeed, in which Freedonia's Dictator, Rufus T. Firefly starts hostilities by calling Sylvania's Ambassador an upstart. 'A war, a war there's gonna be a war!' Instead of a lot of prayers, I always think assemblies such as the House of Commons and the United Nations should begin their business with this same cry. There followed at the Manoel the film version of *Service*. Christopher Phillpotts, who had

JUST A HOGG'S LIFE

played the part of Michael Service, was very cross to hear a girl in the row behind saying, "This one's much better than the one in the play we saw".

Less amusing for the British taxpayer at home, *Hood* and *Renown* had collided; in the Mediterranean two destroyers likewise and the submarine *Oxley*, having caught fire, was being towed to Malta by the cruiser *Despatch*.

On March 5 we were diverted to Phaleron Bay to protect British interests and to report by W/T (Wireless Telegraphy) what was happening in the Greek civil war. The situation appeared to be that all the fighting, confined to the North around Salonica, was snowed up. From Athens the rebels had taken half the Greek Navy to Crete. With life normal in Athens, I took some forty four boys, aided by the Padré and the "Schoolie", Mr. Wyatt, on a sight seeing tour of the Acropolis, the theatres of Bacchus and the Stadium, where the games were played. Lunch in a restaurant and a Laurel and Hardy film, all in French with Greek captions, completed this treat for the boys.

When in Malta we had entertained Westmacott's Aunt Muriel, a very dashing woman with a passion for Gin and Mixed – 'very little mixed please'. On a Hellenic cruise she now paid us a surprise visit with a bevy of her Hellenic fellow travellers. Hailed as Gavin "because you are so like my good looking nephew", I envisaged soaring wine bills enough to get me court-martialled. Fortunately when we promised a special party in Portsmouth, they departed before the gin ran out.

In February at Malta the Commander-in-Chief had accepted the Captain's invitation to walk round the mess decks where literally everything shone. His verdict was that he had expected something pretty good but his expectations had greatly been exceeded. The general feeling was that the ship was the cleanest in the Fleet and the most efficient in the Squadron, due to frequent practice and plenty of spare time work. Now in the last six weeks the ship's company expected some relaxation. The Commander's nick name was 'Nick a bit' (of spare time) and it was certainly true he seldom gave them an extra Make and Mend.

The Captain however, developed an obsession that each part of the ship should in turn practise weighing anchor by hand, which seemed rather pointless unless it was to revive the singing of sea shanties. Another exercise for the duty part at sea was to close all watertight doors and the ventilation during its watch, re-opening on completion. The unavoidable banging of doors and bumping of sleepers in hammocks as men groped past disturbed most of the ship's company. Outside my cabin the Marines, determined to give the Commander a sleepless night for his pains

AN IMPOTENT SCENE-SHIFTER

did for us both. The Captain, of course, sleeping in his sea cabin under the bridge would hear none of this.

At Famagusta, putting on my gaiters and boots, I marched with our 'A' company through the town followed by the local urchins. Fortunately for morale after three miles we stopped at an orange grove whose owner provided succulent oranges and good local beer free for all.

Walking after dark in Haifa, an unreliable member of the Gunroom declared he heard the following two way conversation floating out of an upstairs window.

"Get back in bed you've got to 'ave it!"
"But I don't want it, its too big"
"Get back in bed or I'll throw you in the river"
"What with me 'at on?"
"Yus, with your 'at on".
Pause . . .
"How's that then?"
"Coo that's lovely!"

The pleasures of Haifa were largely confined to social events with the Army, my two acquaintances being Barker who had been in India and expected the Arabs to call him 'Sir' and his friend Trapper-Lomax, who had a really terrible stammer. I was therefore glad when Campbell Lithgow, the Senior Engineer, and Scovell, the younger doctor, asked me to join them on a trip to Tiberias. In a reliable hired car our first stop was Nazareth where an American priest showed us round the two churches, both modern, built over the caves where Mary and Joseph were said to have lived. There was of course a Souvenir Carpenter's shop, where I bought a wooden cross which my mother revered at her bedside for the next forty years.

Tiberias, on the shores of Galilee, was like an American village of the nineteenth century as depicted in American films. The hero rides in; then, having rid it of the cattle thief gang, develops the place, starting with a bank. Next the railroad arrives. Instead of Black Mike's saloon, Tiberias actually had two hotels, surrounded by dingy houses, scrap iron and refuse dumps. Along the lake, recommended by H.V. Morton in his latest book, *In the Steps of the Master*, we liked Tabea where a German Father gave lunches and dinners to tourists in his delightful garden.

Motoring back in the evening sunshine, the women were all out on the way to the wells their pitchers on their heads, while the men went jig-jogging home, riding side-saddle on their donkeys, both aspects of Palestine that could not have changed for 1935 years at least.

My last memory of Haifa was a Rugger match on a ground that we were told would be full of snakes. These must have left the field in protest before we arrived. There was everything except grass growing on this playing field - dandelions, thistles - and patches of gravel galore. Only too small Flanders poppies bloomed in one corner, a reminder that Palestine had suffered war until Allenby evicted the Turks in 1917.

A last week at Malta disembarking stores and saying farewells pleased the golfers, who with the rest of the Fleet still away had the Marsa course to themselves. *The Tiddly Quid* steamed out of Grand Harbour in perfect weather at 1030 on Saturday 13 March. There were Maltese heads craning from every window and balcony along Valletta's Barracca with hands waving handkerchiefs and coloured materials. Vice-Admiral Malta could be seen opposite on the St. Angelo ramparts, while our Squadron Admiral lay in his barge off the breakwater having sent a highly complimentary and valedictory signal on the ship's smart appearance in light Mediterranean grey. It was ironical that when the moment arrived for which all had yearned for so long, one should feel a pang of regret at leaving the island, which we had reviled so often. After passing the breakwater, for the first time in my ten months on board we turned westwards. This was also the moment when Lieutenant Martin Price Royal Marines fulfilled a solemn vow - the removal of his moustache.

So, in the words of a current hit song, we headed for the last round-up, the Gunroom entertaining the Captain, Surgeon Commander Brown and others to a last dinner recorded as : Consommé, Fried Mullet, Sweetbread, Roast Duckling, Glace Chocolat and Cheese, with Hock to drink as our champagne is very poor.

> Easter Sunday April 21 in the Bay was too rough for Divisions and church, our 10 knot economical speed getting a boost up Channel until we anchored at Spithead at 1120 on Tuesday 23rd.

Moving up harbour in the afternoon the ship certainly looked a picture, passing through the narrow entrance lined with people, some cheering, some waving, some holding up children to be seen by their fathers for the first time. Berths alongside the Dockyard were all occupied by Home fleet ships giving leave and looking dirty with their dark grey paintwork unwashed. A buoy had to be good enough for *Royal Sovereign*. Instead of a tug two small Gosport ferries were sent to take our liberty men ashore but they had all gone soon after 5pm.

Motoring home to Epsom for the week-end with my parents, I found the new Guildford and Godalming by-pass had been opened, avoiding at last the drive through the main streets of these two towns. Not so popular was the introduction of that 30mph limit in built-up areas, still with us after fifty seven years.

Rex Madoc RM escorts two American ladies round Rodney.

HMS Revenge *making a near miss during Officer of the Watch manoeuvres.*
Photo taken from Royal Sovereign's *Quarterdeck!*

*Scenes from the Malta Amateur Dramatic Club
production of 'Service' by C.L. Anthony, February 1935.*

CHAPTER 15

1935 – MUSSOLINI'S ABYSSINIA AGGRESSION

Among the passengers cruising in the *Viceroy of India*, was the proprietor of Epsom's Woodcote Garage, Mr. Norman, who now sold me a 1933 Wolseley Hornet saloon, mileage only 8,000 for £95, which proved to be a very reliable vehicle. Throughout May and June during *Royal Sovereign*'s refit, with the noise of riveting and all three officers' messes being painted in turn, life on board was tedious. The ship's company took their foreign service leave in two watches and officers also took some of their entitlements. We still kept an Officer of the Watch on the quarterdeck, except that relaxation in the Wardroom from 1800 to 0400 was permitted.

On May 8 Captain Ramsay was promoted to Rear-Admiral, departing in time for Ascot when his relief, Captain Frank Elliott joined on June 15. Bertie Ramsay was born at Hampton Court on January 20, 1883, his father being a Colonel in the Fourth Hussars. One of his subalterns was Winston Churchill, who remembered Bertie as a boy at Aldershot. Earmarked for high rank, Ramsay's next job was Chief of Staff to Admiral Backhouse, Commander-in-Chief Home Fleet. But in 1936 he resigned and went on half pay because Backhouse could not delegate responsibility. Having resigned he sought advice from Churchill. This and his experience of amphibious operations, first in the cruiser *Hyacinth* when a Lieutenant in Somaliland and secondly in the Dover patrol as Captain of the destroyer *Broke* in 1917/18 with a Mention in Despatches, contributed to his appointment as Vice-Admiral Dover in September 1939.

Dover was where the naval war began. Within ten days the *Adventure*, *Plover* and the converted train ferries, *Hampton* and *Shepperton* laid a deep minefield across to Calais to catch U-boats; and we, in the 5th mine sweeping flotilla, then made a skimming sweep to be sure that no mines were shallow. The following May came Dunkirk, an evacuation for which Ramsay was acclaimed. From Dunkirk 338,226 men were recovered, with about one vessel sunk in every three out of nearly seven hundred rescuing craft. For the successful North African landings 1942 and the Sicily landings 1943 he was the naval Commander-in-Chief. Knighted and promoted a full admiral, this made him the obvious choice for Allied Naval Commander Expeditionary Force for *Overlord*, the Normandy invasion of June 1944.

Within four years he was in command of two Task Forces, one British and one American, that carried the armies of four nations across the Channel to Normandy, with a great armada of ships to support them and not an enemy aircraft to be seen. Only a Norwegian destroyer was sunk on D-Day, sinkings rising – mainly from mines – to seventeen ships and craft after the first twenty-five days. Few men in war can have derived greater satisfaction from achievement than Bertie Ramsay and his staff of planners, matched perhaps by the relief and gratitude of the free world setting forth to liberate Europe.

Then, on January 2 1945, flying from St. Germain-en-Laye to a meeting with Field Marshal Montgomery in Brussels, Ramsay's plane crashed on taking off catching fire and killing all five passengers. He was sixty two.

In Britain the great event of 1935 was the Silver Jubilee of King George V and Queen Mary. Jubilee week began on Monday May 6 in hot sunshine when they went in an open landau to St. Pauls, with other members of the Royal family following in procession for the Thanksgiving Service. Stands were full all down the Mall; window and balcony seats had sold for amazing prices, and along the route there were cheering scenes undreamt of since the Armistice. Huge crowds gathered each night outside Buckingham Palace, the King and Queen making two or three appearances to satisfy them. Londoners danced in the streets and the bonfires on Jubilee night, built as far as possible on the sites of their 1588 predecessors, recalled Macaulay's "Such night in England ne'er was seen, nor e're again shall be".

In Portsmouth I found two jolly companions. The colour-blind Lionel Bonsey, last mentioned on hobnobbing terms with the Commander-in-Chief Joe Kelly, had joined the cruiser *Coventry* as a Paymaster Lieutenant. Eddie Baines had come home in the destroyer *Antelope* with other ships of the Mediterranean Fleet to take part in the Review. A genial rendezvous in Southsea was a small bar at the back of The Bush, a tatty old hotel at the corner of King's Road and Castle Road, Southsea. It's attraction was Valerie Gunnell, a pretty vivacious brunette, who seemed to be 'day on, stop on' as the barmaid. No less a rendezvous was the Wardroom of *Coventry* before lunch. Being the flagship of Rear-Admiral

(D) now ABC (Cunningham), the Wardroom welcomed all officers of the Mediterranean Fleet destroyers to a glass of gin any forenoon. At the cry "Bring gin Mifsud", the worthy Maltese steward appeared with a huge tray of glasses being relied on to charge them to members of the mess on a stripe basis according to seniority.

The married officers still in *Royal Sovereign* encouraged me and John May, a bachelor Lieutenant, to play golf with the Commander, leaving as early as possible after lunch. Turning my head as we left for Hayling in his car, I could see them all looking out from their cabins, not daring to go and join their wives until the Commander had left.

Promotions to Captain and Commander were made twice yearly, on June 30 and December 31. June 30 was the last chance for Leonard Hammersley Bell as already mentioned in Chapter 13 and he was not selected. Tantrums not withstanding I was very sorry. Here was a dedicated man of forty three, Executive Officer, of the smartest capital ship in the Fleet, now about to get it 'on top line' for the Review, with only half a ship's company, passed over after nearly thirty years of working for the Service.*

The refit completed, *Royal Sovereign* sailed on Thursday 11 July to join the ships anchored in their berths at Spithead for the Review the following Tuesday. Stuart Cunningham, an easy going Lieutenant not always sober, and I were to run the *Fumerole*, about the oldest drifter afloat allocated to *Royal Sovereign* for the review period. To avoid lying alongside, rubbing the battleship's paintwork, we berthed in the dockyard each night and could sleep in *Fumerole*. On Friday 12th Southsea awoke to see long lines of Home and Mediterranean Fleet ships stretching westwards from Spithead to Cowes, due to be joined on Sunday by the Reserve fleet and foreign ships too representing their respective countries.

Running the *Fumerole* to and fro in warm sunshine, looking through glasses at all the yachtsmen and their girl friends as they passed along the lines made a pleasant day. On Sunday there was sudden concern that the ships might not be swung East and West when the King passed with the crews lining the sides giving three cheers. Accordingly, afternoons were spent by each drifter trying to pull round the stern of its parent ship.

At 2200 a nightly a stampede of drifters and tugs belched smoke across Portsmouth Harbour taking Libertymen back to their ships, while the

---

*The reason, possibly, was a black mark when *Royal Sovereign* had commissioned. Sailing from Portsmouth was delayed because a large number of men were still ashore on leave. Bell lived to be ninety three; he had been made a Captain during the war and retired with a CBE.

Royal Yacht, alongside South Railway jetty, sent hectic signals to make less smoke. Fumerole seemed to be the heaviest smoker and about the slowest vessel.

JUBILEE REVIEW DAY

The weather was perfect; about 1400 a light southerly breeze dispersing a heat mist swung the ships into their right position. In *Royal Sovereign* there were two hundred guests in the Wardroom and about fifty in the Gunroom, which included my father, brother, sister and her husband Jack Paterson, the *Bimbashi* from Alexandria home on leave. My Uncle A. G. ("Sandy") Hogg, the golfer of repute whose property in Cheshire became the Dunham Forest golf club in the 1950s, I took to *Renown*, where he was the guest of William Dallmeyer, the Torpedo officer.

To keep clear of the formalities, all drifters and ships' boats had to anchor in an area around No Man's Fort throughout the afternoon, so I left my family in the excellent hands of Skottowe, the Australian midshipman. At 1400, greeted with a Royal Salute, *Victoria & Albert* secured to a buoy ahead of *Queen Elizabeth*, while Flag Officers called to meet the Monarch. At 1600 she led the procession, followed by the Admiralty yacht *Enchantress* and the ss Maine with Ambassadors, Diplomats, MPs, and Dominion representatives on board.

Meanwhile in our area every drifter except mine seemed to be dragging its anchor. Unable to use the normal anchor and the drifter's cable because the winch was not powerful enough to lift them, I was puzzled that my light anchor and a manilla rope was holding so well. When eventually I weighed them, a bight of what might well have been the main telegraph cable to the Isle of Wight was firmly entwined round the flukes of my anchor.

A Fly Past by the Fleet Air Arm ended the day's proceedings, visitors getting ashore by 1930 with little hope of dinner in overcrowded hotels. The illuminations began at 2200. Seen from Portsdown Hill that shower of rockets over five mile long made a glorious spectacle. While the Mediterranean ships returned to their station and the Home Fleet departed to Home Ports for leave, *Royal Sovereign* went back to Fountain Lake jetty in Portsmouth dockyard. With the new captain, and a new Commander, Patrick W. Brooking relieving Bell, life became more relaxed. The senior midshipmen took their seamanship exams, Jo Phillips getting a First Class with Seconds for the other four.

The ship was to recommission at the end of August with a Portsmouth crew for the battleship *Barham*, then refitting at Devonport. After taking the Portsmouth crew there, she would go to the Mediterranean. *Royal Sovereign*, recommissioned with a West Country crew, expected to stay at home. Reappointed as Sub-Lieutenant of the Gunroom, I thought life without the senior midshipmen would be dull. Phillips, very practical with a cold-blooded outlook on life and a strange sense of humour; Phillpotts extremely funny, often at my expense; Ellsworth lighthearted and amusing; Westmacott continually moaning; Bruce, the athletic but quiet member; I should miss them all. The Australians too; Gordon, a games all rounder always broke, speaking incessantly of 'Popsies' in Australia, Brewster and lastly Skottowe, facially disfigured from one road accident, who would soon lose his life tragically in another.

My own Summer leave was three weeks from July 31 to August 20. Cars went quite well even in those days. Leaving Portsmouth at 1500 (closing time) the Wolseley Hornet made the Lygon Arms, Broadway by 1800 (opening time). Dinner at Kidderminster and a bed at the Mytton and Mermaid, Shrewsbury, set me up for Old Boys cricket at Brockhurst, Church Stretton. Sadly none of my contemporaries were there, otherwise I would not have made top score of 38. I only remember now sharing the Sick Bay with Bobbie Hereford and the warm welcome for all from the Marshalls, particularly Tony now a Chief Cadet Captain-to-be at Dartmouth.

The Hogg family stayed at the Ferry Hotel on Windermere at the bottom of the hill going up to Sawrey and Coniston, which became a scientific establishment soon afterwards. My brother had chartered Dryad, an old Potter family yacht as well as a motor boat. Our cars took us to Hound Trails (losing money), Sheep Dog trials, over Wrynose and Hard Knott to Wastwater, and back by Buttermere and Honister Pass. Our friends the Scotts at Matson Ground, Bowness took us for picnics on the lake, where Patrick Crossley – still living at Storrs in 1992 – was racing as usual. Though the weather was perfect for a fortnight, bathing in the lake was self-inflicted torture.

Back in *Royal Sovereign* mess bills had to be made out and sent to all those who had left, while on 23 July in pouring rain the old ship paid off and recommissioned with the crew for *Barham*. One by one shipmates departed. Stuart Cunningham, having had a splendid wedding in the Cathedral after the review, left me with his pile of pornographic literature; John May, Martin Price, Peterson and Drawbridge all left, the last named on a bicycle.

THE NEW COMMISSION

What with beer at "The Bush" and learning to dance at the A&B (Arse and Belly Rooms) where even the new Captain and Commander were to be found occasionally, the activities of Mussolini are not recorded in my journal until August 25 1935.

A few Italians murdered in Abyssinia gave Mussolini his excuse for pouring in troops and an offensive was expected. The League of Nations would of course condemn an aggressor but regarded Britain as a Head Boy in a school, who should keep order. Mussolini was parading his strength with manoeuvres in Northern Italy while the Admiralty was preparing for a war with Italy.

At noon on Wednesday August 28 when *Royal Sovereign* sailed for Plymouth I felt like Cherubino the page, (in Mozart's masterpiece) banished to the battle field by the Count and terrified by Figaro singing: *Non più andrai, farfallone amoroso*, (Say goodbye now to pastime and play). However at Plymouth morale improved when a beaming Officer of the Guard greeting us, invited me to dine in the Barracks that evening. It was our old friend and shipmate, David MacPhail now working in the Devonport Gunnery School.

Berthed alongside *Barham* all our officers assembled on the Quarterdeck to meet the Rear-Admiral, another Ramsay, who was transferring his flag to us. No relation of Bertie, this was "Black Ramsay" on account of black hairs in his ears; or, "The Ocean Swell" on account of his rolling gait. Shaking hands he was very civil, but a foreign observer seeing Guards and Bands and over a hundred sailors on parade in both ships, performing various manual exercises with rifles, would have been surprised that all this was because one man was to cross a plank ten feet long from one ship to another.

The following day our remaining men moved bags, hammocks and themselves across to *Barham* before our own new ship's company arrived from the Barracks.

Early in September the Home Fleet was meant to assemble at Portland; we arrived there in fog on the 6th. But with the possibility of war, one third of Britain's capital ships appeared to be in dockyard hands. *Rodney*, having been Guard ship at Cowes, was still giving leave. *Ramillies* had collided in the Channel with a German steamer killing three of its crew. *Hood* and *Repulse* were present, anchored in Weymouth Bay.

On board we only had four watchkeepers; Lieutenants Parker and Hale, myself and our new Royal Marine subaltern P.H. Teek, also a regular at The Bush. Short, the Fleet Air Arm Observer and Senior Watchkeeper, was away collecting *Leeward*, the ship's new drifter. Stirling, an Assistant Navigator and Batten a Lieutenant, were expected to join shortly.

As soon as the drifter arrived I had to take her to a position South East of Portland Bill towing a Pattern VI target for sub- calibre shooting practice. It was a foul morning, very rough with a bucket already on the bridge marked "Captain for the use of". About 0700 the signalman, who was also the cook when necessary, brought me up a hearty breakfast. Foolishly smoking my pipe I brought it up too. Feeling like death, unable to move about steadily trying to fix one's position making only three knots in the Portland race was hell.

The following day, Friday the 13th, all ships were put at four hours notice by the Commander-in-Chief, which restricted week- end leave. To my surprise the Commander saw no reason why I should not go to Portsmouth to collect the faithful Wolseley Hornet provided I spent the night in Weymouth. In Portsmouth meeting Otto Jenner-Fust we discovered that like Flamand,, the musician and Olivier, the poet in Straus's *Capriccio*, we were both after the same girl. Not a Countess in our case, I hardly need add, but Nicky the greengrocer's daughter. When out with Otto, making the Gloucester hotel at Weymouth by 0230 was creditable. The shock came next morning. The Battle Cruisers, Cruisers and the 6th Destroyer flotilla had left at high speed for the Mediterranean at 2200 the night before. In fact within a week of starting their leave, Peterson had been sent to *Neptune* and Drawbridge to *Renown*; with others getting similar "pier-head jumps". I was greatly relieved to find the *Royal Sovereign* still there.

"Where were you when your ship sailed?"

"Learning the rumba in the Arse and Belly Rooms Southsea" wouldn't have sounded too good.

Equinoctial gales sank a Picket boat and damaged the drifter. Wynne, First Lieutenant and Cable Officer, wanted me to clear the PV (Paravane) chains with a vigorous pull from the drifter. I did not like the idea and said so. Inevitably the drifter was swept under the two starboard hawsepipes, where the flukes of the anchor tore away all the woodwork and canvas comprising the port side of the drifter's bridge as we tried to get clear. Determined not to do a Leonard Hammersley Bell I stood there calm, cool and collected. Fortunately his successor Patrick Brooking regarded these disasters with equanimity; indeed the score now being Port ladder bashed twice and two picket boats likewise, there was really no alternative.

Towards the end of September with better weather, attention was paid to Gunnery. Our 15 inch, 6 inch, 4 inch High Angle, Pom Pom and

JUST A HOGG'S LIFE

machine gun shoots were all good. *Nelson*, *Rodney*, the 20th Destroyer flotilla, the old cruiser *Cairo* and *Galatea*, the new one about to replace *Coventry* in the Mediterranean, were all working up at Portland. I spent several days in the tugs *St. Cyrus* and *St. Just* which towed battle practice targets for them. Being in charge of marking parties, recording where and when the shots fell and other data required for analysis was interesting, except that it involved leaving harbour around 0600 and getting back about 1900.

On Friday October 4 the Commander-in-Chief flew to London in *Nelson*'s seaplane for a meeting. Coming back the pilot, forgetting to raise the wheels clear of the water, crashed into Portland harbour. A boat from *Nelson*, with a midshipman in charge thought to be not too bright, got there immediately. This midshipman realising at once that the Commander-in-Chief was underwater unable to get out of the cabin, dived in, opened the door and pulled him out. He undoubtedly saved the life of Admiral Backhouse, who subsequently became First Sea Lord. But in March 1939 Admiral of the Fleet, now Sir Roger Backhouse, was forced to retire due to illness and he died in July that same year.

Summer Time in 1935 ended on October 6. The Italians, advancing with little resistance had captured Adowa. The prospect of gales, rain and fog based at Portland was dismal. Even Commander Brooking seemed to have lost his good humour, ordering me to beat a midshipman, who had damaged his Picket Boat on the ship's Port ladder. After reading in O'Connor's book, "A Picket Boat smashed may one day mean a Battleship saved", I pretended it had been done.

The Home Fleet (Portland) provided scratch sides to play Canford School and Blundells at Rugger. Though we beat the former, by the last ten minutes we had shot our bolt with Blundells who won 19-8, reported in *The Times* no less. Twenty years on I saw that ground again. My son Adam was at Port Regis Preparatory School. It was half term, Blundells were playing Sherborne in pouring rain. Their fly half, here there and everywhere, conspicuous with his fair hair never dropped a pass. "He'll play for England", I said. Sharp did just that, returning there to teach in due course.

The Admiralty decision that we should discharge a hundred and fifty seamen and sixty stokers gave us an excuse to spend a few days at Devonport so that the ship's company could see their families. Among my visitors there were Kitson and David Malim, who had left *Repulse* to specialise in Engineering at Keyham College close to Devonport Barracks. Travelling in Europe after the war one constantly ran into friends of one's youth; at Positano Joan and I met Theo and David Malim at Carlo Cinque's newly opened Hotel Pietro in 1971. David died of cancer in 1985. One of a large family, his father had been the Master of Wellington College 1921-1970.

Fresh from Gibraltar Northey (Dartmouth Exmouth) told us of continuous anti-submarine exercises, darkening ship, patrol work and boom defences. Another visitor Lieutenant J. W. Forrest, a massive Gunnery Officer and England's second row forward, who said the Devonport Services forwards thought nothing could be good unless, like me, *they* did it. I made a spirited reply saying that at Portsmouth Wally Elliott thought rightly that his three-quarters, Harrel and Hogg were novices so we seldom got the ball. When we did it was only natural to try and show one's individual skill. At this point "John Willie", giving a loud bellow hid his face in a large tankard. Once, stopped by the Police driving his bull-nose Morris through Guildford, he explained to the Bench that he felt so ill after being given some awful cocktails at a party in North London that he had to stop in Guildford for two pints of bitter that would put him right. The breathalyser was about twenty years away then, but the fine and the publicity spoilt his chances of promotion to Commander. Back at Portland my journal describes meeting the pilots of the Fleet Air Arm's 822 Squadron at the Breakwater Hotel their daily routine being:

0820 - 1000 Turn out, breakfast etc., Fly occasionally if weather suitable, otherwise try *Times* crossword in hangar. Relate events of night before.

1115 Return to hotel. Drink gin.

1245 (about) Lunch, Return to bar. Drink beer.

1430 Siesta.

1800 Return to bar. Do some young woman a mischief somewhere in Dorset.

Prominent in the Gunroom since recommissioning were: Sub-Lieutenant (E) Cock, Engineer and excellent messmate, nephew of the Engineer Captain Cock retd, a great raconteur always to be found in the bar of the Bedford Hotel, Tavistock. Senior midshipman John Stucley, member of a well known North Devon family went to Dartmouth in 1930, earning a D.S.O. after escorting convoys to Russia. After the war he qualified as a Recorder of the Crown Court and became a Judge, living mainly in London with his wife Natalia. He died in March 1988.

D. W. Piers RCN
On November 25th seven midshipmen took their Seamanship exam in *Nelson* returning late in the evening with two Firsts and Five Seconds. The dinner planned in the Gunroom began at 2030, the Commander and others who had instructed them being the guests. They included W. S. Handcock, the Admiral's Flag Lieutenant and as such, a Signals specialist, who knew exactly what flags to hoist when the Admiral boomed something inaudible. But the star of the seven was a Canadian, Desmond William Piers, who in 1992 is to be found in the British *Who's Who* as Rear-Admiral Piers D.S.C., C.M., RCN retd, living at *The Quarterdeck, Chester, Nova Scotia. BO J 1 JO Canada*. The life and soul of the party he made a speech about absolutely nothing convulsing his audience with laughter. How we borrowed the wardroom piano and who played it I do not recall, but Piers, and others put over, "My brother Sylvest had a row of forty medals on his chest" with great élan. The following day they were gone.

Poor old *Tiddly Quid*! On Friday 29th, en route for Plymouth, her Full Power Trial only managed a speed of 18½ knots. Next day we went up the Hamoaze in a gale with West Country rain pouring down. During the leave period which began on December 5 Admiral Ramsay continued to appear on board daily from 1000 to 1230 or perhaps until 1500. This was necessary to retain his table money, about £2 a day. Absence for 48 hours meant striking his flag and forfeiting the allowance, which was to feed those who messed with him.

He and his wife, with daughter Patricia now in her teens, lived in the imposing Manadon House, a large mansion in park land a few miles north of Plymouth, which has been the Royal Naval Engineering College, formerly at Keyham, since the war. It was customary for officers - and their wives if any - to pay calls on admirals, captains and possibly commanders of the ships in which they served and, said the Captain to me, for days the Ramsays have been sitting daily in front of a huge tea expecting some of the midshipmen. None had come and the Captain said they must call forthwith.

Mountain, our dentist, the Captain of Marines and I had already done so. Rightly named, the *Gipsy Queen* had a head of hair like an O'Cedar mop. With a pedigree by Ocean Swell out of Gipsy Queen, it was fascinating to think of a name for Patricia, whose nursery was referred to as Pat's gunroom. Since cars were scarce all the eight midshipmen we could find crammed into one ancient Austin, descending on the long-awaited tea like a bunch of ravenous seagulls.

Early in December came the astounding news that *Royal Sovereign* would become a Boys' sea-going training ship in January. The Admiral would transfer his flag to *Rodney*, an announcement that caused the Captain to stand on his head and cheer in his cabin, fulfilling an intention he had announced privately from time to time. Anticipating that the Gunroom would close, I up-dated the Gunroom wine and tobacco accounts and all the charts before proceeding on leave myself on December 15.

After spending a few days at Altrincham with my brother Martin working in Manchester, some adjustment to my Wolseley Hornet delayed our start for Epsom on Christmas Eve to spend Christmas with our parents. Stopping for beer and a sandwich somewhere near Lichfield, it was snowing and the roads were icy. Though conditions improved nearer London, it was after 1am on an empty A5 when we passed the 30mph sign entering St. Albans. Suddenly, without warning a woman stepped off the pavement on my left and was carried on the bonnet as I braked and stopped. We carried her into the nearest house and phoned for an ambulance. She died on the way to hospital. The car was dented but serviceable; the police took measurements on the spot and details at the Police Station over a welcome cup of tea. We reached Epsom about 7.30 a.m. dead tired.

Christmas Day was largely spent making telephone and written reports to the AA, who assured us that Counsel would meet us at the St. Albans Court at 2pm on Friday the 27th, half an hour before the Coroner's inquest began. It transpired that the old lady was staying with her son and they went to a party, which she left to go back to his house alone. The petrol station, close to the accident being open, she stopped there to ask the way. Counsel for her family now made out a case that my car was being driven dangerously at over 30 m.p.h. and the police said it should have stopped sooner. My own counsel had not appeared.

Matters looked ugly when a voice behind me said, "Are you Mr. Hogg, what is all this about? Tell me in a few words, I have heard nothing from the AA". I whispered the facts as best I could. In a flash he was on his feet. It took him little time to establish that, making merry, the family had allowed the old lady to go alone at about 1.30 a.m. Next, the petrol station attendant said she was peculiar and had obviously been drinking.

There had been a number of accidents recently in St. Albans that upset the Coroner, who directed the jury that death was accidental but they could find the driver was partly to blame. At this my Counsel immediately stated that they could also acquit the driver of blame. The Coroner said testily that of course they knew that.

Much to our relief the verdict was Accidental Death, exonerating the driver from all blame. Being a child in these matters, I never thought it could be otherwise. But my father the judge, remembering when his son-in-law was the defendant how the great Rigby Swift had misdirected the jury some years before, breathed a great sigh of relief.

Since we can all make errors of judgement I count myself lucky to have retained a clean licence for over sixty years now.

Back on board *Royal Sovereign* in January 1936 I discovered that my counsel, Wilfred Bennett was a close friend of Pat Brooking, the Commander. Both were useful golfers with whom I played two years later at St. Enodoc.

By the end of 1935 my second journal was full so I took to a page a day diary instead. Its pages, each 8 inches by 5 inches, are largely blank until January 20, the day George V died. I remember we were able to hear the Doctors' bulletin on the wireless: "The King's life is moving peacefully towards its close" Unlike our parents we had known no other King and it all seemed very sad. The Press put out that his last words were, "How is the Empire?" But rumour had it later that they were really "Bugger Bognor" in reply to Queen Mary, who suggested that they would soon be back where previously he had undergone convalescence.

Descending from Royal House to Public House, Valerie of The Bush became engaged to Sub-Lieutenant Geoffrey Gabriel, a handsome fellow from Tasmania. Unfortunately, having failed in his courses, his services were no longer required by the Australian Navy, so they booked a passage home for him on board the *Stratheard* sailing from Tilbury on Friday 21 February. The marriage, for which I was best man for the first and last time in my life, was in the Southsea Registry office on Tuesday 18th. *Royal Sovereign* was paying a brief visit to Portsmouth from Portland enabling me to buy the ring for £1.00 and lend £1. 10s. for the Licence. Valerie lived with her mother in the basement flat of 39 Shaftesbury Road close to the Queen's Hotel. Her parents, who had some connection with the stage had separated and no dowry was available from them, though Mrs. Gunnell gave us a good cold lunch. Miraculously however a magician arrived from Portland by car with £100 for Geoffrey. He was Sub-Lieutenant Rudy Wratislaw (Dartmouth, *Rodney*). This repaid me, and probably bought a 2nd class passage for Valerie. Poor Mrs. Gunnell! I took her from Waterloo to Tilbury and back after seeing the couple off. Nobody told her that Geoffrey had lost his job; she expected they would return within two or three years. To my embarrassment they soon had a son calling it Anthony. Valerie had taught me a lot about dancing, but with no Admiralty Manual of Seduction, my passes were still confined to Rugby football. Eight years later with the British Pacific Fleet in Australia, I had ten days leave to visit my uncle in Hobart. To mutual delight and astonishment we met at a dance there. Geoffrey was fighting somewhere at sea; Valerie was working for the local Broadcasting Corporation. Within a month the war was over, I wrote but there was no reply. What happened to the Gabriels? I still wonder.

During February 1936 officers in *Royal Sovereign* were steadily being appointed elsewhere. Teek returned to the R. M. Barracks at Eastney. I was ordered to *Grafton*, one of the new flotilla of destroyers nearing completion by Thornycrofts at Woolston, Southampton. Turning over to my relief, Keith-Roach, I departed on February 19, reporting to the Anti-Submarine school at Portland the following Monday 24th for a week's course. I was delighted to find Terence Harrel on the course too prior to joining the destroyer *Fearless*. Another member of it was Seth-Smith, who was to have a little trouble in London with a car, a bollard and a breathalyser later on in life. In the bar of the Gloucester I met (Charles) C.L. Firth, my next Captain, who said we would take over *Grafton* on March 17 with a steaming party, proceeding to Devonport to commission fully.

February 18th 1936, Southsea. Just married, Geoffrey Gabriel and Valerie Gunnell.

CHAPTER 16

1936 – HMS *Grafton* – Cock of the Fleet and King's Escort

Since the mid-Twenties V and W class destroyers were being replaced at the rate of about one flotilla a year, starting at A. Examples now in service were:

  A - Acasta   B - Brilliant   C - Campbell
  D - Duncan   E - Eclipse   F - Fearless

Very similar the G's, completed in 1936 were *Grafton, Gallant, Garland, Gipsy, Glowworm, Grenade, Greyhound* and *Griffin*. Displacement 1335 tons, length 312 feet, speed 35 knots. Armament Eight 21-inch torpedoes, four 4.7 inch guns. Complement 145. *Grenville*, the flotilla leader, last to complete, displaced 1460 tons and had five 4.7 inch guns. All had Asdic's and Depth Charges for Anti-submarine work.

Appointed to *Grafton* completing in March at Thornycroft's Woolston, Southampton were:

Captain:	Commander C. L. Firth
Lieutenants:	N. E. G. Roper, R. M. Crawford
Sub-Lieutenant:	A. L. S. Hogg
Engineer Officer:	Lieutenant Commander (E) R. A. Gould
Cd.Gunner T	H. A. Mitchell

On Saturday morning 29th February I joined the Captain and Nigel Roper for a first look. Compared to the old *Vidette*, this destroyer was wonderfully spacious with stoves to heat the mess decks. Nigel Roper who gave me lunch at the Polygon Hotel, seemed very nice, keen on tennis, golf and angling.

Dividing my leave between my relations at Altrincham and my parents at Epsom, I sold the £95 Wolseley Hornet for £57.10s. after eleven months use before repairing by train once more from Waterloo to Southampton on March 17, spending the night at the Polygon Hotel.

Next morning *Grafton*, moored head and stern in the stream, looked a picture as our baggage was taken on board. The first of several social events when taking over new ships was a beer party for all the bowler-hatted foremen, which began at 1145. Finding dinner jackets in our baggage, we officers dined that evening with a Dr. Gillespie and his partner Dr. White, who were in some way connected with the builders. The following day a Commander Hill from the Admiralty appeared in plain clothes, that being the custom because the Admiralty was a civil establishment. He too wore his bowler reading out a long questionnaire on the ship's fittings to which Thornycroft's people answered 'Yes' with monotonous consistency. For lunch we officers were the guests of the Company at the South Western Hotel.

The steaming party duly arrived from Devonport. Fire stations were read and after that there was a cocktail party on board, attended by Mrs. Craven Ellis who had launched *Grafton*. "And you must use the silver salver" she said, "Otherwise you won't think of me". Among other guests was my term mate and close friend "Joey" Groome who was involved with the Flotilla of Motor Torpedo Boats, some being built by Thornycroft. In his large Alvis car he took me to the South Western Hotel where we dined well with a bottle of the never-to-be-forgotten Lanson 1921, a good soporific for a first night on board. Subsequently Joey became an Observer and was killed on 30 July 1940 when a Swordfish of 812 Squadron from North Coates, Lincolnshire crashed on a training flight.

Headed by Sir John Thornycroft, a veritable army of departmental managers, some Admiralty people and copious workmen arrived at 0730 and away we went for Spithead, with an old pipe-smoking pilot in charge, without so much as glancing at a chart. Having swung for magnetic compass correction off Lee, we then headed Eastwards at nearly full power, speed 32-34 knots. Lunch and beer were provided by Thornycroft and at 1340 the white ensign was hoisted when the Captain formally accepted *Grafton*.

Having been made Navigator, I wondered how on earth the Captain intended to reach Plymouth that night. Anchoring off Netley to disembark the civilians, we did not leave until 1500. Through the Needles Channel we were doing 25 knots when the steering jambed due to some mistake attributed to Thornycroft's. In all my years at sea, plodding along at economical speeds of 10 or 12 knots, I had never done 25 knots. It was most alarming, but very jolly passing Portland at 1830 and Brixham at 2030 before anchoring in Plymouth Sound about 2230. Navigating by magnetic compass furthermore, since the ship's gyros were not working as yet.

Grafton commissioned on March 24 ammunitioning the following day. My duties involved drawing charts and Confidential Books, which re-

JUST A HOGG'S LIFE

quired careful registration. I was also in charge of the mess decks, the wheelhouse and the bridge, places that had to be spotless. I was also Sports Officer, pleased to find that Nigel, hereinafter No.1, had already given thought to *Grafton*'s colours. Crawford had an MG car so old that it looked like a Morris. When duty on board he lent it to us, whereupon as we headed for golf at Tavistock, a policeman pointed out that the licence had expired.

One evening in the Wardroom, 'Pooh' and another young lady, friends of No. 1 from Budleigh Salterton, stayed to supper and the Captain, who hitherto had talked 'shop', relaxed and was most amusing. At the beginning of April *Rodney* and *Royal Sovereign* arrived for the leave period bringing us more visitors eager to see the latest destroyer.

On April 8 we sailed for Portland steaming up and down the coast between Weymouth and Lulworth firing torpedoes one at a time and picking them up with the whaler, a tricky job because the Mark IX torpedo floated vertically, its nose, usually bobbing up and down, being difficult to hook on. With Good Friday on April 10 long week-end leave was given to as many as possible. I myself managed a Friday to Sunday, hitch-hiking a lift to Bath where the parents were staying at the huge Empire Hotel for a break, a Sunday train at 1600 getting me back to Weymouth before 1900.

On board our latest gramophone records were from *Follow the Fleet*, with Fred Astaire singing topically:

"*We joined the Navy to see the world, but what did we see? We saw the sea.*

We saw the Atlantic and the Pacific but the Pacific isn't terrific and the Atlantic isn't what its cracked up to be".

Crawford and I now bade tender farewells to Vera in the Gloucester Hotel bar, my diary remarking that life seemed to be a succession of farewells to barmaids.

At 1000 on Saturday April 18 *Grafton* in company with *Grenade*, a recent arrival, headed for the Atlantic and Gibraltar doing a 10 hour fuel consumption trial at 18 knots as we passed Ushant on a calm and beautiful night. *L'envoi* it might be but the next day nobody felt like Kipling, selling his tired soul for the bucking beam-sea roll of a black Bilbao tramp. Lacking time to get our sea legs, we were just sea sick and the Captain was rolled out of his bunk. Along the Portuguese coast better weather allowed Range and Indication exercises; Dummy torpedo attacks too and the towing of *Grafton* by *Grenade*. So different from a big ship, I found myself thoroughly enjoying playing with a sextant and handling *Grafton* by myself with a genial Captain calling me a bloody fool in a cheery way from time to time.

Destroyers also had a T.S.D.S (Two Speed Destroyer Sweep) for mines, with paravanes and explosive cutters, which had to be streamed astern, towed and recovered, with parts of the sweep more than likely to foul one another. In the war, I'm told, it was only used once; by destroyers preceding the battleship *Warspite*, entering Vestfjorden, Norway for the second battle of Narvik in April 1940. Though small ships were uncomfortable at sea, in harbour they usually had the advantage of berthing alongside. At Gibraltar three or four destroyers could be alongside each other in 'The Pens' and the buoys in the harbour could each take two, so in the flotilla we got to know each other fairly soon.

Because Malta had no air protection against possible Italian air attacks, the Mediterranean Fleet had been based at Alexandria throughout the winter and spring, maintaining a state of readiness that restricted night leave to 2300. But by May the war was over. Haile Selassie, the Emperor had left Abyssinia for exile in Britain. The League of Nations half-heartedly imposing sanctions had failed. Mussolini had triumphed.

Designated the 20th Destroyer flotilla we were required to make ourselves efficient before relieving the old 1st flotilla of Vs and Ws at Alexandria in June, so for the next three weeks we were at sea three days a week concentrating in particular on Asdic practice with real submarines to detect. In harbour the Rock Hotel just opened was the main attraction and at 62°F the sea became warm enough for bathing.

A particular trial, definitely not in the programme, which had a reassuring result, took place in *Gipsy's* wardroom. Paying an after dinner call one Saturday night a few of us found 'The Chief' and 'Guns' sitting solemnly on the floor beside a bucket. Measuring content carefully they were filling French letters with water till they burst. Supplied free from the ship's Coxswain, acting as Sick Berth Chief Petty officer, the standard Admiralty Pattern Condom would stand up to 17½ pints. Fit for an elephant it would seem! Perhaps *WHICH!* magazine would undertake some comparative tests from EEC sources.

As a rough rule of thumb Portsmouth to Gibraltar, Gibraltar to Malta and Malta to Alexandria are each a thousand miles, taking three days at around 15 knots. Leaving Gibraltar on May 15th the flotilla was ready to berth in Sliema creek about 0700 on Monday 18th. Ships had to turn 180° and then go stern first up this narrow and winding creek to their moorings. My diary reads:

> "A wonderful performance but I had no idea how tricky. Gipsy and Gallant went in first, the former all wrong put her bows into Gallant - no damage done. Charles brought Grafton in magnificently, he certainly does handle the ship well".

Philip Ziegler in his biography alludes to Mountbatten's first attempt, two years before, handling the destroyer *Daring*, his first command. Unnerving, the Commander-in-Chief, William Fisher, 'The Great Agrippa' was still on board having watched an exercise. "A strange feeling controlling 38,000 horse power at 12 knots going backwards – a new form of thrill", declared Mountbatten having done it well. But he went on to say that sometimes there were narrow squeaks besides an occasional signal 'Manoeuvre well executed'. Mountbatten had the extraordinary experience of being told to take *Daring* to Singapore and return with the old *Wishart* instead. Declaring to all and sundry that this old and dirty ship would become the smartest in the Fleet, he endeared himself to his own men by saying the ship was holy, named after God to whom we pray: '*Our father wishart in heaven....*' Winning every race in the flotilla's regatta, *Wishart*, 'Cock of the Fleet', fully fulfilled his prophecy. Whether rowing, gunnery, cricket or water polo, *Wishart* was the top.

We only spent forty-eight hours in Malta exchanging charts with *Witch*. Without the Fleet, business in the island had suffered, the Commander-in-Chief being greatly concerned for all the unemployed *dghaisa* men, for whom a fund was raised. I found a good 'run ashore' partner in Mr. Battersby, the Flotilla's Radio Bosun temporarily accommodated in *Grafton*, but Aunties and such places were lifeless and depressing. On passage to Alexandria the 20th Destroyer flotilla now had a leader, H.M.S. *Douglas* deputising until *Grenville* arrived from Britain, flying the pennant of Captain D20, C. M. Blackman.

After the cancellation of *Royal Sovereign*'s visit to Alexandria in 1934, for me it was quite a thrill to arrive about 0700 on May 23, a hot cloudless Saturday morning in this great harbour, so full of ships that we could hardly spot the oiler, let alone my sister, Brada Paterson, waving a welcome from a smart Police launch. After we had fuelled and berthed in the outer harbour, she came on board at 1130, with Otto Jenner-Fust bearing greetings from many of my friends. A drink or two and Roy Gould, 'the Chief', drove my sister and me ashore in our fast little 16 foot 'skimming dish'. These little 2/4-seater dinghies were first supplied to our flotilla I think, the other power boat being a 25 footer with a cabin. Having kept the Middle Watch I was glad of lunch and a siesta in the charming little Paterson house at Ramleh five miles out from the port.

Born in 1899 to my sister's 1902, her husband Jack Paterson had been unsuccessful in business, but in 1931 was able to follow in his father's footsteps as an Egyptian Police Officer. A good organiser, Jack was currently involved with the British Boat Club Regatta, an Old Etonian dinner, and permanently with sporting events such as Boxing and Shooting by the Police against the Navy. The job itself was no sinecure; there was plenty of crime in Alexandria and strikes by Egyptian workers, who were very accurate throwers of bricks when addressed by Police Officers. The end of the crisis had revived social life bringing former friends in the Grenadiers and the Scots Guards stationed at Alexandria to their little house at Ramleh.

Jack recommended me to hire a car, selecting from Mr. Theodorarkis, the Greek dealer, a Ford V8 coupé for £8 a month; cheap said Mr. T because it was good to keep in with the Police. As the natives wandered all over the place, driving this monster on the Right, unaccustomed to its Left Hand Drive and formidable acceleration, made the trip to and from Ramleh through the suburbs a series of near misses.

On Friday May 29 the Fleet gave a cocktail party in *Glorious* by way of thanks for Alexandria's hospitality over many months, the entire hangar being so full of guests and hosts that speech was well nigh inaudible. The following night Mr. and Mrs. Oswald Finney gave a dinner party. Finney, who needed a block of flats to hold his vast collection of *objets d'art* was considered the richest man in Alexandria. But in Liverpool he was merely referred to as Frank Verdon's agent. The money, at both ends, came from buying cotton in futures, a procedure I do not pretend to understand.

My sister explained that it would be a small party, about fifteen with several naval people included, so I would be quite at home. That celebrated Tatler reporter, Mary Kennard, would have been far more at home. Besides Sub-Lieutenant Hogg, unlikely to be mentioned, there were three Admirals, Wells, Forbes and Evans, Lieutenant-Colonel 'Boy' Browning with his wife Daphne du Maurier, Colonel and Mrs. Mackenzie who lived in Alexandria, my sister and my brother-in-law.

After a magnificent meal our host showed some of us round, while others opted for Bridge or Snooker. There was a startling moment coming to a small dark room when Finney switched on a light. There before us on the wall was a life size picture of Christ. "Christ that's Rio de Janeiro!", exclaimed Admiral Evans. All present were duly impressed by such cultural knowledge, though I think it was Galilee not Rio. Oswald Finney loved showing guests round his mansion. Coming in there was a swimming bath and a marble replica of the Bridge of Sighs in Venice. A pink marble staircase led to the first floor. Dick Riviere called it 'The Smoked Salmon staircase'. Overheard by Finney, he was not asked again. Pictures, lovely tapestries and priceless collections of fine china abounded, but the ballroom and library impressed me most.

Touring cricket teams sometimes stayed in this house. Unable to find the W.C. in the middle of the night, A.P.F. Chapman, England's Captain reached the library and filled a pitcher. Showing him round in the morning, Oswald was only persuaded in the nick of time not to move it for closer inspection.

On Sunday afternoon the social centre became Gabriella Barker's houseboat. Gabriella (Mrs. Cyril Barker) came of an Austrian family and due to a game leg was slightly disabled. This made her achievement of forming a concert party in 1939, which subsequently gave 538 shows, entertaining thousands of men of all three services, mainly in the desert, all the more remarkable. Nearly all British Alexandrian young ladies, in 1956 Gabriella told their story entitled *Desert Angels*, published by herself, with a foreword by Major General Sir Guy Salisbury-Jones, friend of de Gaulle and a distinguished English vigneron as well as a soldier.

In September 1944 two cruisers *Aurora* and *Black Prince* were based at Alexandria for a short time. As a Lieutenant in the latter I was pleased to be mentioned in the book having arranged a performance for each ship's company.

By May 1936 Admiral Sir Dudley Pound had relieved Sir William Fisher as Commander-in-Chief, while Sir James Somerville had relieved ABC as Rear-Admiral (D) flying his flag in the new cruiser *Galatea*. A spectacle never to be forgotten was ABC on his bridge manoeuvring three flotillas or more single handed. Mountbatten, present on one occasion, described it as the greatest one-man performance he had ever seen on the bridge of a ship.

My brother-in-law Jack, invited to a day at sea in *Galatea* by the Captain Guy Warren, imitated this performance in which the Flag Lieutenant Douglas Dobell and the Chief Yeoman of Signals were on the receiving end, converting ABC's verbal orders into appropriate flag signals. ABC heard about this and on a second visit said to Jack,

"I hear you do a good imitation of me, I must see it".

"What on earth did you do?" I asked.

"Alright", he said, "Just toned it down a bit".

Going to sea in mid-week for two or three days, – or just one day in harbour at one hour's notice when emergency destroyer – gave much needed respite from social life. The next cocktail party was given by the Peels (Teddy and Norah). Born in Knutsford Cheshire, in Egypt he was Chairman of a large family firm, earning a knighthood in 1944 at the end of the war, having received a DSO and MC in the first one.

During the Thirties Teddy was more in the news as a yachtsman and tunny fisherman. Jack Paterson was his guest sometimes, in the Red Sea

Tea Party at Sidi Bishr. Left to right: Sue Carver, Jock, Claude Dunbar, A.N. Other, Harry Carver, Hilary Holmes, Leslie Carver.

Fifi Carver takes on Colonel Alan, Jock and Claude Dunbar for a bucket.

JUST A HOGG'S LIFE

and off Scarborough. An exciting experience, strapped in a boat one could be towed rapidly for miles by a hooked tunny fish. Jack, whose life style was always thousands of piastres ahead of his income, once said to me, "I'm a poor man, I can't afford a yacht like Teddy Peel."

My Greynvile term were represented at the Peels' party by Dan Duff, Chief Cadet Captain at Dartmouth and now Flag Lieutenant to Dudley Pound, the Commander-in-Chief. In 1940 Dan would make a long and happy marriage with Barbara his daughter. There were different dinner parties after the cocktail party much the same people meeting again at the Excelsior for dancing and a cabaret. My diary mentions Hilary Holmes, daughter of a local judge, Patience Archer, niece of Geraldine and William Henn, head of the Police and a pair of marvellous dancers in the cabaret. The surprise of the day however was Charles Kennaway with a lovely tall blonde whose identity, like Cinderella at the Ball, none of the locals knew. This was Joice Campion; I thought she was lovely until she forced me to drive her young brother home, thirty six miles there and back one night, getting back on board at 0530. They married in 1937. Unable to take his Captain J. C. Clouston in the destroyer *Isis* ("I suffer in silence") Charles applied for the Fleet Air Arm and lost his life in 1940 as a pilot of a Swordfish in 826 Squadron, raiding German-occupied Holland. A merry fellow, only his mother and sister were left to communicate with his father, made stone-deaf in the first World war.

The Grenadiers' party with Lieutenant-Colonel 'Boy' Browning and his wife Daphne (du Maurier) receiving the guests, was on Saturday 6 June. Here I met Dennis, a younger Peel, the fair haired son of Teddy's brother, also in the family firm. Daphne, a close friend of my sister, was delightful, though we are likely to learn from her biographers in the 1990s that she hated social life, which hindered her real love – writing.

Hereinafter 'CC', my sister had now nick-named Charles Firth 'Champagne Charlie'. Having given him many introductions, the great sparkler fizzed on board *Grafton* as well as among the Brigade of Guards. My sister's name Brada had a curious origin; in fact she was Brada III, following our mother and grandmother, Hultons of Bolton. Pronounced 'Bray-da', it was derived from Bradda Head in the Isle of Man, where an earlier generation had lived. Ten years my senior, Brada had an attractive way with men, though an appendix operation, two Caesarean daughters and a Hysterectomy had reduced her stamina considerably.

On Sunday June 7 after calling with C.C. on Captain Guy Warren and the Wardroom of *Galatea*, my job was to make Sidecar and White Lady cocktails chez Paterson in Ramleh for our party. Barkers, Carvers, Henns,

Holmes's, Pakenhams, Lady Keown-Boyd, Jimmy Ford, Jack Hargreaves were 'the locals'. Otto Jenner- Fust, Rudy Wratislaw, Peter Milburn, the Warrens and from *Grafton*, Firth, Roper, Crawford, Gould were the naval names I recorded. In my eighty-first year now, Roy Gould tells me we are the only officers of *Grafton* surviving, he, aged ninety two, having done it pretty well.

At sea the following week Admiral Pound, Commander-in-Chief, came on board *Grafton* unexpectedly one afternoon to see an Anti-Submarine exercise. At the end of the afternoon I went up to the bridge.

"Sub", said C.C. "Show the Commander-in-Chief....."

Realising immediately the old boy's need I said 'Ay, Ay, Sir' and led the way down to the Upper Deck, throwing open the door of the Heads.

"It's your No.1 boiler room I want to see", he said tersely, with Dan Duff laughing his head off in the background.

June 16 called for a celebration. Becoming a Lieutenant I could now ship my second stripe. Jack had retired to bed with 'flu. Brada was about to return to England with their two girls, now 10 and 7. After dining at the Union Bar with two bottles of champagne for a *jeunesse dorée* that included Hilary Holmes, Joice Campion and Peggy Purvis, it was all the fun of the fair. Dodgems, walls of death, switchbacks and roundabouts were just a prelude to dancing at the Maisonette and the Miami. A Policeboat was persuaded to take me and Charles Kennaway to our ships and a 2.30 a.m. bed.

For some weeks we had been practising for the 20th Destroyer flotilla regatta, the officers' crew doing so at 0715; and a pretty awful crew we looked at that hour with Crawford muttering, "Dear O dear! the things I do on John Jameson" and C.C's oar being dipped rather than pulled.

That evening the Herbert Carvers, who were about to leave for England gave a small party at Bacos, their delightful Ramleh house. Their family were there in force: Leslie married to Sue, so beautiful she should have been preserved in a glass case; Harry, the second son married to Fifi, and the tall Marguerite whose old fashioned waltz with Jack was a pleasure to watch. She, in due course, would marry Charles Earl of the Grenadiers. Only Agnes, the eldest was absent, married to a Commander Farrant Royal Navy, who insisted on a notice over their double bed reading "Efficiency First", so she told me the only time we met.

The next visitor to 8 Rue Station Schutz was Colonel Alan Swinton commanding the Second Battalion Scots Guards. One of the Old Contemptibles of 1914 he had fought through the Great War losing a foot in the very last week. By the end of June everybody was bathing at Sidi

JUST A HOGG'S LIFE

Bishr and our party one Sunday included Colonel Alan, the Adjutant Claude Dunbar and Jock Burns, also of the Regiment. Their custom socially of calling their Colonel by his Christian name, preceded by his rank, was one, I thought, that could be adopted in R.N. and R.A.F. circles too.

In the week before the regatta we, the Wardroom crew, had been practising twice a day. The day before, beating the Communications whaler easily, the ship's company thought we were a marvellous crew. Trained on gin and no sleep! "CC seems more interested in criticising the appearance of the ship. Crawford swears and mutters. No. 1 washes out at the end of the stroke. 'Guns' as coxswain makes wet remarks continuously". (The diary doesn't mention my performance, only that I sleep on the upper deck in the hot damp weather waking at 0430 with the dawn and the flies).

Wednesday July 1 was the day. First the Communications came 6th out of the eight competing crews. The Daymen with three Maltese came 2nd and for the rest of the forenoon all our crews, except the Young Seamen who were 6th, either won or came 2nd. The officers' race was a triumph, winning in the fastest time of the day, Crawford telling us that he had taken half a tumbler of Very Special Old John Jameson reserved for these desperate occasions. So at dinner time *Grafton* led by a few points from *Douglas*, the flotilla leader.

P.M. The Seaman's B let us down coming 6th reducing our lead to four points with one event left, the All Comers. The excitement was awful but *Grafton*'s All Comers won their race and with it the regatta, quickly improvising a Cock and a Chucking-Up party to parade round the Fleet. The result was really a triumph for No.1, Nigel Roper, showing himself to be a first class executive, who could get the best out of a ship's company.

But our ordeal was by no means over. On Monday July 6 we berthed alongside *Douglas* to give us a grandstand view of the Inter-Flotillas' regatta, the Gs being one flotilla, the Fs - *Fame Fearless*, the other. For us the officers' race was a tragedy. *Fame* and *Grafton* drew ahead about half way, but just as we began to draw ahead of *Fame*, 'Guns' our coxswain, mistaking the cruiser *Ajax* for the *Galatea* steered widely to Port. It was sometime before we spotted this, and still more before we made him realise his mistake and correct it. On course again we were still in the lead but lost the race by inches. The error had cost us five lengths - were we annoyed!

However the 20th Flotilla went ahead and the *Grafton* All Comers did well enough for us to win the Aggregate Cup. Our officers' crew were selected to pull in the Orion Cup. I am not sure what this was but C.C declared he was not pulling any more for love or money and opened a bottle of champagne at dinner to wet my second stripe. I was not present when R.A.(D.) James Somerville presented the prizes. Congratulating C.C. he said,

"How do you manage to pull so well, Charles?"

"Training Sir, just training!" was the reply.

"Nonsense, Charles, I've seen you every night in the Excelsior" said the Admiral.

Looking through the old Navy Lists before writing this chapter I found that in 1926 Charles Firth was one of five taking the Signal Course held then in R. N. Barracks Portsmouth, James Somerville being the Director of the Signal Division at the Admiralty. Mountbatten, born 1900 like Charles, had gone on to take the advance signal course at Greenwich and then to become Fleet Wireless Officer in the Mediterranean Fleet before returning to the teaching staff of the Signal School at Portsmouth in 1929. Tall, fair haired and handsome, Charles looked immaculate in his white uniform and as victor in the regatta he had followed in Mountbatten's footsteps.

While Mountbatten taught and wrote a *Handbook of Wireless Telegraphy* besides descriptions of every wireless set in R.N. use, Charles learnt his trade, first as Signal officer in *Campbell*, the Leader of the 6th Flotilla at home, then as Flag Lieutenant to Commodore Dalglish of the Atlantic Fleet flotillas. A step up, in 1932 he was Flag Lieutenant-Commander to Rear-Admiral Rose of the Mediterranean Fleet flotillas. This, as was customary, he combined with being their Signal and W/T Staff officer.

After our regatta victory less than two weeks remained before the Fleet departed for Malta. My diary records a succession of Farewell parties, one on board the flotilla leader *Codrington*, another by Val Goodchild in Ramleh and finally the Fleet's Farewell to Alexandria in the hangar of *Glorious*, very crowded with tasteless, weak drinks. Among my friends J. M. D. "Jock" Gray had found an attractive fiancée in Peggy Purvis and Hilary Holmes would soon marry C. W. 'Kit' Wells, just qualified as a Gunnery officer. As such he lost his life in the Carrier Glorious sunk by Scharnhorst and Gneisenau off Norway in June 1940. They had a son and later Hilary had three daughters having made a second marriage with Sir James Henry, a distinguished member of the Bar. Jock retired as Vice-Admiral Sir John and has since been Secretary of the Oriental Ceramic Society for many years.

At 0815 on Saturday 18 July the Fleet sailed for Malta with a large gathering of the English community on the breakwater and King Farouk

JUST A HOGG'S LIFE

a guest on board *Queen Elizabeth*, the flagship. A great display was given to impress him, destroyers dashing about in all directions. Indeed after only three hours sleep, I drew a reciprocal course on the chart, which resulted in *Grafton* going Eastwards at 30 knots with all other destroyers going West. Unlike the occasion when the Admiral signalled "What the hell are you doing?" and the delinquent Captain replied, "About 30 knots", my mistake was corrected before the wily eye of James Somerville noticed it.

Dissatisfied with our station keeping, he made us take station on a line of bearing throughout the night on the way to Malta, with Officer of the Watch manoeuvres by day such as exchanging stations or closing *Galatea*. Grumbling at first, soon I had never known the four hours of a middle watch pass so quickly. Reaching Malta on Tuesday July 21 *Queen Elizabeth* and *Grafton* respectively led the way into Grand Harbour and Sliema Creek. Antelope being the other destroyer alongside us, I found Eddie Baines ready for a run ashore. He still remembers the evening because only a lightning leap saved us from being killed by an infuriated Maltese taxi driver driving his taxi at us in the narrow Strada Stretta. We swore vengeance and took his number but the incident was forgotten when a signal came saying *Grafton* was to be ready by Saturday for duty as Guard ship at Cannes because King Edward VIII was renting a house there for a holiday.

On Wednesday July 22 Civil War had broken out in Spain. Three destroyers of our 20th flotilla sailed for Barcelona. The 1st and 4th flotillas, on their way home at last, found themselves directed to Spanish ports, required to safeguard British people and interests.

Meanwhile we started 'buffing up'. All the boats were sent to the dockyard. Sailmakers measured for a special ceremonial awning, painters set to in the after lobby, shipwrights measured for wooden gratings to cover bollards. R.A. (D) had arrived at 0700 to wake C.C. and I, finding an important chart missing, went ashore to get it. By Monday 27th all was ready, when due to civil war in Spain and tension in France, the plan was cancelled.

On Tuesday 28th after a visit from Commander-in-Chief, Dudley Pound, back came our boats looking a treat as for a Boat show. Two officers and thirteen ratings joined us for passage and at 1600 off we went for Barcelona. I remember that night so well; off Pantellaria the sea was an absolute mill pond. Another twenty four hours, passing the Balearics, it became rough and stormy. C.C. on the bridge being sea sick into a bucket was handed a telegram. It was from Sue Snelling, a lady he had met in Alexandria, now in Cannes. With fond love it read: "Can't wait to see you here tomorrow night".

Arriving in Barcelona at 0600/30th July we berthed in the harbour alongside *London*, 10,000 ton flagship of the Cruiser Squadron. A French cruiser was nearby. Outside the harbour there were two Italian cruisers, one destroyer, and a German 'pocket' battleship. *Gipsy* and *Gallant* were just off taking British refugees to Marseille.

The situation in Spain was confused. The elected Government was Left wing. General Franco, who had been Governor of the Canary Islands, landed in Southern Spain from Morocco in aeroplanes financed and piloted by Englishmen. His aim was to destroy the lawful Government and substitute a Fascist dictatorship. Europe was in fact governed by fear. Fear of Fascism by the Left; fear of Russia by the Right. In the cities the workers murdered the aristocracy and Franco's troops and supporters murdered all who opposed them as they advanced.

Our role was to take British residents away to safety and in pursuit of this we sailed down the coast twenty five miles to Sitges anchoring close to the Terremar Hotel. But after waiting till dusk our catch was only two British and their dog. Back in Barcelona we secured alongside *Douglas*, busy transferring Captain D and his staff to *Grenville* just arrived.

But at 0400 next morning, August 1, the refugees in strength boarded *Douglas* and *Grafton* before we sailed at 0500 with, in theory, a maximum of seventy five passengers apiece. We made them as comfortable as we could in the Wardroom, Captain's quarters and on the upper deck. But by 0900, approaching the Gulf of Lions they were very sea sick, three women settling permanently with their heads over bath and basins in the bathroom. I felt very sorry for all these uprooted and unhappy people. Reaching Marseille about 1500, the quays on this Saturday afternoon were deserted; not a Frenchman in sight to take our wires. Eventually one clapped-out specimen did appear. C.C. temperamental and mad with irritation, declared he would remain on his bridge until everything aft had been restored to normal, recalling for me Masefield's Consecration:

> *Not the be-medalled Commander, beloved of the throne,*
> *Riding cock-horse to parade when the bugles are blown,*
> *But the lads who carried the* koppie *and cannot be known.*

Returning overnight to Barcelona we called at Caldas de Estrach, thirty miles north of Barcelona embarking a German Jew, his wife, nurse and two children. They said they were the only foreigners left and that there were none at Mataró. A signal having now been received indicating that the King would do a cruise in the Adriatic, we disembarked our passengers and set course for Malta at 1400 on Sunday August 2.

On board I had the job of Cypher officer; messages were in groups of four figures. These one subtracted from another lot of four figures in a Secret book provided. Having done that, reference to another Secret book revealed the words. By Monday we knew that H.M.C. stood for His Majesty's Cruise and that Sir Godfrey Thomas, the King's Private Secretary and one detective would be accommodated in *Grafton*. Running along the North coast of Africa stopping for a tea time bathe off the Cani rocks, CC's bonhomie was quite restored when he remarked that we were on a cruise already and it was such a pity we had to have all these guns and things.

In Grand Harbour we joined *Glowworm*, moving into dock for a bottom scrape. The next coded message from the Admiralty ordered H.M. the King to be met on Monday 10 August at Sibenik. The Captain of *Grafton* would be responsible for His Majesty's safety and should select 'suitable quiet bays for His Majesty to visit'. It was certainly not the safest time for monarchs to travel around the Mediterranean. King Alexander had been assassinated at Marseille; with a left wing government in France, Communists could be active on the Riviera. Instead King Edward chartered *Nahlin*, the 1400 ton yacht belonging to Lady Yule living in the Channel Islands. Time was short and Captain Doyle proceeded direct to Sibenik, a port up the coast from Split.

In *Grafton* we sailed independently, while *Glowworm* went to Brindisi to collect mail, arriving at Sibenik with *Nahlin* at 0600 on Monday 10th. The Royal Party came out in the Orient Express arriving at 0845 to be met by C.C. and cheered by a crowd. About 1100 the *Nahlin* led the way into the Adriatic with *Grafton* and *Glowworm* following in line ahead, arriving about 1530 at Port Tager at the Southern end of Dugi Island. Arid and barren, while *Glowworm* oiled *Nahlin*, the King taking a walk ashore ran into the island's one inhabitant a shepherd, who recognising him shouted, "Christ Mr. King! " and ran away. As far as 'Mr. King' was concerned that was the end of 'suitable quiet bays' and he decided we would make next day for Rab, that popular island and resort about fifty miles up the coast.

Sir Godfrey Thomas 47, who had been Private Secretary to the Prince of Wales since 1919 and looked overworked, had a spare cabin aft and dined with C. C. in his cabin. David Storrier, the King's detective, was given the Captain's sea cabin forward and a three badge Able Seaman called Nobby to look after him. Storrier was a big man; the cabin small.

Nobby looked at them both. "Good job you didn't bring a couple of blood 'ounds with you", he said.

Sending *Glowworm* to Brindisi for the mail we sailed at 1000 with *Nahlin* between the islands to reach Rab about 1630. A charming little port, most of the inhabitants appeared to be out sailing. But ashore the King and Mrs. Simpson were mobbed, not surprisingly in August where many Germans came for holidays. Hoping to avoid crowds we went South the next morning at 0600 between Pag Island and the mainland and at 1000 C.C. and Sexton Blake – as Storrier was now called – went off in a motorboat with the Royal party for a picnic. Peace perfect peace to write up the fair log and correct charts on board! Navigation around these islands, where uncharted rocks might lurk anywhere, required constant fixing of the ship's position and at only 10 knots the engine and boiler room fans failed to keep their inmates comfortable such was the heat.

After a big overnight thunderstorm we resumed the journey South, passing Zadar to the little island of Murter, where all could bathe from *Grafton*. Invited by C.C., the King and some of his guests in *Nahlin* came over for a drink. It was quite informal; the Chief and Guns being on the Quarterdeck were presented to the King; No.1 and Crawford were invited to join the drinks party in the Captain's cabin. Left out, I could only presume that like Cassio I had offended Othello, until afterwards he asked why I had not been there. The reply 'not asked' brought an apology of a sort, but it became increasingly clear that the possibility of an M.V.O. was the prime mover in C.C's life during the cruise.

Our next stop was Port Trogir, ten miles up the coast from Split on its own island, connected by a bridge to the mainland. Its Hungarian Gothic Cathedral dating from 1450 is one of the glories of Dalmatia. Its inhabitants almost all Slavs had driven out the Italians, who had tried to take the town in 1918. Anchoring about 1245 King Edward preferred to pull round the Fleet, as he called the two destroyers, during the afternoon in a dinghy. C.C. dined in the yacht returning about 0100 with £1.10.6., winnings at Poker. Off again next day Saturday 15th, our call at Split was chiefly to pick up Duff Cooper, Minister of War and his wife, Lady Diana. The King was said to have a hang-over and nobody dared ask what he wanted to do. However we moved to a small resort twenty miles down the coast, where he was mobbed once more by the locals.

On board we were having difficulty in amusing ourselves apart from bathing and water polo over the ship's side. There were one or two Wardroom arguments; Chief Roy Gould asserted that to end a dispute or argument there was nothing like socking the opponent on the jaw. A

JUST A HOGG'S LIFE

Wardroom argument, so it was said, had three stages: Downright Assertion, Flat Contradiction, Personal Abuse.

This particular day was sad for Savoyards. Sir Henry Lytton, the most famous of Gilbert and Sullivan Titipu Executioners as well as Strolling Jesters was dead.

Sunday 16th at 0700 saw the yacht and its escorts under way heading for Korcula, the forty mile long island about half way between Split and Dubrovnik. After supper, preceded by many sherries, Crawford and I went ashore to find a charming little hotel on the quay, with tables out of doors in front of it. With a local steamer alongside the pier the place could have been a scene in *White Horse Inn*, the musical of 1929 enchanting London at the Coliseum. Introduced to a Yugo-Slav family we drank quantities of beer and danced on a terrible stone floor. Most of them, students at Zagreb University, were good company.

Leaving at 1030 on Monday we anchored at Dubrovnik in the afternoon between a wooded island and the mainland after cruising through lovely scenery between the islands of Peljesac and Mijet. *Anna Maree*, Lord Dudley's yacht was in the harbour with some tennis enthusiasts on board who welcomed No.1 for a game. Dining ashore the Royal party received a cordial welcome, and enjoyed a two night stay.

On board we were entertained by a naked couple on the island five hundred yards away busy copulating to their hearts content. In the Wardroom Storrier and two local detectives fought for a look through the two scuttles. Settled in Chichester in the 1950s, I related this story to C........ Y............, a friend of my wife's. We checked the date.

"That girl was me", she said.

When we sailed at 1400 there was a similar view from the Bridge of - presumably - another couple. C.C's glasses may have been trained on the ball, they were certainly not scanning the seas for those hidden rocks. Our destination was Kotor at the head of an inlet thirty miles down the coast. Its approach is not unlike a Norwegian fiord. A narrow entrance from the Adriatic opens out into a large expansion of water. The channel leading to Kotor then becomes little wider than a canal before it opens up again into what is described in Scotland as a sea loch with the town of Kotor in its south western corner. All round the sea loch the mountains fall precipitously making it rather a dark sinister place, I thought, when followed by a porpoise while taking a swim in the almost fresh water.

But when night fell on the mountain side, there behind the town, was an entire map of England and Scotland in torch light. A great effort, each light must have been placed or held in position by somebody. The King

HMS GRAFTON - COCK OF THE FLEET

King Edward and Mrs Simpson (right) go ashore at Dubrovnik.

The Yacht Nahlin about to leave Sibenik with HM on board.

JUST A HOGG'S LIFE

did not go ashore because a motor trip into the mountains was planned for the following day. Instead he decided we should leave at 2200 for Corfu. Apart from the unnecessary risk in passing through the narrow passage at night, the discourtesy was inexcusable. We were led to believe that Mrs. Simpson had said, "Darling these mountains are so oppressive I feel so boxed in".

Arriving at Corfu about 1500 on Thursday August 20 the first to climb our ladder was George Assimakis, the Admiralty contractor who was said to be in the employ of at least three Governments. The King and Wallis Simpson went to stay with King George of the Hellenes. In the ships everybody had a 'moan'. Storrier complained that when the King was in *Nahlin* he could not go ashore. C.C, probably suffering from lack of sleep was finding fault generally. I was criticised because the messdecks were not smart enough. The reason was that most of the hands were made to concentrate on the Upper Deck and parts of the ship that could be admired from outside. Much of my time was occupied running up to the chart house to collect charts for perusal in C.C's cabin aft. Captain Doyle of *Nahlin* had a near miss with a local steamer and was said in Southampton to have been to every port in the world and made a cock-up in each of them.

The *Nahlin* was not too comfortable in the hot weather. The Royal Suite, hastily converted from a library, was isolated in the bows below the upper deck. The other guests were crammed into the stern. In *Nahlin* they liked to play a card game on the upper deck until the small hours, surfacing from the arms of Morpheus about 1000 to find themselves at the next port of call. Since C.C. could not bear to miss their company and had to be alert when at sea, this sort of sleepless life did not endear him to the shipmates he commanded.

Continuing South H.M did not like Cephalonia so the squadron reached Port Itea on the North side of the Gulf of Corinth for an 8 a.m breakfast on Monday August 24. In the evening the Royal party and many of our ships' company went to watch *Glowworm* beating *Grafton* 6-3 at water polo.

After dark Dick Jessel, *Glowworm*'s captain and Paul Foy, his First Lieutenant went water skiing using the ship's 16 foot dinghy as their towing boat. The dinghy driver released Foy on skis to cruise up to *Glowworm*'s after gangway, but at speed with the bow in the air he could not see a short way ahead from the driving seat of these dinghies. Jessel, swimming off the forward gangway, dived too late, suffering shock, loss of blood and compound fractures of both legs.

Surgeon Lieutenant-Commander Keating patched up his Captain on the upper deck there and then. *Glowworm*, under the command of Foy, sailed for Patras within the hour, returning at 0845 next morning saying that Jessel was as comfortable as possible in hospital, asking for beer.

Dick Jessel died on 14 February 1988 with an obituary in *The Times* of 16 February and the small piece about the accident added by me. Though in theory he was unfit for sea service he commanded the destroyer *Legion*, winning finally a D.S.O., O.B.E. and bar. Invalided home after the *Legion* had been sunk, the hospital ship was sunk, those on board becoming prisoners of the Vichy French. As Senior officer in their notorious Lagouat Prison in Algeria, he was a tower of strength described by Commander Charles Lamb in his book *War in a String Bag*, the Stringbag, being the Swordfish aircraft.

On the afternoon of August 25 *Nahlin*, *Grafton* and *Glowworm* (Paul Foy now Captain) proceeded through the Corinth Canal with all the locals for miles around crowding the banks and the one bridge overhead until we anchored off Piraeus, the port of Athens, for four days. With the Royal party all ashore, Evans the second detective showed me round the yacht. The two rooms forward occupied by Edward and Wallis were full of photographs of each other. Aft, the accommodation for the other guests seemed to me to be marvellous but for the staff it was very poor.

Roy Gould and I dined with an interesting Greek Foreign Office official who had been up at Oxford. Ouzo never became my favourite drink and the meal took longer in coming than any I remember. By invitation the King inspected the *Grafton*'s ship's company and then the *Glowworm*'s. Placing myself in command of the Royal Guard in beautifully polished boots and gaiters, everything went well – I only poked my sword through the ceremonial awning once.

Somewhere in the distance we spotted the Athens Golf Club to which No. 1, Roy, Storrier and I proceeded in the dinghy getting soaked with such a load. The course was all sand, but sand of all kinds so there was some variety. No.1 and I returned to play at 0730 the following morning followed by a bathe and a real English breakfast on return.

Sailing for Skiathos in the Sporades at 2100 on Sunday 30th, the weather had become very rough by the next morning with *Nahlin* rolling considerably, much to the delight of Storrier, because Wallis was a bad sailor. Instead of proceeding through the Ora channel into the Aegean the three vessels anchored in the lee of Euboea, that eastern province of Greece that would be an island but for the swing bridge of Chalkis. Back to normal weather the next morning sailing at 0700, we reached the swing bridge about 1130, width 181 feet, with one hell of a tide running through it in our direction. There was no sign of any pilot.

Going first much too slowly, *Nahlin* was swept against the jetty, damaging all her boats on the starboard side. Increasing speed as we went through C.C. did it well. Telling Foy in *Glowworm* what to expect, he went hell for leather followed by a huge wave. Enough for one day, we anchored at the North end of Euboea not so far from Ossa and Pelion, those mountains famous in fable. Anchored close to us, units of the Greek Navy fired a Royal salute and cheered.

September 1. Sailing at 0700 brought us to Skiathos at 1130. With their marvellous bathing beaches, these islands looked lovely and George Assinakis was on the spot to greet us. C.C. changing into a shirt and shorts waited to be asked to join H.M.'s picnic party looking like a dismal dog not getting a walk. The signal came in due course asking him and Alan Lascelles, who had taken the place of Sir Godfrey Thomas, to join them. The old Engineer from *Nahlin* paid us a call, while the Chief and 'Guns' went to *Nahlin*, to meet two of the maids they fancied. C.C. transformed into a dog with two tails, returned having been invited to a whole day's picnic next day.

September 2. With this picnic party back on board we sailed at 2000 for Suvla Bay en route for Istanbul, where H.M was to meet Kemal Ataturk, the Turkish Head of State. The little town as we left was illuminated with coloured lights. The cloudless, calm night with a full moon was exceptionally beautiful. "The isles of Greece!, the isles of Greece! where burning Sappho loved and sung". One began to understand Byron's love for Greece. I had been reading Masefield's book on the Dardanelles campaign and keeping watch from midnight to 0200 tried to imagine those men steaming towards the peninsular at about the same hour, on April 25 1915, expecting a victory but meeting a massacre.

September 3. Our rendezvous with two Turkish destroyers took place at 0915 in Suvla Bay. This area of the Dardanelles campaign is twelve miles up the coast from Cape Helles at the entrance only two miles wide, around which the beaches formed the other area. Anzac, named after the Australian and New Zealand companies was just south of Suvla Bay. Steaming slowly down the coast those well kept cemeteries were clearly visible. The friendly Turkish officer, who came to *Grafton* brought a wreath which he wished to drop where the battleship Triumph had been sunk by a U-boat on 25 May 1915. Reaching Cape Helles about 1100, the King, with Lascelles and Storrier, landed close by at Seddel Bahr. I would have liked to have been with them. The War Graves records read as if every man in Lancashire perished at

Gallipoli. As for the Australians and New Zealanders, that they returned once more to fight for Britain in 1939 is a debt we can never repay.

The Straits are thirty five miles long and rarely more than two miles wide. The two Turkish destroyers stationed themselves one on either side of *Grafton*; Chanak, the town at the narrowest point fired a 21-gun salute and Turkish troops lining either bank cheered loud and long. There must have been 10,000 of them. It was most impressive. Probably to make a spectacular arrival in daylight, we anchored in the Sea of Marmora about eight miles short of Istanbul.

September 4. Flags galore, crowds lining the shore, Sir Percy Loraine, Britain's ambassador to Turkey in his barge and the English community in another, our Royal trio anchored at noon off Dalma Bagtche Palace with a background of mosques and minarets.

The King's mission with Kemal Ataturk was to ensure that Turkey's interests did not conflict with Britain's in Egypt and the Suez Canal. In this he was successful and as a result of their meeting Britain pipped Hitler's Dr. Schacht on the post by getting contracts for the Dardanelles refortification recently agreed with the League of Nations.

Sight-seeing tours were arranged for our libertymen giving them their first real run ashore since we left Malta. I was duty on board while C.C., No. 1, Foy and Dr. Keating were taken to lunch by a Captain Macdonald R.N. retd. The King and Wallis returned to *Nahlin* after sight-seeing to give a small cocktail party for Ataturk and other important Turks. Ataturk was a gay dog; a few days before, he had sent the King a telegram saying he was demonstrating the pleasure of the King's forthcoming visit by dancing at the Palace Hotel.

After dark everything in sight appeared to be illuminated – Leander's tower, lots of 'E's',, Prince of Wales feathers, all the boats, with some fifteen of them making a procession round the Bosphorus. The ships too – masts, funnels, bridges, all lit up; a marvellous show.

September 5. This Saturday was quite a day. Ataturk and his Turkish ministers were expected to walk round *Grafton*, partly because their Italian-built destroyers were not too good and they wanted British. Unfortunately they couldn't pay. At 1100 the Prime Minister led the party inspecting my Guard and the Ship's Company before the walk round and champagne in the Wardroom. Said the P.M.

"I have never seen a destroyer so clean, so smart, so perfect ... but then it is a British ship".

Where there's a British community, there is a cricket club. Having collected five *Glowworm*s and six *Grafton*s we were met that afternoon by

JUST A HOGG'S LIFE

their Captain Perkins and Jean Madge, as pretty a scorer as one could wish to meet. The ground was small, the matting wicket not very true and the outfield awful. Electing to bat we were 40 for 3 when Telegraphist Gregory and Captain Hogg came to the rescue. No cricketer, I was immensely proud making 56. To our 142 they were all out for 220.

The next item was a cocktail party given jointly by Mrs. Ross, wife of the Military Attaché and Mrs. Kernick, wife of *The Times* correspondent in, I think the latter's pleasant house, with lots of local lovelies present. Dancing to the gramophone Mrs. Ross enjoyed learning the rumba, Cuban style with Arse and Belly Rooms, Southsea variations. Next C.C., No.1, Foy, Woodhouse, Crawford and Dr. Keating arrived from a tea party in a Turkish battleship. Mrs. Kernick then played the piano with all present singing sea shanties, Scott Gatty's Plantation songs and a little Schubert, the pianist adding her own descant from time to time. The scorer, Jean Madge, small with golden hair, freckles and a turned up nose was musical too.

For dinner the party broke into groups. I found myself with the Rosses, Jean, Foy, Crawford and the Doctor crossing the Bosphorus to Moda where we dined about 2300 and got to bed about 0300. It was not until Easter 1979 that I met another Kernick. We were lunching with Robin and Elsa Reid at Croft's Port wine Quinta Roeda at Pinhâo up the Douro. I mentioned the party at Istanbul. "My parents", said Robin Kernick. For some years now he has been the Managing Director of Corney and Barrow, the London wine merchants, with a son also in the business.

September 6. At 1000 we moved to Prinkipo Island for H.M to bathe. At 1430 we moved to Moda to see a regatta and to receive the guests for a final At Home. The lovely Jean Madge fell a little from her pedestal being rather bossy and "a little schoolmistress-ish"; which was not surprising for that was her profession.

At 1930 we made yet another move – back to our original berth. The King with Wallis and his staff boarded a royal train for Vienna that evening. C.C. went to see them off returning at midnight with the M.V.O. 4th Class*, a cigarette box, special cuff links from H.M and a gold cigarette case from Ataturk. Jessel and Foy also received cuff links. We poor souls got nothing, except a portion of what H.M had left in the larder.

So about 0100 we departed for Malta at 20 knots. *Glowworm* had already sailed to call on Jessel in hospital at Athens.

---

*Member Victorian Order

In the light of the King's abdication, which we never expected, the *Nahlin* cruise became part of British history. For me, though tedious at times, it was certainly a unique experience.

Back in Malta on September 8 *Grafton* and *Glowworm* were each given a three week refit and rest. *Grenville* was now in harbour and the Twentieth flotilla now became the First, our V and W predecessors having been put into reserve. Most of the Mediterranean Fleet was away in Spanish waters, observing and reporting events with Germany and Italy now openly helping Franco. Though back in Bighi hospital, Dr. Keating came to dine in *Glowworm* and encouraged us to take more exercise with squash courts close by. He also analysed a new seasick prevention pill sent me by my mother, which had been useful on the cruise. "Principal drug Hyoscine used for quieting maniacs and inducing twilight sleep", he said.

C.C. hiring a large Ford V8 and sleeping in chambers at the Union Club when the ship was in dry dock, appeared to have few friends at present in Malta, and seemed content to mix with us and other officers of the flotilla. The most hospitable couple were Kay and Bill ("Closet") Moss of Garland, who had a house on the sea front by Sliema Creek. Gipsy returned from refugee rescue; her captain, Ransome, later had a fall from his own bridge which was fatal. Bobbie Burton paid a call to announce that the *London* was about to go home after a month in Barcelona and that he would be married on November 14 to Molly, a union that both families had intended for years.

One morning I was required to take charge of a funeral of an Able Seaman from *Gipsy*, who had died in Bighi Hospital. From the hospital mortuary we set off in procession about 0800, the firing party preceding the gun carriage on which the coffin was placed. There were no mourners from Gipsy, but a photographer took pictures to send to his relatives. Wearing my 'solar bowler' I marched behind the gun carriage finding the smell of the corpse most unpleasant as it jolted over the cobbles during a twenty five minute march in the sun. The burial ground was barren and untidy with hardly a tree. As I wondered whether I should doff the 'solar bowler', a priest appeared to read the Burial Service. Soon it was all over, except for a 'Stand Easy' and a smoke outside the gates.

Towards the end of September the 40th Division returned from Spain so that the whole new 1st Destroyer Flotilla with its new leader *Grenville* berthed together in Sliema Creek. Required to go to sea alone to test some new Gunnery gadget, getting out from the inner end of the creek was relatively easy to getting back going astern. We were all relieved that C.C's ship handling was so good.

On the 29th Crawford, who ran the office and opened the mail, gave me a note, which appointed me to the aircraft carrier *Glorious*, date October 16, relief named Somerville. I was flabbergasted; having escaped from big ships to be sent back after only six months to a life of teak treading was awful. C.C. seemed upset too and went to see Captain D, who said that destroyers were not entitled to three Lieutenants and Admiralty policy was to give young officers as wide experience as possible. I could only console myself that when Somerville arrived we would probably be in Spain and *Glorious* in Greece.

With *Queen Elizabeth* and *Repulse* available to be 'attacked' by *Glorious* aircraft, the submarine *Clyde* and our flotilla, we sailed for three days of Dummy torpedo attacks, Fleet manoeuvres, Night Encounter exercises and some smoke laying practice all in rough weather. The following week returning to Lazaretto Creek, on the other side of Manoel Island from Sliema Creek, a cross wind caused considerable delay when berthing, and quite a few bumps, but no damage fortunately.

On October 12 the 39th Division (*Garland*, *Grafton*, *Gipsy*, and *Gallant*) sailed with *Galatea* for Spain. Exercising most of the way in foul weather, including thunderstorms in the Balearics, we made for Cartagena and *Gallant* for Malaga. Arriving P.M. October 14 we learnt from *Arrow* that the town was a Red stronghold, not raided by the insurgents yet. The atrocities were dreadful; one man had been soaked in the harbour and then burnt to death under a petrol pump. When the town blacks out we should follow suit. Franco's two cruisers, Canarias and an older one are based at Cadiz: if they pass through the Straits into the Mediterranean we have to go and anchor at night at some quiet spot ten miles away.

The next ten days can be given in diary form. ***October 15***. Dashed off at 0400 for Alicante at 22 knots taking a constipated stoker to a Medical Officer. Arrived 0730 transfer Stoker O'Shea and Chief Stoker (with tonsilitis) to light cruiser *Despatch* for Gibraltar and thence to *London*, going home to U.K. Returning to Cartagena by noon, found a German destroyer in *Arrow*'s berth. Decoding a 137 Group cypher learnt that a Russian Steamer, S. S. *Stavi Bolshevik* was in the port with forty nine tanks, eighty lorries and crews totalling three hundred men trained in aviation. Two more ships expected.

October 16. Battersby, 'the radio bosun', living in *Grafton* again, was a help to me decoding cyphers that arrived daily. C.C. returned from the town with Mr. Leverkus, a British subject about to become Hon. Vice

Consul for Cartagena (a post he was to occupy with distinction all through the 1939-1945 war). A big man with a beard like St. Peter's he had a calm outlook, well aware that the locals would kill him if they thought he was giving information. The tanks had been driven through the streets, their Russian crews getting a great welcome, all of which had to be reported to the Admiralty in a long coded message. C.C. gave a good talk to the ship's company on the situation and regaled us in the Wardroom with his 1919 trip to Australia as a midshipman in *H.M.A.S. Sydney*.

October 17. The Red fleet, one cruiser, three flotilla leaders and one submarine, left Cartagena looking a real shambles. Each ship was said to be run by a committee seen congregating on the bridge having butchered their officers. Their other squadron based at Bilbao, included the battleship *Jaime I* manned by a cut throat crew, who too had murdered their officers. A local General came on board; appearing to be pale pink politically, he said if things went wrong he'd be shot by the Reds.

October 18. At 0630 three planes high up bombed Cartagena and another two about 1100. At noon Leverkus, Gregson (A Vickers Man) and a Scot called Maclean came on board. They said ten bombs had been dropped causing great damage. The town's water pipes had been split and the people rushed the gaol to kill the prisoners, their way of getting revenge. Leverkus explained that most people cannot read or write; they are really uneducated children – but dangerous. All his friends were dead or in gaol and he would be too if he was not a British subject.

October 19. I went ashore with C.C. and an interpreter. They had killed all those in gaol and some corporals of the guns' crews for inattention to duty during the raids. The German Consul had been arrested and taken to Madrid. His Spanish wife told us he was safe and they would both leave in a German warship. The attacking planes were believed to be German. *Jaime I* and two other Red warships arrived, anchoring unhealthily close to us. The Master of *Nela*, a British ship with some millions of eggs to unload said to be drunk as a rule but sober today, asked C.C's advice on their disposal. C.C. advised him to go to Alicante but the old fool still hesitated. Expecting another dawn attack, we moved our position five cables (1000 yards) to the westward. October 20/21. When the air raid began at 0345, in *Grafton* we all leapt up on deck in dressing gowns. There must have been four to six planes, one acting as a decoy flew over the sea with a light on, drawing the fire of the shore batteries. Three times they went away and returned. About 0445 gazing upwards one came right over us; then suddenly a whistling whine. C.C. nipped behind a gun shield; "Radio" and I through the screen door. This bomb fell about a hundred yards away and the ship shook. Just as well it was not a *stick* of bombs! C. C., murmuring about locking the stable door behind the horse, decided we should go out to sea. Returning at 0830 the water was strewn with dead fish. Collected by our whaler, these subsequently appeared on the luncheon menu as *Cadeaux de Franco*. According to reports forty to fifty bombs had been dropped with little damage as most had fallen outside the town. Many people were dispersing into the country. Relieved by *Gipsy* at 1400 we went slowly down the coast taking four refugees, two women, one man and a child, calling at Almeria next morning to pick up fifteen more refugees. These were lucky to leave, some months later a German Pocket battleship shelled this small but ancient port as a reprisal for some event with which it had not been involved. 24 knots brought *Grafton* to Gibraltar the same evening, October 21, with *Gallant* joining us in the Pens having brought a hundred refugees from Malaga. Evenings ashore in Gibraltar usually ended at the Royal, a restaurant/night spot where competition was hot to spend a night with a tall dazzling blonde called Elaine. I did well to get a dance but not speaking Hungarian or Italian, she fell an easy prey to an American engineer officer from a ship in the harbour, who had more 'dough' than we British.

October 29. After eight lovely autumn days in which I longed to be at Sunningdale or Walton Heath, while the ships' companies enjoyed plenty of football, *Grafton* sailed for Alicante taking mail and some ratings to our Submarine Depot ship *Resource*. Back at Cartagena Leverkus came to lunch on board most days while at sunset we moved to Subida Bay down the coast. On November 6, my twenty-fourth birthday, we embarked nineteen refugees as well as one woman and her ten children. The other women were mostly the widows of shot naval officers. Dressed in deep black with contrasting ashen faces, they made a tragic spectacle. Joined in the Pens at Gibraltar by *Gipsy* bringing many more refugees from Malaga, the jetty looked like Victoria Station platform with the Boat train just in.

For the Armistice Day parade on the Rosea parade ground, the Navy contributed a detachment of a hundred men, who needed a rehearsal the day before. Lieutenant H. W. Acworth as the officer instructor was superb; by tact and skill he worked everybody up into a mood of enthusiasm, the officers even managing to draw and sheath their swords in unison with the men fixing and unfixing their bayonets. Packing to leave was a task. Besides uniform suits, blue and white, we needed plain clothes, from dinner jackets to 'dog robbers' (tweed coat and flannel trousers), bed linen and towels, shirts, shorts, shoes and socks for all occasions. Cocked hat and epaulettes travelled in their own special Tin box, the 'solar bowler' in another. No. 1 uniform was a button-up-the-centre tunic and trousers with a wide gold braid stripe, but for Lieutenants this was not yet compulsory and the cocked hat and epaulettes could be worn with the frock coat. Then, of course, there was the Great coat for cold weather and the blue Burberry for wet.

Even for midshipmen a couple of Gieves trunks needed augmenting with a wooden packing case about forty inches long, eighteen wide and fifteen deep, usually made free in a big ship's shipwrights' workshop. The case could be unscrewed and stowed away in a store room after unpacking.

Leaving *Grafton* to join the light cruiser *Despatch* for passage to Malta, I also had a portable radio and gramophone and my bag of golf clubs, a suitable receptacle for my sword too had it not been required for the Armistice parade.

The Parade went well; Somerville, my relief, arrived and *Grafton* sailed that evening for a further spell of Spanish patrol. After saying my goodbyes throughout the ship I received my flimsy with some very kind words from C.C. As I climbed over the guard rails on to the jetty, *Grafton* cast off and departed. It was a very sad moment. I felt that destroyers would be the life for me. But in fact, far from life, almost the next one was nearly the death of me.

The flimsy was a small form on which every Captain of a ship or naval establishment had to insert in his own handwriting the conduct of each officer, who had served under his command. It gave the dates of joining and leaving and was a summary, given to the officer, of the Confidential report which the Captain had also to make when either he or the officer was leaving the ship.

The Captain inserted his remarks after the printed words: *He has conducted himself:* "To my satisfaction" or "To my entire satisfaction" normally followed. When in the zone for Commander or Captain remarks such as "Deserving and ready for immediate promotion" were usually included if this was the case.

Of course there were many jokes about flimsies "Entirely to his own satisfaction" being one and "I have seen this officer sober not once, not twice, but three times", being another.

❖ ❖ ❖

TEN DAYS IN *DESPATCH*
Joining a ship was rather like going to a boarding school. In the Wardroom the chap you thought looked nice did not speak a word to you, although

in the fullness of time he became your best friend. In *Despatch* I was given the Navigator's cabin opposite the Wardroom door. Where the Navigator had gone I cannot remember. In no time however I was 'bullied' into the ship's hockey team and, inevitably, into the Watchkeepers' Union. Being alongside, this was not too arduous; at night the chief requirement was to be on deck when Captain Jackson came on board, which was likely to be in the 0200 or the 0400 boat sent in shore for him.

On November 13 we sailed across the Straits to Tangier to show the flag for a few days. The Commander asked me to a private supper to help entertain Admiral Sir Guy and Lady Gaunt. An ancient, egotistic mariner talking about 'anchoring here' when offered a chair, Sir Guy was the great bore of Tangier, if not the world. His young wife, whom he called "child", was charming; a widow, having come to Tangier in response to some advertisement, she married the old basket. 'Bet she regrets it!' declares my diary.

Despatch gave a 6 to 8 party on the quarterdeck under a smart blue and white ceremonial awning. The Italian Admiral's Flag Lieutenant was a smooth operator who took it upon himself when the party was coming to an end to hail boats alongside in the correct language, French, Portuguese, Italian or English while, at the same time, clicking his heels and kissing the ladies' hands before departure. The Italian Gunnery officer did not like him. "He is", he confided, "How you say... a snaike?"

Going ashore the next afternoon for a round of golf with Coldham, the Sub-Lieutenant, I returned on board after it at 0545 in a rowing boat with Fisher, the Torpedo Officer. After the 19th hole there had been an excellent concert somewhere by a harmonica band twenty five strong. This had been followed by Mr. and Mrs. Kingsmill's dinner party at the Embassy restaurant, with a look at Tangier night life after that. Losing my companions at one stage I had been threatened by four toughs, who said I had not paid the bill. Although pretty sure our host had paid, it seemed prudent for me to pay up forty francs rather than be beaten up.

I recalled talking a lot to the band and Fisher decorating the place by strewing a toilet roll, which seemed a most natural thing to do at the time. And so to bed, back on board, with a precautionary three aspirins.

The next thing I saw was the doctor by the bed saying it was 1330 and was I alright. My servant had summoned him with,

"I've been calling Mr. 'ogg at half hour intervals and all he does is to groan".

"Never mind", said the doctor "No hurry, the Wardroom is running a sweepstake on when you'll come round"

Having a terrible head I slept on until 1530.

Summoned by Hutton the Commander, he said that as I had missed General Drill, I would be required for duty at the cocktail party in *Lima*, the Portuguese destroyer that same evening, a punishment that certainly fitted the crime. Among the guests was Mrs. Kingsmill, who reminded me of things I did not remember.

We docked in Grand Harbour on November 24. Bidding each other Goodbye, the Commander said I had been of great assistance for ten days out of eleven.

1936. HM Destroyer Grafton. *Courtesy of Vosper Thorneycroft*

Gabriella Barker's troupe of young ladies.

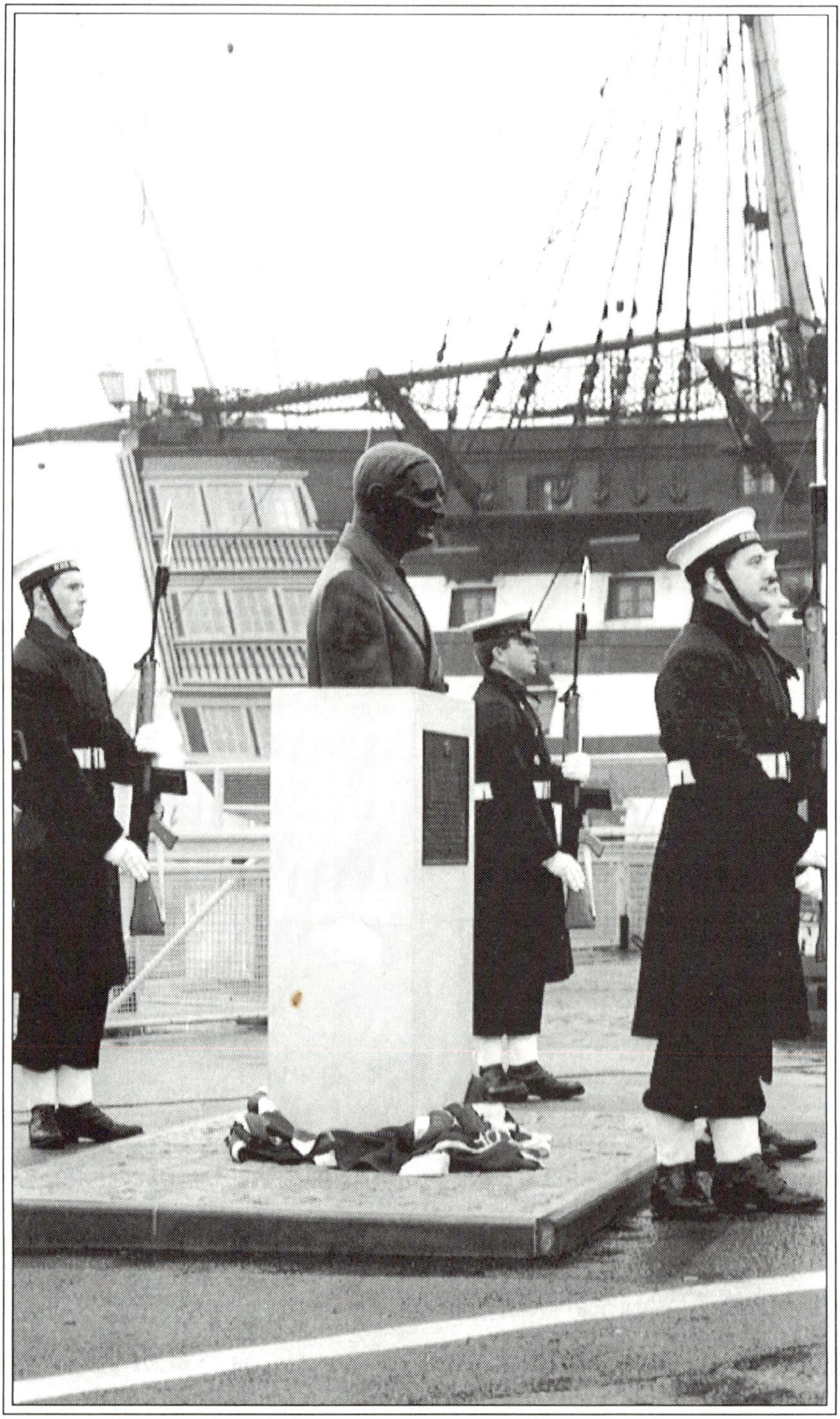

CHAPTER 17

1937 – Bruce Fraser's *Glorious*

Joining *Glorious* about noon it was nice to be greeted by a few familiar faces. Among them were Patrick Milner-Barry, Fanning formerly an RNR officer, Tom Jameson and Malleson, a Dartmouth Hawke. All four were observers. When in Malta the pilots lived at Halfar aerodrome with their aircraft. The observers, who were mostly divisional officers as well, stayed on board to keep watch; and in the case of these four to play chess occasionally, for Milner-Barry's brother Philip, was about to become Chess correspondent of *The Times*. A Commander came up and said, "I don't expect you remember me but you chaperoned your sister Brada when I met her in Manchester in 1920." My sister was then eighteen, I was eight and he was twenty four. This was Mackintosh of Mackintosh (The Mackintosh) to give his full title, of Moy Hall, Invernesshire. Currently the Senior Observer in *Glorious*, this rather shy, quiet man would command three large carriers during the war, retiring in 1950 as Vice-Admiral Lachlan Mackintosh CB, DSO, DSC. His only son retired as a Lieutenant-Commander in 1963, six years after his father's death, needed for public work in the County.

My impression after looking round was that *Glorious* was a creation of the devil quite unlike anything which has ever floated. The quarterdeck at the stern was only about a dozen paces long overhung by the flight deck, which was where Divisions and Church services were held unless it was raining. The hangar of course was useful for Fleet cocktail parties. The cable deck forward, also overhung by another deck, could not be seen from the bridge located on "the island" on the starboard side housing the funnel. My cabin was inboard, small and very dirty. Only a letter from Hilary was some consolation; another proved to be Kay Moss, still living at the Villa Maresca in Sliema, who gave lots of parties to amuse her guest Esme Henderson, an attractive young lady from Sevenoaks.

This of course was the refitting period for the Fleet. *Glorious* lay at Parlatorio wharf in French Creek across Grand Harbour from the Custom House. There must have been ten of us in the Watchkeepers 'union' when

---

Opposite: Leslie Punter's bust of Admiral of the Fleet Lord Fraser of North Cape unveiled close to HMS Victory by HRH Prince Philip, 9 November 1990.

JUST A HOGG'S LIFE

in harbour but watches were boring because so little happened. Many officers had their own, probably rented, cars alongside and *dghaisas* lay off the gangway like a taxi rank to take people across to Valletta. One almost longed for Leonard Hammersley Bell to appear reading the riot act. The Executive officer, Commander Crane used to disappear if he was displeased. On going to sea he was usually on or near the Bridge to take one's report, "Part of ship secured for sea, sir". If however one was late he disappeared, making sure that it took fifteen minutes to find him.

A great misfortune befell the Gunnery Officer, a senior Lieutenant J.W.F.D. Cowgill. His assistant P.H. Wormell known as "Hookey" went somewhere else and Cowgill had to put up with me. My first job was to examine a Gunnery Training Class in stripping. Fortunately there was a Gunner's Mate to instruct me; I had not seen a gun pulled to pieces for two years, let alone done it myself.

At home on December 7 Edward VIII announced his intention of marrying Mrs. Simpson. His choice was plain; give up his crown or his woman. By Sunday December 13 he had abdicated, sailing from Portsmouth to France in the destroyer *Fury*, while his brother the Duke of York had been proclaimed King George VI. How sad that a Prince, who had done so much so well during his father's life could find no suitable mate with whom to share his own!

Returning to Malta from Spain in December, *Grafton* docked close to *Glorious*. Based mainly at Valencia, her patrol had been uneventful with frequent gales that made life at sea most uncomfortable. Crawford had applied and been accepted for the next long Anti-Submarine Course at Portland and, relieved by a fat South African called Barnett went home on December 16. He had an idea that those who did badly in the course were retained as instructors to the next course. Attempting this he in fact failed and within a year was back in the Mediterranean in a destroyer not half as nice as *Grafton* under C.C.

By degrees I seem to have become Sports Officer, trying first to collect the best *Glorious* Rugby XV to play the best regimental Army side, a difficult task because communicating with Halfar, either the chap wanted was in the air or the telephone line was engaged or broken. Frustrated, Cowgill's instructions to do some Gunnery job went begging partly because he never explained what he wanted. However, much to my surprise we beat the soldiers 22-8 in those days when a try and a penalty goal were each 3 points, a dropped goal 4 and a converted try 5.

I also had another job. Aware that we all lifted the elbow too much, my mother stood me a Regent Correspondence Course to keep me writing not drinking. There were a dozen lessons by post each requiring the submission of a short article for criticism. With luck after four or five lessons one's tutor suggested sending it to an appropriate periodical. If accepted, regarding oneself as a potential Priestley with nothing more to learn, the course was apt to be given up to the satisfaction of the Regent Institute, which could take on another pupil. My particular masterpiece which eventually graced the pages of *Men Only* was called *Sidelights on Malta*.

December was dancing time. The Commander-in-Chief, Admiral Sir Dudley and Lady Pound gave a ball at their residence, the superb old Admiralty House in Valletta. Dan Duff, still Flag-Lieutenant, was superb, encouraging everybody to dance old fashioned waltzes and one-steps, here, there and everywhere.

On Christmas Day in *Glorious* many wives, friends and families came to Matins. Taken by the Captain B. A. Fraser there was no sermon because the Padré, name of Biggins, went mad and had been sent home. Among the carols inevitably there was:

> *Hark the herald angels sing*
> *Mrs. Simpson's pinched our King.*

The thirst after righteousness was then relieved with champagne in the Wardroom, the important guests being the Casson family. Lewis Casson, great actor and theatrical producer was married to Dame Sybil Thorndike, the great actress, and they were in Malta to see their son John, a pilot in the *Glorious* and his attractive wife Patricia.

The next social event in the ship was a Children's Party four days later in which John Casson revealed himself as a first class conjuror, supported by a cabaret that included a grand little dance by an Engineer Artificer's daughter and a real sailor's hornpipe. The flagship *Queen Elizabeth*'s dance came next before the New Year's Eve ball at the Sliema Club.

After a Rugger match in the afternoon I donned my overall trousers, Spanish sailor's hat, red shirt and all the badges of the Spanish Communist Trade Unions gathered I suppose in Cartagena, C.N.T., F.A.I., J.S and others. Otto Jenner-Fust appeared as Hitler; Charles Kennaway was half Hitler and half Stalin; Lionel Bonsey an anaesthetist.

WORLD EVENTS
1936. Britain, United States, France sign London Naval Convention. Spanish Civil War Franco captures Badajoz, sets siege to Madrid. Edward

VIII abdicates. George VI's accession. Mussolini and Hitler proclaim Rome-Berlin axis. Olympics in Berlin, Jesse Owens wins four gold medals for U.S.A.

1937. Out at Halfar on New Year's Day the annual meet of the Halfar Hunt was a remarkable event. The quarry was a cat, the mounts ten donkeys. In the evening Charles Kennaway and I saw *Show Goat*, a very good revue staged in Floriana by the Malta Amateur Dramatic Club. The MADC chorus, looking most decorative, included three RN wives, Patricia Casson, Noreen Moultrie and Molly Clutton. Stuart Perowne, in a Douglas Byng role, was outstanding as 'Freeboarding Freda'.

On the last day of January our 'chummy' carrier *Courageous* arrived from England and I dined at the Union Club with the two friends I knew on board. One was Christopher Jelf and the other R. J. H. (Dagon) Stephens, who had recently married Audrey of the Hills family in Epsom. Chris was flying Nimrod fighters, "Dagon", or "Boff" Stephens to the Navy, was in a Swordfish squadron. Having discovered that Spring weather was better for flying in the Eastern Mediterranean, the two carriers sailed for Alexandria on 2nd February.

On Friday the 5th the weather cleared with Alexandria in the distance, for a massed Torpedo Bomber attack. Two planes crashed in mid-air; Lieutenant Vardon of *Glorious* and Overall, his Torpedo Air Gunner were lost. The other plane lost height and landed close to *Comet*, the attendant destroyer which, stationed for that purpose, picked them up.

The attack abandoned, we proceeded into an empty harbour, by former standards. Landing at 1640, I found my sister, Brada, waiting to welcome me at that smelliest of landing places, No.6 Gate. The English community were not exactly bright and cheerful. By the terms of the Anglo-Egyptian treaty British Government would end in 1937 and the Police Officers would go home to unemployment. At the Ramleh house my nieces June and Jacqueline, now ten and seven respectively, gave me a warm welcome, Jack's beloved tropical fish had been augmented by a second tank and Gip, an Alsatian puppy that ate one's shoe laces.

On Sunday, by invitation, John Westall, Major of Royal Marines in *Glorious* appeared at 0500 and off we went with Jack in a police car for duck shooting. Arriving in the dark at some delta outpost we walked a mile along a railway line, thence rowing in little punts to the butts. A pastime entirely new to me, the birds soon came over but not in the numbers I expected. I blazed away at flying ducks and sitting ducks until 0815 with no success whatsoever. The bag was Hogg 0, Paterson 1, Westall

10. Westall stayed on after snipe. We went home for breakfast, he joined us for lunch. No wonder such a marksman became General Sir John KCB, CB, CBE, Commandant General Royal Marines 1952-55 before he retired to his home land, New Zealand!

Monday to Friday should have been spent at sea by the carriers but the Swordfish had defective under-carriages so after a Memorial Service for Vardon and Overall and a flip for the fighters we returned to harbour. A dinner at the Carvers and a bouquet from me celebrated Marguerite's birthday and a Cuban band somewhere, when we danced played Blue Moon as well as Harpo Marx in the film.

A Police Boxing tournament in which *Glorious* figured in nine out of seventeen fights was preceded by a dinner for guests and officials at the Union Club. Bruce Fraser was the only Commanding Officer to attend, the attendance generally being disappointing. By the time my sister had got to work on my Captain, I had been granted three hours extra leave though what for I could not tell.

At the Boxing I sat between Marguerite Carver and Elsa Pilley, a Police Officer's wife, who accidentally dropped a lighted cigarette for which I grovelled under the seats in vain. Then suddenly the P.M.O's wife sitting in front leapt to her feet crying, "Help my bottom's on fire!" In some extraordinary way the cigarette had lodged on the back of her seat burning a hole in her dress. Marguerite got the giggles and so did I. It was of course very funny, though not for the victim. Back in the mess they said, "It'll be castration for you next time you have to report to the Sick Bay".

On Sunday Lachlan Mackintosh returned Paterson hospitality by giving us lunch on board. By 3 p.m. I was playing rugger for the ship against a local Hawkes XV. By teatime I was chez Paterson helping to entertain a party of Henns, Mackenzies and others who came to see films of Jack's Sinai trip and *Glorious* entering harbour. By 8 p.m. I was dining in a young mixed party at Reynard Bleu, with dancing and a 3 a.m. bed. And at 7.30 a.m. I was catching a train with my sister for a day in Cairo. This was life in one's twenties; today I wonder how one survived.

By accident or design we shared a carriage with Billy Henn, Colonel of the Alexandria Police, who insisted on standing us breakfast. The train reached Cairo at 1015. Brada left me to see the Sphinx and the Great Pyramid where I found the climb to the King's chamber half way up quite enough. Meeting again at Mena House, we found the cheapest drinks - two glasses of champagne - most refreshing before lunch. Our return was in an 8-seater *Dragon* aircraft, flying time fifty five minutes.

JUST A HOGG'S LIFE

The next day Tuesday 16th the Captain and officers were expected to see the Police Mounted Troop stables but failed to turn up because the carriers were at sea looking for Gerry Lake and Macdonald whose plane was lost and never found. Magnificent horses marvellously kept, they were rehearsing a new musical ride in which a few hundred Egyptians would sing Ramona in Arabic. The City's cinemas were now showing "Follow the Fleet", not the best of Fred Astaire and Ginger Rogers films but very acceptable to sailors sweating in the giant Esse cookers called capital ships. The Captain and officers paid the visit to the Mounted Troop stables two days late.

Bruce Fraser also gave a large dinner party on the 18th in his spacious day cabin, the guests being, Bill and Geraldine Henn, Brada and Jack, Geoffrey Mills, who had married Kathleen Carmichael of Alexandria, Michael Elliott and his wife, Tom Jameson and his wife Willa, Lachlan Mackintosh, Joan Brachi, a niece of the Henns and myself.

A record was broken on Friday 19th when Neville Cummins landed an Imperial Airways Experimental Flying Boat in Alexandria at 8 p.m. after leaving Southampton Water at 4 a.m. Allowing a further three hours between Egyptian time and British Summer Time makes a nineteen hour flight time, which was unheard of by a passenger-carrying aircraft then. It was of particular interest to us as Neville and his wife Jean had become our close neighbours at Epsom. A farewell cocktail party was given in *Glorious* that evening.

For the Finneys' ball beginning at 2200 on Saturday 20th, I donned my white tie and tails. Champagne flowed like water and there was a lovely supper set up in the billiard room, but the crowd was great and the heat uncomfortable. By 0200 the guests began to thin out. Brada and Billy Henn were together most of the evening, partly because he was flying home next day for an interview. The job was Chief Constable of Gloucestershire and he would leave Egypt in June if, as happened, he got it, which he did.

'Boff' Stephens was rather tight but naval guests behaved well on the whole. Faced with Seven-a-Side Rugby within twelve hours, I left at 0400. The finals began at the Sporting Club at 1400. Playing for *Courageous* A, 'Boff' Stephens, a forward who had played for the Navy at home, blatantly socked an Egyptian opponent on the jaw and laid him out plain for all to see. It was a disgraceful exhibition and to our embarrassment he was coming to supper with us that night. We went to an opera called *Der Rosenkavalier* which bored me so much I left after Act I.

Fifteen years later, having become besotted with Beethoven and Mozart, I had to play Richard Strauss over and over again with the librettos and William Mann's book in my hand before at last the penny dropped. But it would be the *Capriccio* sonnet that I would pack first for *my* desert island.

Glorious and *Courageous* sailed next day at 1415 for Malta, practising those torpedo attacks that were to lead to the triumph of Taranto in 1941. Records, records, records! We filled the Gunnery office with paper for analysis which never seemed to be completed.

Early in the afternoon "Crash in the Sea", "Crash in the sea" boomed the loud speakers throughout the ship. The luckless pilot of the Swordfish shot off the flight deck by the accelerator was 'Drunky' Lewin, last mentioned in Chapter 12 having difficulty with a bicycle. He and his aircraft were recovered unhurt; the fault lay with the material not the man, who seemed to take it all in the day's work. Crashes and collisions when taking off and landing on, were a constant threat to crews in the Fleet Air Arm.

My parents were the next visitors to Alexandria. My mother always longed to see her daughter and her two grandchildren, whom she had largely brought up during Brada's absence due mainly to operations. My father's heart was troublesome so on February 15th they took the train to Venice, sailing in the ss *Marco Polo* the next evening to reach Alexandria on March 3, where they stayed at the Cecil Hotel. But the visit was slightly marred by the grandchildren becoming seriously ill with temperatures of 103° for the best part of a fortnight. Even the Alsatian puppy got hysteria and had to be put away.

In warmer weather the return voyage in the ss *Esperia* must have been pleasant. Alexandria dep. March 28, Syracuse arr. a.m March 29, Tour with Guide. March 30, Naples Arr. a.m. Trip to Pompeii. March 31, Arrive Genoa 0730; At leisure till Rome Express dep 1855. April 1, Arr.Paris 0800, dep.1030. Arr. Boulogne 1400. Dep. Folkestone 1600. Epsom from Victoria arr. 2030.

Back in Malta on February 25 there was just time to see *Mr. Deeds Goes to Town*, the Capra comedy that added "doodle" and "pixillated" to our language, before we sailed westwards with *Courageous* and the Fleet. But the weather was too rough for flying and "Guns" directed me to work on a scheme that would provide hot meals for Action Stations in war. Consomeé de volaille, Sole Dieppoise, Filet de Boeuf Madère, Crème Brulé. Some war!

With the weather worsening as we went through the Straits into the Atlantic plans for the usual Home Fleet/Mediterranean Fleet battle were abandoned and *Glorious* anchored in Gibraltar Bay on March 6. Having been appointed 2nd in command of patrols I landed to meet Lieutenant-Commander H. C. Browne, 1st in Command, a submariner better known as a forward in the Ireland XV. Together we went to the Garrison Mess to find our sleeping quarters close by. Having delivered an oration to the patrols at H.M.S. *Cormorant*, the naval base, he walked me and two Warrant officers all round the town visiting patrols. Browne took Duty the first day Saturday 6th, leaving me Sunday 7th and alternating after that. My afternoon rounds paused at *Grafton* in No. 1 Dock to hear that CC was pursuing the lovely Linette, Guy Warren's daughter and was too love sick to be seasick at sea. By 2100 two drunks had been brought into the Picket House. One was a young stoker who objected to being called a bastard, but placed in the cells called everybody a bastard without ceasing.

Needing me as a watchkeeper I returned to *Glorious* for three days of flying exercises. The weather was good on one day and for me it was back to patrolling ashore on the third. Calling on one's friends in the ships for pre-brandial gins before lunch, and either joining them in the 'joints' or attempting to get them to leave them in the small hours if on duty, was not the best training for the Inter-Fleets rugger match.

The Med Fleet XV was Lieut Jameson; Duff, PO Criddle, A.B. James, Lieut Hogg; A.B. Bailey, Hunter, Pay Lieut Watkins, Sgt Kelly, RM., E.R.A. Doggett, A.B. Attwood, Lieuts Shaw, Lake, Lewin, Savage.

Though the better team, we played badly and making mistakes lost 13-5. Discussing the match afterwards Willie Wood, the Navy's best sprinter said to me "I have always regarded you as a match winner in an inter-ship game, but in first class Rugger the speed of the game defeats you."

The truth hurts, but as Milton has it:

> *Fame is the spur that the clear spirit doth raise*
> *To scorn delights, and live laborious days;*

Provoked, I recorded in my diary that I should prove Mr. Wood wrong. We had in *Glorious* two former Rugby players well qualified to assist me. William John Abbott Davies OBE, born 1890, had captained England, the Royal Navy, Hampshire and United Services Portsmouth in 1921, 1922 and 1923. In 1913 he had joined the Royal Corps of Naval Constructors and from 1935 to 1938 was Fleet Constructor officer of the Mediterranean Fleet. Playing fly half his partnership with Lieutenant C.A. Kershaw R.N. as scrum half in the Twenties was unsurpassed.

Living in Malta with his wife, he was a quiet Welshman always willing to referee; tennis was his game now and he refused to play golf until he was too old for tennis. At flight deck hockey he kept goal and, though almost teetotal himself promised me a sherry for every goal I scored against him. He lived to be 77.

John Dudley Bartlett was another Welshman born 1907, who had joined *Glorious* in February in place of the Chaplain, who had gone mad. Short, tubby and very fast he played on the wing for Cambridge University, Llanelli and Wales in 1927-8. Declaring that the third Chaplain would certainly not go mad, he drank measure for measure with the chaps ashore and afloat and usually remained sober. A keen golfer his surplice taking Matins was sometimes a little too short to hide the plus fours underneath. I lost touch with Dudley during the war; after it some horrid complaint confined him to a wheel chair. He and his wife lived on Hayling Island where he died in 1967.

Returning to Malta, the Long Range Reconnaissance and Striking Force had a good day making an attack on *Hood* and *Repulse*, Lachlan Mackintosh deriving much satisfaction from having all his observers airborne at the same time. And the night before the pilots flew off to Halfar, Cornabe revealed his talents at the piano with impersonations of Leslie Hutchinson, the cabaret pianist and 'Fats' Waller, playing the latest tunes.

Flying from *Courageous* off the Isle of Wight, Christopher Jelf was the first of our Greynvile Term to be killed. I felt stunned. We had met sitting in the corridor of that General Strike train to Dartmouth. Being an 'H' and a 'J' our beds were close enough for rags after Lights out and when he or I were called to be beaten he would bounce on his bed saying "Cuts are good for the bottom". Then, dining in the Club so recently, how keen he had been that we should all meet his fiancée! During the next five weeks from March 23 to April 26 *Glorious* was mostly in harbour with two or three excursions for a few days to practise gunnery and flying. The ships' football teams, as well as playing each other, took on the Malta clubs such as Floriana. With excellent hockey on hard grounds, squash rackets and golf, we all became fitter in theory. The golf course, playable after the winter rains was at the Marsa inside the race course. Prominent among our players were: Dudley Bartlett, Dick Kearney, Tom Jameson and his wife Willa, Malleson, Playfair and myself.

On April 3 the Khedive boat called taking the Henns home for him to become Chief Constable of Gloucestershire. I went on board to greet them in a cabin full of gifts, mostly flowers and silver cigar boxes from Alexandrian friends. The Khedive line, landing passengers at Marseille, enabled them to reach London by an overnight train in less than twenty four hours. Also leaving Egypt for the last time, my sister and her two daughters following about three weeks later, reached the family home at Epsom a day before *Glorious* arrived at Spithead for the Coronation Review.

Compared to Alexandria our farewell cocktail party in Malta needed only half the hangar. My own guests were Fisher and his wife from *Despatch*, he having survived our Tangier all night party *without* going to bed. Bobbie Burton now married to Molly, Mrs. Roy Gould and his sister Nancy Langdon. Among the naval wives much admired were Pam, née May, married to James Buckley, Lieutenant-Commander and Senior Pilot of 802 Squadron and her sister Peg, married to an R.N Surgeon called Coulter. These two exceptionally pretty girls were said to own an island in the Seychelles, a joke that gave rise to the following by the Milner-Barry brothers perhaps:

> *There were two young ladies of Malta*
> *Whose morals were n'er known to falter*
> *But when in the Seychelles*
> *Those smug little belles*
> *Would have to dispense with the altar.*

The Captain spoke to all the officers about a Marriage Allowance Scheme. Briefly officers over thirty would lose 2/- a day and married ones over thirty would get 4/- a day, plus 2/6 for one child and 1/- for each additional one. I think this was introduced soon afterwards. Another talk by Bruce Fraser was on the principles of war saying that they were much the same as those of life, security for example being practised whenever one bolted a lavatory door.

The passage home began with a full power trial, reaching 30 knots. Our aircraft were practising Torpedo attacks as usual and in the vicinity of Spain we manned half the High Angle Armament ready to shoot at any Spanish aircraft that threatened us. One morning practising High Angle firing at a drogue towed by an aircraft, I got in a bit of a muddle opening fire and firing two salvoes before the order to do so had been received. Consternation on the Bridge, I was sent for and 'blown sky high' by 'Guns' Cowgill. The Captain also spoke to me not unkindly and this was typical of Bruce Fraser; he knew I knew I had made a fool of myself. There was no need to shout or humiliate the offender.

Anchoring for the Review at Spithead there was another example of this, an incident so well remembered forty years later that it is described by Richard Humble in his biography *Fraser of North Cape*. Because the cable deck could not be seen from the Bridge, a young signalman was posted on a small platform projecting outwards from the cable deck so that he could pass messages from the Bridge to the Cable officer. Leading the way, *Courageous*, the flagship, hoisted the flags for "Prepare to Anchor". Watching this and knowing its meaning, the young signalman shouted 'Let go' when it was hauled down. Thus one bower anchor was dropped before *Glorious* had quite reached the required position. Fortunately Fraser managed to drop the other anchor so that the ship was moored in the right berth.

Sternly rebuked for his impetuous act, first by the Cable officer and then the Chief Yeoman of Signals, the lad was put in the Captain's report. What would be the judgement of Solomon? We waited anxiously behind the Captain seated at the small table. The answer was a Caution, with a gentle explanation that the Captain must decide when to anchor, not the signals department.

When building, *Courageous* and *Glorious* began as battleships but the Treaty of Washington in 1922 forbade battleship construction for ten years. The eight 15 inch guns were replaced by sixteen 4.7 inch guns, the 4-shaft turbines were designed for 30 knots and the complement fixed at 1216. The two decks under the flight deck were hangars designed to take thirty six aircraft in three squadrons; 802, 823 and 825 in 1935. When *Glorious* commissioned after a long refit and Bruce Fraser became Captain, faced with a possible war with Italy, his most difficult task was to make the flying people happy and efficient. In the Fleet Air Arm, over half the pilots were R.N holding RAF rank. Ashore the flying crews came under the RAF discipline Act; afloat it was the Royal Navy's Act. Commander Crane was the Executive officer, Wing Commander Halley (RAF) in charge of flying and Commander Stevenson in charge of the Flight deck.

Fraser had a remarkable capacity for getting on with people, senior or junior to himself. A natural flair, it may well have become stronger after being a prisoner of the Bolsheviks in 1920 when officers and men had to live together in one cell. His excellent ship-handling, much admired by all on board, had been perfected in his previous sea appointment, Captain of the cruiser *Effingham* on the East Indies station.

"Fraser, of course was the most magnificent man ever, and relations on board were always very good", said my friend Flying Officer George Seymour-Price, a Nimrod pilot then of 802 Squadron and now an Air Commodore retired living at Hambledon.

Coming up the Channel on May 5 all the aircraft flew off to Lee-on-Solent at 0900 leaving a void, which was always rather depressing like standing on the empty platform when the train has left. *Glorious* anchored at Spithead at 1100 proceeding up harbour at 1330 to a buoy, not alongside. Off watch next day I returned home to Epsom in a small £7 a week Ford. We were back at Spithead for Coronation Day, May 12 listening to the Service in Westminster Abbey on the wireless in the Wardroom. Greatly moved by the choir, I hastened to buy a record of Zadok the Priest. Next came Divisions in No. 1's before a Royal Salute at noon. Drinking the health of King George VI in champagne, the order 'Splice the Main Brace' was received, this being the only occasion when officers were issued with a tot of rum.

The next day we departed at 0800 to meet the Mediterranean Fleet, which elected to make an impressive arrival by coming through the Needles channel to berths at Spithead. The Review was not until Thursday May 20 giving a week to complete painting. Our boats had to be lent to the *Cuba*, a ship that had broken down several times on its way from - yes - Cuba and appeared to have no boats at all. One morning unexpectedly the liner *Queen Mary* steamed through the lines outward bound. A wonderful sight, it seemed inconceivable that men's hands could build a ship so huge yet so beautiful. She gained the Blue Riband from France's *Normandie*, crossing the Atlantic at a mean speed of 31.7 knots. And, as a troop ship in the war, she must have carried at least 750,000 troops, 811324 being the figure for her younger sister *Queen Elizabeth*.

For Review Day the hangar was nicely arranged with chairs, tables and fire places for our guests who started arriving about 1100. My father, sister Brada and brother Martin arrived in time for the buffet lunch, but hoisting the boats on one side and falling in on the Flight deck from 1500 till 1710, I saw little of them. Including many friends from Alexandria, they all went ashore about 1830, my family having booked rooms at the Queen's, where they enjoyed the illuminations at closer range than last time.

Enjoying even more the hospitality of H.M.S. *Nelson*, Lieutenant Commander Thomas Woodroofe, 1899-1978, making the first live outside broadcast for the BBC, repeatedly declared, "The Fleet is all lit up"; his speech a trifle blurred, hit the newspaper headlines next morning and is now enshrined in *The Oxford Dictionary of Quotations*.

Glorious sailed for Devonport at 1645 the day after the Review. Finding *New York*, flagship of Admiral Harold Stark U.S.N. who would later be Commander-in-Chief US Naval Forces in Europe, going down the Channel too, Bruce Fraser asked if *Glorious* could take station astern and come under his command. Just an act of courteous modesty which would be remembered when liaison with the Americans became vital in the war.

Catching the Cornish Riviera, fast train of the day to Paddington, I now had ten days leave because I was one of a party of officers and men of the Fleet appointed temporarily to take *Saltash*, *Elgin* and *Lydd*, three old minesweepers from Chatham to be placed in reserve at Malta. At Epsom my father was ill, bidden to sit up in a chair and drink lots of whisky as a heart stimulant he badly needed after the exertions of Review Day.

In Manchester *Radiac* shirts were selling well and Martin was driving a Marmon V8 saloon which took us comfortably to his rooms in Altrincham on a Sunday between 1500 and 2230, dining at Stone. While he went to work, I had calls to make. Mabel Lady Crossley, my deputy godmother since her son Brian was killed in 1915, now needed an ear trumpet. A widow for thirty three years when she died in 1943, she had lived all her married life at Glenside, a large house with a conservatory close to St. Margaret's Church, with her cousin Amy Anderson, sister of the R.N Chaplain, who became Bishop of Portsmouth and finally Salisbury. Next I always had a rendezvous at noon for a pint at The Stamford Arms by Bowdon church with James Berry, our former gardener who declared I was a harum-scarum young bugger when I crashed my bike across his flower beds, the six-letter word being taken as a term of endearment in Lancashire. Annie, the parlour maid of my childhood, lived in a council house by the Bridgewater Canal with her husband Bertie Willie. Her saying "There's nothing soft about us in the North – except our water" deserves a place in *Unfamiliar Quotations*. In Altrincham itself, a welcome and two cigars always awaited me from Mr. Wainwright and Mr. Dean, leading grocers, whose premises in Railway Street by chance fell into our hands in 1966 when I had become Sales Director of Peter Dominic.

In summer after 4 p.m one could usually join my Uncle Sandy at the Bowdon Golf Club for a cup of tea from Miss Blease and nine holes before dinner at his house Tirbracken, looking across at the trees and bracken of Dunham Park. The property of Lord Stamford, Bowdon's nine holes were ploughed in the war and Tirbracken and it's surroundings became the Dunham Forest Golf Club after it.

Back in London on *The Mancunian* (dep. London Rd. 0945, arr. Euston 1300 on time) I lunched with Joan Powell at Gennaro's before a matineé of the successful Rodgers and Hart musical:

> *See the pretty apple, top of the tree*
> *The higher up the sweeter it grows*
> *So my friend, you've got to be-up*
> ON YOUR TOES.

Two other numbers became famous, the ballad *Slaughter on Tenth Avenue* and *There's a Small Hotel.*

For several years Joan had been working at the St. James's Theatre for Gilbert Miller, the American impresario, who leased it but spent most of his time producing plays in New York. Her job was to see and report on new plays being tried outside London which Gilbert might consider for West End production. The only one outstanding as 'Good Box Office' was called *French without Tears* by a new author named Terence Rattigan.

"Why haven't I been told about this? screamed Gilbert after its long run had begun at the Criterion theatre.

"But you have, Mr. Miller, a favourable report was put on your desk by Miss Powell", said Gertrude Butler, who was his secretary based at St. James's.

The report was produced. Of course, probably with his mind obsessed on how to meet the Prince of Wales for he was an enormous snob, Gilbert had overlooked the report completely. But he did have the grace to give Joan a rise to £5 a week. He also staged Laurence Houseman's *Victoria Regina* at the St. James's with sets designed by Rex Whistler and that was a great success.

At his house Drungewick Manor in Surrey he had installed a white piano for the coloured singer, Josephine Baker to play to Prince George in the expectation that the combination would excite the Prince beyond measure. The money came from his wife Kitty, daughter of Jules Bache, a New York millionaire. An intrepid character, Gilbert had his own plane and the most alarming invitation in the theatrical world was to fly the Atlantic as the one passenger, with Gilbert in the driving seat.

There were so many of her Alexandria friends in London that my sister had taken a flat somewhere near Mount Royal in Oxford Street where it was said when the bell rang at 0730 everybody went back to their own room. Colonel Alan Swinton, who had a house in Eccleston Square, was much in evidence and was kind enough to give me a bed there occasionally when up from Chatham during the next few weeks. I actually joined *Saltash* at 23.30 on June 2 after a delicious cold sole mayonnaise, a speciality of the Buttery at the Berkeley Hotel, then at the corner of Berkeley Street and Piccadilly.

It was nice to find Philip Bekenn, a Public school friend, who had done Sub-Lieutenants' courses with us, was First Lieutenant, being senior to me by a few months. The next morning we met our Captain, Lieutenant-Commander R. L. Pearson Royal Australian Navy, a P & RT (Physical and Recreational Training) specialist. I managed to escape to London that night, where Colonel Alan kindly gave Brada, Joan and me dinner at Pruniers before the first night of *Yes my darling Daughter*, an amusing play with Sybil Thorndike, Margaret Bannerman, Jessica Tandy and Evelyn Roberts.

In *Elgin*, Fenwick, an observer from the *Glorious*, was First Lieutenant with an RNR called Davies No.2; in *Lydd*, Frankie Morgan and the younger Collett brother were Nos 1 and 2 respectively. I fancy we were all made honorary members of the R.N Barracks Wardroom, because my diaries mention a variety of friends there, Pog (A. A. Havers) and 'Tatters' Drawbridge among them. The latter said he had pinched my Seamanship Manual in *Royal Sovereign* but added nothing at all about returning it. Destroyers giving leave included *Brilliant* (Eddie Baines and Pat Havers, Pog's young brother) and *Garland*, Bill Moss with Kay often on board.

Rarely at home in mid-June myself, Colonel Alan motored Brada and me to the Aldershot Tattoo in his 25 h.p Wolseley overtaking all other cars regardless of corners. The Tattoo was a great display spoilt by rain which, sitting in a box, did not affect us but was miserable for the majority. The following day was my mother's sixtieth birthday and my father, sufficiently recovered to take an aperitif at Tyrrells Wood, was given a warm welcome there. With Mr. Farmer the Boatswain now on board, all three ships were inspected by the Commander-in-Chief The Nore, Admiral Evans of the *Broke*, wearing more medal ribbons on his chest than any Admiral I had ever seen before. The ordeal over, on June 16 we moved to buoys in the Medway to ammunition. It now seemed probable that we would do a spell of Non-Intervention patrolling along the Spanish coast before reaching Malta. Nigel Cox, the King's Harbour Master, who came to check our compasses, thought that it would be appropriate because "after all, these ships were built to be blown up by mines".

An evening spent at The Deanery, Canterbury with my godfather, Hewlett Johnson, known as the 'Red Dean' because of his politics, was exceptionally interesting. Visiting Spain recently he had seen Durango bombed by German planes and pilots, under orders it seemed to kill every living thing within a five mile radius. He had seen the battlefield from Madrid and interviewed prisoners. If only the Germans and Italians could be got out, the elected Government would defeat Franco very quickly. He had purposely made a speech in Strasbourg which would pass by word of mouth into Germany, where the Press under Nazi suppression had made no mention of Durango nor of Guernica. If Franco wins, Germany could get control of Bilbao's iron ore. Italy might get Ceuta or Palma but, supporting the Right, the British public did not appreciate these dangers.

At home that week-end, the last before sailing, I went up to Epsom College in the evening after Speech Day. Arnold Powell, the headmaster was fawning over Charles Taylor, a former head boy and his saucy wife, who was a sister of Winifred Shotter, heroine of many an Aldwych farce; who – said *Punch* – had very little to do – or undo. Perhaps Arnold was after money for some College project. Charles, MP for Eastbourne from 1935 to 1974, the safest Tory seat in the country, was very rich.

Half way to Plymouth Captain "Beefy" or "Boify", as he had now become, said he dreamt we had put in to Weymouth where masses of yachts were at anchor in the Bay. As Officer of the Watch I kept hitting each one in turn saying, "Bang goes another one!" Far from a dream our real trouble was that the starboard engine had packed up. However the Chief said that idling it would do 6 knots and the port engine 11 knots, thus with the aid of a tug our trio were alongside the coaling jetty in Plymouth dockyard by 1900 on June 22.

These three minesweepers, built in 1917/1919 for a complement of 73, took 185 tons of coal to give a range of 1500 miles. Coaling next day took over three hours a ship. It was customary for everyone to take part, ending with coal dust in every orifice of one's body, difficult to remove in bathrooms inadequate for so many at the same time. Across the Hamoaze in the old wooden ship *Impregnable*, Peter Gretton and Frank Woodward, both Greynviles of 1926-29, were not too busy training two hundred boys to refuse a game of golf, so Peter drove me out to Yelverton. His father owning Lillywhites, enough lessons were forthcoming to bring his handicap down to single figures, so I was well beaten. Crossing the Bay Boify and I became quite engrossed in taking sights by day and at dusk, but with the wind astern blowing coal dust, and the funnel discharging something similar the results were rather peculiar. After passing Cape St. Vincent when I relieved Philip at 0400, there was a written instruction in the Captain's Night Order book that we should both take sun sights at 0900 and at noon. After keeping the two night watches, a bath and breakfast were customary so we were not prompt, which greatly incurred his displeasure. Approaching Cape Trafalgar and the Straits, sun sights were pointless. Boify trying to be super efficient was rude to officers, men and stewards; he never offered to keep part of a watch and had disliked giving the men a Make and Mend when the other two ships wished to do so before we left Plymouth. I never served under such a difficult man until I met Captain John Hughes-Hallet (known as Hughes-Hitler) in HMS *Vernon* after the war. With hindsight, they must each have had an unhappy childhood.

On Sunday the Captain's plan of a service with many hymns was foiled by the total absence of hymn cards; instead he read a large number of prayers in his Australian twang. Grafton appeared from Almeria, looking as smart as when on the Royal cruise. Roy Gould assured me that the Cathedral lacked basses at Evensong so we donned surplices and trooped in with the choir such as it was. The experience gave me much pleasure because henceforth I could claim to have been a Cathedral chorister in my time.

Weekday nocturnal music was much the same with many new girls at the Royal and the Embassy, where a new little thing gave me a Hungarian lesson at a cost of one 'sherry' a word.

Young German sailors were much in evidence. We had passed *Admiral Scheer* returning to Germany at 22 knots on our way out. Now another pocket battleship *Deutschland* appeared. She had been bombed some weeks before with casualties thought to have been over forty killed or wounded. This had brought about the reprisal shelling of Almeria.

Augmented from Malta by a Lieutenant Parker R.N.R., we sailed for Cadiz on July 6 in weather so hot that it was difficult to sleep on board. Cadiz was Franco's naval base but our patrol was uneventful and we were back in Gibraltar a week later cheered by the news that Henry Cotton had won the "Open", with Englishmen not Americans in the first three. Coaling ship in the heat was hell. We divided into four parts, taking it in turns for a Stand easy. Armed with a shovel I was just about done when each 'Stand Easy' came round. 90 tons took 4½ hours. A sea bathe did not help much afterwards, then there was no fresh water and Pond's cream protecting my back against sunburn became Pond's black tan. Eventually repairs to the fresh water system returned us to white men by mid afternoon.

The following day, giving no notice to anybody Philip decided there should be a *Saltash* cocktail party. Forte and Hallet, two Army officers, a Mrs. Chapman, the attractive little thing from the Embassy, and Eleanor Fenwick and Charles Kennaway duly arrived and Boify attended. Charles for some reason having moved to *Isis* declared he could no longer afford a hang over with "Father" Clouston in command.

Our next patrol, off Malaga, lasted from July 16 to July 19. The 1st Minesweeping Flotilla came out from Portland to take over non-intervention patrols for a month, *Speedwell* relieving *Saltash*. Saying our 'Good-bye' to the *Royal*, who should appear but Noel Coward. Hardly in search of new talent, he had come in the cruiser *Arethusa* from Cannes as a guest.

Our trio left Gibraltar on July 22 a tedious thick fog along the N. African coast reducing our speed to 7 knots until it cleared beyond

Algiers. Passed by *Isis* towing her TSDS at 24 knots, inspired us to finish with a Full Power trial. All three ships ran smoothly at 15-16 knots for two hours, allowing another hour to tidy up before entering Grand Harbour to berth in French Creek. Philip returned to his parent ship, the cruiser *London*, almost immediately. Boify also spent much of his time in *Barham*, where he was playing some part – villain I presume – in amateur theatricals. This left me to wind up the paperwork, deck log, wine books, correspondence, muster and return Confidential books etc. And having completed those of *Saltash*, so many juniors had departed from the other two ships that I had to wind up for them too.

In July ABC had arrived from England to relieve Admiral Blake, Second-in-Command of the Fleet, who was ill. Flying his flag in the *Hood* I thought I would write my name in his Visitors Book. Found doing so by James Munn, the Flag Lieutenant, I was entertained in the Wardroom by Willie Dallmeyer and others before being summed to *the Presence*. Ten minutes genial talk over a pink gin, ABC seemed pleased to have had so young a visitor.

Later that day I paid another call, on my term mate Bill Dobbs, recently married to Ann Stoker of Seaview, Isle of Wight and now a pilot in the *Glorious*. Bill appeared after a while, no longer the wild Irishman who sang about Paddy McGinty's goat in his cups at Dartmouth, I felt he had settled down with a charming wife, who had helped him to recover from a Rugger accident in which his neck had been more or less broken.

After Boify had read prayers for the last time on Sunday August 8, Fenwick and I gave the last *Saltash/Elgin* cocktail party. Among the guests were: Eleanor Fenwick, Kay Moss, Flight-Lieutenant and Mrs. (Eileen) Wisher, Lieutenant-Commander 'Bog' Beard and Mrs. Beard, Lieutenant and Mrs. Dobbs, Lieutenant Bobbie Burton and Mrs. Burton, Lieutenant Commander and Mrs. J. J. Casement, Captain Bruce Fraser, Chaplain Dudley Bartlett, Lieutenants Roper and Barnett from Grafton and Lieutenant "Joey" Groome whose M.T.Bs had arrived in Malta.

Having left our ships clean with a little repainting here and there, the Dockyard decided to dock and refit them starting on Monday 16 August. Boify had continued to find fault most of the time, so I expected a terrible flimsy but to my astonishment it read, "Entirely to my satisfaction, has ability and initiative".

Without my diary I would not have remembered much about these months in *Saltash*, except the sweltering heat that kept one awake in the Valletta dockyard. Returning to *Glorious* on August 15 it was literally a breath of fresh air finding temporarily an outside cabin with an open scuttle. The jolly life and not-so-jolly hangover ended on August 23 when *Glorious* went to sea and embarked all three squadrons while many *Glorious* wives set out for home in the *Knight of Malta*, the little ship that plied almost non-stop between Valletta and Syracuse in Sicily. Not far behind, *Glorious* was expected to pay off at Devonport in November.

Discussing my own future with Captain Fraser it transpired that William Davies had written to the Navy Selector suggesting that it might be useful to give me a year's Rugger, which the Captain thought was a good idea too.

The setting for a big exercise presumed that in a war with Italy, Malta was untenable and the Fleet would leave for a base in the Greek Islands. *Malaya* and two cruisers represented the Fleet, which *Glorious* aircraft, MTBs and submarines were to find and attack. As usual lots of sinkings were claimed before we all anchored in the great bay of Cephalonia by the fishing port, Argostoli. A party of six that included Bill Dobbs, Joey Groome and myself landed there on Saturday 28th, finding a car that would take us near to the top of Mount Nero, 5000 feet high and fifteen miles away. Walking down in the heat from where it left us took from 1230 to 1830 which was quite long enough.

Heading next for Alexandria, Bruce Fraser – always the innovator – asked R.D. Franks* the Captain of *Comet*, the escorting destroyer, to dine with him. A boat would be lowered and he would be hoisted on board in a boatswain's chair. For a Captain to leave his ship at sea was most irregular but it encouraged Captains to trust their subordinates. Returning to the Mediterranean after the review, Fraser himself had sent for Lachlan Mackintosh saying "You take over, take a good observer as your navigator and call me when you sight the Rock". They ran into fog, but "sweating a bit", so he told me later, Fraser remained in his after cabin.

Approaching Alexandria, Drunky Lewin persuaded me into the back seat of his Swordfish. First we climbed to, and dived from 8000 feet in a dummy torpedo attack on *Coventry*. What with this and steep turns I felt dizzy. Next an aerial look round the City was more in my line but with the noise, the slipstream and the heat, an hour and a half was quite enough for me. That my friends did this for pleasure earned my astonishment and, still more, my admiration when we were at war for five years.

Our six days at Alexandria with my own family and most of the English colony away was a shadow of previous visits. Hilary Holmes just married to Kit Wells writing to thank me for a present of Maltese lace, said that he was to be Gunnery officer of *Glorious* in her next commis-

---

* Franks, now a Captain retd, says he was only 1st Lieutenant then.

sion. To be bossed by the husband of my favourite girl friend certainly did not auger well for my future.

Returning to Malta on September 16, at 1300 there was a real ACTION STATIONS alarm. Somebody had seen a torpedo track passing ahead and the Captain of *Comet* had reported a periscope. But there was no further evidence of an attack as we legged it at 25 knots and sent up six aircraft armed with live bombs. After a brief stop we headed West from Malta and I received a cable that my father had died, which I had expected for some days. The rest of the family were there at Epsom having brought him back while on holiday in Southern Ireland, a horrible journey for a sick man. I was upset but his survival would have meant retirement and a wheel chair. My parents had had thirty six years of a happy marriage and the Obituaries in the Press praised him as a County Court judge. He was sixty-seven and with another World War to come it was a good time to die. But for my mother, whom we all adored, the future must have looked bleak and lonely.

Quite why *Glorious* anchored at Mersch-el-Kebir on the evening of September 22, nobody knew but a fleet of buses took us into Oran. Bill Dobbs and I treated ourselves to two Champagne cocktails, dined well at the Tavern Alsacienne and finished with a Cabaret at the Coq d'Or. This was a case of the Fleet following the girls, for most of them had gone west from Rexfords, and gave us a tremendous welcome celebrated by dancing the Conga. Alas the boat back was at 2300.

The next patrol went Eastwards as far as Cape Matapan with more deck hockey on the flight deck than Cruising or Action Stations. And I was so absorbed reading *Gone with the Wind* that *Progress in Gunnery* - not at all a long work - got a little behind schedule.

Back again in Malta I discovered that Crawford was back too in the destroyer *Ivanhoe*, having failed the A/S (Anti-Submarine) course. *Sotto voce* he still mumbled away, his addiction to John Jameson in no way diminished.

In a large Wardroom such as that of the *Glorious*, for jocular purposes membership was divided into two, the S.O.Bs (Silly Old Buggers) and the B.Y.Fs (Bloody Young Fools). Looking back, it always amuses me that the dividing age was about thirty. Another group, The Deadbeats' Corner, consisted of old persons such as the First Lieutenant, the Chief and the Senior, the P.M.O (Principal Medical Officer), the Paymaster Commander and the Captain's Secretary, a very staid body you will agree. However, one day they all went for a picnic in the gig and became very drunk throwing bottles and glasses at one another. Deciding to sail back they overturned the boat and were picked up by the Captain. Badly cut in the face the Secretary needed five stitches. What Bruce Fraser said to them was never divulged.

On Wednesday October 13 the Wardroom entertained the Captain to dinner. After Lachlan Mackintosh had proposed his health, Bruce Fraser made a speech describing what the Mediterranean Station would be like in 1952. There would be Air Marshal Sir Robert Halley, Air Vice Marshal Heslop, Group Captain Pryde, Constructor Admiral Davies. He had them all weighed up touching on their idosyncrasies with much humour. Last came Archdeacon Bartlett whom nobody could find until they looked in the London Bar at 2 a.m.

Walking down the hill to the Customs House to catch a *dghaisa* the London Bar was the last port of call for that great reviver, the Prairie Oyster.* If after midnight it was always the custom – though Heaven knows why – to buy a hard boiled egg to present to the Officer of the (middle) Watch. I shall always remember Dudley Bartlett making me run up and down the Flight Deck to get fit, undoing the good work at some party or other afterwards, which ended at the London Bar.

On October 19 before entering Grand Harbour all the aircraft flew off for a display around *Enchantress*, the Admiralty yacht with Duff Cooper, the First Lord doing a tour. 802, the Fighter Squadron, returned while the others landed at Halfar. As usual Bruce Fraser put the ship neatly alongside Parlatorio jetty where the road was up creating considerable problems for me, appointed Baggage Officer expecting to hoist various cars on board for the voyage home. However by the 25th all seemed right with the world. A corrected version of my *Sidelights on Malta* had been accepted by *Men Only*, even *Progress in Gunnery* had been completed and the Dobbs were ecstatic with a son, Noel.

With everybody on the Flight Deck to cheer the other ships as we passed, *Glorious* sailed at 1400 under a blue and cloudless sky. Then came the planes diving down as close as they dared to the Flight Deck coinciding with the M.T.B's buzzing round our path. Then came sub-flight Torpedo "attacks" on either side; then a fly past in flights; then back again down each side and finally a fly past *en masse*. There was fun too, throughout a party sat on the after lift under a parasol playing dice. Les Levis towing a flag and making smoke puffs burst around it gave a good imitation of the last H.A. shoot. On the flag as he passed we read, "Ladies half way". Finally George Heycock after clowning around landed on his

---

* Pour into a wine glass one teaspoonful of Worcestershire Sauce and one of Tomato Juice, the yolk of one raw egg and two dashes of vinegar, taking care not to break the egg yolk. Add a dash of pepper.

JUST A HOGG'S LIFE

fighter as he was going home in the ship. This intrepid pilot aged twenty eight, who always attracted a bevy of spectators when landing on, became an Air Commodore CB, DFC, retiring in 1965.

Bloody old Malta! Awful old *Glorious*! Our grumbles faded away. It had been fun to serve in a carrier. It had been fun to know so many people, particularly the RAF, a cheery crowd and excellent messmates. On the way home they continued to fly as opportunity offered. A flight deck being the best "field" for deck hockey we made the most of our last chances. The chess players, myself included, enjoyed themselves. Cornabe was active at the piano into the small hours.

The weather report for November 3rd being unfavourable, 802 Squadron and three Swordfish on board flew off to Roborough (Plymouth) whilst *Glorious* anchored in Cawsand Bay before going up harbour to berth alongside the following evening. With relations trying to come on board, libertymen trying to go ashore, cot cases and then cars being hoisted out, the jetty presented a scene of happy chaos. I was Officer of the Watch; about 2200 when all was calm Terence Harrel, Greynvile term mate walked over from *Fearless* to welcome me.

The Commander Edward Evans-Lombe, much to our delight, decreed that Officers of the Watch on their days off were entitled to a Make and Mend. Very soon our numbers dwindled to four and our status became Officer of the Day. The four were Fenwick, Griffiths, Moultrie and myself. An unlucky tossing of coins gave me the job of correcting the ship's charts. Taking over an empty cabin with a view of the gangway enabled me to work on them when Officer of the Day.

A timely lift from Peter Gretton enabled me to catch the Cornish Riviera and be at home for my birthday for the first time since I was seven. Peter Gretton was displeased to be sent to Dartmouth as a Term officer when he wished to be at sea again. He could hardly foresee how, soon enough, the cruel sea would bring him five years of strain and stress as well as fame and honours.

At Epsom, Barbara and Geoffrey Hulton, the two young children of Sir Roger, head of my mother's family, were staying. That I should write a large book about them in my seventies was indeed one of life's improbabilities.* Once again the admirable Woodcote garage supplied me with a good car, a Morris 12 4 cylinder saloon. An interview with a Commander William-Powlett at the Admiralty indicated that a Devonport Rugger job might be a possibility. After lunching with Joan Powell and her brother Michael, she took me to a play and then to the Ritz to meet

---

The Hulton Diaries 1832-1928. A Gradely Lancashire Chronicle.

her young friend Prim, another former pupil of Miss Penrose in Florence. After a while in this august hotel there appeared a dark girl in great distress. Only sixteen, she had been taught to believe that only one affair was necessary for a girl to become pregnant. This was Leonora Carrington, today almost the last of the Surrealists, whose latest exhibition in London (Serpentine Gallery) moving to Preston and to Bristol has been such a success in 1992.†

Although there were few dual carriage ways, there was relatively little traffic and the Morris would average 37 - 40 mph over the 211 miles from Epsom to Plymouth along the A.303. Back in Plymouth I found myself selected to play in the Devonport Services A team beating the Glosters, the local regiment on Wednesday and losing 13 - 11 to Paignton on Saturday. By mid- November four fifths of the ship's company had gone on foreign service leave, relieved by a mere one fifth of the new commission. The ship was moved into dry dock for a brief refit before recommissioning early in January. The Captain told me I should remain until then before taking my foreign service leave.

Promoted to play against Bristol and Redruth these matches were both lost but not by much, but a minor injury prevented me playing for the Royal Navy versus The Police. December passed pleasantly with Dudley Bartlett coaching us twice weekly at the Rectory Field, Devonport Services' ground and playing an occasional game of golf with me at Yelverton or Tavistock. The trouble with West Country rugger was mud, the greasy leather ball was difficult to hold and the forwards tended to dribble on regardless. However, we did have a dry day in which to beat Guy's Hospital in a grand open game.

"Quite like old times seeing you going through", said Master-at- Arms Luddington, the most capped Navy player and England international, to me.

Whether it was Christmas leave or Foreign Service leave, I seem to have been at home every other weekend and from December 19 to December 26. Jack Paterson had returned for good from Egypt by flying boat for an interview for the post of Chief Constable Suffolk which was not successful.

At Epsom, the best Christmas entertainment was at our local, *The King's Head* opposite the Parish Church. Mrs. Carr, widow and licensee, would shake her fist in its direction saying "There's that Vicar taking good money out of us poor honest folk's pockets". The elder son Ernie, slightly disabled, ran the place with her. Then came "Beau" pronounced Buff

† Followed by her life story on film, BBC TV *Omnibus*, 10 November 1992.

JUST A HOGG'S LIFE

because he was so beautiful and then the pretty daughter, Olive. The great moment came when Mrs. Carr in her cups at the piano played and sang, "God send you back to me" with the tears rolling down her cheeks.

1937 World Events
Baldwin resigns. Chamberlain becomes Prime Minister. Japanese aggression in China. Britain signs naval agreement with Germany and Russia. Riots begin in Sudeten part of Czechoslovakia. Butlin's first camp.

1937. L to R. Wing Cdr Halley, Captain Fraser, Lt-Cdr Tupper-Carey (Navigator) Comdr (O) Lochlan Mackintosh on the bridge of HMS Glorious.

BRUCE FRASER'S GLORIOUS

1937. Glorious at Spithead for the Coronation Review.

In the hangar, 1938, Chaplain Dudley Bartlett christens my godson James Dobbs before his parents, Bill (far left) and Anne (centre).

ROYAL NAVY XV 1938

Cdr William Powlett   Lieut Hogg   Lieut Jameson   Sub-Lieut Crawford   Sub-Lieut Whitworth   Surg-Lieut (D) Goldsworthy   Ldg Tel Stovell   Surg Cdr (D) Osborne
AB Atwood   Pay Lieut Lyddon   Pay Lieut Watkins   Lieut (E) Evans   Lieut Hammond   Lieut (E) Callaghan   Lieut (E) Kirkby
Lieut Vavasour   Lieut (E) Wickham

Note: AB = Able Seaman; D = Dental; E = Engineer Officer; Ldg Tel = Leading Telegraphist.

CHAPTER 18

Victory at Twickers

1938   Q   *Are you a b—r ?*
Or do you play Rugger ?
Do you like pederasty ?
Or think it quite nasty ?

       A   *Well I recommend P—g*
And be sure I'm not joking
For F—g is in
And no longer a sin
But considered a must
By our own upper crust
Who go to great trouble
And put it in double
To get twice as much pleasure
From half as much measure
Which deserves an ovation
In times of inflation.

Never having heard an answer to the question, I challenged Cyril Ray, who wrote the above in the space of ten minutes over the port at his own dinner table.

Even more amusing was that Ray, the smallest forward ever, played the game for Manchester as a hooker. Held up by a hefty forward on each side, he claimed that his airborne feet did a splendid job.

Though United Services Chatham and Royal Naval College Greenwich fielded Rugby teams, only United Services Portsmouth and Devonport Services could be said to have first class fixture lists. At Portsmouth on Saturdays they could field three XVs nearly all officers; at Devonport perhaps two, of which the first XV relied greatly on lower deck players and on officers and men of the local regiment, the Gloucesters at this time. Since however their main object was to win the Regimental Knock-Out, they were not regularly available, which made good team building difficult for Devonport Services.

JUST A HOGG'S LIFE

On New Year's day we lost 16 - 3 to our near-by rivals Plymouth Albion, a team containing quite a few policemen. Leaving *Glorious* for good the next day, my seven weeks leave were punctuated by returning to play at the week-ends. The Great Western Railway service from Paddington, taking less than four hours, enabled teams such as London Hospital, Guy's Hospital and the Old Blues to arrive for a 2.30 kick off returning that evening or by the over-night sleeper.

I think I owed my inclusion in the Navy team to an injury to Lieutenant Roy Casement. There were three Casement brothers: Roddy, JJ and Roy, all pretty good at the game. Roy had played against the Army in 1937. Our practice matches began at Bristol on 12 January. The going was so slow that *The Daily Telegraph* said that even the referee's watch was affected, the first half lasting forty eight minutes. The ground was a mud heap and our defeat 11 - 6 was largely due to two dropped goals by Morris, Bristol's international fly half.

A fortnight later at Blackheath on a dry day we won 14 - 0. All I remember about this game is a bang on the head after fifteen minutes and next seeing the clock with ten minutes to go and our score, 10 - 0. It seems I had been playing rather well, my team mates joking that a kick on my head before each match would be efficacious in future. Aware that alcohol must be avoided, I suffered no ill consequences from concussion. Our next effort was a victorious 28-3 at Plymouth against the Civil Service. At a dinner afterwards one of their speakers said, "You really couldn't expect us to beat the Navy on water", referring to the ground not a beverage.

With seven men in the Navy side, Devonport Services took a strong team to Bath losing 6 - 0, failing to score being largely due to R. A. Gerrard, their England centre-three quarter playing full back and repelling all attackers. Then a week before the RAF match at Twickenham, United Services Portsmouth came to Devonport defeating us by 8 points to 7. However, the selectors, Commander William Powlett and Surgeon Commander (D) Osborne made no changes, so this Navy side met at the Grosvenor Hotel by Victoria Station going on to Greenwich in a motor coach for a final practice on the afternoon before the RAF match at Twickenham on Saturday February 19. This team was:

ROYAL NAVY — Lieutenant T. G. C. Jameson (H.M.S. Furious), back : Lieutenant (E) J. P. Kirkby (H.M.S. Drake), Lieutenant A.L.S. Hogg (H.M.S. Drake), Surgeon Lieutenant H.M. Goldsworthy (H.M.S. St Vincent), and Sub-Lieutenant W.B. Whitworth (H.M.S.

Alresford), three-quarter backs ; Lieutenant G.W. Vavasour (H.M.S. Iron Duke) and Sub-Lieutenant D.T. Wickham (H.M.S Vernon), half backs ; Lieutenant (E) N.L. Evans (captain) (RNE College, Devonport), Sub-Lieutenant (E) D.N. Callaghan (H.M.S. Iron Duke), Leading Telegraphist R.G. Stovell (H.M.S. Drake), Paymaster Lieutenant H.C. Lyddon (H.M.S. Victory), A.B.H. Attwood (H.M.S. Drake), Sub-Lieutenant W.H. Crawford (RAF Station Leuchars), Lieutenant R.J.L Hammond (H.M.S. Iron Duke) and Paymaster-Lieutenant J.K. Watkins, (H.M.S. St Vincent), forwards.

Our strength lay in the back row. Watkins was an English international, his white head always conspicuous in the loose. Crawford, a Scottish cap, excelled at converting tries and Hammond, known as 'Wally' after the Gloucestershire batsman, was a tower of strength in attack or defence. Thought too light for England, he had the rare distinction of being selected to play for The Barbarians without being an international. Specialising in Engineering at Keyham Jerry Kirkby played for the Navy in 1933-34 and 38, and I fancy for Devon too at times. This tough little man on the wing, going like the wind, was a formidable opponent. A useful golfer too, we became close friends.

The RAF strength lay in their halves, Sowerbutts and Graham Walker, who scored a try in the first ten minutes. A penalty made them 6.0 at half time, but two goals in the second half, contrived by Vavasour and Goldsworthy, with Crawford converting, gave us a 10 - 6 win. Risking our limbs again the following Saturday with a drawn match at Portsmouth against the Harlequins, there were no casualties. Still trying to meet young ladies of higher quality than those at the Bush and the Barley Mo, led me to spend the night at The Manor House, Havant with my fair cousins. Cyrene's husband, Captain Cecil Hulton-Sams R.N., forced into a wheelchair by paralysis had died in 1931, Cyrene with her daughters, Valerie now 22 and Cyrene 20, made an attractive and very amusing trio. A collection of *Tatlers* in the downstairs lavatory, fit for a Baronial Hall, gave them encyclopaedic knowledge of such persons as 'Jumbo' Jolliffe and 'Fruity' Metcalfe.

The next Saturday March 5 was sunny with scores of friends picnicing in the Twickenham West car park. On paper the Army were the better team with England's centre three quarter, Leyland, likely to be troublesome and a giant of a man named Ford on the wing being marked by Jerry Kirkby. At half time the score was 5 - 3, Crawford having converted our try and the Army failing to do so with theirs. In the second half they scored two more tries and, leading 9-5, all seemed lost for us. Then suddenly, pressing them in their own 25, the ball came out from a loose scrum to Attwood – Hammond – Vavasour who, missing me out made a long pass to Jerry, running like a rigger to score in the corner. The silent service was never more silent as Crawford prepared to kick. A magnificent conversion! Two more minutes and we had won the match and the championship 10-9; the first time for six years. The Army should have won but they had missed penalties and fallen to our vigorous tackling.

Our two selectors threw their bowler hats high in the air. While after the war, 'Ginger' Osborne became an England selector and managed the Lions in New Zealand on the very happy tour of 1949-50, he never forgot this game, sending good wishes before every Service championship to the Navy selector. Becoming Deputy-Director General of Naval Dental Services in 1954 he was made a Rear Admiral (D), though whether this was for dentistry or football nobody was quite sure. It was said that knowing he was out of practice when required to extract the tooth of an admiral's wife, he had a Lieutenant (D) ready, who approached unseen from the back of the room to do the job while he chatted up the patient. Dying in 1989, he was 88.

My family were thrilled at the match and enjoyed the dance at The Dorchester. Those of us who returned to Devonport were invited to drinks in the house of Commodore and Mrs. Davies, Commodore being an honorary rank given to Captains commanding Barracks known as stone frigates. I even had a personal letter from Bruce Fraser, promoted Rear-Admiral on January 11 and about to become Chief of Staff to Admiral Sir Dudley Pound in the Mediterranean.

Though we held Bath to 6-0, local rugby was rather an anti-climax for us and for the Gloucester regiment which had won the Army championship. Gloucester, the town, we held to 18-13 but for entertainment I preferred *A Day at the Races*, Marx Brothers' version, at a Plymouth cinema the same evening.

By coincidence, on Friday March 11 Hitler marched into Austria as we were rehearsing mobilisation, an exercise controlled by two or three Writers from the Central Regulating Office (C.R.O). Knowing the number of men each Devonport-manned ship required to increase to war complement, they detailed them off accordingly. In Austria Von Schuschnigg, the Chancellor, had arranged a plebescite for Sunday on whether his country should remain independent. Forestalled, he was forced to resign in favour of a Hitler-appointed Nazi as Hitler's troops swiftly occupied his country. For Lieutenants in the Barracks our main duty was to be Officer of the

Day in rotation. The Commander, First Lieutenant and Officer of the Day each had an office in the small administration block across the road from the main entrance and Guard room. A day on started at 0830, witnesses required for Commander's defaulters at 0945 appeared in good time. The OOD signed unimportant correspondence for the Commodore, made sure signals were answered and did rounds at certain times. Relieved at 1230 for lunch he took the 1300 parade, where classes marched off for instruction or other work. His tea was sent up from the Wardroom before Fire Parties were exercised at 1630. In the Wardroom there was early supper for officers going out in plain clothes. But before dinner in mess undress (bow tie) a Petty Officer steward, calling others to attention, would climb a step ladder to remove Drake's sword from its case and place it by the President's place at table. This ceremony was always witnessed by the Officer of the Day.

Although in non-working hours there was often time to write letters, or even a diary, there were many interruptions. People kept coming in with signals or to draw keys for beer bars. On my first day a woman wanted to get her husband home from the *Glorious*. A man whose child had died had to be given money to get him to Rosyth. £5 was kept in the safe for such cases. There was a bathroom and a bed, which one left in the middle watch as a rule to do the rounds of the Barracks seeing that sentries were at their posts.

Soon I was made responsible for one large Dining Hall, which entailed little more than taking a cup of tea at 1100 and doing a football pool in conjunction with the Chief Petty Officer under me. Real responsibility, including painting the place lay with the Civil Engineer's Department, except for one large plate-washing machine. Since our standards required painting far more frequently than those of the Civil Engineer, we drew sufficient paint by frequent requests "for washing machine". Probably enough to paint the Forth Bridge, they were never questioned.

Early in April when Roy Casement went to sea again, I was able to take over his cabin, a spacious room on the ground floor of the Officers' Block facing west across the Barracks cricket ground. Cooks and stewards under instruction looked after us and with a Decca portable radiogram and an open fire in winter I was very comfortable.

Carleton Walker ("Uncle Ritz") last mentioned with his niece Joan Powell in Malta, lived in Liverpool, where she and her two brothers, Michael and Philip, often stayed with him. Being a benefactor of the Anglican cathedral he knew Bishop David, formerly Headmaster of Rugby. For his own retirement and the enjoyment of his wife and four children, the Bishop had bought, Skippers Close, a house on the top of a hill at Trebetherick on the North coast of Cornwall. Of passing interest, this house had been built by the parents of John Betjeman, who found it too breezy.

Knowing nothing of Cornwall I was delighted when Michael Powell, down from Cambridge, who was staying with the David family, suggested an 1800 (opening time) rendezvous at the Rock Hotel. Michael lived for pubs and pubs lived for – or rather off – Michael. Fair haired Bill made lame by polio and Diana, his vivacious sister always in trousers, introduced me to darts in the hotel bar. After supper at the house we sang hymns as we washed up and returned to the pub. This was a quiet evening as none of the locals had drunk enough beer to sing *The Farmer's Boy* so we next called on Mrs. Ann Channell, Rock's best known character. My brother Martin vaguely wanted to come to Wadebridge for Easter; hearing my report we booked at the Rock Hotel forthwith.

I cannot tell whether West Countrymen are more musical than others. Certainly at the Rectory Field there was often a sing-song of rude Rugger Songs with the beer after matches. The leader was Able Seaman Attwood, who was, on the field, what Wade Dooley has been to England. Retiring after the war he became the Swimming Instructor at Cheltenham Ladies College. I hardly think Miss Buss and Miss Beale would have approved this appointment.

Easter at Rock was fine, sunny and fun. Everybody met everybody by sitting with a glass on the wall in front of the hotel, with the Camel estuary on the other side. On the far bank was Padstow, then the Southern Railway's terminus, with trains moving in and out along the estuary to Wadebridge and London.

Johnny Walker of the Lancashire and Yorkshire regiment was with his blonde attractive wife Joyce and somewhere around was her young, blonde brother David Jackson, an Etonian with a lovely girl friend, Pamela Durrant. The large Jackson family lived in a big house near Titchfield. Ann Channell stopping her car called "The Flying Commode", seemed to be inviting anyone in sight to a Good Friday evening party.

In the bar of the Rock Hotel visitors of both sexes mixed freely with the locals, some of them caddies. This suited them well since they took us on at darts winning as a rule; so, as losers we kept them in beer. The local character was Archie Luke, cobbler at Wadebridge though he seldom seemed to be there. He had had a nameless dog for some years, "B'aint had time to give her a name", said Archie. But he had found time to train the animal to retrieve any packet of cigarettes lying about, which in the crowded bar went into Archie's pocket unnoticed.

Less than a mile up the road towards Wadebridge was the Dormy House Hotel, owned and run by Commander Bannerman DSO retd. and his wife. A difficult gentleman by all accounts, the Commander, a very good golfer, quarrelled with the committee and forbade entry to his hotel by any young lady in trousers; hardly good for business when the habit was growing fast. Better appointed than the Rock, the Dormy House had a billiard table and tennis courts. Known as Pam the Good, Pamela Durrant was a niece of Mrs. Bannerman. Pam the Bad, known as 'The Dormy House Vamp', was a smasher too, carefully chaperoned by her very large Aunt Tizzie Young. Though she might have taken a course in waggling from Marilyn Monroe, her innocence of life had hardly progressed beyond babies under the gooseberry bush, so she shared a room with Aunt Tizzie.

On the links the crowd dwindled after noon. My brother Martin hit the ball as if he was driving a tent peg with a mallet, which made him a trifle erratic, but he enjoyed the game and on the course we met Pat Brooking and Wilfred Bennett, who had defended me at the St. Albans inquest.

Back to work, the Gas Course of former days was now the Passive Defence course. Taking this for a week I found my respirator was obsolete and the new one gave protection against nerve gases such as DM. An Experimental Officer from the Chemical Warfare establishment at Porton gave an interesting lecture as did a Portsmouth Air Raid Precautions officer. The best part was a demonstration of an air raid on the dockyard. We sat in the Bomb and Gas proof ARP Headquarters with smoke bombs making a frightful din outside. The raid completed, signals came in giving details of the damage, also shown on a large map. The Devonport Passive Defence Officer then explained how he would deal with it, provoking much discussion among the many Dockyard managers doing the course. Finally one of them stood up saying he had a small point to raise.

"I'm afraid you'll find things more difficult than you think", he said. Then, pointing to an incident on the chart, he continued, "I'm afraid that HE bomb must have severed the town's main electrical supply so that alone would take several days to repair".

The assembled company were somewhat shaken.

Going home that week-end, I was well equipped to talk Air Raid precautions with my brother-in-law Jack. After applying for two Chief Constable posts unsuccessfully, he had become a Civil Servant doing much the same course in London, which would result in him becoming Principal Civil Defence Officer for the Midlands during the war.

Down at the Rectory Field on the evening of May 4, the ground had never been so full. There was a band, boys brigade and field guns crew display, which all the relations of the participants had come to watch. Every year at Olympia, Portsmouth and Devonport field guns crews of seamen and stokers competed against each other in the Royal Tournament. A highly dangerous affair crews of twenty manhandled their gun and limber over a five foot wall before dismantling them for swinging over a bottomless chasm. With wheels first removed and then replaced, the whole carriage was reassembled for the final run. All this in a time less than three minutes. Jerry Kirkby and Warwick Bracegirdle R.A.N, a recently qualified Gunnery officer, who were in charge respectively of Stokers and Seamen departed for London with their crews a few days later*.

Although my diaries give the impression that we had little to do except play golf and end the day inebriated, as Officers of the Day we were only four. Hodgson, the senior, had risen from the Lower Deck and was as efficient as he was pleasant. Next came Emmanuel a Dartmouth cadet, three years my senior. Then came Bill Boaks, who in his retirement after the war frequently stood for Parliament as a Nut-Case candidate. I expect he enjoyed it but who would have paid his deposit?

Extraneous duties included visiting foreign vessels and our own merchant ships with passengers as Officer of the Guard bringing greetings etc., from the Commnder-in-Chief Plymouth. In a ship called *Narkunda*, arriving from Australia, I found my Uncle Arthur Hulton, who had served before the mast in the clippers to and from Australia as a young man. Settled near Hobart and now sixty, he had come to see his British relatives before it was too late.

Relations of any deceased officer or naval rating were entitled to a free R.N. burial if they so wished. On May 18 we buried a commissioned Gunner Curtain at Pennycomequick cemetery about 1½ miles from the hospital at Stonehouse. The march back to the Barracks took nearly two hours. I was Officer in Charge.

The diary mentions a resolution to spend less money. As a Lieutenant on promotion I received 13s. 6d. a day, say £20 a month. The mess bill is given as about £11.10.0 a month which left £8 or £9 a month, with £12 a month unearned from £1000 left to me by my Uncle Lee of Portrush when he died in 1925. Running a car is estimated at £3.4.0 a month and

---

*In recent years there have been three competing crews from Portsmouth, Devonport and the Fleet Air Arm, bringing the record time down to 2 minutes 40.6 seconds.

it may be part of my pay was being committed to, perhaps, Gieves. Going home to Epsom, perhaps twice a month, and back by train 3rd class (there was no 2nd) would have cost £3 return. In Plymouth a run ashore usually included a grill at the Royal Hotel close to Lockyers. The place had the most revolting carpet, but to eat one chose one's sole or one's mixed grill in the dining room where they were displayed. The chef then grilled them while one drank half a pint of bitter in the bar.

Lesser places for lesser meals were Malcolms and the Falstaff; and for refreshment, the Athenaeum bar along Union Street presided over by a large lady called the Duchess. There were plenty of cinemas and the Palace Theatre that survived the war put on variety shows each week.

A few other examples of pay on promotion, taken from The Navy List June 1939, were per day:

Officers:	Sub Lieutenant 9/-
	Commander £1.16.2
	Captain £2.14.4 with 3/-per day
	if in command of a ship.
Ratings:	Ordinary Seaman 2/9
	Able Seaman 4/-
	Leading Seaman 5/3
	CPO 8/6

Enchanted by St. Enodoc, Martin flew from Manchester to Plymouth (Roborough) for the Whitsun weekend. The plane being late we paused for a round of golf at Tavistock. To arrive at most golf clubs on a Saturday afternoon, pay a green fee of five shillings perhaps and then play a round seems incredible today. On Sundays at St. Enodoc it was only twelve holes, the land with the six round the church being owned by an old lady who disapproved of play on the Sabbath. An after dinner discovery was Major Pellew's Constantine Bay Hotel. A great raconteur he was amusing company in his own bar, decorated with murals by the Zinkeisen sisters. Little heed was paid to the 10pm closing time, which applied to all imbibers not actually staying in hotels. The Major had three sons all lost on Active Service during the war.

Our party of about a dozen for the Wardroom's Barracks Ball on June 16 began with an excellent dinner at the Yacht Club on the Hoe. Joan Powell came from Epsom as my partner, Warwick Bracegirdle was back from Olympia, Nigel Roper too in the *Grafton* at the end of her two year commission. Dancing was in the two spacious ante rooms, Guard and Band beat the retreat on the lawn and supper was served in the Drill shed.

But the Barracks had its own station, on a loop off the Great Western main line, very convenient for embarking drafts. This, *The Railway Inn* had been transformed with advertisements etc., into a beer bar to end the party. A train of course was drawn up, enabling Bracegirdle to combine the role of wheel-tapper and station master, but some young officer in drag was even better as the barmaid.

Playing cricket most Saturday afternoons, the Barracks team were saved from defeat on June 18 by the bat of Lieutenant Pope RNVR doing his annual training. Over a drink I suggested taking him to Westward Ho! for golf next day. Old Uppinghamians, as were my father and brother, one Pope brother was England's scrum half and this one had a golf handicap of 9, defeating me with a hole in one at the 16th. The custom then was to make the hole-in-one golfer the guest of the club for the rest of the day (drinks only) which, I'm happy to say, included his opponent.

Nowadays the player is expected to stand a round to all present and a Gilbey pensioner, doing it twice on Sunday mornings within three months, had to ask his firm for help. They promptly replied with a case of Gilbey's gin to the club. I myself did it once at Hayling's first hole finding the bar empty when we finished the round. I rewarded the Greenkeeper with £10, he being the man who had put the hole in the right place. That, I think should be the custom.

Towards the end of June we did our first test mobilisation, an unsolved problem being how to feed and accommodate hundreds of reservists coming in when the regular occupants had not been moved out.

The half yearly promotions on June 30 made Lochlan Mackintosh a Captain, Geoffrey Gowland and Colquhoun Commanders, all three of *Glorious*. Kay Edden of the Devonport Gunnery School and Stokes, Captain of *Griffin* became Commanders, as did 'Blossom' Stewart, Captain of Eddie Baines destroyer *Brilliant*.

About to visit two Russian hydrographic vessels as Officer of the Guard, I was instructed to tell their Captains that it was not necessary for them to call on the Commander-in-Chief. It was made clear to me that our Admiral Hon. Sir Reginald Aylmer Ranfurly Plunkett-Ernle-Erle-Drax had no use for Russians, which made him just about the worst possible choice to lead the Military mission sent to make some sort of entente with Stalin a year later.

Staying with David Meredith, the Club Secretary and his wife, I had my first introduction to Saunton at the end of July. The great big Saunton Sands Hotel, had just opened. Conspicuous even when seen from Westward Ho! on the far side of the Taw estuary, it belonged to John Christie of Glyndebourne. About twenty years later it would be bought by Paul Dauthieu, founder of Peter Dominic in 1939 with his one wine shop in Horsham, for whom I would then be working as Sales Director. The Merediths, promised a new house three years before, lived in the smallest bungalow with splendid views across the Braunton Burrows and the links. In perfect weather, David played with me in the afternoons and found me a partner in the mornings.

Used by tanks in the war, the old course was soon restored after it. But it was not until 1976 that the new, designed by C. K. Cotton and Frank Pennink, was ready. Even so, that glorious 1976 summer kept it unplayable for some time.

The annual Armada dinner was held in the Wardroom on July 27 the Commodore and the Commander-in-Chief each making a speech. The latter, attributed Drake's success to prayer, forgetting that Spanish Catholics prayed a damn sight harder than Drake's buccaneers. For a press preview of Navy Week I walked round the Dockyard with Mr. Bennett, the Times correspondent, who seemed to know more about the Navy and its week than I did.

The family holiday was fourteen days in August at Rock. Martin and I stayed in the Rock Hotel; my mother, Brada, Jack and their two girls now twelve and nine at Penmayne House, a small hotel across the road. With plenty of sand and surfing, pleasant young people and informal parties almost every night, as well as golf on a delightful seaside links, I found it thoroughly enjoyable. The last day was the best; surfing at low tide at Daymer Bay with Diana, Pat youngest of the Davids and a cousin Colwyn Hemsley seemed better and warmer than at Polzeath. That evening, catching the last ferry at Torpoint, looking back at Cornwall, I felt as sad as Napoleon banished from France for ever.

But of course the next day but one being Saturday, I was back, introducing John Inverdale to the wonders of such a place. Lieutenant (D) J. B. Inverdale and I had become closely acquainted when he remarked, "That one filling you said you needed is at least seven and it'll take me some months to make you dentally fit". A very nice fellow, Rock was really no place for him. He was a very bad golfer and could not swim. Surviving the war nevertheless, he became Surgeon Captain (D) with a C.B.E. for his services to Royal Naval Rugby. On 12 March 1987 soon after he died, there was a crowded memorial service in the Chapel of Haslar Hospital with much fraternising among those present on this sunny afternoon. The hymn tunes - I hardly need say - included *Cwm Ronda*. His son, John, often heard on BBC Sports News, now wakes us at 6.30 a.m. with his own *Morning Edition* on Channel 5.

THE PROPER DRILL
When I was a Surgeon Lieutenant (D)
I filled and polished in the R.N.B.
Of chaps in the Barracks my chair took a load
But I filled in time with the handling code.
I ran and I dribbled at The Rectory*
And very soon they passed me as a referee.

With my drill and whistle I did aspire
To be 'That bright young Toothy who should go far',
Through cervical margins and dental decay
With a jink and a swerve I would drill my way
I drilled and I whistled so successfully
That very soon they gave me a brass hat (D).

I would think as I used to say 'Open wide!'
(They must practise dummy scissors on the open side.)
And as those fillings I packed hard down -
(I'd rather have The Triple than a jacket crown.)
And to all those fillings I gave such a gleam
That now I am the Hon. Sec of the Navy team.

Now officers (D) I advise you all
Keep a drill and a whistle and an oval ball
Volunteer for Hon. Sec., but never be caught
Turning up at Twickenham with one man short.
Then, with conscience clear, you can shout "Navee"
And look forward to promotion to a Captain (D)
A.S.H.

During September Mobilisation Orders arrived day by day. On September 13 Hitler spoke of three million German brothers being bullied and tortured by fifteen million Czechs, which was of course rubbish. On September 15 Chamberlain, the Prime Minister making his first flight aged 70, flew for talks

---
*Devonport Services' ground.

with Hitler, flying back the next day. At home Mrs. Keelan, almost a member of the family who had been our cook since 1913 died of a heart attack.

While the Czechs accepted a British plan it was much criticised and Chamberlain returned to continue conversations with Hitler on the 22nd at Godesberg on the Rhine. On Friday 23rd about 2300, when the Wardroom had just ended a farewell dinner to the Commander-in-Chief, came the order to send off drafts totalling at least 800 men. The Czechs were reported to have mobilised, with Germany sending troops up to the frontier.

Earlier in the month Jan Aylen, a Lieutenant (E) had been made Captain of Devonport Services and I became Team Secretary. The Blackheath XV, having been beaten by Plymouth Albion on Saturday, were staying in the Barracks to play us on Monday. Apart from our scrum half, drafted to a destroyer, our team was still in Plymouth so we played losing 12-11.

All through the week beginning Monday September 27 the situation grew worse. Class A and B reservists were called up on the 28th. Roosevelt sent appeals to Hitler, as the servers in our Dining Halls tried to feed the incoming men. Relatives and friends gathered dismally outside the Barracks gate.

It was on the afternoon of Thursday 29th that Chamberlain, making a doleful report in the Commons, received the note that Hitler had agreed to a further meeting creating emotional scenes of relief. The Four Power agreement was reached in the small hours of Friday. With the Dining Halls standing the strain, I combed the Dockyard to make up a scratch XV to play Bristol next day at the Rectory Field, reinstating the fixture that had been cancelled. There was a good crowd and the team looked good on paper but we lost 23-0. As to the crisis Germany was allowed to takeover the Sudetenland and by degrees we learnt that Chamberlain's, "It will be alright this time" was the reverse of the truth. Nevertheless the year gained for the production of Spitfires, Hurricanes and radar equipment may well have prevented our defeat.

❖ ❖ ❖

During October Jerry Kirkby acquired a girlfriend called "Copper" and Warwick Bracegirdle, inevitably "Braces", introduced me to a small brunette called Daphne Norman. She worked in a Knightsbridge beauty parlour but had a basement flat in Sussex Place, no distance from Paddington Station. This was very useful; staying with us at Epsom we could return to the flat late on Sunday evenings by train and tube and I could catch the 0140 to Plymouth which arrived there at 0615. Usually I could get one side of a carriage to myself, sleeping to Exeter; if not, only 9s.6d. was needed to transfer to First Class. Stopping at stations after

Exeter, hearty Chief and Petty Officers smoking *Digger Cut Plug* made the carriage a pollution zone.

Claud Line a Lieutenant (E) and his wife Greta were a most hospitable couple in their flat near the Hoe. Wishing to give Greta a present, Braces arranged for Daphne to post him a parcel of cosmetics. Greta was all dolled up giving her Aunt dinner when we all arrived to present the parcel. Out of it however, far from cosmetics a pair of Gunnery officer's black leather gaiters landed on Greta's lap. Braces had lent them to a fellow Gunnery Officer who had returned them. Sudden dismay turned to hilarious laughter.

For some time I had been in charge of the Guard and the Commander now said I was to continue until I left the Barracks. He then asked if I would care to join the new cruiser, *Gloucester* completing at Devonport in January. I replied that I was hoping to finish the rugger season.

Since the *Gloucester* was sunk with heavy loss of life off Crete in May 1941, this may well have saved my life.

I was now quite busy with the Guard and Band, in charge of Rodney division and Dining Halls. Much of the forenoon was spent investigating cases of defaulters and seeing request men. I discovered too that I was President of the C.D.A. mess, the letters standing for *Caught Disease Ashore*, the disease being Venereal. I had - I hasten to add - no qualifications.

Admiral Dunbar-Naismith, suitably saluted by Hogg's Guard and Band took over Commander-in-Chief Plymouth on October 24. Moreover the Changing of the Guard ceremony rated by No. 1 ("Ruckers") as "Fairly bloody", which was the most one expected from him, suddenly became "Surprisingly good". This was timely; at the end of October four new Lieutenants (G) just qualified at Whale Island - 'Oafie' Custance, Jock Gray, Frankie Morgan and Jas. Miller - whom I knew well joined the Devonport School and would be critical.

On November 8 I decided I needed a new reefer (double breasted uniform jacket), receiving an awful shock that Gieves' price was £8 made to measure. In 1992 the price is £896. Two new discoveries were Camembert cheese in the Mess, French fern soap at Boots.

Devon played their annual match v The Navy at the Rectory Field winning 5.-0. John Willie Forest was now the team selector and I was very disappointed not to be selected even as a reserve. Devonport Services had barely won a match; Able Seaman Bailey, our fly half, was injured and I was considered to be out of form. When he was fit again, we recovered a little by beating Aldershot Services 14-3. Five of them stayed over the weekend to form part of a scratch side that played a sort of exhibition match against the College at Dartmouth. Defeated 18-11 we stayed on to supper and the College Dramatic Society performed The Middle Watch, though recalling Jane Baxter in the London production, the girls hardly gave me a swing on the Menotti, an expression coined by Braces in some elementary electrics class.

Ten days before Christmas I motored Jock Gray to Dartmouth, where we were to play for the officers and masters v the Devon Barbarians, mainly Plymouth Albion and Aldershot services volunteers. We won 34.0. But the interesting feature was Mark Sugden, playing full back and moving to scrum half in the last fifteen minutes. An Englishman educated at Trinity College Dublin, between 1925 and 1931 Mark made twenty four appearances for Ireland, a feat no other scrum half had then surpassed. He then taught French and Spanish, first at Glenalmond then at the Royal Naval College Dartmouth.

Famed for his elusive running, in this match he scored a try under the posts after selling dummies to all and sundry from the half way line. And his passes from the base of the scrum dispatched the oval ball vertically at a speed that knocked you down if you failed to catch it. He survived until 1990 aged eighty seven.

The College officers allowed themselves 'a jolly' in Plymouth once a term, Jock and I being invited to dine with them at Genoni's. Wully McKendrick, Peter Gretton and Walter Starkie were three of the House (no longer Term) officers singing with gusto when Harry Piggott sat down at the piano. This, I think, was the occasion when Walter, finding their motorcoach had gone back to the College, girded up his loins like Elijah and ran the thirty miles. Good training no doubt for his next appointment – Flag Lieutenant to Commander-in-Chief Mediterranean Fleet, A. B. Cunningham.

Most of Britain had a white Christmas. Arriving home at Epsom on December 23rd, we had a quiet family Christmas before I returned to duty by overnight sleeper on 27th.

1938. World Events
The year ended with Mussolini shouting for Tunis and Corsica and Hitler demanding colonies. In Germany the persecution of the Jews intensified; their property was being confiscated and they were being forbidden to go to certain places of entertainment, even to certain streets. Lord Baldwin, former Prime Minister raised a fund for relief and care of refugees. Anthony Eden had resigned as Foreign Secretary, Lord Halifax had taken over.

COLTS RUGBY XV - R.N.C. DARTMOUTH - DECEMBER 1928

A.S. Hogg   D. Groome   R.C. Burton   D.G. Hallwright   G.P. Darling   H.N. Custance   P.W. Griffiths   H.C. Ashton   G.W. McKendrick
C.F.S. Robinson   R.A.W. Dobbs   F.P. Baker   W.N.R. Knox   J.W.H. Bennett   G.B. Barstow   B.B. Bordes
C.B. Jelf   K.W. Ross

There are thirteen Greynvies in this picture, most of whom readers will have met among my pages. The others are four Exmouths and one Anson, Warrie Ross. Unbeaten in 1928: "Why were we born so beautiful? . . . Why were we born at all?"

CHAPTER 19

1939 – NOBBY CLARK'S HARRIER

In the Half Yearly promotions the Commander de Winton had been made a Captain and the ebullient J.H. Ruck-Keene, became a Commander. Relieved as First Lieutenant by Lieutenant-Commander S. M. Else serving under him, "Ruckers" soon departed to command the destroyer *Shikari*. We had got on fairly well enjoying some jolly four balls and he suggested I might like to go to *Shikari* as No.1 when Wilson, the present one, would be due to be relieved in May. A few months later, fearing I might be destined for a Yangs-tze gunboat, I wrote reminding him of this, receiving a typical reply, "I can't have been sober".

Commanding some other small ship during the war, it was said that "Ruckers" developed a habit of putting his officers under Close Arrest in their cabins for trivial offences. Finding all his messmates so placed, the Chief approached "Ruckers" requesting their release because he had nobody in the Wardroom with whom to have a gin.

A duty, not so far mentioned, undertaken by Lieutenants in the Barracks was to attend the civil court whenever ratings were charged with committing offences ashore, such as theft or being drunk and disorderly. We attended for only one purpose; to testify as to the defendant's character if asked to do so by the magistrate or judge. Listening to other cases before one's own was normally boring but in the Callington Police Court a case of carnal knowledge proved very different.

A young Electrical Artificer had been playing slap and tickle with his girl friend in the back of his car and her parents noticed a stain on her dress. Asked to explain what happened and how far up her leg his hand had gone, the shy young lady was inaudible.

"Speak up, speak up", cried the Police Sergeant, "These gentlemen here, pointing to the Bench, are men of the World. They think no more of these things than they do of eating their dinner."

I could see the Chairman asking the colleague on his right, "What exactly is carnal knowledge, Claude?"

Cases that arose in ships or naval barracks coming under the Naval Discipline Act were summarily dealt with by the Commander or Captain,

Minesweeper HMS Harrier, 1937.

National Maritime Museum, Greenwich.

or tried by Court Martial if serious. Such a case was that of Leyton,* a V.D. patient in the Sick Bay, who sat astride an Ordinary Seaman's hammock and forced the occupant, Ordinary Seaman Brand to have oral sex. I was required to be Leyton's friend. The Commander, now Captain de Winton, was to prosecute. There were several Ordinary Seamen in hammocks close to Brand. They had all been boxing and were possibly drowsy or asleep in this dimly lighted space. Both Leyton and Brand were accused of gross indecency, an officer called Davenport defending Brand.

My talks with Leyton had been no help at all. Experiments with the lighting showed that it was not so poor that Brand would not recognise what was happening and call for help from the Staff. Nor had he reported the incident to them later.

The case was heard in the Wardroom library on February 24 before a court of three Captains and four Commanders. Both Davenport and I cross examined the witnesses, but I was advised that to put Leyton in the witness box would be fatal for him. The verdict was that both were guilty of gross indecency. Leyton was given two years imprisonment and dismissal with disgrace, the maximum for the offence. Brand received six months and dismissal with disgrace.

With hindsight I think sending Brand to prison was wrong. These Ordinary Seamen were north country lads educated only to the age of 14 and now just over 18. Waking up to find a large man astride him, possibly drunk, when his face had already been punched in a boxing bout would force him to obey through fear.

Jerry Kirkby, a wit who loved a joke, but not one against himself, dubbed me "Sir Horace Hogg K.C., the man who got his man the maximum sentence". He also gave an imitation of Commander de Winton dealing with defaulters.

"Well Smith, I have listened to your excuses carefully but hearing the good report your Divisional Officer has just given you, I am able to deal with you somewhat more leniently than otherwise would be the case".... Pause.... "Death".

Early in February came a signal from *Glorious*, practising night torpedo attacks off Alexandria. Having dropped their torpedoes, two Swordfish had collided. Bill Dobbs in one, Henry Newcombe (Dartmouth Exmouth 1926-30) in the other. Two Leading Seamen and two young pilots were with them. All were lost.

I was distressed beyond measure. Poor Anne a widow with two boys at twenty five! She remarried after a while becoming Mrs. MacCaw, but after

---

*Names are fictitious.

JUST A HOGG'S LIFE

separating, she reverted to 'Dobbs'. Anne lives in Farnham and is well. The two boys Noel and James both became chartered accountants. Noel and his wife Susan live in London and have three children. James, my godson, once sailed the Atlantic single-handed. Based now on Antigua he is in the charter business.

With West Country weather wetter than usual, there was even less open play on the Rugby field. Nevertheless Devonport Services had a 10-3 win against Guy's Hospital at Honor Oak Park and lost narrowly 3-0 at Bath. The Royal Naval College Keyham had a great triumph beating Plymouth Albion. For the Navy side I was only a reserve winning at Bristol 6-3.

The Navy XV, with McCleod a very good centre three quarter, was probably stronger than in 1938 and duly beat the RAF 8-3. But against the Army, last year's hero Crawford failed with three penalties, one of them right in front of the posts resulting in a 6-6 draw. Then three weeks later to general astonishment the RAF defeated the Army 18-6, which gave the Navy the championship once more.

Since October, in sessions twice weekly, John Inverdale had been drilling out great holes of decay in my mouth substituting soothing temporary fillings and replacing them with permanent structures of amalgam polished finally like brasswork on a flagship's quarterdeck. Local anaesthetics were in their infancy and I cannot say it had been a painless experience. However, with repairs now and then, this old antique shop has lasted into my seventies and I was grateful to John, who departed late in March to H.M.S. *Ganges*, the boys' training establishment at Shotley across the Stour estuary from Harwich.

On March 16 having stirred up a crisis between Czechs and Slovaks, Hitler marched his army into Prague, deposing Dr. Hacha, leader of the Czechs as he had deposed Sehuschnigg and taken over Slovakia as a German protectorate. Munich was now a farce. And when on Good Friday April 7, Mussolini invaded Albania, few in Britain doubted that war against these evil dictators was inevitable.

Due for some leave I spent the last weekend in March enjoying the hospitality of the Merediths at Saunton again, playing Rugger for Devonport Services against Barnstaple on Saturday afternoon. The opposing forwards were so occupied having their private battles, lectured in vain by the referee from time to time, that the ball never emerged from the scrum and the best thing the referee did was to abandon the match before time. The golf, on the other hand, was friendly and delightful.

After my father's death my sister and brother-in-law took a share with my mother of Richmond House, our stately home at Epsom. Given a house there was no stopping Jack Paterson building on to it. I found the kitchen out of action, food being cooked in the cottage at the back while a large sitting room was added with a double bedroom and bathroom above. To avoid the shambles Brada had gone out to Alexandria to stay with friends, Colonel Alan, taking my mother, drove out to Rome, then picked up Brada at Genoa, the three of them returning via the 1914-18 battlefields, where he had fought with the Scots Guards.

Invited to lunch at Epsom College on Sports day I found three young Powells, Joan, Michael and Philip there. Michael, a long distance runner, had just missed his half-blue at Cambridge being 'cheated' by the captain, who chose his best friend, John Wright instead. Michael however achieved his ARIBA and Philip, asked later why he chose to be an architect, always said, 'Because my brother was an architect'. For the same reason although only five feet seven, Philip just eighteen, put up a great show in the half mile.

Michael Powell became Principal Architect (Education) in the Greater London Council's Department of Architecture and Civil Design between 1950 and 1971, when he died never having enjoyed good health. Serious professionally, he disguised it well in a cloud of follies and nonsense, which delighted officers and committee members, not to mention his brother-in-law which I became.

Philip Powell and his partner Hidalgo Moya (Jacko) qualified at the A.A. School of Architecture, winning the open competition in 1946 that resulted in Churchill Gardens, the conspicuous blocks of flats on the Embankment near Pimlico. Next came the two small houses in Chichester, one for Philip's father Canon Powell, the other for his sister Joan and me, where I still live since her death in 1982. The Chichester Festival Theatre followed in 1962. Seven hospitals, extensions to Oxbridge Colleges, Wolfson a new post graduate college at Oxford, the London Museum and Queen Elizabeth II Conference Hall are some of their major works. A full list can be seen under their names in Who's Who. Recently retired, the work of Powell, Moya and Partners has been recognised with a Knighthood and a CH for Philip and a CBE for Jacko. That the partnership lives on will soon be seen when the extension to the Great Ormond Street Children's Hospital is opened.

Visiting the Admiralty next day I learnt that HMS *Vernon* had one vacancy for the Long T (Torpedo) course starting in May and my name had gone forward with two others. A cruiser was likely if I was not chosen.

For golfers there can be few more enjoyable outings than playing thirty six holes on a warm spring day over the Old course at Walton Heath. My companion was Francis Carter, another Greynvile. I stood myself a *two shilling ball* for the occasion and slinging our bags over our shoulders we played a little below our handicaps of 16 and 13, going home to Epsom for lunch and tea. Awarded a D.S.C. Francis survived the war and retired to South Africa, where he died of a sudden heart attack in 1978, leaving his wife Elisabeth, a son and a daughter.

That evening we had a family party of seven: my mother, Brada and Jack, Martin and his friend Cynthia Sandford, Daphne Norman and myself dining at the Ivy and then seeing *The Gate Revue* at the Ambassadors theatre across the road. At the Ivy, where Noel Coward and Victor Gollancz had their own separate tables, Jack was always welcomed as a VIP by Abel the proprietor/manager. Back in 1921 he and his fellow Grenadiers had discovered and patronised Abel's place, setting this Italian *restaurateur* from San Marino on the road to fame.

The Gate Revue with Hermione Gingold and Walter Crisham was a splendid little show, full of delightful satirical sketches; the equivalent of our post war Sloane Rangers being Kensington girls from Kensington Gore ('We've given up our war work because of the war'). But what pleased me most was Walter Crisham's Dirty Post Card seller, unable to keep his two wives and kiddies because 'the Daily Press keeps giving pictures twice as nice at less than half the price'. The music was mainly by Geoffrey Wright, composer of the hit, *Transatlantic Lullaby* and elder brother of John Wright, the Cambridge runner. Supplied with words and music, I sang it myself in 1949, when in the cruiser *Birmingham*, we put on a show at Mombasa. Eminently suited to the British community up country, where the definition of a gentleman was *one who lays down his wife for his friends*, nobody told me the evening performance would be preceded by a children's matinée.

The Captain of the *Birmingham*, T.A.C. Pakenham (short title: Tampax) who unfortunately was not made an admiral, became a Deacon in Holy Orders up country in Kenya. Surprisingly he thought the song unsuitable for his future parishioners of all ages.

Such was our determination to make Rock for Easter, that Martin and I spent Maundy Thursday driving 315 miles from Altrincham via Exeter where I had left my own car. Including a good stop there for dinner we were on the road for twelve hours. The weather was lovely all that weekend. Johnnie Walsham* and his wife Sheila, daughter of the Dormy house Bannermans were there as were the two Pamelas and Aunt Trissie. Diana and Bill David played a foursome with the Hogg Bros. Johnny Walker and Joyce, with her brother David Jackson stayed like us at the Rock. With tennis too, trips to Tintagel and St. Merryn, a walk to Smugglers Walk and singing at St. Mabyn, led by the bass "grave-digger", the holiday was most agreable and David stayed an extra day to play on the links with me. Back in barracks no sooner had we given a farewell dinner to Commander, now Captain de Winton, than I saw my name in the Press among those appointed to Vernon for the long T course, while every country in Europe appeared to be calling up troops and Mr. Chamberlain made speeches guaranteeing support for Greece and Rumania in the event of invasion of their countries.

Having examined various Able Seamen in practical work for Leading Seaman and turned over my Guard and Band duties to a Lieutenant Duncan, I left by car for home on Sunday April 23 joining my future colleagues in Vernon a week later. We must have been eighteen all told, a third of them conscripts not looking at all bright and cheerful at the prospect of becoming masters of mines, minesweeping, demolitions, the ins and outs of torpedoes and finally a ship's electrics, from dynamos to the Wardroom toaster.

On Monday morning we met in turn: the Captain, Denis Boyd, the Commander Sidney Paton, who had been 'Torps' of *Rodney* with ABC in 1930 and Commander Willie Dallmeyer, in charge of all instruction, whose parties I had been to in Malta. To my surprise Captain Boyd had a special word with me over a gin before lunch. "Congratulations Hogg", he said. "We have never before selected for the Long Course a Sub Lieutenant who got only a 3rd class here in his exam. There were three candidates; one was probably an alcoholic and the other a homosexual. Even so you only got it by a casting vote".

Under Willie Dallmeyer came 'Porky' Veale, a passed over Lieutenant Commander, who had become a good lecturer after supervising the last few Long Courses. It seemed however that our course would be abandoned or postponed while we went to sea in small ships being brought out of Reserve. But since they were not ready we began at Greenwich on May 4th as planned, 'Porky' having had time to describe the horrors of minesweeping, which he had undergone in the First World War and we were likely to find far worse in the next. Our arrival coincided with the opening of The Painted Hall as the new mess room for three hundred mouths.

Rear-Admiral Sir John, distinguished engineer, died October 22, 1992.

This magnificent place, with Thornhill its painter holding out his hand for more money as you go in, was one compensation for Physics, Applied Mechanics, Mathematics and Chemistry all week, including half Saturdays. The other was having two girl friends working in London. Wednesday however was a half day and I soon discovered a fellow golfer, Charles Cameron and the excellence of the Addington course. There had just been time to dine Jack Paterson in The Painted Hall and show the wonders of Wren to my mother and grandmother before, on May 19, our sea-going appointments arrived. Mine was to *Harrier*, a minesweeper at Chatham; at least it was younger than *Saltash* and burnt oil. Out of their scientific depth already, Healey and Ingram promoted from the Lower deck, were glad to go and so was I. Understandably our professors, taken aback, were disappointed so, still in the classroom for another week, we tried to look attentive.

Four of us joined the four minesweepers on the night of May 31 lying alongside one another in a basin of Chatham dockyard. In commission since the previous September, they had been well maintained by small daily working parties. A. H. Rowlandson went to Halcyon, the Senior Officer's ship operating the bar. Healey went to *Skipjack*, the one for eating. Russell to Speedwell and Hogg to *Harrier*, where his cabin was clean and comfortable. Lieutenant-Commander L.V. Lloyd recalled from retirement appeared next morning to explain that we would commission with Reserves on 15 June, a Captain and a Sub-Lieutenant joining each ship some days earlier. The Engineer officers were already there ours being Lieutenant (E) Wynne. There was of course no duty free drinking in shore establishments; consequently the pre-luncheon gin session in *Halcyon* gave me quite a shock.

In Britain the disappearance ten miles off Llandudno of the submarine *Thetis* when undergoing acceptance trials from Cammell Lairds of Birkenhead caused great distress. Four men escaped using Davis apparatus, others were expected to follow but didn't. The air in the boat was thought to be foul and by Sunday June 4 all hope of more survivors was given up. At home on Sunday 11 June invited to play tennis at Epsom College, Joan and Philip Powell our hosts departed at 3.30 pm in evening dress for a mysterious place called Glyndebourne. They had eight pence between them for food and beer. This was not Joan's first visit; she and her Uncle Carleton had been there in 1935, the second year of this now famous opera house. A devoted supporter I have not missed a season since it re-opened in 1950.

The Captain Brian Clark (Nobby) joined about 2030 on the 13th. A small but pleasant character he had last been to sea in *Dunoon*, a minesweeper in 1932. Then, in civil life, he had been a recruiting officer for Walls Ice Cream, not much of a job and he just couldn't wait to be back on the Duty Free. Next came the Sub-Lieutenant Richard Wilson with his father, a Captain R.N. (retd) and a "Springer" (P. and R. T. specialist standing for Physical and Recreational Training), who seemed to know several of our Commanding officers.

The ship's company arrived bit by bit during the afternoon of the 15th. Sitting in the Wardroom I greeted each man, trying to give him a job that he would like. These men were good seamen having already served their twelve years. Many became postmen and wore their coats on board when the weather became cold. They wasted no time in embarking stores and ammunition, nor in completing the painting.

At 1100 on Monday 19th the tugs were secured and the only man missing was Captain Nobby who had been hopping round the other ships and now hopped on board his own. The day before he had appeared for Divisions in a shocking old moth eaten frock coat and later in the day was rather tipsy after lunching with Leggatt, the Captain of *Selkirk*. *Selkirk* was an old Forres/Saltash coal fired minesweeper ordered to join us, the Fifth Minesweeping flotilla. Into the lock, out at 1230 and then to the oiling jetty half way to Sheerness, we finally secured with two bridles to a buoy at Sheerness. All had gone well and leave was given to half the *Harrier*, complement 80. The following day the flotilla moved on to Harwich, *Harrier* and *Selkirk* sharing a buoy, the latter wrecking one wing of his Bridge against our motorboat davit by approaching too fast.

Going to sea under Harold Lloyd, the Senior officer in *Halcyon* on two or three days in mid-week, we learnt how to handle our Oropesa sweeps by degrees without accident. Invaluable as a seaman, our Able Seaman Watson, "Hector" to the ship's company, was still a regular doing his first twelve years. "Hector" was a huge man in charge of the Bosun's locker aft and all the sweeping gear stowed in it. When going to a buoy he would jump on it pulling the *Harrier* with one hand and handling her bridle of cable with the other, said his messmates. Eveleigh on the foc'sle was the expert with the heaving line and the grapnel, thrown as if he played grapnels instead of darts; a useful accomplishment when picking up dan buoys.

Among the captains, Proudfoot in *Skipjack* had never handled a ship because he had left the Navy as a Sub-Lieutenant. Tim Healey his No. 1, who had not had much practice either, showed him how to do it. Leggatt in *Selkirk* was apt to curse and shout from the Bridge when things went wrong and Ingram his No.1 thought there might be trouble with the men. Giving weekend leave appeased them at least temporarily. An exercise in rough weather in which the sweepers attempted to be hostile ships entering Harwich was soon ended by the Army's searchlights, blinding Nobby on the Bridge who missed an unlighted buoy by a few inches.

Berthed nearer to H.M.S. *Ganges*, the boys training establishment at Shotley than to Harwich, our chief recreation was paying them a call. Their Wardroom included Pog Havers, who had not been made a Commander, Peter Baker, Frankie Barchard, the First Lieutenant, formerly of *Despatch* and others who played tennis with us.

In mid-July *Harrier* had to stay in a given position out in the North Sea to be one of several 'Safety Ships' in an R.A.F. exercise. Richard Wilson took many sights and we asked some fishing vessels where we were. Answers varied from off Yorkshire to off Suffolk. When it ended we sailed for Sheerness. Totting up the wine bills I found Nobby had reached 126 shillings for July and he had not even paid for June in spite of my verbal requests. A new minesweeper *Hussar* now joined us captained by Lieutenant Commander T.G.P. Crick, who had played for the Navy against the Army at Twickenham, no fewer than five times being Captain in two of them.

July 20 was the Sub-Lieutenant's twenty first birthday. Fifty three years on I am happy to say that he is still with us in Chichester having been West Sussex County Councillor, Richard Wilson for some years. Having reached Sheerness, *Harrier* was ordered to send a Lieutenant to Rosyth to bring back the old destroyer *Verdun*, which had been on the sales list for about ten years. It seemed that officers in the Barracks could not be spared. Greatly indignant I wrote myself a First class Warrant, spent Saturday night at home and caught the 1300 on Sunday from King's Cross, which reached Edinburgh with one stop, Newcastle, at 2020. All bars and pubs in Scotland were closed on Sundays except that *bona fide* travellers were legally entitled to a drink.

My diary reads: *"Walked along Princes Street not seen for seven years, listening to the tub thumpers and admiring the looks of the girls. What a magnificent street with or without them!"*

A 2100 train got me to Inverkeithing at 2120 and thence to the depot, HMS *Cochrane*, in a stray taxi. Surveying the crowd of dead beats in the wardroom, I thought they should have been covered up with a dust sheet. Keeling, Commanding Officer of *Verdun* for the trip took me to the old vessel in his car saying she had last been at sea in 1927 and bits of deck falling to bits must be expected. Frank Talbot, principal boy friend of my cousin Valerie Hulton-Sams, appeared from his submarine H.28 taking me back to *Cochrane* where a number of jovial submariners had replaced the elderly 'dead beats'.

Next morning we got away about 0900 in calm and sunny weather doing 15 knots. The Chief reported from the engine room that he would be delighted to do 25 knots but, thinking the vibration might topple the mast, we said 'No thank you'. The Gunner for the trip took the afternoon watch, I did the First Dog while I noticed Keeling, needed glasses to see the chart and was probably over fifty.

Communications were a little difficult. The Type 53 lent for the trip only transmitted on 1000 kws and above and was used only by the Admiralty at night. But unfortunately its range was only 12 miles. However we made good time to Sheerness, found a buoy off the Dockyard and secured to it. Keeling had good reason to be pleased; he had never done it before.

Rejoining *Harrier* we returned to the rest of the flotilla two days later at Harwich. *Hussar* had replaced *Selkirk* which was now operating with trawlers from Dover and Sheerness. Thinking his young fit lads would win, Crick suggested a pulling regatta. A meeting held in *Hussar* agreed to eight races on Friday August 5. Now the reservists were all men over thirty and with war probable, all they wanted was to see their families as much as possible. I told the *Harrier*s with a few four letter words that I thought the regatta was inappropriate in the circumstances. But I said, based on my own experience, the most depressing outcome was not to win it. The next day when the rest of the flotilla had gone to sea we put in a little quiet practice, a 3 knot tide nearly killing Clark, Hogg and Wilson, the Wardroom crew. I was also able to have a word with MS5 about my captain's messbill when the other ships returned.

In the first week in August *Harrier* towed *Halcyon* successfully at 10 knots, ships carried out a shoot, and regatta practice was in full swing. A formal dinner at Shotley in mess undress (bow tie and bum freezer) was not the best night-before-regatta training for me, but our seamen and stokers in whalers and skiffs won the first four races giving *Harrier* a formidable half-way lead. The Officers' skiff race came last when we had already won The Cock but by coming third, without Captain Nobby having a heart attack, we were not disgraced. I do not remember who stayed on board but by 2100 I was home in Epsom celebrating my brother-in-law's fortieth birthday as well.

From Tuesday 9 August to Sunday 12th the flotilla was spread about the North Sea acting as safety ships in another big exercise, aircraft flying in to a country blacked out from Hull round to Portsmouth. Acting on

JUST A HOGG'S LIFE

MS5's private instructions, I had told the Captain that his mess bill was now £32 unpaid and that I should have to report the matter to MS5 unless he paid up. Much to my surprise rather secretly he passed a cheque for £25 to the Chief.

In the next exercise starting on August 15, *Harrier* and *Hussar* were the local defence flotilla sweeping from Harwich approaches to the Barrow Light Vessel starting at 0600 daily. The other ships went to Dover. Friday was a disastrous day with sweeps parting; Saturday just the reverse, back in harbour by 1640 instead of 1800 or 1900. C-in-C then signalled sweepers to make good defects. John Inverdale back at Shotley from leave had been to the wedding of Jock Gray and Peggy Purvis, a great party which took place in the Barracks church at Devonport.

To the Sunday press prospects of peace were negligible J.L. Garvin the famous Editor of *The Observer* was as pessimistic as Commander Stephen King-Hall, a retired Torpedo officer whose political newsletter was widely read. Playing golf at Woodbridge with Marcus Vertue, a naval person who features frequently in my diaries, though I cannot now remember him, we ran into Walter Cobbett, my father's and my Uncle Sandy's close friend and Solicitor in Manchester. Great golfers, he and his daughters, Rachel and Eleanor, insisted on us supping with them at the Crown Woodbridge, a merry evening in the circumstances.

Duty free drinking being so much cheaper, Nobby brought his wife, and daughter Kitty on board frequently and occasionally their other daughter Rosemary, an attractive nineteen year old. His mother too, a sporting 75, was a visitor when three rasping ladies from Harwich were brought on board by two Sub-Lieutenants. The third must have been a present for Nobby for he bore her away to his cabin as if to emulate Don Giovanni in his prime.

As to smoking I suppose 80 per cent of officers and men over eighteen did so, with duty free tobacco and cigarettes available at little cost. I remember in *Rodney* there was a large smoking space forward, while in the Gunroom a half Corona cigar cost ten pence and ship's pipe tobacco came in one pound tins at 1s 6d each from the Pusser's stores. It was only now when ships were darkened during these night exercises and the atmosphere in our small Wardroom became intolerable that my diaries mention tobacco.

On August 22 came the news that Soviet Russia had agreed on a non-aggression pact with Germany mistrusting Britain, whose military mission had been negotiating unsuccessfully for months. The fact was that Stalin mistrusted the capitalist west when many people in France and Britain preferred Fascism and feared Socialism.

On August 24 *Harrier*, *Hussar* and *Skipjack* were ordered to Dover. At sea our bad days were always Fridays and on Friday September 1 when the news came that Hitler had invaded Poland both our sweeps were foul of wrecks. Getting clear took three hours with the loss of one otter and fifty fathoms of sweep wire. Back in Dover who should join *Harrier* but a navigating officer, Lieutenant (N) McEwan, and next day all three ships swept a channel without trouble.

The next day Sunday September 3 at 1100 Britain declared War on Germany and the first Air Raid Warning sirens sounded at 1130. Clutching tin hats and gas masks we went to Action Stations. Luckily it was a false alarm; mine sweepers had no control system for shooting down aircraft. Operating during the first week in lovely weather outside the Goodwin Sands we swept up some of Vernon's sand-filled dummy mines, which at least gave confidence that our gear did the job. Occasional air raid warnings came to nothing; indeed the greatest hazard was emerging from the Grand Hotel, a popular rendezvous, into the black out. By mid-September minelayers *Adventure*, *Plover* and the converted train ferries were laying the cross-channel barrage over which we would do skimming sweeps to remove any mines accidentally moored too shallow. Meanwhile *Hussar*, *Skipjack* and *Harrier* in turn moved into the Western docks for boiler cleaning giving 36 hours leave to each watch.

Train services being peculiar, my mother, with grandchild June Paterson, now 13 came by car at breakfast time to take me home, calling on my godfather Hewlett Johnson in the Deanery at Canterbury. Trained as an engineer he was, with professional advice, having the crypt made into a protected shelter for all the services, surrounded by much criticism. "Nothing would please the Nazis more than to destroy our City and Cathedral", he said. A prophetic statement! When they did their best in the 'Baedeker' raids of 1943, even the *Daily Telegraph* conceded that the Red Dean's organisation had saved the Cathedral.

At home Doctors descended on Epsom where the Asylums at Horton were to be evacuated and made into hospitals. Living temporarily with my mother in Richmond House were Mr. William Gilliatt (later Sir William) the gynaecologist and his wife, Mr. Richards, a bachelor anaesthetist, who often worked with him and a Dr. and Mrs. Hilton. My sister was working at Epsom's Control centre, Jack Paterson had taken up his post as Principal Civil Defence Officer, Midlands in Birmingham and my brother Martin had left the firm to our Uncle Sandy in Manchester, while he became an Acting Pilot Officer R.A.F, stationed somewhere near Warrington. This I think he enjoyed, though unlikely to be a pilot at his age of 36.

With only one day I chose to give Daphne lunch at the Ivy, which being a Saturday was sufficiently empty for Abel to greet me as if I was Noel Coward himself. We lunched on Hors d'Oeuvres from that memorable trolley and cold grouse. Nearly all the inmates of Daphne's No.3 house had evacuated and I felt low and depressed leaving this lone little figure in an enchanting blue dress on her doorstep. These war time goodbyes, how ghastly they were to be for so many!

At home Colonel Alan appeared from Pirbright to tell us all about Marguerite Carver's wedding to Charles Earle of the Grenadiers which he had attended at Chippenham that afternoon. Next morning at 0600 Joan Powell took me back to *Harrier* in Austin 7, FPK71, made possible by the postponement of petrol rationing. A very kind act after going to bed herself at 0200, she stayed to lunch and slept in the Wardroom while we moved out to a buoy by the pier. Yet another parting, like the moment returning to Dartmouth when the College appeared round the corner from the railway.

Russia had now invaded Poland leaving us nothing to do but drink to the damnation of Stalin as well as Hitler.

On September 18 our three ships began the skimming sweep with a new R.N.R. navigator, Higson who had relieved McEwan. All seemed to be going well as I sat in the sun reading *Rebecca*, Daphne du Maurier's best seller. First four mines bobbed up and floated past, then *Skipjack* signalled he had a most unwelcome visitor; a mine had appeared five or ten yards from the stern when winching in the sweep. Eventually she cut the sweep leaving the mine on the bottom secured to the otter.

This was the day when a U-boat, disregarding two destroyers in attendance torpedoed and sank the carrier *Courageous* with the loss of 518 lives in the Atlantic.

On September 20 about 1900 the sloop *Kittiwake* struck a mine near the Goodwins. Only half a mile away we lowered our whaler and stood by her. Our efforts to tow failed and a tug arrived to do so about 2000. Out of fifty one only the five men in the Engine Room were missing. The mine was one of ours recently laid. Confusion as to the ship's position probably arose because the Goodwins Light Vessel had just been moved to confuse the enemy. The Captain E. R. Conder soon took over the destroyer *Whitshed* instead, playing a gallant part in the evacuations before and after Dunkirk in 1940 with successes against U-boats in the Atlantic later.

Slowing down when sweeping for any reason caused the sweep wires to sag and mines to go off in the sweep with a great bang and a splash that obliterated the nearest minesweeper from view. I remember, due perhaps to countermining (the explosion of one mine detonating its neighbour), these bang/splashes from the ship ahead coming nearer and nearer in a ripple. It seemed a funny way to spend a Saturday afternoon; quite a change from rugger at Bristol, except that wetting one's pants was a strong possibility out here too.

Our attempts to sink mines with Lewis guns or rifles took ages or failed. With a trawler or two following to do the job, things went better. Once cut by the sweep wire and floating on the surface, the main switch in moored mines was opened rendering them safe, a requirement of the Geneva Convention. But, of course, assumptions when handling explosives are not very wise.

During September the 5th Minesweeping Flotilla had been augmented by *Sphinx* and *Salamander*, two new mine sweepers. *Sphinx*, mostly at Harwich, was the Senior Officer. When *Halcyon* joined us at Dover on October 2, I felt I must report to Harold Lloyd that my Captains's unpaid mess bills now totalled £45, making it impossible in a small Wardroom to pay our creditors. Sent for by Harold, Nobby returned somewhat shaken and upbraided me for not giving him notice. I replied that having asked him to pay frequently, I had only obeyed Harold's instructions.

With leave extended to 2200, one Sunday evening I took train and bus to Canterbury. The crypt was full with some 400 people eager to hear the Dean preach at Evensong. After losing his first wife Mary from cancer, Hewlett had married in 1938 Nowell Edwards his second cousin, young, pretty and a talented artist. Soon they would have two daughters, biblically named, Kezia in 1940, Kerin in 1942, with a house Hewlett owned at Harlech in which to live during the *blitz*, while he remained alone in his badly damaged Deanery.

By mid-October Hitler, having knocked out Poland, was making peace proposals. Harold Lloyd departed for a shore job in Chatham, the new Senior Officer in Halcyon being an Active Service Commander, rather short and plump, called St. John Cronyn.

I particularly remember October 12. My gramophone in the Wardroom was playing some tune when a large 18 stone officer, wearing one wavy R.N.V.R. stripe, walked in and said:

"How do you like that tune?"

"Not much", we said.

"A pity", he replied, "I wrote it".

JUST A HOGG'S LIFE

This new arrival was Richard Fisher, novelist, script writer of songs for the ("We never closed") Windmill Theatre, speaker of Arabic and German, who had been on the staff of the *Morning Post*, a daily like the *Telegraph*.

With the laying of mines along the French coast and subsequent skimming sweeps, our task in the straits was nearly over. Three U-boats had been sunk in this barrage of about 7,000 mines enough to achieve its aim of forcing German shipping to go round the North of Scotland greatly decreasing the operational range of the U-boats in the Atlantic.

October 14 was the night that a U-boat penetrated the defences of Scapa Flow to sink the battleship *Royal Oak* with the loss of 833 lives. Struck by three torpedoes at 0116 she capsized thirteen minutes later. One survivor was the navigator, Dick Gregory, who owed his life to being in the Wardroom playing Bridge. When Commander of the cruiser *Black Prince* in the last two years of the war nothing would persuade him to sleep before 0130.

Relaxing at Dover with a game of soccer and a sing-song on deck, rumours of a refit for *Harrier* became true and we found ourselves heading for Chatham and berthing at No.4 Riversdale. One watch went on four days leave immediately, but after a dockyard conference had examined our defects this was extended to seven, with telegrams sent as necessary. Nobby met an old flame, a Mrs. Rand, getting rather tipsy and confiding to me that women had always been his undoing besides mess bills. By Saturday 21st the only officers on board were Higson and Fisher besides myself.

Fisher, taking over the Sub-Lieutenant's job, sorted out the contingent account taking it to Paymaster Captain Whittington-Ince in the Barracks for his approval. Treated with great civility by such a V.I.P. he declared it was a great honour, like walking down an Underground escalator with Lord Ashfield (Head of London Transport at that time). His wife, Helen Colley, was a singer on the stage and also a friend of Daphne Norman, so they both came to a Saturday lunch on board which the four of us bought ashore since the ship's galley was out of action. Rooms at The Sun were adequate and the Sun's restaurant rose to roast partridges. On Sunday the portable galley by the ship provided a lunch, and Hodges - one of the ship's company, brought my car from Shotley. The petrol allowance was six gallons a month.

Lunching in the Barracks waited on by very efficient Wrens, I met Willie Dallmeyer and Wheeler, the Australian Lieutenant, who had continued his Long T Course at the wishes of his Government. Willie said they hoped to re-start the Long Course in *Vernon* in December with fewer chaps but he'd try to fix me in. The Barracks had built close by a shelter 100 feet deep, dug out of a hill to hold 8000 people; a most impressive place like an Underground Station. *Halcyon* arrived after being near missed by German aircraft attacking a convoy. A squadron of British fighters had appeared in time to destroy four of them.

During my own week's leave Dick and Helen Fisher gave Nobby and me a superb lunch at the Carlton Grill (closed later) and free seats at a Windmill theatre matinée. A second edition of *The Gate Revue* being more in our line, my brother, looking pretty smart in his RAF uniform, stood our girl friends lunch at the Ivy beforehand. Unexpected and better still was a piano recital at home by Dr. Hilton playing extracts from Gilbert and Sullivan, *The Beggar's Opera* and Bach, that took my mother nostalgically back to the days when she sang in Lancashire with Roger Quilter.

Returning to *Harrier* I found Nobby, having called the Sub 'a brown-eyed bastard' had fallen down a ladder and fractured two ribs. Helping him to his cabin, the Sub was rewarded with 'God Bless you Sub'. Sadly missed, Richard Fisher, appointed elsewhere had departed.

The Captain of the Dockyard, Cecil Sandford was a bachelor, provided with a delightful small Georgian house. Lonely, he was anxious to renew acquaintance with my sister after former days at Alexandria, so she and Joan Powell stayed two nights with him coinciding with my birthday on November 6. Of ruddy complexion, they called him "The Over-Ripe Plum"; he sat on their beds in turn into the small hours, each one trying to persuade him to go to the other or better still, to his own.

Suffering from bronchial asthma, our much loved engineer, 'Chiefy Wynne' had to leave. His relief, Slade, had been in *Verdun*. My own relief, Lieutenant Hoare RNR joined too. Captain of a tanker he had had mine sweeping experience in the last war and if Commanding Officers approved, these RNR reliefs would take over after a month.

By November 13 we were groping our way North in thick fog, hopefully in the swept channel, alert for ships without lights. Entering the Humber we anchored near the trawlers, two miles off Grimsby whence shore steamers would collect and return the libertymen. Working with *Sphinx*, *Salamander* and *Leda*, a trawler, we were off at 0600 sweeping the Channel northwards to Bridlington. Arriving there at about 1700 it was about turn at 0400 next morning. *Salamander* had swept a mine identified as one of ours. The weather was cold and the sea rough, enough to make those who had been ashore for a fortnight sea-sick.

The Germans had increased their aircraft attacks but many alarms turned out to be our own American Hudsons. Moreover I do not remember any silhouettes of our own and enemy aircraft issued to aid recognition. Wrecks however - Norwegian, Danish and Swedish - were plain to see after

JUST A HOGG'S LIFE

leaving Grimsby, in shallow water which pointed to ground mines laid by aircraft at night. With a break towards the end of the month, we swept from 0600 on the Bridlington run daily except on one or two days when the weather was too rough. Mines bobbed up occasionally though whether they were British or German it was hard to tell. But with three of our merchant ships being lost weekly in the North Sea the talk was of the enemy's magnetic mines. Not that these were new; both sides had them at the end of the 1914-18 war. But no antidote could be devised until the principle on which they worked was discovered.

Until December 8 when *Harrier* docked in Grimsby to boiler clean, we lived up to the minesweeper's hymn that goes to the tune of *Holy! Holy! Holy!* the words being:

> "*Sweeping, Sweeping, Sweeping,*
> *All we do is Sweeping.*
> *Early in the morning until the blackest night.*"

A month having passed, Hoare was ready to relieve me and I, after sending my heavy luggage to Waterloo, took a train to Manchester being met by Jack and Martin, who were staying at Tirbracken with Uncle Sandy Hogg. I had enjoyed *Harrier* until recently, when there were so many RNRs in the ship, their conversation going little further than sea-faring, the last war and dirty stories.

Tirbracken was not quite the same since Nicholson the butler had died. His widow Mrs. Nicholson and their daughter lived on in the house and ran it as best they could. Sandy himself was rather deaf; and the war, with its petrol rationing precluded trips to shoot at Woodhead or to play golf, other than at the Bowdon club a mile away. And that would soon be ploughed up for vegetables by its owner Lord Stamford. Sandy was glad to die in 1942 aged 75.

Old friends and relations had to be seen, notably Annie, our old parlour maid, coping in her small council house with three evacuated children, two dogs and her husband Bertie Willie. Martin now based at Cuerdley Farm on flat land near Liverpool was associated with barrage balloons, but for Sunday lunch he thought the Adelphi Hotel would be better than the Cuerdley pub.

Having spent a night in Birmingham being shown Jack's ARP headquarters, I found a telegram at Epsom saying "Appointed *Vernon* for Long T Course December 14th," which happened to be the next day.

Assembled at *Vernon* for the course were: Dickie Stubbs, Tim Healey, Charles Cameron, Frank Fletcher (another Brockhurst boy) and Ingram.

'A' and Oropesa Sweeps

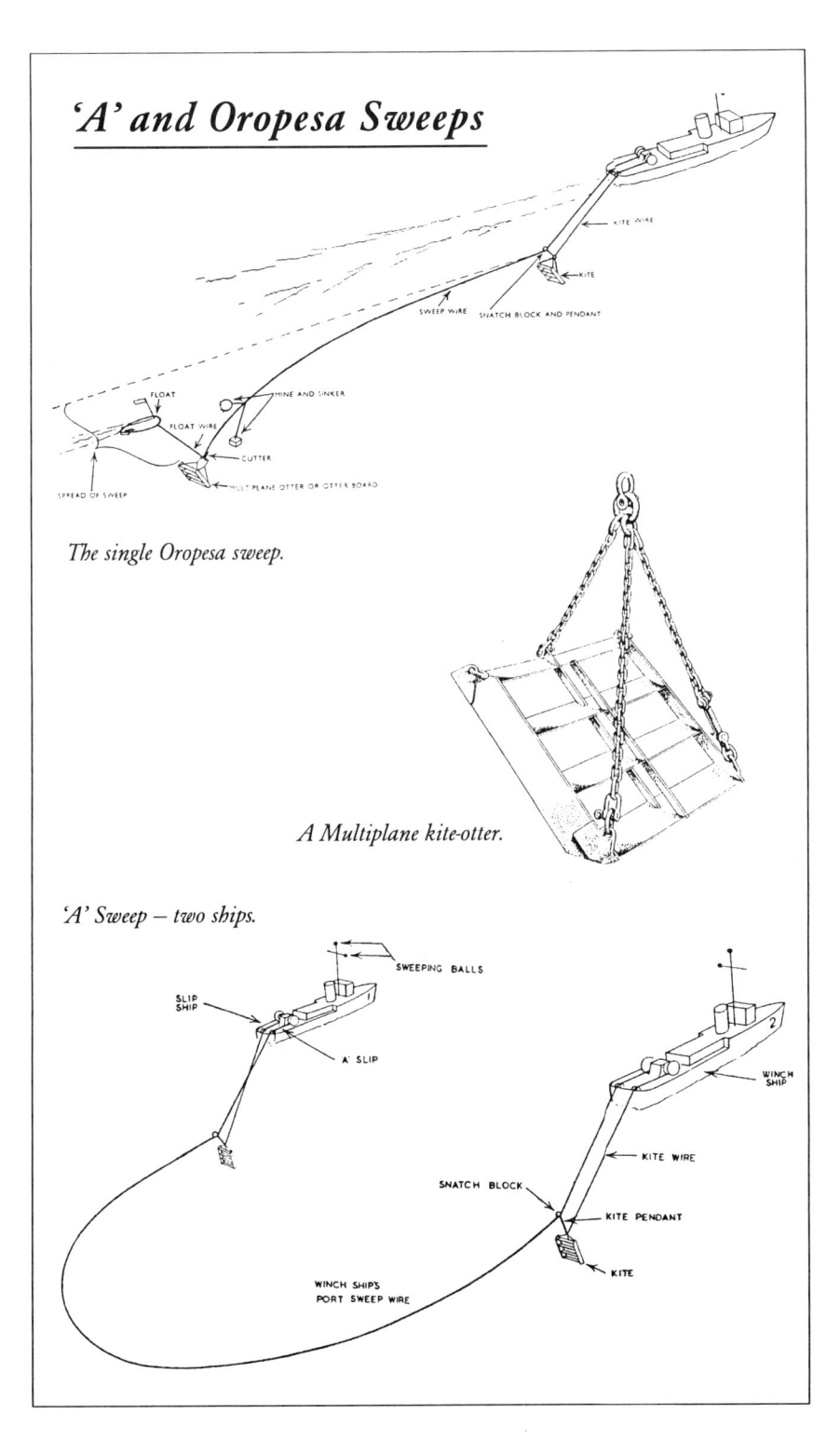

The single Oropesa sweep.

A Multiplane kite-otter.

'A' Sweep – two ships.

Rodwell was sick and Arthur Rowlandson and Nigel Tibbits, younger brother of Terence, must have joined later. The Commander was now Porky Veale, who signed all his letters with the stamp of a pig. "School" which meant theoretical electrics, magnetism, dynamos ... had already started but the following Tuesday 19th we were to have 14 days leave.

The excitement of the moment however was the battle off Montevideo in which *Exeter*, *Ajax* and *Achilles* had forced the pocket battleship *Graf Von Spee* into that port. Over the weekend the world held its breath. Would she be forced to leave this neutral port and fight again ? On Monday 18th my Leading Wren called me saying she had scuttled herself. Two of my Greynvile term mates received D.S.Cs. McBarnet, wounded in the head, controlled *Exeter*'s main armament; Duncan Lewin piloting *Ajax*'s aircraft reported the movements of the *Graf Von Spee*.

On the 19th at 0950 King George VI walked into our classroom. Lower Deck was then cleared for him to present a D.S.O. to Commander John Ouvry and to Lieutenant Commander Roger Lewis, who had rendered safe and captured the first German magnet mine in the mud at Shoeburyness. Lieutenant Glenny dealing with a second mine, received a D.S.C, Chief Petty Officer Baldwin and Able Seaman Vearncombe each a D.S.M. The mines were on show; the largest 1600lb. being similar in shape to and half the length of a torpedo.

Considering it was wartime we were lucky to have a family Christmas round the tree. My mother's three children, son-in-law, two grandchildren and step mother Blanche Hulton were all there. Jack however had an appalling cold and was ordered to bed by our Doctor conveniently living opposite. And out came the Victorian song books, *The Wraggle Taggle Gipsies* and Scott Gatty's *Little Songs for Little People*, which I hope my younger grandchild, Florence, will play and sing herself one day.

Sad for us Canon Arnold Powell retired as Headmaster of Epsom College and with his wife Winnifred went to be the Rector of Graffham near Petworth in Sussex. For the time being Joan, Michael and Philip, all working in London, remained in Epsom.

This brings to an end my naval saga of The Thirties. But since 1940 was to be the most traumatic year of my life, bringing my diaries to an abrupt end, a final chapter must follow.

Sub-Lieutenant Richard Wilson (now a West Sussex County Councillor) takes charge of the Harrier's rifle party trying to sink floating mines.

CHAPTER 20

From a War to a Wedding

1940. In October the Soviets had launched their attack on Finland. The Finns fighting bravely had created a deadlock by 1940. Western sympathy naturally was with them, with talk of sending troops. France intended 50,000 troops and Britain agreed to send fifty bombers. Only Churchill, still First Lord at the Admiralty, recognised that the enemy was Germany. Fortunately peace was signed in March and Britain began to realise that the Baltic ports were vital for the USSR's defence.

In HMS *Vernon* our Long Course proceeded according to plan. I went home to Epsom some weekends from Noon Saturday to Sunday night unable to read in a blacked-out train. On Friday January 14 Wheeler said he had nearly finished his Long Course and would like to turn over his TOP SECRET job to me. I replied I would like to know something about it before accepting.

"Impossible" he said, "It's TOP SECRET".

After two gins, and remembering I had volunteered to do dangerous jobs on some form I had filled in, I capitulated, finding myself in charge of a Demolition party, training at Chatham, which would destroy Dutch harbour installations in the event of a German invasion of Holland.

"But I haven't done the Demolition part of the Course yet", I protested.

"Not to worry", said Wheeler, "Nothing will happen for months yet; just go home for the week-end and forget it."

Doing just that, at 0845 on Sunday I was called to the telephone.

"Go to Chatham via Admiralty at once", said the speaker.

The Sunday paper headlines read: *Another Holland/Belgium scare*. Arriving at 1000 wearing my great coat in a freezing fog, I was told to report to the Imperial Defence College, 9 Buckingham Gate. Pausing in the doorway of a large upstairs room, I saw half a dozen Army and Navy top brass pouring over a large map. It might have been a film.

"If Hitler goes there, the British Army moves here", said a voice, giving a great swing of his left arm. And seeing me in the doorway he boomed,

"Here comes the Demolition expert!"

I must have gone green at the gills, for next came,

"You are the Demolition expert, aren't you?"

"Yes, sir of course", I managed to say.

Those present, most of them known to me, were Rear Admiral Vivian, Captains Herman-Hodge and Friedburgher, Commanders Caslon, Stanford and Goodenough. Suitably briefed I repaired to Chatham lunching on the 1235 Pullman to be warmly greeted by Sam Smith, the Commander of the Barracks, who had been most kind and helpful to us in *Harrier*. Wheeler soon arrived from Portsmouth.

On Monday we discussed Demolition arrangements in the new Torpedo school. Three RNVR Sub-Lieutenants, Whittle, Paterson and Hindson were attached to a large Demolition party, which would be trained at Chatham by the Royal Engineers in the use of FID (Fuse Instant Detonating) and Cordtex, not yet used in the Navy. A lecture and practice took place on the Thursday, the "panic" having subsided. After making a report to Captain Friedburgher, a call to Vernon approved my resuming the interrupted week-end.

After our Sub-Lieutenants' courses Walter Knox (Willie) had taken up an appointment in the Far East. Getting some mysterious infection I had last seen him in the Hospital for Tropical Diseases in London. Having married, his wife became mentally unstable and he, greatly distressed, had been in the R.N. Hospital Haslar for a while. Delighted to see him again I was invited to dine as his guest in H.M.S. *Dolphin*, the submarine base across the harbour mouth from *Vernon*, where he was doing the qualifying course. Sitting next to me one moment, he had vanished under the table the next.

"Hush", said the chap on my other side. Then, just as Willie 'surfaced' so to speak, the President at the far table leapt to his feet crying,

"Christ! my shoe laces are on fire!".

It seemed to me that Haslar, with an overdose of some *Bucku-uppo* had turned a fairly normal chap into a slightly crazy extrovert, for some weeks later during a cabaret at The Polygon Hotel in Southampton his performance was repeated. When an outraged Colonel came to my table saying, "You have a lunatic in your party", one glance at his shoes and one sniff made it all too clear what had happened.

Willie was lost in April 1943 when commanding the submarine H.M.S.*Regent*, which never returned from a patrol in the Adriatic. He had won a D.S.C. but when we last met a year earlier in Greenock I thought he was too tense to be fully fit.

In February the 5th Mine Sweeping Flotilla lost its leader. *Sphinx* was bombed and sunk while being towed in heavy seas with the loss of about fifty lives. Reggie Caple, only recently relieved as No. 1, was in Portsmouth.

JUST A HOGG'S LIFE

Better news was how the destroyer *Cossack* (Commander Philip Vian) with Peter Gretton his First Lieutenant, had intercepted *Altmark*, a German supply ship, releasing 299 British prisoners, largely crews of the ships that the *Graf Spee* had sunk.

The 1940 diary records only one golf match, one Sunday at Liphook in the Spring. Willie Knox and I played two R.N.V.R. doctors, Mac and Freddie Grant. What gave it distinction was that the two Vavasour girls chose to walk round with us for 36 holes. Captain Sir Leonard Vavasour the 4th Baronet had three children. Geoffrey the youngest, playing stand-off for the Navy in our victorious team was a good all rounder. Betty lost her R. N. husband Michael Walters in the earliest days of the war. Josephine, her younger sister, married Derick Hetherington in 1942. Retiring from the Navy in 1961 as a Rear-Admiral C.B., D.S.C., he became Domestic Bursar and Fellow of Merton College Oxford until 1976. Betty's second marriage in 1942 was to a soldier, Brigadier Bird. Happily they are still with us; the Birds near Heathfield, the Hetheringtons near Oxford, and Geoffrey in London.

At Liphook we had lunch at the Royal Anchor and supper at the Red Lion, Petersfield, where my friends Joan and Michael Powell joined us from Graffham. With the place more or less to ourselves, the proprietor Captain Shields joined us at the piano until it was time to drive Willie, now full of beer back to Portsmouth. When the raids came the gallant Captain banged away with a 12-bore from his garden at any Hun flying low enough.

❖ ❖ ❖

Busy making a garden myself from 1950 to 1961 after finding two thirds of an acre in Chichester for a house, I gave up golf. Then for the first time, in 1961, Liphook had built its own Club House. Though the club was 21 miles away I joined, getting my handicap down to single figures when over 60. Singles, foursomes - mens and mixed - match play knock outs, summer and winter, what a pleasure it was to compete on one of the finest inland courses in Britain until about 1987 when my old arthritic hogsback could take it no longer.

❖ ❖ ❖

In March Russia and Finland signed a peace treaty, Russia taking a bigger slice than that she originally demanded. As to aid from Britain, Finland had received very little, the only possible routes were through Norway and Sweden and fear of Germany prevented their co-operation.

As to our course, by Maundy Thursday when we sat the exam in Torpedo Control (very well taught by 'Sandy' Villiers), Mining and Whitehead (the torpedo) were all behind us.

Leaving Portsmouth by road at 1400, Joan Powell and I dropped Joyce Walker off at Yeovil, making Rock by 2015 to find Martin and Cynthia already there, with the usual warm welcome from Pete Passmore and Mrs Lane at The Rock and from the Bannermans at the Dormy House. The Davids too were at home, excepting the Bishop celebrating Easter in Liverpool. Much older than his wife, when at Rock he usually retired to a room above their garage, while Mrs. David, sister of Barrington-Ward (then Editor of *The Times*) loved to organise walks in this the beloved country. David Jackson brought a young Army friend called Gordon Alston, re-named the Laughing Hyena before very long. Five lovely days; meanwhile at home my mother and sister had German measles so badly that a nurse was required.

All the London theatres had been closed since the war began so March 29 was a red letter day when the Glyndebourne Opera Company staged a revival of *The Beggar's Opera* at the Haymarket Theatre, with Michael Redgrave as Macheath the highwayman and Audrey Mildmay as Polly Peachum. Good though Michael was as an actor, his untrained voice among the opera specialists was a little incongruous. We were lucky to hear Audrey Mildmay; she succumbed to German measles after a few performances. Coming later HMV's six records were a cherished possession.

"April 1 All Fools' Day started another gas course. The old place at Tipner looking just as it was four years ago."

In case there was an exam, Friday April 5 seemed a good day to put in an appearance at Chatham. Porky Veale having approved I arrived in time for lunch, discussing matters with Whittle and Hindson. I also ran into J.O.M. Hunter, now a Sub-Lieutenant R.N.V.R. who had been so popular in *Royal Sovereign*'s gunroom.

On April 9 the Germans invaded Denmark and Norway, taking the Allies completely by surprise. Our parties at Chatham went to 12 hours notice. The submarine depot ship *Maidstone* being in Portsmouth, the best I could do was to get myself dentally fit in John Inverdale's dental surgery. The battles of Narvik have long been history. Captain Warburton-Lee, who won a posthumous Victoria Cross, having led the way up the fiord in the flotilla leader *Hardy*, was the brother-in-law of our friend Colonel Alan Swinton.

While we tried with difficulty to study High Power electrics, some members of the Long Gunnery Course went to Norway in the British Expeditionary Force that landed about April 15. At Epsom nothing had

JUST A HOGG'S LIFE

*A swimming party at Rock, 1939.
Left: David Jackson.
Right: Johnnie and Joyce Walker.*

*Pamela Young,
The Dormy
House Vamp.*

been heard from Jack Paterson in Birmingham for some time until on April 18 he appeared the day after giving a big Civil Defence exercise for the King and Queen. This was so realistic that a bomb fragment hit Lord Dudley to the delight of the Monarch.

In *Vernon*, Russell, who had been relieved as First Lieutenant of *Speedwell*, told us about the end of *Sphinx*. The bomb had gone through the wheelhouse exploding somewhere below the Sick Bay. Casualties were mostly those on the bridge. Taken in tow in dreadful weather becoming worse, nobody thought that *Sphinx* would not stand the storm but suddenly she capsized. Rescue work was the hell of a job and the cries of the men were so distressing that he dreamt of them for weeks.

April 25 was a lovely day for Betty Vavasour's wedding to Michael Walters at the R.C. Church in Gosport High Street, Best man, Robin Scott. I went with my cousins Cyrene and her daughter Valerie Hulton-Sams, joined by the genial golfing Doctor MacGregor.

On Sunday 28th, when Duty Officer in *Vernon* I met a friend of my brother's called Selby Armitage, whose life was largely spent sailing his own boat round the British coasts. Chess was also a hobby and he had little difficulty in beating me. By the end of 1940 he was an active member of the Render Mines Safe party in the Mining Department, having worked with Glenny on the second German magnetic mine. Later he was awarded the George Cross for rendering land mines safe in London. Invited to go to America to teach them how to do it, his first reaction was to refuse. "It would interrupt my postal chess matches", he said. Met by the Mayor at some airport on his travels there, he was handed a copy of the local paper. To his horror its front page headlines were, "Armitage arrives today swears he'll drink U.S. dry". Just a joke by the Mayoral leg puller!

By May 1 the Demolition Parties were at 12 hours notice while in the *Vernon* I was doing my best to understand the workings of the Gyro Compass with the prospect of an exam on this whirl-a-gig contraption at the end of the week. Clearly my place of duty was at Chatham. Captain Hermon-Hodge in the Admiralty supported my view; Porky Veale likewise. My visit coincided with the opening of the new Torpedo school. Fallen in with the others, my hand was shaken by the Commander-in-Chief, Admiral Hon. Sir Reginald Aylmer Ranfurly Plunkett-Ernle-Erle-Drax, followed by the Commodore of the Barracks Bob Burnett, who greeted me with a more than bonhomous "Hee! Hee! Hee! Old Boy".

Escaping to the Drill Shed I found Commander Michael Goodenough had come from the Admiralty to brief the men involved. It was as well that I spent a night in the Barracks: there were matters to check, not least

JUST A HOGG'S LIFE

Christmas 1939 at Richmond House, Epsom. L to R Anthony Hogg, Daphne Norman, Cynthia Sandford, Pilot Officer Martin Hogg.

The morning pint on the wall at Rock.

the stores and the arrangements for loading them at the port of embarkation. I was also glad to give dinner to Pat and John Osborne, kind hosts to me so often. John, Engineer Officer of the destroyer *Hotspur* was just back from Narvik; with her steering controls damaged by a German shell she was lucky to make her escape in the battle.

After lunching with Captain Herman-Hodge at his club the *Carlton*, I took Joan home feeling unwell. "Yet another case of Rubella", said the Doctor without difficulty. Driving me to Effingham in the snow and the black out to get back to Portsmouth, our relationships had become closer; we had even talked half jokingly of getting married when I became a Lieutenant-Commander in 1944.

The telephone call to me in *Vernon* came from Captain Herman- Hodge at 0645 on Friday May 10 and I was on the road to Dover by 0720. A lovely cloudless morning, war seemed absolutely remote as I drove along the coast expecting to reach Dover in three hours, though in fact it took four to reach the Eastern Mole.

Our destroyer bound for Imjuiden, the port of Amsterdam, was *Whitshed*, commanded by Ray Conder lately of *Kittiwake*; his First Lieutenant was Sam Lombard-Hobson, whose book *A Sailor's War* describes this operation and many others in the next few weeks.

With the stores embarked Michael Goodenough stood on a bollard saying a few words to the effect that Hitler couldn't take it, the war might be a bloody one but it would soon be over. *Whitshed* sailed at noon crossing the Channel at 30 knots expecting to arrive at 1700. The demolition party consisted of nine officers and 158 naval ratings and sappers, the aim being to destroy oil storage tanks, the lock gates and other installations of value to the advancing Germans. The boxes of T.N.T charges for this work were piled high on the quarterdeck and in the lobby below X gun that led down to the Wardroom and the Cabin Flat.

As we sped up the coast of Belgium at nearly 30 knots on this calm glorious day, smoke over Ostend showed the *Luftwaffe* already doing its worst to civilians of a neutral country. Twenty miles short of Imjuiden *Whitshed* was attacked by JU88 bombers; flat on my face on the upper deck I noticed a tear in my trousers and a hot splinter close by it. I thought my baptism of fire could have been worse. Though there had been many near misses and some minor casualties, the ship had not been hit. While firing all she could, the 4.7 guns could not elevate over 30° and the close range anti-aircraft weapons were difficult to aim with the ship taking avoiding action at high speed. As a passenger I found it difficult to know where to go.

In the next attack I was standing on the upper deck, starboard side by the door leading into the after lobby stacked with the boxes of TNT. Suddenly a man from X gun's crew above me was blown overboard just as I was engulfed in flame. I thought this was the end of me, but turning into the lobby, I was able to walk out through the Officers' Galley to the port side. Thinking the Bridge would be a safer place, I went forward, but somebody took me to Surgeon Lieutenant David Pugh R.N.V.R. the ship's Medical Officer.

The tin hat had covered my head but no anti-flash gear was issued then, so my face and hands were severely burnt. The flash fortunately had been momentary caused by a red hot splinter igniting a cordite case at X gun. There was also an explosion, which blew every member of X gun's crew over the side and started a fire near and below the T.N.T. boxes. No.1 with every available hand put it out with hoses. But there were other cases of burns and concussion, although thanks to Conder's bomb dodging, the aircraft had scored no actual hits.

Sitting there helpless I began to realise my predicament, when three more JU88s attacked as the ship entered harbour. Busy trying to avoid a collision with a tug, Conder was actually going astern, the bombs exploding well ahead, merely soaking those on the Bridge. With *Whitshed* alongside to cheers from the Dutch, the landing party and their stores were soon ashore.

I was placed in the spare cabin forward anxious to get back to Dover as my eyelids now swelled until I was blind. A *schuyt* (local Dutch vessel) was sent to find any survivors from the first attack, possibly on the floats dropped by *Whitshed* at the time. It returned with three injured men but five others were lost. Other casualties were three killed by bomb splinters, eight badly injured or burnt and fifteen officers and men, including the Captain, slightly hurt. Escorting two bullion ships *Whitshed* sailed about 2200 to reach Dover at 0515. Placed in a cot I was carried down Dover's most slippery steps into a hospital boat and then by ambulance to the R. N. Hospital at Deal.

So far I had little pain but cleaning up and dressing with tannin, in spite of anaesthetics, was hell. It was consoling however to find myself in the hands of Surgeon Commander Keating, who had attended Jessel on our *Nahlin* cruise. By evening my mother and sister appeared, driven by our family Doctor Wilde, followed next morning by my brother who had driven through the night from Cheshire.

A few days later my visitors were my godfather, Dean Hewlett Johnson and our Epsom Vicar Hugh Warner. There was general anxiety that I might be blind, dispelled fortunately by Monday when I began to see a little. On Wednesday, to make way for further casualties, many of us were moved to Chatham by bus, where I was given a cabin and well looked after for fifteen days.

At Chatham I could not read for a long time so visitors made a great difference. Cecil Sandford put up Brada and Joan alternating with my mother. Goodenough, Whittle, the Torpedo Gunner's Mate and Lieutenant Colin Madden, who had taken my place, came to say they had done the demolitions without losing a man, returning in a Dutch boat paying the large sums of money, Dutch and British, taken for such purposes. Some weeks later I remembered I too had been issued with £400, which was still in my reefer. Returned to the Admiralty the receipted reply read, *"Many thanks, we had written it off by enemy action"*. Sisters Stonely and Carroll did everything for me; I often wonder what happened to them.

The next move was on 29 May in a hot uncomfortable 'hospital' train, my coach being a converted cattle truck from which one could not see out. We reached Bristol at 1415, buses taking us to Barrow Gurney four miles out where a former mental asylum was now a naval hospital. Joan spent a week staying with a friend near by. After a month I was allowed home for a weekend and on Saturday July 6 discharged on a month's sick leave. On July 27 I took Joan to lunch at Barry Neame's celebrated hotel, the Hind's Head at Bray. Although I felt nobody could want to marry a man with a face like a beef steak, I hired an electric canoe and proposed under Maidenhead Bridge. The affirmative answer was rather pathetic, "I thought you were never going to ask me," she said.

We were married on 7 September in her father's little church under the Sussex Downs at Graffham. Some twenty to thirty guests drank champagne on the lawn of this lovely old rectory on another glorious summer's day. Dan Duff and Peter Gretton representing the Navy returned to man the road between Havant and Emsworth; invasion by Germany was believed imminent. The guests returning to Epsom witnessed the first German Blitz on London that night.

Two nights after the wedding we arrived in FPK71 for our honeymoon at the Rock Hotel, Rock to be greeted by Mrs. Lane.

"What a time to arrive!" she said. "They've landed you know. Pete in the Home Guard is out repelling them now. So if you hear a noise in the night, Mr and Mrs Hogg, you'll know that the Germans have really reached Rock."

THE END

JUST A HOGG'S LIFE

*Wedding at Graffham,
7 September 1940.*

*A joke with Uncle
Sandy and Colonel
Alan Swinton.*

*Austin 7 FPK 71
awaits us.*

Appendix

THE BATTLE SCENE
from
GASOLINI's
Opera

L'APPREZIAZZIONE DELLA SITUAZZIONE

SCENE: The Bridge of a Battleship

Admiral, Flag Captain, Flag Lieutenant, Staff Officer (Operations)
and Chorus of seamen.

Based on themes from the following operas:

'The Play' from Leoncavallo's Pagliaci
Trio and Finale from Gounod's Faust
March of the Priests from Verdi's Aïda
The Prologue from Leoncavallo's Pagliaci
Samson et Delilah by Saint-Saëns
Madame Butterfly by Puccini
'Home to our mountains' from Verdi's Il Trovatore
Duet: Butterfly & Suzuki, Puccini's Madame Butterfly
Soldiers Chorus from Verdi's Il Trovatore

Transcribed by Michael Walsh

NOTE: The following musical score gives an exact transcription of how Anthony Hogg recalls the piece's original performance, rather than a strictly 'correct' version of these themes.

JUST A HOGG'S LIFE

THE BATTLE SCENE
from Gasolini's Opera
L'APPREZIAZZIONE DELLA SITUAZZIONE

Admiral: Smoke there! Smoke there! Tell the En-gin-eer Com-man-der.

Chorus: Tell the Eng-in-eer, the En-gin-eer Com-man-der: too much smoke. The

Admiral: e-ne-my Sir have turned a-way. Then I will close their rear and break their

Chorus: line. Close their rear and break their line.

S.O.O.: There is no re-fer-ence, Sir, in the bat-tle in-struct-ions to such a move as that,

Chorus: such a move as that, as that, as that, as that.

Admiral: And who are you, pray, to ques-tion my de-cis-ion? Yes,

Chorus: who in-deed are you?

S.O.O.: I am the Staff Of-fi-cer (Op-er-a-tions). My du-ty is to see the War Man-ual is o-beyed. I car-ry a foun-tain-pen-in case, a ream of ser-vice fool-scap, a piece of in-dia rub-ber. And in this belt a-round my waist, I car-ry thir-ty-two grains of As-pirin, Two Star, Mark Four. And in my heart I

322

A MUSICAL APPENDIX

car - ry a dou - ble al - low - ance of mo - des - ty. Hum - ble mo - des - ty,

All kneel and sing with Chorus

hum - ble mo - des - ty. Hail mo - des - ty. We praise thy name kneel - ing in

a - do - ra - tion. Thou who all oth - er gifts ex - cell - ing Mak - est

our Staff thy claim thy true ha - bi - ta - tion. Their hearts thy cho - sen

Exeunt Chorus S.O.O.

dwell - ing. Thy cho - sen dwell - ing. Sir, your de -

Admiral

stroy - ers can - not ex - e - cute that move - ment, They none of them know the Ad - mi - ral's in - ten - tion. Ah,

no. A - las, you are right. They none of them know my in - ten - tion.

Ah in my scan - ty hours of leis - ure, Los - ing

balls twixt tee and green. I might have spent my time en -

sur - ing that my in - ten - tion was fore - seen.

323

JUST A HOGG'S LIFE

F.C. Ev-ery fleet of-fi-cer knows what your golf is, Sir, But

S.O.O. no-bo-dy knows this move you pro-pose. Would there were some in-ven-tion to ex-plain his in-ten-tion to show what he thinks by his round on the links. His in-

F.L. ten-tion to ut-ter with a stroke of the put-ter, his pur-pose to speak with a click of the cleek.

Admiral Ah in my scan-ty hours of leis-ure, los-ing balls twixt tee and green, I should have spent my time en-sur-ing that my in-

S.O.O. ten-tion was fore-seen. *f* Take heart! for you must see, Sir,

324

A MUSICAL APPENDIX

strat-e-gists all a-gree, Sir. Mo-rale will count as three, Sir, Phy-si-cal force as one.

F.C.
Yes he's right. Three to one. I think I read it in O. U. 5 8 9 1.

Admiral **F.L.**
Tab-les for sol-ving tac-ti-cal prob-lems. Ask my gal-lant sea-men if their mo-rale is good. Be-

low there! Be - low there! Is there good mo - rale?

Chorus (below)
Our mo-rale is grow-ing ev-ery sec-ond it will short-ly be gi-gan-tic when the

S.O.O.
bat-tle is be-gun. Joy, oh joy, mo-rale is al-ways rec-koned (though I

Admiral
hate to be pe-dan-tic) at the rate of three to one. Yes, Na-po-le-on the Great so his-

tor-i-ans re-late, worked the val-ues out and made them three to one.

Enter Chorus singing
ALL
Our mo-rale is grow-ing ev-ery sec-ond we can clear-ly see the foe will be de-fea-ted.

Will be de-fea-ted, will be de-feat-ed. Will be de-fea - ted.

Anon.

INDEX

Ranks after page numbers are those finally attained.
Names in brackets are maiden names.
Abbreviations: Adm = Admiral; Capt = Captain;
Col = Colonel; Comdr = Commander; Lieut or Lt = Lieutenant;
Mid = Midshipman; (E) = Engineer; (D) = Dental Surgeon.

Abel, Restaurateur, 294, 302
Abyssinia, 208, 219
Acasta, HMS, 148, 180
Achates, HMS, 180, 186
Achilles, HMS, 37, 307
Active, HMS, 180
Acworth, H.W., Lt.-Cdr, 242   Cdr.
Admiralty, 107, 110, 145, 208, 310
    Hydrographic Dept., 104
Adventure, HMS Minelayer 63, 91, 96, 98, 203, 301
Air, Short course, 175-6
Ajax, HMS, 37, 226, 307
Albania, 292
Aldershot Services, 261, 287
Alexander, King of Yugo-Slavia, 185-6
Alexandria, 171-2, 177, 219-227, 229, 250, 252, 258, 265, 293, 305
Algeciras, 103
Algiers, 67-68
Alicante, 241-2
Allenby, General, 6
Allright, Chief Petty Officer retd, 163-4, 318
Almeria, 242, 263
Alpha Class, RNC Dartmouth, 33
Althing, Iceland Parliament, 77
Altmark, German Ship, 312
Altrincham, 3, 213, 216, 259
    St. Margaret's Church, 1, 6, 9
    Orchard House, 4
Anderson, Rev. William, Chaplain, 41, 259
Andrew, M. F. Mid., 51, 70, 82   Capt
Antelope, HMS, 189, 204, 228
Antigua, 99-100, 292

Mr. Henzell, 99
English Harbour, 160
Athens, 235
Aphrodite, statue, 173
Ardent, HMS, 148
Arethusa, HMS Cruiser, 263
Argus, HMS, 139
Armitage, Selby, Lieut RNVR, 315
Arrow, HMS, 240
A Sail for a Sale, Musical, 122, 126-7
Ashby, A.N. Pay Cadet, 104
Astaire, Fred, 147, 157, 218, 252
Ataturk, Kemal, 236-7-8
Atkinson, A.H., 8
Attwood, Able Seaman, 275, 278
Aurora, HMS Cruiser, 222
Austin, family, 125 - 127
Austin, FPK 71, 302, 320
Aylen, Jan, Lieut. (E), 285
Azores, 96, 120, 121
Backhouse, Adm. of the Fleet Sir Roger, 203, 210
Bailey, Bill, Able Seaman, 287
Bailey, O.N. Mid, 104   Captain
Baines, E.F. 'Eddie', 189, 204, 228, 261
Baldwin, C.P.O., 307
Baker, F.P. Cadet, 43, 51, 68-9, 70, 95, 104, 117, 119, 129, 130, 135, 139, 298   Captain
Bamford, Bros, 9
Bannerman, Comdr Retd., 279, 313
Barbados, 123, 124, 125, 126, 127
Barcelona, 229
Barchard, Frank, Lt Comdr., 298
Barham, HMS Battleship 64, 71, 72, 75, 82, 91, 206-7-8

326

INDEX

Barker, Family, 224
Barker, Gabriella, 222
Barnes G. Dartmouth Master, 34 Sir George
Barracks Ball, 281-2
Barrow Gurney Hospital, 320
Barthou, Monsieur, 185
Bateman, C. R. Mid, 135
Bartlett, Rev, 255, 264, 267, 269
Bascombe, A. W., Actor, 71
Bath, 218, 274, 276
Battersby, Flotilla 'Radio Bosun', 220, 240
Bawler, Mr. Boatswain, 183, 185
Baxter, Jane, *Midshipmaid*, 48
Beard, Lt-Cmdr 'Bog' and Mrs, 264
Beckett, John, 21
Beggar's Opera, The, 305, 313
Bekenn, Philip, Sub-Lieut, 144, 260, 263 Lt-Cdr.
Belgrade, 186
Bell, L. H., Comdr., 167-8, 170, 171-2-3, 183, 192, 198, 205, 209, 248 Capt.
Bellairs, R. M., Captain, 94, 110, 111
Bennett, C. J. 'Wiggie' Lieut, 169, 183, 191-2
Bennett, Wilfred, Barrister, 214, 279
Benians, F.H.A. Mid., 167
Benstead, C. R. Inst. Lt-Cdr, 73, 78
Betjeman, John, 278
Betteridge, Mr, Tailor, 24, 25
Between the Bollards, Musical, 102
Bilberries, 23
Bird (Vavasour) Betty, 312
Birmingham HMS, 191, 294
Birmingham, City 306, 315
Bismarck, German battleship, 91
Blackheath, 141, 153, 274, 285
Black Prince, HMS, Cruiser, 114, 122, 173, 191, 222, 304
Blackman, C. M. Captain, 220
Blake, G.P., Mid., 17
Bloomer, L. G., Mid., 17
Boaks, William, Lieut., 280
Boiler Cleaning, 101-2
Bonsey, A.L., Pay Lieut, 113, 204, 249
Boothby, Lieut RM, 169, 175 Maj.
Borrett, Simon, Lt-Cdr., 187 Captain

Boulestin, Marcel, Chef, 161
Bowden, H.D. Mid., RAN, 65 Retd.
Boyd, Denis, Captain, 295 Adm Sir Denis
Bracegirdle, Warwick, Mid. RAN, 65, 280-1-2, 285-6 Comdr
Bray, Hind's Head hotel, 320
Brewster, H.C.W. Mid. RAN, 167, 178, 184, 207
Bridlington, 305, 306
Brilliant, HMS, 261
Brindisi, 230
Brioni, 180-1
Britannia, HMS, 27, 49, 121
Britton, Joe, Pay Lieut, 171
Brockhurst School, 8 - 21
Brooking, P.W. Comdr. 206, 209, 210, 214, 279
Brown, J.F.B. Mid, 51, 69, 70, 82
Browne, H.C., Lt-Cdr, 254
Browning, Lt. Col. Sir Frederick, 'Boy', 221, 224
Brownrigg, J. S. Mid., 167, 183
Bruce, M.A.M., Mid, 167, 183, 207
Bryant, Sir Arthur, 148-9
Buchanan-Dunlop, D, Lieut., 195-6
Buckley, James, Lt. Comdr., 256
Buist, Colin, Mid, 104
Bullocke, J. Professor, 145
Burnett, R.L. 'Bob',Comdr. 49, 50, 59, 64, 65, 66, 67, 68, 69, 73, 82, 88, 89, 90, 94, 158, 315 Admiral
Burns, Robert, 1
Burton, R. C. 'Bobbie' Mid. 165, 175-6, 239, 256, 264 Comdr.
Burton (Dixon) 'Molly', 239, 264
Burton-Brown, 'Beachie', 22, 23
Bush Hotel, 204
Cairo, HMS, Cruiser, 121, 210, 251
Calvert, T.F.P. Captain, 131-2, 136-137, 139, 140 R.Adm.
Calcutta, HMS, 50
Callender, Geoffrey, Prof, 145, 148
Callington, 290
Cammell Laird, 296
Cameron, Charles, Lieut. 296, 306
Campion, Joice, 224, 225
Campbell, Sir David, H.E. 190
Campbell, Lady, 190

Campbell, Jean, 190, 195-6
Camozzi, Phyllis and May, 195-6
Cannes, 85, 228-9, 263
Canterbury, 303
Carstairs, HMS Sloop, 79
Carlton Grill, London, 305
Carrington, Leonora, Painter, 269
Carroll, Sister, 320
Cartagena, 240-1-2, 249
Carter, Francis, Lieut. 294
Carter, Lady Gilbert, 126
Caruana's Bar, 176
Carver, family, 224-5, 251
  Marguerite, 302
Catherine the Great, Film, 191
Casement, Bros, 274, 277
Casement, J. J. Lieut., 69, 70, 94, 264, 274   Captain
Casson, family, 249, 250
Centaur, HMS. Old Cruiser, 91, 112, 115, 116
Centurion, HMS. 66
Chalkis, 235
Chamberlain, Neville, Prime Minister, 284-5, 295
Chanak, 237
Channell, Ann Mrs, 278
Chapman, A.P.F., Cricketer, 222
Chappell, E. B. Prof. 145, 148
Chatfield, Adm. of the Fleet   Baron.
  C-in-C Atlantic, 71
  C-in-C Med., 73
Chatham, 88, 108, 111, 118, 259, 260, 296, 304, 310, 313, 315, 320
Chelmick, Shropshire, 14
Chemical Warfare (Gas Course) 93
Chester, Frederick, Entertainer, 14
Cheltenham, Ladies College, 21, 278
Chichester, 126, 232, 298, 311
Christian, King of Denmark, 77, 94
Christie, John, 164, 283
Christie (Mildmay), Audrey, 313
Church Stretton, 8, 9, 207
Churchill, Winston, 203, 310   K.G.
Clark, Brian 'Nobby', Lt Comdr, 297, 298-300, 303-5
Clements, F, Pay Mid. 167, 183
Clements, G. Pay Mid. 167, 183
Clouston, J. C. Comdr, 224, 263

Clutton, Molly, 250
Coaling Ship, 262-3
Cobbett, Sir Walter, 300
Cochrane, HMS, 298-9
Cochran, Charles B, 147, 189
Cochrane, Edward, Captain, 121
Cock, Sub-Lieut (E), 211
Cockburn-Mercer, J. Mid. 44   Retd.
Codrington, HMS., 180, 183, 227
Cody, Mid. RAN, 167, 176
Coleby, R. Paymaster Mid. 52, 104
Coldwell, J. C. Mid., 17
Cole, A. B., Sub-Lieutenant, 90
Collins, Mid. RAN., 167, 176
Colville, G. C. Lieut., 131, 138, 140 Comdr.
Comet, HMS, 250, 265
Conder, E. R. Comdr., 302, 317, 318
Condom, Trial of, 219
Constantine Bay Hotel, 281
Co-optimists, Theatricals, 14
Corfu, 234
Cormorant, HMS, 254
Cornabe, Fl. Lieut RAF, 255, 268
Cornwall, HMS., 18, 22
County, 278
Coronation Review, 258
Cossack, HMS., 191, 312
Cotton, Henry, Golf Champion, 263
Counter Mining, 303
Courageous, HMS Carrier, 132, 134, 139, 194, 250, 253, 257, 302
Court-Martial, 291
Coventry, HMS Cruiser, 204, 265
Coward, Noel, 147, 195, 263 Knight
Cowes, 205. 208
Cowgill, J.W.F.D., Lt.Comdr, 248, 256
Cox, Ian, Lt. Comdr., 40
Crane, H. D. Comdr. 248, 257
Crash Whaler Race, 182, 183, 184
Craven-Ellis Mrs, 217
Crawford, R. M. Lieut., 216, 218, 225-6, 238, 240, 248, 266
Crawford, W. G. Sub Lieut., 275
Creasy, G. E. Comdr., 50, 70
    Adm of the Fleet Sir George
Crick, Rev. Thomas, 41
    Chaplain of the Fleet
Crick, T.G.P. Lt. Comdr. 298

INDEX

Critchley, Julian, M.P., 12, 20, 21
Croatia, 180
Cummins, Neville, 252
Culme-Seymour, G. H. Mid., 135
Cunningham, Stuart, Lieut., 169, 205, 207
Cunningham, Andrew "ABC", Adm. of the Fleet, Baron. 49, 50, 51, 63, 65, 66, 67, 76, 77, 78, 79, 80, 83, 90, 92, 94, 111, 121, 205, 222, 264, 287
Cunningham, (Byatt) Lady Nona, 49
Curate's Egg, Musical, 102
Cypher Officer, 236
Daily Telegraph, 274, 301
Dalglish, J. S. Cadet, 104   Captain
Dallmeyer, William, Comdr. 264, 295, 304   Captain
Dardanelles, 172, 236-7
Dartmouth, Royal Naval College, 17, 82, 118
  Alpha Class, 33.
  Greynvile Photograph, 35
  Pass in Interview 16,
  Pass Out results, 44
*Daring, H*MS. 220
Dauthieu, Paul, 146, 161, 283
David, Bishop of Liverpool, 277
David, (Barrington-Ward) Mrs, 313
David, family, 278, 295, 313
Davidson, A. G. Pay Mid., 52
Davies, Mr. Rhys, M.P., 76
Davies, W.J.A., Fleet Instructor, 254-5, 267   Comdr
Daymer Bay, 283
Deal, RN Hospital, 318
Deck Hockey, 133
Delysia, Alice, Actress, 316
Demolitions, 315
  Antigua, 99
  Holland, 310
De Pass, D, Comdr. 131, 137, 138, 140   Captain
Desert Angels, Book, 222
Despatch, HMS. Cruiser, 198, 243, 244
Deutschland, German battleship, 263
Devonport, 72, 83, 93, 110, 111, 208, 217, 268, 292
  RN. Barracks, 88, 277, 280

Mobilisation, 284-5
Services XV. 269. 274, 285-6-7, 292
Devonshire, HMS Cruiser, 171-2, 184, 189
Dobbs, R.A.W. Cadet, 43, 190, 264-5, 267, 291   Lieutenant
Dobbs (Stoker) Anne, 190, 264, 267, 291-2
Dobell, Douglas, Lt. Comdr. 222
Dolphin, HMS, 311
Domvile, Admiral Sir Barry, 148, 153-4
Dominic, Peter, Wine Firm, 146, 161, 259, 283
Dorrien-Smith, family, 80-81
Dorsetshire, HMS. Cruiser, 108, 120, 126
Douglas, HMS., 220, 226, 229
Dover, 118, 203, 301, 303, 317-8
Downside School, 42
Doyle, Captain of Nahlin, 230, 234
Drawbridge, 'Tatters', Lt Comdr., 167, 170, 176-7, 207, 209, 261
Dryad, HMS, 161-2
Dubrovnik, Town, 232
Dubrovnik, Yugo-Slav destroyer, 185-6
Duck Soup, Film, Marx Bros. 197
Duff Cooper, 231, 267
Duff, Dan, Mid, 43, 224-5, 249, 320   Comdr.
Duff (Pound) Barbara, 224
Dunbar, Claude, Major, Scots Guards, 226   Major-General
Dunham Forest, Golf Club, 206
Dunbar-Nasmith, Adm. Sir Martin, 33, 286
Dunkirk, 203
Durango, Spain, 261
Durban, HMS. Cruiser, 189
Durness, Kyle of, 155
Durrant, Pamela, 278-9, 295
Eagle, HMS, Carrier, 108
Earle, Charles, Major, 302   Lt. Col.
Edinburgh, 139, 298
Edward VIII, King, 228, 230, 231-3-4-5-6-7-8, 248
Edwards, Nowell, 303
Effingham, HMS, Cruiser, 257
Queen Elizabeth II Conference Hall, 293

329

Elgin, HMS, Minesweeper, 259, 264
Elliott, Frank, Captain, 203
Elliott, Fl. Lieut and Mrs, 252
Elliot, W, Lieut. 158   Captain
Ellsworth, R.F.G. Mid. 167, 185, 207
Emmanuel, T. Lieut., 280
Emberton, 3
Emerald, HMS, Cruiser, 135
Emery, Able Seaman, 114
Emperor of India, Old battleship, 91
Enchantress, Admiralty Yacht, 206, 267
Epsom, 200, 213, 216, 269, 270, 320
  Richmond House, 44, 141, 292
  College, 163, 165, 262, 293, 296
  Downs, 163, 165
Erebus, HMS, Monitor 79, 143
Evans, A. R. E. Mid., 104   Captain
Evans, D.P. Lieut., 189
Evans-Lombe, Edward, Comdr. 268
                                Rear Adm.
Eveleigh, Able Seaman, 297
Everett, A. R. Cadet, 104
Exeter, Bishop of, 41
Exeter, HMS, 37, 120, 307
Excellent, (Whale Island) HMS, 155, 156-159, 168
Falcon-Steward, Lieut, 108
Falla, Guy C., Sub Lieut., 131, 137-8
Falmouth, 80, 81, 82, 83
Famagusta, 170-71, 199
Fame, HMS, 226
Farnhill, K. H. Pay Cadet, 104
Farouk, King of Egypt, 227
Fasson, F.A.B. Mid., 104
Fayal, 121, 127, 128, 134
Fearless, HMS., 226, 268
Fegen, Captain Fogarty, V.C. 165-6
Fenwick, C.E. Mid., 51, 82, 261, 263, 264   Comdr.
Feuerheerd, family, 84-5
Finland, 310, 312
Field Gun Crews, 280
Firth, C.L. "Champagne Charlie", Comdr., 215-6-7, 219, 224-5, 227-232, 236-8, 239-243   Captain
Fisher, Admiral Lord, 119
Fisher, Adm. Sir William, 170, 186, 220, 222
Fisher, Richard, Sub-Lt., RNVR. 304-5

Fisher (Colley) Helen, Actress, 304
Flecker, James Elroy, Poet, 170
Fletcher, Frank, Lieut., 17, 306
Fleet Air Arm, 90, 91, 106, 176, 206, 211, 257
Fleming, James, 20
Flimsy, The, 243
Floral Dance, The, 14
Follow the Fleet, Film, 218
Forres, HMS, 39, 79
Forrest, J. W., Lieut, 99, 211, 286
Foy, Paul, Lieut., 234-5, 238
Flying Boat Record, 252
Flying Down to Rio, Film, 157
Franco, Spanish General, 229
Fraser, B.A., Captain [Fraser of North Cape], 246, 249, 251-2, 256, 257, 258, 264-5-6-7, 276
                Adm.of the Fleet.Baron
French without Tears, Play, 260
Frobisher, HMS. Cruiser, 64
Fumerole, HM Drifter, 205
Furious, HMS., Carrier, 65, 108, 169, 174-176, 194
Fyffe, Lieut-General Sir Richard, 195, 196
Fyffe, (Moore-Gwyn) Lady Diana, 195, 196
Gabriel, Geoffrey, Sub Lieut, RAN, 214-215
Gabriel (Gunnell) Valerie, 214-215
Galatea, HMS., Cruiser, 210, 222, 224, 226, 240
Gale, D. T. Mid., RAN, 65   Comdr.
Gallie, Brian, Lieut, 167, 169, 178
Gallant, HMS., 216, 219, 229, 240, 242
Ganges, HMS, Boys Training, 292, 298
Gardener-Brown, Matron, 10, 14
Garland, HMS., 216, 239, 240, 261
Gate Revue, The, 294, 305
General Drill, 65, 80, 134
General Election, 114, 115
Geneva Convention, 303
George V, King, 131, 134, 204, 214
George VI, King, 62, 248, 258, 307
George, Prince, 132, 150, 189, 219
Gibraltar, 64, 71, 96, 102, 177, 194, 219, 242, 263,
  Rock Hotel, 219

INDEX

Gieves, Mr. Robert, Chairman, 25
  Long RN Association, 26-27
  The Naval Officer's Life, 27-28, 96, 286
Gilchrist, Don, Author, 18
Gilliatt, Sir William, 301
Giovenezza, Fascist song, 181
Gipsy, HMS., 216, 219, 229, 239, 240, 242
Glasgow, HMS., Cruiser, 144
Glasspool, C.P.O., 193
Glenny, D.E.M., Lieut, 307
Glorious, HMS., Carrier, 128, 148, 191, 221, 227, 240, 247-258, 261-270, 274, 291
Gloucester, HMS., Cruiser, 286
Gloucester, Regiment, 276
Glowworm, HMS., 216, 230-1-4, 235-6-7-8-9
Glyndebourne Opera, 296, 313
Gneisenau, German battle cruiser, 92, 147, 227
Godwin, A. Lieut Comdr, 44
Golf, RN and RM Meeting, 162
Gone with the Wind, Novel, 266
Goodchild, Val, 227
Goodenough, M.G. Comdr. 311, 315, 317, 320   R.Adm
Goodhart, G.A.J., Cadet, 135   Lt-Cdr
Goodwins, Light Vessel, 302
Gordon, C. S. Mid., RAN, 167, 178, 184, 207
Gould, R. A. Lieut Comdr(E), 216, 220, 225, 235, 256, 263   Cdr
Graffham, 307, 320
Grafton, HMS., 215-6,
  Gibraltar, 218
  Malta, 219
  Alexandria, 220
  Wins regatta, 226
  Diverted to Barcelona evacuates refugees, 229
  becomes King's escort at Sibenik, 230
  Cruise ends, 238
  Patrols Spanish East Coast, 239-243
Graf Von Spee, German battleship, 37, 307, 312
Gray, J.M.D. "Jock", Mid., 189, 227, 286, 300   V.Adm. Sir John

Gray (Purvis) Lady, 225, 227, 300
Gray, Gordon, T.S. Mid., 144   R.Adm.
Greenwich, 295
  History, 141-143, 145
  Night Pageant, 148-154
  Painted Hall, 154, 296
  Rugby XV, 146, 274
  Staff College, 117
Gregory, R. Comdr. 304
Grenada, 124-125
Grenade, HMS., 216, 218
Grenville, Sir Richard, 121
Grenville, HMS., 229, 239
Gretton, P. W. Cadet, 30, 41, 111, 189-90, 262, 268, 287, 312, 320   V.Adm. Sir Peter
Greyhound, HMS., 216
Griffin, HMS., 216
Grimsby, 305, 306
Groome D, "Joey", Sub-Lt., 217, 264-5
Gruning, C.L. Cadet, 104
Guernica, Spain, 261
Guildford, 200, 211
Gunnell, Valerie, see Gabriel
Gunner's Mates, 156, 190
Gunroom Traditions, 57-58
Guest Night, 65, 200
Haifa, 199-200
Hailsham, Viscount (Quintin Hogg), 1
Haile Selassie, Emperor of Abyssinia, 219
Haines, G. M. Mid, 65   Retd.
Halahan, Lt. Comdr. 82   Captain
Halcyon, HMS Minesweeper., 296-7, 298-9, 303
Halfar, Air Station, 247, 250, 267
Halley, Wing Comdr. RAF 257, 267, 270
Hamilton, Sir Robert. MP., 76
Hammond, R.J.H. Lieut. 275   Comdr.
Hampton, HMS Minelayer, 203
Hankey, A.S., Cadet, 135
Harlech, 303
Harley Bros. 18
Harman, J.C.M. Cadet, 30   Lieut.
Harper, K.J. Lieut., 144
Harrault, Prof. French, 146
Harrel, H. T. Cadet., 43, 158, 215, 268   Captain

331

Harrier, HMS Minesweeper, 296-7-8, 299, 300-01-02-04-05-06
Harrison, 'PTH' Master, Dartmouth, 34, 42
Harrison, P.R.H., Mid., 135
Harry, Tll, Brockhurst master, 12
Harwich, 292, 298, 300
Haslar, RN Hospital, 156, 311
Havers, A.A. "Pog", Lt. Comdr, 37, 43, 44, 261, 298   Comdr.
Hawick, 1
Hawkins, HMS, 63, 64, 96, 98
Hay, Ian, Playwright, 48, 71
Hayling Island, 129, 189, 205, 255, 282
Hayter, Lt. Comdr., 98
Healey, A 'Tim', Lieut. 296-7, 306
Henn, William & Geraldine, 224, 251-2, 255
Henry, Sir James, 227
Henry (Holmes) Lady, 224-5, 227, 247, 265
Herbert, A.P. Writer, 189
Herman-Hodge, The Hon., 117, 311, 317   Captain
Hermitage, Village, 20
Hetherington (Vavasour) Josephine, 312
Hewat, Bros., 17
Heycock, George, Fl. Lt. RAF, 267 Air Commodore
Hickley, J.A.V. Cadet., 104
Higson, Lieut. RNVR, 302, 304
Hill, R. H. 17
Hill, Rowley, 17
Hindustan, HMS, 27
Hitler, Adolf, 161, 249, 250, 276, 284-5, 287, 292, 310, 317
Hoare, Lieut RNR, 305
Hobart, R. H. Cadet, 135   Lt-Cdr
Hodges, Elizabeth see Kimmins
Hodges, Adm Sir Michael, 75, 100, 110, 111
Hodgson, F. Lieut., 280
Hogg, Adam 1832-1897, 2
Hogg, Adam, 1943-, 157, 210
Hogg, (Gilfillan) Eliza 1838-1895, 2
Hogg, Alex G, 'Sandy' 1867-1942, 2, 4, 85, 206, 259, 301, 306

Hogg, Anthony Spencer
passim, birth 1
Brockhurst School, 8
RN College Dartmouth, 29
Cadet and Midshipman
battleship *Rodney*, 52, 64, 100
destroyer *Vidette*, 108,
battle cruisers
Repulse 119,
Renown 131, Sub Lieutenant
RN College Greenwich 141,
Courses, Gunnery Torpedo and Navigation at Portsmouth 156
battleship *Royal Sovereign* 167
destroyer *Grafton* 216
promoted Lieutenant 227
cruiser *Despatch*, 243
Aircraft carrier *Glorious* 247
RN Barracks, Devonport 276
RN Rugby XV, 277
RN College Greenwich to start long torpedo course, 296
course abandoned, appointed minesweeper Harrier, 296
war declared 301
sweeping from Dover and Grimsby, 306
Vernon Portsmouth, torpedo course re-assembled 307
Wounded, severe burns, in charge Demolition Party at Imjuiden 318
in hospital May-July, patient of McIndoe facial surgeon, 320
married September 320
honeymoon Rock, 320
Hogg, Joan (Powell) wife of Anthony Hogg *see* Powell.
Hogg, Brada II (Hulton) (1877-1974), 3, 24, 293, 301, 305, 318
Hogg, Brada III, *see* Paterson, Brada
Hogg, David, MP, 2
Hogg, Eliza, 'Betty', 1872-1954
Hogg, Florence, 4
Hogg, Vice-Admiral Sir Ian, 144, 167, 185
Hogg, James 'Ettrick Shepherd' 1770-1835, 1, 2
Hogg, Lee Robert, 1866-1925, 2
Hogg, Martin Spencer, 1903-1962, 3,

INDEX

85, 155, 206, 258, 278, 281, 306, 318
Hogg, Percy, 1876-1906, Captain, Royal Scots Greys, 2
Hogg, Quintin, See Hailsham,
Hogg, Spencer, Judge, 1870-1937, 2, 3, 4, 6, 85, 87, 206, 258, 266
Hogg, William, G, 1874-1949, 2
Hogg, Mitchell, Londonderry, 2
Holloway, Stanley, 14
Holyhead, 79
Hood, HMS, Battle cruiser, 119-121, 125, 127, 131, 132, 134, 135, 136, 198, 208, 255, 264
Hoskyns, Chandos, Lt. Col. 195, 196
Hotspur, HMS, 317
Hulton, Arthur 1878-1974, 280
Hulton, (Martin) Blanche, 1860-1944, 161, 191
Hulton, Jessop, 1848-1928, 3
Hulton-Harrop, Paul, 10
Hulton-Sams, Cecil, Capt. RN retd., 1882-1931, 275
Hulton-Sams, family, 275
Hussar, HMS, Minesweeper, 298-9, 300, 301
Huxley, family, 22, 23
Iceland, 1930, Visit June 24 to July 1 by HMS *Rodney*, 76-79
Illustrious, HMS, Carrier, 92
Imjuiden, Holland, 118, 317-8
Imperial Defence College, 310
Impulsive, HMS, 187
Ingram, Lieut, 306
Inguanez, Baroness, 190
Inverdale, J. B. Surg Lieut (D), 283, 292, 300   Surg.Capt.(D)
Inverdale, John (son) BBC Sports, 284, 313
Invergordon, 73-74, 90, 106, 109, 110, 129, 135, 136
Isis, HMS, 224, 263
Isle of Wight, 90, 94, 109, 111, 206, 264
Isola Bella, restaurant, 44
Istanbul, 236-238
It Happened One Night, film, 193
Italy, 265
Itxassou, 84

Ivanhoe, HMS, 266
Ivy, restaurant, 294, 305
Jackson, David, 278, 295, 313
Jaime I, Spanish battleship, 241
James, Admiral Sir William, 136, 139
Jameson, T. G. C. Lieut, 247, 252 Captain
Jazz Varieties, "Aunties", 176-7, 179
Jelf, C. B. Cadet, 30, 43, 44, 250, 255 Lieut.
Jellyfish, 96
Jenner-Fust, Otto, Lieut. 209, 220, 225, 249
Jervis Bay, S.S. and HMS, 165-6
Jessel, R. Lt. Comdr, 234-5   Comdr.
Johnson, Hewlett, Very Rev. Dean of Canterbury, 6, 135, 261, 301, 318
Johnson, Mary, (Taylor) 1st wife d.1931 6, 135, 303
Johnson, (Edwards) Nowell, 2nd wife, 303
Johnson, Kerin, 303
Johnson, Kezia, 303
Journal, Midshipman's, 51, 168
Jubilee, Review, 206
Juno, HMS, 185
Junod, Mlle, 10, 14
Keating, Surg. Comdr. 235, 238-9, 318
Keeling, Lt. Comdr., 298-9
Kelly, Admiral Sir John, 111-113, 132, 204
Kempson, Rachel, actress, 42
Kendall, family, 17
Kennard, J.N. Cadet, 104
Kennaway, C.S.H, Mid., 135, 224-5, 249, 250, 263   Lieut.
Kernick, Mrs, 238
Kernick, Robin, 238
Kershaw, C. A. Comdr. 254
Kewley, Bros., 18
Keyham, RNE College, 210, 292
Kimmins, Anthony, Lt. Comdr. retd., Playwright, 37-38   Captain
Kimmins (Hodges) Elizabeth, 37
King-Hall, Comdr. retd., 48, 71, 300
Kingsmill, Mr. and Mrs., 244
Kingsland Grange, School, 14
Kipling, Rudyard, 11
Kirkby, J.P. Lieut (E), 275, 280, 285,

291
Kirke, D. W. Cadet, 135   R.Adm.
Kitson, P.W. Sub-Lieut., 210
Kittiwake, HMS, 302, 317
Knapton, E.G.P.B., 52   Comdr.
Knox, W.N.R. Cadet, 44, 52, 65, 68, 102, 104, 107, 119, 129, 135, 139, 311, 312   Lt. Comdr.
Korcula, 232
Kotor, 232
Lamb, Charles, Comdr, 235
Lambert, A.A., 11
Lamington, Lord, 76
Langridge, A.W. Mid., 167, 183, 184
Larken, E. T. Lieut. 123, 126, 129 Captain
Lavender Sisters, 177, 179
Lascelles, Alan, 236
Law, Bonar, Prime Minister, 11, 21
Law, Admiral Sir Horace, 144
Lawson, H. F. Lieut, 60 Comdr.
Lead and Line, 138
Leadley, K. R. S. Mid, 104 Lt. Comdr.
League of Nations, 68, 208, 219, 237
Lees, D.M. Lt. Comdr, 122   R. Adm.
Legion, HMS. 235
Lenin's Tomb, 53, 56
Leverkus, Mr. Consul, 240-1-2
Levis, L. Pilot Officer, RAF, 267   Air Commodore
Lewin, E. D. G. Mid, 37, 253, 265, 307   Captain
Lewis, Roger, Lieut, 62, 122, 307 Captain
Lieutenant, Pay and Expenses, 280-1
Line, Claud, Lieut(E) and Greta Line, 286
Liphook, 312
Lithgow, Campbell, Lt.Comdr.(E), 199
Llanbedr, 15
Lloyd, L.V. Lt. Comdr. 296-97, 303
Loch Ewe, 106
Lockyers, Hotel, 89
Lombard-Hobson, Sam, Cadet, 118, 317   Captain
London, HMS, 229
London Museum, 293
London Bar, Valletta, 267
Loraine, Sir Percy, 237

Lucia, HMS Submarine Depot Ship, 64, 68
Luddington, Master-at-Arms, 269
Luke, Archie, 278
Lydd, HMS, Minesweeper, 259
Lytton, Sir Henry, 232
Lyme Regis, 83
McBarnet, D. T. Cadet, 37, 119, 135, 139, 307   Comdr.
McCall, H.W.U. Lt. Comdr. 29, 31, 37, 117   Adm. Sir Henry
McEwen, B. S. Cadet, 104
McKendrick, G.W. Cadet, 185, 287 Comdr.
Mackenzie, C.M.G., "Jock", Eng. Comdr, 129, 189
Mackenzie, G. C. Mid, 51
Mackintosh, Lochlan, Comdr. 247, 251, 252, 255, 265, 282 Vice-Adm.
McIntyre, Hogg, Marsh & Co., Radiac shirts, 2, 4, 155
McLaughlin, Patrick, 167, 170 R. Adm.
Macphail, David, 178, 187, 188, 190, 208   Lt. Comdr.
Madden, Colin, Lieut, 118, 162, 320 R.Adm.
Madge, Jean, 238
Madoc, R. W. Maj.Gen. RM., 52
Maidenhead Bridge, 320
Makarska, 183
Malaga, 242
Malaya, HMS, Battleship, 64, 72, 75, 82, 91, 107, 139, 265
Malim, David, Lieut (E), 210-11
Malleson, C.V.S., Lieut, 247
Manadon House, Plymouth, 212
Manchester, 247, 259, 273, 301, 306
Malta, 165, 173, 176, 177, 187-8, 189-193, 198, 200, 219, 239, 249, 256, 264-5
Malta Amateur Dramatic Club, 'M.A.D.C' 188, 190, 195, 250
Marina, Princess of Greece, 189
Marlborough, HMS, Old battleship, 91
Marks, Lord, 76
Marlston House, 9, 20
Marriage Allowance, 256
Marris, family, 18
Marseille, 185, 229, 230, 255

INDEX

Marshall, Reginald, P 'RPM', 8, 9, 10, 13, 14-22
Marshall(Trelawney-Hare) Mabel, Wife of RPM, 8, 10, 21
Marshall, Anthony, 'Tony', 8, 17, 21-22, 207
Marshall, Rest of family,
  Catherine, 'Ba', 8, 11, 21
  Hannah, 'Bobbie', 8, 21
  Norah, 8, 14, 21
  Jean, 'Jane', 22
Martin, Blanche, *see* Hulton Blanche
Martin, Kingsley, Ed. New Statesman, 11, 76, 77
Martinique, 99
Marx, Brothers, 147, 276
Mary, Queen, H.R.H., 204
Masefield, John, Poet, 229, 236
Matapan, Cape, 266
Matthews, Mark, 190-1, 196
Maude, Cyril, Actor, 42
Maurier, Daphne du. Novelist, 221, 224
May, John, Lieut., 205, 207
Medd, P.N. Mid., 104, 108 Lt. Comdr.
Men Only, magazine, 249, 267
Meredith, David, 164-5, 282-3, 292
Mersch-El-Kebir, 266
Midshipmaid, The Frontispiece, 48, 71
Milburn, Peter, Lieut., 225   Comdr.
Mill Mead, School, 14
Miller, Gilbert, Impresario, 260
Mills, Sir John, Actor, 147
Mills, Geoffrey, Fl. Lieut., 252
Mills (Carmichael) Kathleen, 252
Milner-Barry, Bros. Patrick and Philip, 247, 256
Milos, 172, 173-4
Milton, J.W.T., Lieut., 144
Minesweeping, 132, 311
Mister Deeds Goes To Town, film, 253
Mitchell, H. A. Gunner T, 216
Mobilisation, 284-5
Montgomery, Field Marshal Sir Bernard, Viscount, 204
Montserrat, 99
Moore-Gwyn, Diana, see Fyffe
Morrison, T.K. Mid., RAN 65 R. Adm.

Morse, J.A.V., Comdr, 121, 122, 123, 126, 129   Comdr
Moss, Mrs. R.L.W., "Kay", 239, 247, 261, 264
Moss, R.L.W. Cadet, 52, 104, 108, 114, 117, 118, 119, 139, 190, 239, 261 Comdr.
Mosta, 196
Mosley, Sir Oswald, 82, 146, 154
Moulin Rouge, 176
Moultrie, Norah, 250
Mountbatten, Adm. of the Fleet, Earl, 144, 188, 220, 222, 267
Mountifield, R.A.P. Mid, 135, 139 Comdr.
Mount Nero, 265
Mudros, 171
Munn, James, Lieut., 264   R. Adm.
Mussolini, Benito, 27, 208, 250, 287, 292
NAAFI, 49
Nahlin, Royal Yacht, 230-1-3-4-6, 237-8-9
Naval Review, 1924, 15
Navarino, 174
Nazareth, 199
Nazi Occupation, 173-4
Nela, s.s., 241
Nelson, Horatio, 100
Nelson, HMS. Battleship, 46, 59, 62, 63, 64, 67, 71, 72, 73, 75, 82, 91-92, 96, 100-103, 107, 111-113, 127, 132, 139, 210, 212, 258
Neptune, HMS Cruiser, 136, 209
Newcombe, Harry, Lieut., 291
Newton, Lord, 76
New Zealand, 22
Nicholl, A.D. Lt. Cdr., 108, 117   R.Adm.
Nichols, A. H. Mid, 104   Lieut.
Niels Juel, Danish battleship, 76
Nimitz, Admiral, US Navy, 107
Norfolk, HMS, Cruiser, 91, 108-9
Norman, Daphne, 285-6, 294, 302, 304
Observer, The, 191, 300
O. C. Official Caning, 39, 43
O'Connor, Rory, Cdr, 136, 210   Capt
Oliver, G.N. Lt. Comdr., 50, 70, 82, 92   Adm. Sir Geoffrey

335

On Your Toes, Musical, 259
Osborne, L. D. Rear-Admiral (D), 274, 276
Osborne, John, Lieut (E), 217
Oscar II, Swedish Battleship, 76, 78, 79
Ouvry, J.G.D., Lieut Comdr, 62, 122, 307
Overall, Air Torpedo Gunner, 250-1
Overlord, Normandy invasion, 204
Oxford, 3
   Trinity College, 2
Oxley, HM Submarine, 198
Paddington, 29, 109, 274, 285
Padstow, 278
Palma, Bay of, 69
Pakenhams (of Alexandria) 225
Pakenham, T.A. C., 294   Capt.retd.
Paravanes, 61
Park, John and Nicolas, 20
Parker, J.M. Lieut, 208
Pasley-Tyler, Henry, Lieut, 195-6
Passive Defence Course, 279
Passmore, Pete, 313
Paterson (Hogg) Brada, 3, 86, 206, 220-1, 251-2, 255-6, 258, 261, 293, 301, 305, 318, 320
Paterson, Jack, S, 84, 85, 86, 87, 206, 220, 222, 223, 252, 269, 279, 296, 301, 306
Paterson, June, 301
Pay & Expenses, Lieut & others, 280-1
Pearson, R.L. Lt. Comdr RAN, 260, 262, 263
Peek, Richard, P. Mid. RAN, 167, 176   V. Adm.
Peel, Dennis, 224
Peel, Sir Edward, 'Teddy' and Norah, 222-3
Pellew, Major, 281
Penelope, HMS. 'The Pepper Pot', 117
Perowne, Stewart, 196-7, 250
Perry, Alfred, Golf champion, 164
Peterson, Lt. Comdr. 191, 207
Phillips, J.A. Mid., 167, 183, 185, 206-7   Comdr.
Phillpotts, C.L.G., Mid, 167, 183, 185, 195-6, 197, 206-7   Lt. Comdr.
Phillpotts, Vivien, widow; Simon son, 196

Physical Training Instruction, PTI, 48, 75, 76
Picket Boats, 81-82, 184
Piers, D. W. Mid, RCN, 212   R. Adm.
Piggott, Harry, Dartmouth master, 34, 39, 287
Pinhão, Douro, 238
Player, E. H. Cadet, 104
Plover, HMS Minelayer, 301
Plunkett-Ernle-Erle-Drax, Hon, 71, 282, 315   Adm.
Plymouth, 90, 96, 128, 208, 212, 217, 262, 274, 281
Poland, 306
Pollensa Bay, 68
Pope, Lieut., RNVR, 282
Portland, 60. 62, 131, 208, 218, 248
Porton, Chemical Warfare Establishment, 279
Portrush, 75
Port Regis, School, 210
Portsmouth, 60, 68, 88, 90, 91, 92, 94, 103, 112, 129, 185, 204
Positano, Hotel Pietro, Carlo Cinque, 211
Pots, Chamber, 53, 54
Pound, Admiral Sir Dudley, 222, 225, 249, 276
Powell, Canon Arnold C, 165, 262, 293, 307
Powell, Joan, 165, 196, 259, 261, 268, 277, 281, 293, 305, 312, 320
Powell, Michael, ARIBA, 163, 268, 277-8, 293, 312
Powell, Philip, ARIBA, 277, 293   Sir Philip C.H.
Powell & Moya, 293
Power, Terence, Mid., RAN Cdr. 65
Prairie Oyster, 267
Prelate and Pirate, Musical, 68
Price J. C. H., Mid, 52
Price, Martin, Lieut., RM., 170, 183, 194, 200, 207   Col.
Principal Civil Defence Officer, 279
Prior's Field, School, 22
Promotions and Opportunities 27, 28
Proper Drill, The, verses, 284
Proudfoot, F.B. Lt. Comdr., 297
Pudden, Jonathan, 20

INDEX

Pugh, David, Surg. Lt. RNVR, 317-8
Punter, Leslie, Sculptor, 247
Purvis, Peggy, see Lady Gray
Queen *Elizabeth*, HMS Battleship, 102, 169, 171-2, 174, 184, 187-8, 206, 228, 240, 249
Queen Mary, liner, 258
Queen's House, Greenwich, 141
Quilter, Roger, Composer, 305
Rab, resort, 290-1
Ramillies, HMS Battleship, 65, 208
Ramsay, B.H. Captain, 168-9, 170, 173, 184-5, 192-3, 198, 203-4 Admiral
Ramsay, C. G. Rear Admiral, 208, 212-3
Rattigan, T.Mid, RAN, 65   retd.
Rattigan, Terence, Playwright, 260
Ray, Cyril, Writer, 273
Rebbeck, Bachie, Eng. Comdr. 189 Admiral
Redgrave, Michael, 519
Regatta, Pulling, 75, 107, 168, 174, 225, 226, 299
Regatta, Sailing, 82, 134
Regent, HMS/M, 311, 516
Renown, HMS Battle-cruiser, 75, 82, 103, 107, 119, 130, 131-140, 198, 206, 209
Repton School, 8, 20
Repulse, HMS Battle-cruiser, 63, 72, 75, 107, 118, 119, 120-130, 131, 208, 240, 255
Resolution, HMS Battleship, 169, 176, 184, 187
Revenge, HMS Battleship, 108, 187, 195, 201
Review, Silver Jubilee, 204, 206
Rexfords, 176
Reykjavik, 76, 77, 78, 79
Rhodes, 169-170
Ricasoli, Pistol Range, 190
Richards, Dr. Hugh, 301
Roberts, P. L. Lieut, 144
Robinson, C. F. S. Cadet, 52, 65, 68, 82, 104, 117, 119, 129, 139, 147 Lieut.
Robinson, Surgeon Lieutenant (D), 171

Rock, Hotels and Village, 278, 283, 295, 313, 320
Rocket Display, 347
Rodgers, Lt. Comdr 'Haleeb', 116
Rodney, HMS Battleship, 46, 47, 49, 51, 55, 56, 60, 62, 63, 64, 65, 66, 67, 68, 69, 71, 72, 73, 75-79 Iceland. 80-83, 88, 85, 91-94, 96-104, 107-113, 116, 118, 127, 132, 139, 208, 210
Rodney, N.R.H. Mid. 17   Comdr.
Rogers, Ginger, 157, 252
Roper, N.E.G., Lieut. 216, 217, 225-6, 264, 281   Capt.
Rosemary, HMS., 159
Rosyth, 109, 110, 111, 115
Rowlandson, A.H. Lieut., 296, 307 Captain
Royal Air Force, 91, 292
Royal Court, Hotel, 29
Royal Engineers, 311
Royal Oak, HMS Battleship, 65, 136, 304
Royal Sovereign, HMS Battleship, 136, 165, 167-173, 174-178, 180-2-3-4, 186-7-8, 191-3-5-7.
End of commission, 200.
New commission 208-215
Royal Tournament, 280
Ruck-Keene, J.H. "Ruckers", Lt. Comdr. 290   Captain
Ruddy, J.A. Eng. Lieut., 108   Comdr.
Rugby Football, 269, 272-3-4-5-6; 285-6-7, 292
Rum, 127
Russell, G. V. Lieut. 296   Comdr.
Russia, Soviet pact with Germany, 300, 302.
War with Finland, 310, 312
Saccone & Speed, 116, 194
St. Albans, 213
St. Barbara, 187
St. Cyrus, H.M. Tug, 62, 210
St. Dunstans, 23
St. Enodoc, 214, 281
St. Genny, H.M Tug, 62
St. Issey, H.M. Tug, 169
St. James's Theatre, 260
St. John Cronyn, Comdr. 303

337

St. John, Knights of, 170
St. Just, H.M. Tug, 210
Sr. Mary's Loch, 1
St. Vincent, HMS Boys Training Estab., 130
St. Vincent, Island, 98, 99, 125
Salamander, HMS Minesweeper, 303, 305
Saltash, HMS Minesweeper, 259, 263, 264
Samos, Greek island, 171
Sanders, Lieut, RNVR, 122, 129
Sandford, Cecil, Captain, 305, 320
Sandford, Cynthia, 294
Saumarez, HMS, 16
Saunton Sands Hotel, 164
Sawdust Club, 96
Scapa Flow, 75, 304
Scarlet Fever, 13, 14
Scharnhorst, German Battle-cruiser, 92, 148, 227
Schneider Trophy, 91, 109
Schwerdt, C.M.R. Comdr. 94, 110-111, 118
Scilly Islands, 79-80
Scott, Sir Walter, 1771-1832, 1
Scott, Walter, Cadet, 52, 104, 119, 125, 139   Comdr.
Scovell, F. R. G. Surg.Lieut. 170, 199
Searle, J.H.C. Prof. 145
Seely-Bohm at School, Book, 18
Selkirk, HMS, Minesweeper, 297, 299
Service, C.L. Anthony, 'Dodie Smith', Play, 195-6
Service, Film, 198
Seychelles, 256
Seymour-Price, G. Air Commodore, 257
Sharp, C.E.R. Mid., 51, 82   Lt-Cdr
Sheer, Admiral, German battleship, 165-6, 263
Sheerness, 118, 120, 128, 129, 135, 297-8
Sheffield, Hugh, 163, 185
Shepperton, HMS Minelayer, 203
Shrewbury School, 14, 17
Shields, Captain, Hotelier, 312
Shoeburyness, 62, 307
Sibenik, 230

Sidelights on Malta, Article, 249, 267
Simpson, Wallis Mrs., 233, 234, 235, 237, 248
Simon André, 161
Skiathos, Greek Island, 235-6
Skipjack, HMS Minesweeper, 296-7, 301-02
Skottowe, N.B. Mid, RAN, 167, 178, 184, 206-7
Slessor, Paul and Hope, 195-6
Sliema Club, 189
Sliema, Creek, 219
Smeeton, R. Mid., 106-107 V. Adm. Sir Richard
Smith, C.E. Pay Cadet, 104
Smith, P.S. Lt Comdr, 82, 104, 311
Snapdragon, HMS, 62, 66
Snelling, Sue, 228
Snotties' Nurse, 51, 102, 122
Somerville, Admiral of the Fleet, Sir James, 222, 227, 228
Southampton, 216, 234
 Polygon Hotel, 311
Southsea, 157, 204-5. 209, 214
Spain, Civil War, 228
Spartan, HMS Cruiser, 168
Speedboats' Limit, 341
Speedwell, HMS Minesweeper, 296
Sphinx, HMS Minesweeper, 303, 305, 311, 315
Spithead, 205, 258
Splice the Main Brace, 134, 258
Split, 183, 231
Squire, J. C. Poet, 34
Stacey, H.A. Cadet, 135
Stalin, 302
Stari Grad, 185
Stark, Adm. Harold, USN, 258
Starkie, Walter, Lieut, 287
Stephens, R.J. 'Boff', Lt. Cdr., 250, 252
Stewart, R.G. 'Blossom', 282   Comdr.
Stonely, Sister, 320
Stoker, Anne, *see* Dobbs
Stokes and Harvey, 116, 194
Stokes, G. H. 282   Comdr.
Storrier, David, Detective, 230-1-4-5-6
Strauss, Richard,
 Der Rosenkavalier, 252
 Capriccio, 253

INDEX

Stubbs, R. Lieut, 306
Stucley, John, Lt. Comdr retd., Judge, 211
Suffren, French cruiser, 76
Sugden, Mark, 287
Sukum, Nitya Siamese Navy, 143, 144, 156-7
Susak, 180
Sutton, A.W.F. Mid, 135   Captain
Sulva Bay, 236
Sweden, Crown Prince, 77
Swift, Mr. Justice Rigby, 214
Swiftsure, HMS, 168
Swinley, C.S.B, Lt. Comdr., 122, 123, 128-130   Captain
Swinton, Alan, Colonel, 225-6, 260-1, 293, 313
Swordfish, 'Stringbag', Aircraft, 91, 187
Tabea, 199
Tangier, 244
Taprell-Dorling, 'Taffrail', 76
Taranto, 92, 253
Tarling, Keith, Schoolmaster, 12, 13
Taylor, Charles, MP, 262
Taylor, Pete, 22
Taylor (Marshall) Jane, 22
Teek, P.H. Lieut., RM., 208   Maj.
Teignmouth, 21
Telegraph, Daily, 274
There's Always Juliet, Play, 195
Thesiger, Ernest, Actor, 16
Thetis, Submarine disaster, 296
Thingvellir, 77-78, 95
Thomas, Sir Godfrey, 230, 236
Thorndike, Dame Sybil, 249, 261
Thornycroft, Woolston, 215-6-7
Tibbie Shiels, 1782-1878, 1
Tibbits, C.T.B., Mid, 52, 88, 89
Tibbits, Nigel, Lieut, 307
Tiddly Quid, 167-173, 176-178, 193, 200. 212
Tiger, HMS Battle-cruiser, 63, 72, 75, 103
Times, The, 43, 91
Timetable, RNC Dartmouth, 32
Tippet, family, 15
Tito, Marshal, 182
Toasts at Sea, 128
Tobago, 98

Tomkinson, Wilfred, 119, 125, 134-5 V. Adm.
Topp, R. E. Mid, 52, 70, 100, 104   Comdr.
Tothill, G.C. Prof, 145
Totton, Capt. 96, 99, 100
Trinidad, 96, 122, 124
Tripp, R.T. Mid., 52, 88, 89, 100, 103-4
Troughton, H. D. Mid., 135
Tufnell, M. N. Cadet, 104   Captain
Tug-of-War, 64, 73-74
Tulloch, A.G. B., Sub. Lieut., 108, 114
Tunstall, W.C.B. Prof., 145-6
Twickenham, 274-5, 292
Twiss, F.R. Mid, 51, 69, 70, 82   Adm. Sir Frank
Two Speed Destroyer Sweep, 219
Tyrrells Wood, 130, 164, 261
Tyrwhitt, L. A. K. Lieut., 108
U-Boats, 304
Union Club, Valletta, 189
United Service Club, 'The Senior', London, 25
United Services Rugby Football Club, Portsmouth, 158, 273, 274
Valhalla, HMS, 63
Valiant, HMS Battleship, 107
Valletta, 128
Vardon, Lieutenant, 250-1
Vavasour, Betty, see Bird
Vavasour, G. W. Mid, 312   Comdr. Sir Geoffrey
Veale, "Porky", Comdr. 295, 313
Verdon, Frank, 221
Verdun, HMS., 298-9
Vearncombe, Able Seamen, 307
Vernon, HMS., 62, 122, 157, 159-160, 262, 294-5, 304, 310, 315, 317
Verrey-Wurst Male Choir, 70
Versatile, HMS, 117
Vian, Adm. Sir Philip, 107, 192, 312
Viceroy of India, P & O, 196-7
Vickery, A. F. RM., 73-74
Victoria & Albert, Royal Yacht, 129, 132, 134, 189, 206
Victoria Regina, Play, 260
Vidette, HMS., 108, 109, 110, 114, 117
Vivien, HMS, 116

JUST A HOGG'S LIFE

Wadebridge, 279
Wales, Prince of, 132, 134, 150
Walford, B. Mid., 51, 82
Walker, Carleton, 196-7, 277, 296
Walker, John, Major, 278, 295
Walker(Jackson), Mrs. John, 278, 295
Wallace, HMS., 50, 63
Walls, Tom, Actor, wins Derby, 131
Walpole, HMS, 116
Walsham, Rear Adm. Sir John, 295
Walsham, (Bannerman) Lady Sheila, 295
Walthall, L.E.D. Cadet, 128 Captain,
Walton Heath, 163, 294
Walwyn, J.H. Cadet, 104
War, declaration of, 301
Warburton-Lee, Captain, V.C., 313
War in a String Bag, 323
Ward, N.E. Cadet, 104
Warhurst, Photographer, 76
Warren, Ella, 195-6
Warren, Guy, Captain, 222, 224-5, 254
Warren, Kay, 195-6
Warspite, HMS., 91, 132, 139, 219
Warwick, HMS., 139
Watkins, J. K. Pay Lieut., 275
Watson, Able Seaman, 'Hector', 297
Webb, Sir Aston, 1884-1930, 27, 30
Wells, C. W. 'Kit', Lieut. 227, 265
Westall, John, Maj, 250-1 Gen.Sir John
Westmacott, R.E. Mid., 169, 183, 207
Westmacott's Aunt, 198
West Indies, 96, 120, 121, 127, 138
West Wales, Collier, 103
Westward Ho! Golf Club, 282
Weymouth, 132, 135, 209
Whale Island, 156-159
   Elephant on Parade, 158-9
Whatley, P.M. Comdr., 144, 157
Wheadon, G.M. Mid., 52, 100, 104
Wheeler, W.G. Lieut, RAN, 304, 310
Wheen, C.K.T., Pay Mid., 43 R. Adm.
While Parents Sleep, Play, 38
Whinney, 'Bob', Sub Lieut., 65, 89-90, 110-111   Capt.

Whistler, Rex, 260
White Horse Inn, Musical, 123, 232
Whitford, Q.P. Lieut., 99
Whitshed, HMS, 118, 302, 317-8
Whittle, Sub Lieut, RNVR, 311, 320
Whittaker, Mr. Brockhurst Master, 12
William-Powlett, P.B. Comdr., 268, 274
   Vice Adm. Sir Peveril
Willis, J. B. Lieut., 135
Wilson, Paul, Lt. Comdr(E) RNVR, Lord
   Wilson of High Wray, 114, 174
Wilson, Richard, Sub Lieut, 297-8
Windermere, 4, 85, 207
Wine & Food Society, The, 56, 161
Winton , Francis de, Comdr, 290, 291, 295   Capt.
Wishart, HMS, 220
Wisher, Fl. Lieut & Mrs. Eileen, 264
Wolseley Hornet, Car, 203, 207, 209, 213, 216
Woodroofe, Thomas, Comdr, BBC., 258
Woods, G.A.L. Mid., 52
Woodward, Frank, Cadet, 262 Lieut.
World Events, 1934, 193
World Events, 1936, 249
World Events, 1937, 270
World Events, 1938, 287
Wratislaw, Rudy, Sub Lieut, 214, 225
Wright, Geoffrey, Composer, 294
Wright, John, Athlete, 293-4
Wyatt, Schoolmaster R.N., 198
Wynne, Eng. Lieut., 296, 305
Yarlet Hall, 13
Yarrow, boilers, 197
Yes, My Darling Daughter, Play, 261
Yonge, Philip, Lt. Comdr., 144 Comdr.
York, HMS., 120, 124
York Minster, 100
Young, Pamela, 279, 295
Yule, Lady, 230
Zagreb, 180, 186
Ziegler, Philip, 220
Zinkeisen, Sisters, 281